International Trade Theories and the Evolving International Economy

This book is dedicated
to the memory of Paul Smith

International Trade Theories and the Evolving International Economy

By R. A. Johns

St. Martin's Press, New York

All rights reserved. For information, write:
St. Martin's Press, Inc., 175 Fifth Avenue, New York, NY 10010
Printed in Great Britain

First published in the United States of America in 1985

ISBN 0-312-42374-8

Library of Congress Cataloging in Publication Data
Johns, Richard Anthony.
    International trade theories and the evolving international economy.

    Bibliography: p.
    Includes index.
    1. Commercial policy.   2. International economic
relations.   I. Title.
HF1411.J52   1985   382   85-18333
ISBN 0-312-42374-8

Printed by SRP Limited, Exeter

Contents

All italics used in quotations are original to their respective authors.

Tables

Figures

Acknowledgements

This book would not have been possible without the insights I have obtained over many years from teaching international economics to Principal Economics and International Relations students at the University of Keele, and from evaluating their positive reactions to and frustrations with the subject. Furthermore, the resultant product could not have materialised in the form it has without the invaluable, extensive library facilities that have been available to me at the University of Keele, both in terms of its stock of books and the indulgent use of its inter-library loan facilities kindly permitted me by Mr J.M. Wood, the University Librarian. In the latter respect I am most grateful to Anne Heath and Kathryn Procter for their courtesy, efficiency and tenacity in pursuing and satisfying my requirements. I have also benefited from visits to the libraries of the London School of Economics and the School of Oriental and African Studies at the University of London. The final preparation of the manuscript owes much to the term's leave of absence granted to me by the University of Keele in the autumn of 1984; and, most particularly, the typing of an early rough draft of the manuscript by Pamela Davenport and Sylvia Beech, secretaries in the Department of Economics and Management Science, and the final typing of the manuscript by my wife, Brenda, to whom I owe more than can be expressed here.

Preface

The literature on comparative advantage is so valuable and fascinating that it ought to be part of everyone's education.

Olson (1982: 137)

I must give notice that we are now in the region of the most complicated questions which political economy affords; that the subject is one which cannot possibly be made elementary; and that a ... continuous effort of attention ... will be necessary to follow the series of deductions. The thread, however ... is in itself very simple and manageable; the only difficulty is in following it through the windings and entanglements of complex international transactions.

J.S. Mill (1909: 396)

Traditional orthodox textbooks on international trade theory often beg more questions than they answer and ignore other central questions. This book does not claim to be superior to such texts, but seeks to provide a much needed wider focus and complementary framework from which to approach and extend the often narrow outlook of formal textbook studies. It is also intended to give a self-contained introduction to the subject for non-specialist but interested social scientists and lay readers alike. Its 'originality', if that is the right word, is in the wider than usual range of field-relevant knowledge it attempts to communicate to the student in Part I; the concentration in Part II on a discussion and critique of the ideas and concepts that have evolved in this subject area, rather than the technical nuts and bolts to be found in textbooks, and the additional consideration of some of the methodological aspects of international trade theory; and, in Part III, the inclusion of material that has not as yet commanded attention in textbooks, either because the more recent approaches outlined are still confined to fairly inaccessible professional journals, or because it has traditionally been thought to be the province of other sub-areas of economics or related subject disciplines. It is hoped that as a result of these inclusions, the student will receive a more rounded view of the subject than has been conventional, though it is stressed that this book is only an introduction and does not purport to include all field-relevant elements.

Some words are perhaps required in support of the above innovations. I would justify the contents of Part I and the discursive ideas of Part II by the fact that most students unfortunately tend either to have little knowledge of economic history, or little facility for its exemplar use in international trade discussions; and, additionally, do not have a retained view of the methodological aspects of theorising that condition the effectiveness of the subject's scientific pretensions and circumscribe the significance of the end product as social science fiction, social science fact, or some indeterminable mixture of the two, social science 'faction'. I would further justify these inclusions by reference to a recent statement by Kindleberger (1983: 9) to the effect that:

Mathematical economic theory and econometric testing have been crowding conventional economic history out of undergraduate and graduate economic curricula, and economic intuition has been sidetracked at the expense of elegance in the manipulation of Greek-letter symbols and number-crunching.

The intention behind the inclusion of Chapter 3 is not the provision of a complete world economic history as such, but an eclectic outline of the changing parameters of external trade and their differing implications for national industrial structuring and the international division of labour. It is hoped that this contextual schema may be used by students as a mental frame of reference when they attempt to evaluate for themselves the efforts made by theorists to simulate the forces that may underlie, or indeed undermine, international exchange, whether such theories are ideologically biased, empirically oriented or rooted in introspective imagination. In this respect I am attempting to respond to the exhortation made by Phelps Brown in his classic, but little heeded, article 'The Underdevelopment of Economics' (1972: 7,9) that 'the economist's studies should be field-determined, not discipline-determined ... [and that] the economist is not trained who is not numerate but neither is he trained if he is not historiate'.

The effective success of trade economists and their grasp of the extent and complexity of global activities depend upon the degree of empirical content they seek to project into their theories and the rigour of the methodology they apply thereto to reveal the nature of their determination accurately. The analytical relevance of the latter is necessarily limited by the extent to which awareness of the current state of the universe is being maintained and the processes of change which it is undergoing are being monitored. Part III seeks to outline how the academic subject has evolved as a result of particular detected structural changes in the international economy since the 1950s. Harry Johnson (1970: 9-10) once made the point that:

> it is ... important and necessary to recognize a crucial difference between the role of theory in the context of empirical research, and its role in economics generally. In the context of economics as an empirical science, the function of theory is to cast up empirically testable and refutable explanatory hypotheses, and the value of a theory is to be judged by its explanatory power in comparison with its rivals. In the broader context of economics as a systematic approach to the understanding of economic phenomena and as the organization of disciplined thinking about these phenomena and about policies relating to them, however, the purpose of theory is to abstract from the complexity of the real world a simplified model of the key relationships between dependent and independent variables, and to explore the positive and normative implications of changes in the 'givens' of this hypothetical system ... The theory of international trade has always been primarily theory in the second sense.

However, since the above was written, the body of theory and knowledge of actual trade structures have been significantly expanded, as Part III will show, such that this judgement now requires some modification.

Anthony Johns

Department of Economics and Management Science,
University of Keele,
Staffordshire

January 1985

PART I

Trade and the international economy

Distinctive economic structural strengths and weaknesses as well as political
ideologies and even cultures give the major individual players in international
trade policy differing objectives, approaches, and domestic constraints on
foreign commitments.

Cline (1983: 220)

A nation is a political unit, but it is only as a consequence of its political unity
that it becomes an economic unit

Hicks (1959: 162)

International economic intercourse... confines the freedom of countries... by
embedding each country in a matrix of constraints.

Cooper (1968: 45)

The state... is not an isolated unit, but lives in an environment of other political
organisms, and its external activity is conditioned by this fact.

Beer (1908: 1)

The study of international exchange involves the causal investigation of
particular activities which necessitate the crossing of national territorial
borders and an assessment of their geographical impact. These activities
include:

On the production OUTPUT side the inter-country transfer of goods and
services, of which:
(a) *Visible trade* constitutes trade in primary (raw material) and secondary
    (manufactures/processed) industrial products; and,
(b) *Invisible trade* includes the provision of services (such as transport,
    insurance and banking) to promote visible exchange; unilateral
    financial transfers (aid and migrants' remittances); and international
    tourism.
On the production INPUT side the international circulation of the means of
production as a result of:
(a) labour migration, whether at the managerial, skilled or unskilled
    levels; and
(b) inter-country capital movements and investment flows.

Orthodox trade theories specifically exclude the latter types of international transfer and concentrate on the former, thereby ignoring the
possibility that such resource transfers may promote or substitute for
visible and invisible exchange. As Kojima (1975: 4) has generalised with
respect to capital flows:

if foreign investment is complementary to product trade, it creates and/or expands the opportunity to import one product and to export the other product ... [and] is trade-creating or trade-oriented.

Symmetrically, if the initial capital outflow decreases or eliminates the opportunity to import one product and to export the other product ... foreign investment 'substitutes' for product trade and is thus 'trade-destroying' or 'anti-trade-oriented'. This is the case ... when ... foreign investment induces ... competitive production in the host country.

Actual inter-country product flows and resource shifts occur within a real world context of five populated continental land masses (Europe, Asia, Africa, the Americas and Oceania) set in seven seas (the Arctic, North and South Atlantic, North and South Pacific, Indian and Antarctic Oceans) each continent being differently arranged by latitude within a specific spectrum of natural climates that ranges from the polar, the cool temperate, the warm temperate, to the dry climes of steppe and desert, and the differing tropical climates of the savannah and the equatorial rain forest. Each interstitial country is further differentiated by its individual topography, historical heritage and degree of economic development.

Economists as contemporary theorists, applied technicians, historians or policy advisors are necessarily interested in many separate, but interrelated, levels of analysis of the interregional international exchanges within and between the above continental land masses, whether such interchanges are given a historical, contemporary or futurist focus. As theorists, they are interested in the notional abstract properties of isolate, pre-trade, 'closed' economies, as compared with the alleged theoretical niceties, both positive and negative, that arise when economies are 'open' to trade. As applied technicians and/or historians, they desire to examine empirically propositions that purport to relate to the reality of why trade has taken place, either in general or in particular, in the past and why it is taking place in the present. As policy advisers, they seek to provide, from the viewpoint of a particular national interest, *ex ante* guidelines for the establishment of trade and development strategy objectives. Finally, from the cosmopolitan supranationalist viewpoint, economists need to provide a paradigm model of international political economy towards which attempts may be mounted at a multinational level to correct, by interventionist engineering, 'unfair' competitive differentials, trade asymmetries and other market imperfections in satisfaction of some proposed world welfare criterion.

Whatever the focus of the analysis attempted, the operational significance of geo-political boundaries and the potential geo-economic domains of production activity, within which internal patriate and externally owned economic resources may circulate, cannot be ignored. Their importance and degree of conflict of interest are conditioned by the net impact of three basic groups of factors enumerated in Chapters 1 and 2: facilitative boundary-transcending technologies; basic micro-structural forces that shape the actual gains from trade; and circumstantial macro-structural factors that determine any country's particular trading propensity.

The above factors have to be appreciated within the changing context of international economic history to which theories must relate, and, according to which, be refined. Chapter 3 attempts to outline the changing parameters in which external trade has taken place. While some quantitative aspects of each phase of that history are included and some qualitative features highlighted, the outline provided is not intended as a complete economic history, but as a thought-orienting framework, from which the various theories of exchange discussed in Parts II and III may be approached, and to which their particularities of outlook and interpretation may be subsequently related. The outline is eclectic and adopts neither a 'presentist' (see Seidman 1983) reconstructive perspective, in which events are asserted to be organised in a continuously cumulative systematic way, nor a 'historicist' perspective that assumes discontinuities between each time-phase as a result of changing problems and subject matter.

1 Boundary-transcending technologies, trade development, and the micro-structural activities of firms

An industrial system comprises the operating units i.e. the actors, the functional relationships between those units, and the interactions between the units and the external environment.

Hamilton and Linge (1979: 6)

Given that the oceans of the world 'cover nearly three-fourths of the earth's surface [and that] when from the remainder are subtracted those sections which are entirely unsuitable for economic development because of unfavourable relief ... the agricultural, extractive, and manufacturing industries [are confined] to approximately a tenth of the earth's total area' (Donaldson 1928: 10), it is evident that improvements in transport and communication technology are a *sine qua non* for trade development. The internal integration of geographical areas that became countries and their development of external trade relations required the conquest of the oceanic and terrestrious frictions of time and space that otherwise isolate land areas and continents, and circumscribe both their capacity for trade and the effective, but separate, operational domains of governments and economic actors. Every improvement in transport and communication technology promotes an effective geographical extension of the market area that can be supplied with goods and services and the area from which raw material and other production inputs can be sourced. Each new discounting of the above-mentioned frictions makes trade technically more feasible in terms of ease of business operation and a lowering of the associated transaction and information costs involved. Every such development, whether it results from greater transport accessibility on or through land, by sea or in the air; or personal contact via postal, telegraphic, telephonic or telecommunications; or changes in allied technologies, such as cargo-packaging and preservation techniques, becomes an invariable prelude to changes in the territorial division and specialisation of labour; the volume, ubiquity and variety of trade; and the geographical extent of supportive multi-country commercial networks that are established. These improvements encompass a series of economy mutations now discussed.

ECONOMY TYPES, TRADE DEVELOPMENT AND THE OPERATIONAL DOMAIN OF PRODUCTION

With respect to the main geographic progression of bounded economy operation contained in the historical sequence of trade development, Bücher (1893) has outlined three basic mutations, to which Donaldson (1928: 68–73) has added a fourth, each stage describing the largely self-contained domain within which the circulatory process of production, exchange and consumption is normally completed:

1. *The independent domestic economy*: where the family, or extended family such as the tribe, limits the circulation process.
2. *The town economy*: where there is some functional division of labour on an inter-industry basis, but where it remains largely absent at the intra-industry level.
3. *The national economy*: where, following the advent of what is generally referred to as the Industrial Revolution, industrial specialisation takes place between regions and division of labour occurs within industries. Areas necessarily produce more of their specialized product than they can consume locally. The economy is based upon an intra-national, inter-regional interchange of products. It must be emphasized that the boundaries relevent to this economy type are not necessarily always those of the national state, for economic life within geographically large states may be regionalised to the extent that they envelop more than one effective economic system. So it is that the economy of Brazil is thus segmented, and the Pacific seaboard of the United States partially segmented from the centre and east by mountains, deserts and arid plains (Edwards 1980: 117–8). Indeed, these circumstances often obtain in federal states, where the policies of provincial governments may make 'the discontinuity of economic relations ... as marked, or even more clearly marked, at the borders of each state as at the borders of the federation (Svennilson 1960: 3).
4. *The world economy*: where there is such a degree of 'industrial interdependence of nations' that few of them 'could long subsist, at least without radical and even violent rearrangement of their entire economic structures, and [would suffer] general economic decline, were their foreign trade totally stopped' (Donaldson 1928: 69). It is, of course, possible for 'enclave economies' to exist within a country largely separate from its surrounding area that are world economy directed: for example, free trade zones, free ports, and colonial economic bases.

At each progressive stage of economy development, according to North (1984: 263), the resources devoted to the organisation and integration of the production and marketing of goods and services to 'capture the gains from trade' will tend to become a growing proportion of total costs and increase the size of the transaction sector for three main reasons:

> First, growing specialization and division of labor means an ever-increasing number of exchanges, each of which requires specification and enforcement, necessary whether across markets or within firms. Second, the cost per exchange tends to rise as impersonal exchange replaces personal exchange. And third, government's increasing control over property rights enables groups that acquire influence over decision-making governmental bodies to *raise* the cost of transacting to other parties to exchange and thereby redistribute income to themselves.

The transaction sector includes not only the wholesale and retail trades, banking, finance and insurance, but also 'the expansion of legal, accounting, personnel and marketing departments'. Much, however, depends on 'the role of government as an impersonal third party to specify and enforce contracts' (North 1984: 255).

Naturally, the stages of evolutionary progression outlined are neither completely discrete nor spatially synchronic within or between countries: a lack of 'perfect morphological coordination' of territorial development (Donaldson 1928: 619) is necessarily to be found at any one time. Indeed, the initial process of world economy formation began in some countries while their town economies still predominated, because internal topographical difficulties made it much easier for coastal trade and certain types of high-value low-bulk oceanic trade to develop prior to the unification (and even the settlement) of their geographical interiors and the creation of national markets by inter-regional linkage of local markets. The internal frontier of trade development tended to remain difficult to extend until the advent of railways, until which time economic frontiers were often technically more significant between provinces and towns within countries, rather than around countries.

The impact of the various nineteenth-century transport, industrial and commercial revolutions and their twentieth-century consolidation has been to change the operational nature of the firm corresponding to the market extension from the independent domestic to the town, national and world economy stages, its evolutionary progression being from a single to a multiple unit/function/location/market production entity, as the 'industrial action space' within which it derives its inputs and undertakes its production activities and the 'commercial action space' (Hamilton and Linge 1979: 9) within which it markets its products are both extended. Economy stages 1 and 2 outlined above exemplify different levels of closed economy development, and stages 3 and 4 of open economy development. Production organisation in the former stages can be either on a single product, single-plant basis, where all the output of firms is sold to consumers in that economy who also purchase all their goods from these same firms (Dunning 1974: 577); or on a multi-plant, multi-product basis within the same overall geographical constraints. Stage 3 corresponds with Dunning's 'Open Economy Stage I' (which might be called the international stage), where 'the market for any given product can be supplied by firms producing outside [the economy] and ... firms located in the [economy] can export part of their output' – exchange is between different firms in different countries (Dunning 1974: 578). Stage 4 corresponds with Dunning's 'Open Economy Stage II' (which might be called the transnational stage (Dunning 1974: 579) when firms diversify not only their markets across national boundaries, but their production facilities as well: international exchange becomes denationalised, being essentially trade between parts of the same corporate body operating in two or more different country locations.

In practice, the organisational nature of the transnational firm in Stage 4 can become quite intricate, as Edwards (1960: 118) has indicated:

> One business undertaking may express itself in a considerable number of corporate entities bound together with varying degrees of tightness by ownership, common management, and communities of interest created by contractual arrangements. The linkage among these corporate entities is sometimes so complex as to arouse dispute as to where the boundaries of the undertaking are located.

World-wide integrated communication systems, once established, enable global intra-firm internationalisation of inter-country exchange to take place and 'economic and technical progress [to] burst through the narrow boundaries drawn by monarchs and nationalists in the eighteenth and nineteenth centuries' (Rustow 1967: 212). This has the consequence that:

> different aspects of production, once integrated within the same work unit and work place, are . . . 'emancipated' to be carried out in different places. . . Firms are not so limited . . . by the necessity of carrying out the entire production of a product in one country; further, they are not constrained to carry out within one workplace different processing phases which might profit from work at several different locations. [Caporaso 1981: 375–6.]

Thus world economy production involves an internationally dispersed network of plants, each owned by the same firm, within which production circulates often from the raw material stage, through the various processing and assembly stages to its end-product forms. Individual plant specialisation is based on a central management plan, rather than national factor endowments or competitive conditions. The prices of such inter-country exchanges are company-determined rather than market-determined, such transnational sector integration challenging the very significance of the nation-state as the focus for the analysis of external trade and resource transfers.

Furthermore, 'as in the case of the firm, there has been a transsubstantiation of the nation-state over the last century' (Paquet 1972: 7). Using the three-stage development of the nation-state proposed by Byé (1959: 4–9) – from the 'nation-as-a-firm', to the 'nation-as-a-block-of-factors-of-production', to the 'nation-as-a-group-of-groups' – Paquet emphasises how each stage corresponds to 'new partitionings, new links between parts, and new rights sanctioned by the social contract between individuals and the pact between the leaders and the led' to indicate that the state too is an essentially adaptive organisation:

> the Mercantilists identified the national community with the state and the state with the king: this simplified greatly the problem of reconciling individual wants with the public interest, since for all practical purposes, the valence of individuals was negligible. For a laissez faire ideology. the mercantilistic notion was unacceptable. The nation was a block of factors of production more or less immobile and subject to the same set of collective rules. However, the valence of the individual parts was heightened, and the pact between the national leaders and the citizens left the former with very limited rights.
> The modern notion of nation is more 'social': each transactor may pursue his goals alone, but he soon realizes that it would be highly inefficient. Consequently, in the same way as he found it useful to form production clubs like the firm, he also finds it convenient to enter into a number of other associations with other transacters. . . The nation-state constitutes only one of these clubs, although it is also simultaneously an envelope for families of smaller-size clubs. The nation is therefore subject to a dual series of pressures as a result of any revaluation of the importance of the national clubs, and their preferences or as a result of the restructuring of the component clubs [Byé (1959: 4–9), and see Olson 1965].

All the above mutations, however, were only possible as a result of the forging of and improvements in transport and communication links on a global scale.

TRADE AND THE FORGING OF GLOBAL TRANSPORT AND COMMUNICATION LINKS

Given the importance of the oceans (even in 1977 sea transport accounted for 95 per cent of all international commerce by weight (Rinman and Linden 1978: 15)), it is not surprising that 'all through history, almost up to the present the relative cheapness of transport by water has given an advantage to those who have access to navigable water – first to riverine, then to maritime states' (Hicks 1959: 173). Prior to the general development of an international economy in the nineteenth century and the internal integration of countries by railways, trade tended to develop most in countries such as England and Holland that had good systems of inland waterways and extended coastlines. Long distance trade was confined to high-value, low-bulk 'rich trades' such as spices, silks, ivory and precious stones, rather than high-bulk low-value goods. During this period, aboriginal oceanic links were made as a result of voyages of discovery which subsequently led to the settlement of undeveloped virgin land areas. The emergence of the climacteric of the industrial revolution and the factory system in the eighteenth century created the possibilities of mass production, which required for their fulfilment the formation of national markets at home and abroad and access to resources often separated by geography. The developing capitalist societies required cheap raw materials to service the evolution of the industrial complexes, external markets to absorb their rising levels of production and provide investment outlets for their rapidly accumulating capital, and food supplies to feed their newly urbanised populations.

Despite some prior development of trade in the new industrial products as a result of canal building, the main geographical links for the above were essentially forged in the nineteenth century by the railways and the steamship, and further promoted by the electric telegraph, uniform postage and the development of refrigerated transport. For the first time, commerce in industrial bulky goods was made feasible and predictable in terms of the speedy dispatch and receipt of goods, services and commercial information; and substantial international economic interdependence was established between the relatively developed, less developed and undeveloped areas of the world. White (1899: 105) emphasised the importance of oceanic communication thus:

> modern civilization is crystallizing through the affinity of world intercourse, and is developing greater and greater solidarity... The ocean is ... the great Amalgamator. All highly developed nations are pressing towards it cutting canals from their chief inland emporia towards their nearest seaboard, piercing isthmuses that obstruct free maritime intercourse, building transcontinental railways and uniting oceans – thus opening up new routes, by rail and steamship, for international commerce.

Railways overcame the internal natural barrier of geographical distance within countries and within continents, unifying their internal markets in a more consistent way than heretofore. For example, prior to the building of railways in the United States, the interior terrain of the country made direct transport and the westward movement of the settlement frontier to the Pacific coast difficult, the Pacific seaboard being partially separated from the centre and east by mountains, deserts and arid plains. Here the railways initiated and promoted the 'settlement trails' that were essential for the completion of the process of internal colonisation, as indeed was the case elsewhere (Fieldhouse 1982: 252):

> in Canada ... the westward movement of the settler frontier from the older provinces on the St. Lawrence eventually established the mid-western provinces – Manitoba, Saskatchewan and Alberta, linking them with British Columbia. ... The internal frontier was important also in South Africa and Australia. In the former it produced the provinces of the western Cape and the two Boer republics – the Transvaal and Orange Free State; in Australia movement away from Sydney established Victoria and Queensland.

In respect of the advent of the steamship and refrigerated transport, A.G. Hopkins (1973: 150) has summarised their impact thus:

> The speed of the steamship made it possible to transport a wider range of perishable goods, and it enabled traders to complete their transactions more quickly, thus helping them to economise on capital. Finally, the steamship, being less dependent on natural conditions than was sail, could guarantee regularity of service. Fore-knowledge of the steamer's arrival enabled traders to purchase and prepare goods for shipment. Greater readiness reduced the time spent in port, and so lowered running costs.

Long-distance communication was further promoted by the arrival of cable (Farnie 1969: 161):

> The cable transmitted commercial and financial information, especially market-prices, commodity-orders and news of changes in the political structures of economic life. It thereby laid the mechanical basis for the emergence of a world market. It increased the certainty of business, permitted the reduction of commission, facilitated the entry of small merchants into the India trade, increased the use of the telegraphic transfer in place of the bill of exchange and encouraged the rise of tramp shipping carrying goods 'to orders' received from Europe.

The drawing of the International Date Line through the uninhabited wastes of the Pacific Ocean in 1884 made possible the introduction in 1885 of an international standard time and completed the conquest of the world by metric time. Twentieth-century developments in road and air transport and telecommunications further completed and perfected the process of geographical linkage and the possibilities of a round-the-clock pursuit of international business. Finally, the emergence of modern container technologies changed the independent nature of sea and air modes of transport to mere extensions of the land transportation system. By such means, these revolutions established the infrastructures for international commerce and trade development, enabled previously virgin areas to be settled and developed, made available new products, and conferred international importance on particular sites as entrepôt centres and as nodal junctions of the corridors of global oceanic traffic flows. In the latter case, the construction of two particular oceanic links were crucial in furthering the process of international communication and industrial specialisation: (a) the Suez canal, joining the Mediterranean with the Indian Ocean; and (b) the Panama Canal, uniting the Atlantic with the Pacific Ocean.

(a) The Suez Canal

Whereas effective communication between Europe and India awaited the discovery of the Cape route in the fifteenth century, the pace of nineteenth-century development awaited a direct link between the Mediterranean and the Indian Ocean that did not involve the trans-shipment of cargoes. This happened in stages (Allen and Donnithorne 1957: 210):

> In the early nineteenth century both the British and the Dutch colonies in South East Asia were linked with their motherlands by way of the Cape of Good Hope. Then, in 1840, the Peninsular and Oriental Steam Navigation Company introduced a service for mails, passengers and light freights to India and the Far East via the Mediterranean and the Red Sea, with land transport across the Sinai Peninsular. In 1844, when it extended its services to Hong Kong, the company necessarily took in the Straits as well, and in 1853 it started its fortnightly mail services to the Far East.

Other companies soon followed, and with the opening of the Suez Canal in 1869, 'the trade of the Far East was brought within the acquisitive grasp of the steamship owner and his agents' (Hyde 1973: 21). The canal became the principal gateway to the East, and in Bismarck's words (quoted in Hallberg 1931: 10) the 'spinal cord' of the British Empire: the link connecting India, Australia, New Zealand, Hong Kong and the British settlements on the east coast of Africa with the mother country. A major geographical restructuring of trade inevitably resulted.

1. It shortened the voyage from Europe to India by some 4,000 to 5,000 miles, or about two weeks' steaming for the fastest vessels of the time: the 11,560 sea mile trip from Liverpool was cut by 3,197 miles; for Mediterranean countries it saved 61 per cent of the former Trieste/Bombay and 59 per cent of the Marseille/Bombay journeys. The saving in time was effectively greater on the return route, for while 'the westerly winds and currents pushed the ships along on the outbound voyage [this] increased the time of the return voyage via the Cape by nine or ten days' (Fletcher 1958: 563–4). The new route caused a realignment and loss of much of the European entrepôt trade, and led to significant shifts in the pattern of Australian and Eastern trade. Mediterranean trade with India increased and the return voyage from Australia used this route for the rapid shipment of wool and meat, although in the latter case the outward route often remained via the Cape to avoid canal duty.
2. It promoted the rapid substitution of steam for sail and the scrapping of a large number of sail vessels specially designed for transit through the narrow channel. New shipping technology led to the replacement of the paddle-wheel by the screw-propeller, the substitution of iron-plating for wood, and the displacement of the single-cylinder engine by the compound engine. Harley (1971: 219–20) has calculated the costs of the inputs required to produce a million cargo ton miles by steam and sail in 1855, 1865, 1872, 1881 and 1891. The inputs required for steamship transport are shown in Figure 1 as equal product curves and those for sail are plotted along the horizontal axis. The results indicate that:

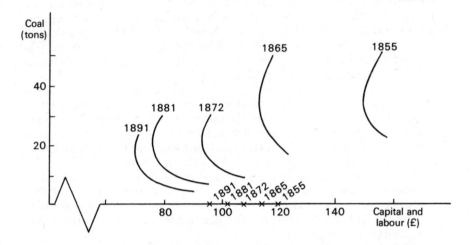

Figure 1: *Production functions per million ton-miles, voyage 5,000 miles length: 1855, 1865, 1872, 1881 and 1891*

Source: Harley (1971: 220, Figure 2)

the dramatic reduction of coal consumption . . . had a twofold impact on the production function for steam transportation. First, the coal input itself was reduced; second, the amount of ship, crew, and coal devoted to the transportation of bunker coal was reduced. The second impact was greater on long voyages where a considerable portion of the deadweight capacity of the ship was devoted to coal for bunkers in contrast to short voyages where bunkerage was a small proportion of capacity.

Table 1: *Cost of round trip voyage per 1,000 tons of cargo capacity by steam and sail, various dates and trades*

Destination	Distance from UK in miles	Year	Cost of	
			Sail	*Steam*
New Orleans	5,000	1872	1,230	1,400
		1876	1,100	1,180
		1881	1,310	1,280
Bombay via Cape	11,500	1865	2,839	3,901
via Suez	6,200	1872	2,610	2,165
Calcutta via Cape	11,500	1872	2,610	2,640
via Suez	8,000	1873	2,950	3,040
		1881	2,470	2,839
San Francisco	13,500	1881	2,840	3,140
		1891	2,000	2,100

Source: Harley (1971: 227, Table 2)

Figure 1 and Table 1 indicate that the competitive edge of steam over sail occurred after 1869: in the early 1870s on the London/Bombay route; the late 1870s on the London/New Orleans and London/Calcutta routes; and the late 1880s on the London/San Francisco route. The impact of reduced fuel consumption was felt first by the Far East trades. This increased the demand for coal and coaling stations on the new Suez route. Frequency of coaling stations was essential to the saving of bunker space that made available the extra cargo space from which higher profits were made possible. Gibraltar, Malta, Aden, Ceylon and Hong Kong now became just such a chain of coaling stations, as well as protective fortresses and naval bases: Hong Kong additionally becoming the great entrepôt for the trades of Southern China.

3. The existence of the canal diminished the importance of the Cape route. Colonies such as Mauritius and St. Helena now lost much of their former prosperity, as they were no longer situated along the main route to India. On the other hand, the new route made East Africa more accessible for trade.

The refrigeration revolution soon followed. The first cold store was opened at London's Victoria Dock in 1882 for the meat trade with Australia, New Zealand and South Africa. Trade now became structured by the exigencies of the international specialisation process and transport economics:

> The growth of population and industry in Britain ... increased the pressure on the supply of food while the growth of wealth ... increased the consumption of meat per head as prices rose. The import of meat from overseas necessitated the extension of the techniques of refrigeration to the transport of large quantities over long distances and through the tropics. The successful development of refrigerating machinery gave the Canal a new traffic, which was a northbound rather than a southbound trade [Farnie 1969: 353.]

> British ships could load partially with the manufactured goods and textiles demanded in such great quantities in India, then take on coal or iron – but especially coal – to round out their outbound cargoes. Part of the coal was dropped off in the Mediterranean ports before the Suez Canal was reached, but sufficient was retained to give the British shipping entering the north end of the canal in 1912 an average load-index of .76. Return cargo from India was available in such abundance that the homeward index very nearly reached 100 per cent – .98. When these load-indexes are compared with those for the British tonnage engaged in the Atlantic trade – .2 outward from Europe to the United States, .63 return in 1912 – it is easy to realize why India was well supplied with British tonnage [Fletcher 1958: 568–9.]

(b) The Panama Canal

In similar fashion, the United States planned a 50-mile maritime canal in Panama. Freedom of use was guaranteed by the Hay Pauncelote Treaty of 1901 which made the eastern seaboard of North America equal to Western Europe as regards trade with East Asia and at a slight advantage over Japan. White (1899: 100) prognosticated that:

> when the ... Canal is built, a new stage of International development will be

reached, namely, that on which the Pacific shall vie with the Atlantic for supremacy in human interests, in the same way that the Atlantic competed with the Mediterranean after the discovery of America. The course of empire moves ever westward, and with it the centre of gravity of world power ... by the inauguration of an inter-oceanic canal in Central America, a new nodal point will be created, by which International commerce will be profoundly affected.

These observations are borne out by Hallberg's (1931: 151) comparison of the two routes as shown in Table 2:

the dividing line in the East between the two routes would seem to be somewhere from Hong Kong to Manila. For European trade with Eastern Asia, including Australia but not New Zealand, the Panama Canal offers no competition with Suez. The only points where the Panama Canal can compete with Suez are

Table 2: *A comparison of the savings in marine miles effected by the Suez and Panama routes between specified destinations.*

	Savings via Suez over Panama (marine miles)	Savings via Panama over Suez (marine miles)
London to Freemantle	5,210	
New York to Freemantle	593	
London to Melbourne	1,803	
New York to Melbourne		2,294
London to Sidney	28	
New York to Sidney		2,460
London to Wellington		1,077
New York to Wellington		4,597
London to Calcutta	9,310	
New York to Calcutta	4,790	
London to Singapore	7,339	
New York to Singapore	2,819	
London to Manila	4,700	
New York to Manila	180	
London to Hong Kong	4,729	
New York to Hong Kong	219	
London to Shanghai	4,989	
New York to Shanghai		1,081
London to Yokohama	1,748	
New York to Yokohama		2,772
London to Coronel		837
New York to Coronel		3,118
London to Valparaiso		1,417
New York to Valparaiso		3,732
London to San Francisco		5,538
New York to San Francisco		7,853

Source: Hallberg (1931: 150–1)

north-eastern Asia, eastern Australia, New Zealand and the west coasts of North and South America.

The canal was not opened until 1914, and was owned and controlled by the United States and subject to the law of that country.

Given that the above-mentioned facilitative boundary-transcending technologies set the operative parameters within which trade takes place, the micro-structural factors that shape actual exchange flows must now be examined.

MICRO-STRUCTURAL FACTORS AND THE APPROPRIATION OF THE GAINS FROM TRADE

Primary and secondary production require the co-existence of a complex relational network of tertiary (service) activities to facilitate their sourcing of inputs and marketing of outputs that needs to be extended beyond national frontiers if full participation in global exchange is to occur. Leaving aside the existence and efficiency of finance and transport facilities and the potential structuring influence of their indigenous or foreign ownership, two activities are crucial for the appropriation of gains from international exchange: (a) the restructuring processes inherent in continuous trade participation, and (b) the competitive actions of firms.

(a) Restructuring processes inherent in continuous trade participation

International trade participation is conventionally regarded as generating certain positive effects of a tangible, practical nature that can obtain as a result of both its static and dynamic impact. Realisation of these results is, however, contingent on whether, in particular cases, the enterprise and organisation exist to effect the required structural changes, and whether the economic environment is one that acts in a manner that furthers the domestic national interest, or a particular domestic sectoral interest at the expense of the national domestic interest:

Static gains from trade

These are alleged to arise from the once-and-for-all restructuring of domestic industry and its concomitant national resource reallocation incurred on entry into the international trading system, and required by the new inter-country national industrial specialisation pattern. However, such business gains are only appropriated by those industrial sectors that are favoured by competitive international exchange. While it can be shown that domestic consumers of the imported products receive a benefit in terms of its purchase at prices lower than those that would exist under autarky; that either more goods can be produced and their equivalent in higher consumption achieved, or the previous output level of goods can be produced with a lower resource cost and a gain made in leisure, these benefits occur at the expense of the internationally non-competitive industries, whose outputs must contract to release the economic resources needed for the expansion of the domestic internationally competitive industries. Olson (1982) has argued that potential or actual injured parties of such de-industrialisation are usually capable of organising themselves into 'distributional coalitions' that seek by political means to pre-empt or severely limit the extent of such market disruption, and that a number of such special interest organisations and collusions accumulate in stable economies, especially those of industrially advanced countries, and retard structural change, there being a tendency for 'regulatory restraints imposed by the "visible hand" of political power [to] shape markets just as surely as economic power does, but in ways designed to create or perpetuate economic power' (Kane (1977: 55); see also Stigler (1971)). Some argue (Owen and Braeutigam 1978) that such institutional behaviour, by slowing down or mitigating the changes imposed on economic agents by market and technological forces, can lead to a more orderly adjustment than impersonal market forces would afford, although strategic abuse may nevertheless occur which enhances the profits of the latter. However, all such activities are at the expense of national welfare gain and slow down overall growth, unless domestic export producers thereby disadvantaged can mount a counter-pressure. 'Tariffs ... furnish a classic example of the type of action taken by vested interests on their own behalf; these subvent the general welfare, especially that of consumers who are too diffuse and separately too little concerned to organize effectively' (Kindleberger 1983: 6).

Putting aside such political manoeuvering, the problem of industrial restructuring *per se* is not to be denied. 'Trade is an *invitation* to gain ... Not ... a *guarantee* for gains ... [so that] if a country lacks the capacity to respond to the challenge of trade, the effects of trading may not be advantageous', Thus when trade is 'opened-up', as from autarky to free trade, or from some protection to less protection, what matters is a country's 'reallocative ability in the form of response to profit opportunities' from the creation of what Linder terms '*more of what already exists*' and '*what does not yet exist*' (Linder 1961: 41,71). In both respects, countries with an ability to reallocate factors of production will tend to maximise their gains and to accumulate them faster over time, whereas those with a lack of reallocative ability will under-achieve their potential benefits because of various factor inflexibilities. Since there is no automatism in the realisation of gains from trade, the gains of less-developed countries tend to be less and the gains of developed countries more than otherwise might be the case. Thus Kindleberger (1956: 307) argues that such industrial restructuring 'may well be easy in developed countries, hard in under-developed countries, and this whether in manufactures or in primary goods'; and Hicks (1959: 173) asserts that:

> once a country has reached a certain stage of development, it does appear to acquire (or to be able to acquire) a kind of resilience against changes in its comparative advantages. One of the great advantages of 'advanced' specialisms is that they carry with them the *capacity* of doing other things; thus, if an 'advanced' country is driven off one specialism, it does not find it insuperably difficult to grow another.

In reality, many countries became incorporated into the international trading system via colonial subjugation or, as in nineteenth-century Latin America, in 'unequal' circumstances that compromised the direction of economic affairs.

Dynamic gains from trade

Once economies previously 'closed' are exposed to trade, reallocation gains merge with the gains from economic growth and the continuity of international trade relations allegedly transform the coefficients of production and alter the production possibilities available to each particular country. These growth-transmitting, micro-structural effects of trade are allegedly positive for all countries. In the nineteenth century, J.S. Mill (1909: 581–2) called them 'indirect' or 'widening' effects which 'must be counted as benefits of a high order'. Apart from his optimistically alleged intellectual and moral effects of trade, which he considered of the greatest importance – its mutually civilising impact, and its role as 'the principal guarantee of the peace of the world ... [permitting] the uninterrupted progress of the ideas, the institutions, and the characters of the human race' – Mill identified two primary economic effects:

(a) The tendency of every extension of the market to improve the processes of production. A country which produces for a larger market than its own, can introduce a more extended division of labour, can make greater use of machinery, and is more likely to make inventions and improvements in the processes of production.

(b) There is another consideration, principally applicable to an early stage of industrial advancement. A people may be in a quiescent, indolent, uncultivated state, with few wants and wishes, all their tastes being either fully satisfied or entirely undeveloped, and they may fail to put forth the whole of their productive energies for want of any sufficient object of desire. The opening of a foreign trade, by making them acquainted with new objects, or tempting them by the easier acquisition of things which they had not previously thought attainable, sometimes works a complete industrial revolution in a country whose resources were previously undeveloped for want of energy and ambition in the people; inducing those who were satisfied with scanty comforts and little work, to work harder for the gratification of their new tastes, and even to save, and accumulate capital, for the still more complete satisfaction of those tastes at a future time.

With the benefit of twentieth-century hindsight, Haberler (1959: 11) has put forward four positive economic effects of trade that emphasise its power to transmit development internationally:

First, trade provides material means (capital goods, machinery and raw materials and semi-finished products) indispensable for economic development. Secondly, even more important, trade is the means and the vehicle for the dissemination of technological knowledge, the transmission of ideas for the importation of know-how, skills, managerial talents and entrepreneurship. Thirdly, trade is also the vehicle for the international movement of capital, especially from the developed to the underdeveloped countries. Fourthly, free trade is the best anti-monopoly policy and the best guarantee for the maintenance of a healthy degree of free competition.

Nevertheless, national abilities to realise in full the effects posited by Mill and Haberler are not equally distributed. Historically some countries have been spectacularly more successful than others. Deutsch (1981) has suggested a number of developmental factors that have favoured 'Western' countries (Western Europe, the United States, Canada, Australia and New Zealand):

(a) Geographical: geographically decentralised diversity (many relatively small valleys, rivers, lakes and ports); water supply of dependable moderate rain; plenitude of woods and use of metal.
(b) Characteristics of economic and technological culture: sustained capacity to learn from other cultures; sustained stream of autonomous innovations and discoveries; respect for manual labour; segmented and dynamic sense of time; use of power-driven machinery; industrial capital for capital equipment; efforts at material self-transcendence.
(c) Political and social practices and institutions: preference for the rule of law; the dualism of church and state; long-lasting autonomy of many small groups; self-governing cities; major political influence of merchants and industrial capitalists before 1850; the rise of critical thought; major social revolutions before 1900; individualism; tolerance and a heritage of enlightenment; major autonomous labour movements before 1900.

Deutsch (981: 89) argues that 'in the course of history, the earlier and stronger presence, the longer duration and the cumulative interaction of its characteristic traits have made the West unique – though not necessarily forever'. In the latter respect, changes may occur either as a result of 'catching-up' in other countries, or because of technological change in the direction of a more appropriate technology, or a labour-saving technology, or a de-skilling of previously essential activities. Where incorporation in the world-wide transport network pre-dated the formation of the country-wide market, there was a danger, even in formally 'independent' countries, that foreign agents would initially be primarily responsible for managing economic change and performing vital specialised commercial functions in the establishment of nation-wide markets and their linkage to the emerging world-wide system, and in providing valuable connections between consumers and suppliers and the provision of freight and investment services – in ways that compromised indigenous interests.

The free and receptive environment of post-colonial nineteenth-century Latin America exemplifies the ways in which economic power can initially be exerted by foreign merchants. The lack of a pre-existing indigenous entrepreneurial class and a local supply of rural capital made foreign control of the export and import trades inevitable: competition was not 'open', markets were not 'neutral'. Trade was initially inhibited because, as a witness said at the time (Graham and Humphreys 1962: 290) 'articles are not wanted, because they are not known; and their necessities must be created before supplies for them can be asked for', and populations were small, scattered and with low purchasing power. In these circumstances an important consideration was the simple matter of shipping economics: the impossibility of securing a sufficient return trade in Latin American produce because of the economic backwardness of the countries. As Woodbine Parish (1838: 356) commented: 'it is ... to the increase and multiplication of the native productions that we must look for the stability and improvement of ... trade'. Once the deficiencies of internal communications were overcome by the advent of the railways, development could proceed. Meanwhile, the initial low levels of import business encouraged foreign merchants, whether shipping agents or shippers, to diversify into the handling and marketing of local produce abroad, given their superior possession of access to capital and trade contacts. Furthermore, as Greenhill (1977b: 175) asserts:

> local commodity markets further reinforced the position of expatriate merchant houses. First, exporters remained consistently better informed through their many overseas contacts. Although the low level of local market information in Latin America impeded all sectors of trade, the foreign merchant was better placed to exploit confusion, and sophisticated enough to ignore bias and misleading reports. And without formal standards and price differentials, most careful businessmen, even if honest, imposed their own rough, rule-of-thumb gradings which lowered prices. The less scrupulous offered still lower prices which producers could not refuse. Second, ... lack of storage space forced producers to sell soon after harvest, thus depressing prices and preventing them from holding for a rise.

Thus, Encina complained with respect to Chile after 1850 (quoted by Greenhill 1977b: 161) that: 'in less than 50 years the foreign merchant suppressed our expanding commercial enterprise abroad; and in our own backyard eliminated us from international traffic largely replacing us in every respect'. European migration further generalised foreign involvement:

> German merchants had, by the '80s, taken over virtually the entire export business of Bahia in tobacco and sugar. By the early '90s they were the principal exporters of Chilean nitrates. French and Belgian houses handled the major part of Argentine wool exports ... German and North American houses were responsible for the bulk of the Latin American coffee exports from Brazil, Venezuela, Colombia [and] Central America. [Platt 1972: 139]

Elsewhere economic involvement extended to the financing of the urbanisation process and the introduction of sanitation, water, gas and electric supplies.

Shipowners were also able to exploit the fragmented and uneducated market for shipping services (see Greenhill 1977a; b) by means of their often exclusive ownership of dock and storage facilities; their use of exclusive contracts and concessions and tying arrangements which limited the merchant's choice; their demand for subventions prior to calling at particular ports or islands; their use of deferred rebates, of 'fighting' ships to displace rate-cutting outsiders and of exclusive through agreements with railway companies; and the subsequent resort to shipping conferences to regulate price and competition once freight rates fell, such that 'the free play of competition [was] more or less paralysed by the influence of "rings" ' (Platt 1972: 175). In one spectacular case, that of the American United Fruit Company formed in 1899, it was possible for a giant multinational firm to have a foreign involvement in the economic development of more than one country: building the railways, owning and leasing the new plantations and marketing the produce. By 1913 this company owned 1,098,995 acres and leased 1,210,443 acres of land in nine countries (Columbia, Costa Rica, Cuba, Honduras, Jamaica, San Domingo, Guatemala, Nicaragua and Panama (Adams 1914: 297)), and owned and operated 907.04 miles of railway and 532.09 miles of tramway in these countries (Adams op. cit.: 304), which it used for the cultivation and distribution of a variety of primary products, as is shown in Table 3.

Table 3: *The international locations, acreages and types of cultivation undertaken by the United Fruit Company, as on 30 September 1913*

Product cultivated	Colombia	Costa Rica	Cuba	Guatemala	Honduras	Jamaica	Panama	Total
Fruit								
Bananas	22,790	47,723	111	27,122	9,037	8,767	34,903	150,453
Oranges		52	694			88		834
Sugar cane		5	58,972					58,977
Miscellaneous								
Coconuts			123		97	4,122		4,322
Cocoa	47	441	846			77	1,143	2,554
Rubber		66			21	15		102
Other land	9,989	20,115	45,440	1,111	1,423	15,157	2,860	96,095
Total acreage	32,826	68,402	106,186	28,233	10,578	28,216	38,906	313,347

Source: Adams (1914: 300)

The unequal exchange relations outlined and the associated problem of undue external influence on development they raise will be addressed in Chapter 10, when the importance of modes production and societal organisation as determinants of structured international exchange will be examined. Suffice it to add here the following stricture laid down by Roepke (1942: 237):

> It is a truism to say that the phenomena which we call economic are ultimately determined by forces lying outside the sphere of economics and rooted in those aspects of the human mind determined primarily by education, tradition, religion, psycho-physical influences, the natural and the social milieu, and by the structure of the society and of the state. Whether it is desirable to bring the 'sociological' frame-work of economic phenomena to the surface will depend on whether we are entitled to regard it as a more or less constant factor or whether a profound change has occurred in the sociological frame-work. If the latter is the case, then we can hardly afford to confine the study of an economic phenomenon of major importance to its immediate aspects without unearthing its deeper sociological significance and causation. Such a procedure would be unrealistic and superficial.

Indeed, some would argue that 'the fundamental problem of modern social scientific theory ... [is] the separation of ideas about exchange from those about the social construction of the units involved in exchange' (J.W. Meyer 1980: 110).

(b) The competitive actions of firms

Goods and services that are transferable across national borders are either globally 'competitive' or 'uncompetitive'. H.P. Gray (1979: 82–4) defines these in a precise manner: 'competitive goods' are defined as goods that 'can be made in ... all countries using combinations of factors of production that are easily transferred from one product to another'; and 'noncompetitive goods' as 'goods . . . usually not competitive with domestic production and must be imported'. Gray distinguishes three types of noncompetitive goods: type A (or absolutely) noncompetitive goods that the importing country is incapable of producing; type B goods, 'gap-fillers', which fill the gap between domestic demand at the going world price and maximum domestic output; and type C goods, for which the technology is not available in the importing country.

Within the international structure of trade-participating states, upward and downward mobility of countries rests, in the absence of state-imposed industrial bias, on two factors: (a) the ability and/or willingness of business to effect favourable changes in established geographical and commodity trade patterns, or to react appropriately to unfavourable changes therein; and (b) their enterprise in and reactions to investment in technological progress. Dynamic competitiveness and growth not only require changes in the production coefficients of 'old' products and increases in the supply of existing factor inputs, but also that the domestic evolutionary potential of 'new' types of factor inputs and products is realised. Such changes alter old national orders of competitive/noncompetitive goods and services and have implications for new patterns of industrial specialisation, the potentials for which have to be actualised if competitive gains are to be maximised and/or competitive losses minimised. If this is not done, domestically produced goods will be uncompetitive against foreign produced goods both in the home and the foreign markets. As Rothschild (1975: 225) has written:

> 'competitiveness' does not consist exclusively in the ability to serve *given* demand patterns at low prices, but to a large and growing extent in the *creation* of demand for 'new' products through product innovation, attractive brands, marketing strategies etc. Supply does not – as the market equilibrium model suggests – simply adjust to an exogenous international demand structure; on the contrary, the structure of international trade flows is constantly modified by the supply side through the activities of 'pioneering' export innovators who discover openings for new products and product differentiation. Other exporters and exporting countries may then, as 'imitators', follow this lead and score successes by adjusting to the structured opportunities so revealed.

Failure to adjust in the ways indicated above will have important implications for the balance of payments in the short run, and the growth prospects of the economy in the long run. Uncompetitiveness internationally will inevitably lead to a loss of export markets abroad and increased imports in the home market as a result of greater foreign competition and penetrative abilities in all markets.

Technological change necessarily causes product shifts in trade flows as 'new' products arise and 'old' products are made redundant. Furthermore, the number of products exchanged is likely to increase, as new distinctive forms and stages of fabrication emerge and extend the variety of both intermediate and end products created, making production progressively more 'roundabout' (Kuznets 1967a: 25).

During the last two centuries, the process of industrial change and economic growth has been intimately related to a succession of industrial revolutions which have progressively transformed the internal industrial structure of national economies and the nature and purpose of their external links with the rest of the world. Svennilson (1954: 7) saw the main elements of this structural transformation process as involving five activities:

A change of production methods, mainly in the direction of more advanced mechanization;

A change of input–output relations between raw materials and end-products;

The development of new end-products, and shifts in the distribution of consumption between various products;

Changes in exports and imports in relation to the output of domestic industry; [and,]

A redistribution of manpower between different industries and occupations [and locations].

Such reallocations of economic activity centered on the ability of individual countries to pioneer and react to new sources of energy and their associated new technologies. Summarised in terms of leading industrial sectors, these were for Britain (the first industrialised country) in succession: cotton textiles, pig-iron, railroads, steel, electricity, motor vehicles, sulphuric acid, nitrogen, plastics and resins, synthetic fibres in the period 1783–1972, as dated by Rostow (1978) and indicated in Table 4.

Ability to be technologically avant-garde requires a perception of the need for technological progress, an understanding of its various forms, and the provision of a receptive environment in which to apply its innovations. There are two basic forms of technological progress: process-technological progress – 'producing the same goods at a lower cost'; and product-technological progress – 'the expansion of the characteristics of a good i.e.

Table 4: *Approximate dates of the principal leading industrial sectors in Great Britain and the United States, 1783-1972*

Sector	Great Britain 1783-1972			United States 1790-1972		
	Peak expansion rate	Leading sector duration Start	Finish	Peak expansion rate	Leading sector duration Start	Finish
Cotton textiles	1780s	1780s	1860s	1805–15	1820s	1870s
Pig iron	1790s	1780s	1880s	1840s	1840s	1910–20
Railroads	1830s	1830s	1870s	1830s	1830s	1890s
Steel	1870s	1870s	1920s	1870s	1870s	1920s
Electricity	1900–10	1900–10	—	1880s	1900–10	—
Motor vehicles	1900–10	1920–29	1960s	1900–10	1910–20	1950s
Sulphuric acid	1870s	*	1890s	1870s	*	1920s
Nitrogen	1940s	*	—	1940s	*	—
Plastics & resins	1940s	*	—	1940–45	*	—
Synthetic fibres	1920s	*	—	1950–55	*	—

* Industry not of sufficient scale to be regarded, in itself, as a leading sector.
Source: Rostow (1978: Tables V-2 and V-7)

an improvement in [its] "quality"... The creation of an entirely new set of characteristics will, of course, imply a new good' (Borkakoti 1975: 384–5). Technology as a source of comparative advantage is not, as some writers and commentators on trade and trade policy seem to believe, a free good capriciously and invidiously distributed by nature among the nations of the world (see Johnson (1975a: 5); and Stewart (1977: 3)). Technological innovation is not a 'production' process in the sense that a given combination of inputs leads to a predictable quantity or quality of output. It is basically a cumulative process of learning and experience, of making mistakes and taking risks which initially may be quite costly and perhaps unproductive (Lall 1976: 4). Magee (1977a) has described this process as specifically involving a five-stage investment sequence: investment must be made in information (i) to discover new products, and (ii) for product development, (iii) the creation of the production function, (iv) the creation of product markets, and (v) appropriation of the returns from an investment in new information. Fransman (1984: 10) has described 'technological capabilities' generally as including the following kinds of activities:

> the search for available alternative technologies and the selection of the most appropriate technology; the mastering of the technology . . .; the adaptation of the technology in order to suit specific production conditions; the further development of the technology as the result of minor innovations; the institutionalised search for more important innovations with the development of R & D facilities; the conducting of basic research.

Given the above, the market for technology tends to be a highly imperfect one in which information is limited, and monopoly usual. New production knowledge will undoubtedly confer temporary competitive advantages that can be protected by a patent system, which if conditionally and selectively relaxed by a licence system, may be used to maximise global profits. The uneven geographical incidence of expenditure to acquire such knowledge is illustrated by a UN Report (1970: 73) which estimated that 98 per cent of all expenditure on research and development, excluding the Second World socialist countries, takes place in rich nations (of which 70 per cent occurs in the United States and only 2 per cent in less-developed countries). Griffin (1974: 8) argues that inequality at the world level is increased when trade expansion is accompanied by technical change, as there is a strong likelihood that the gains from trade of LDCs will be reduced given their greater resource immobilities (for example, widespread illiteracy and a generally poor educational system means that labour cannot readily be shifted from one sector to another). Griffin quotes Hicks (1969: 165) to the effect that:

> the labour that is thrown out (as a result of technical change) may be in one country, and the expansion in demand for labour, which is the effect of the accumulation of capital that results, may be in another. The English handloom weavers, who were displaced by textile machinery, would (in the end and after much travail) find re-employment in England; but what of the Indian weavers who were displaced by the same improvement? Even in their case there would be a favourable effect, somewhere; but it might be anywhere; there would be no particular reason why it should be in India. The poorer the country, the narrower will be its range of opportunities; the more likely, therefore, it is that it

will suffer long-lasting damage, now and then, from a backwash of improvements that have occurred elsewhere.

Griffin further argues (1974: 10) that this is a cumulative process:

> The effect of technical change is continuously to raise factor productivities, the level of income and rates of growth in the rich countries. This acts as a cumulatively disequilibrating phenomenon, the result of which is that the technologically progressive countries tend to attract all mobile scarce resources from the underdeveloped countries. On balance, savings and skilled personnel flow not from rich to poor countries but from poor to rich. In the process international inequality is increased and underdevelopment is accentuated.

What matters then, within the international trading system is the process of inter-country technological transfer. Johnson (1975b: 32–41) suggests four alternative methods of technological diffusion:

 (i)   Through successful imitation by domestic producers in the former export markets.
 (ii) Through a decision by the innovating firm to establish a subsidiary or affiliate plant in the foreign market.
 (iii) Through the sale, or lease in return for royalties or a share of profits, of productive knowledge by the innovating firm to a domestic firm in the foreign market.
 (iv) The disappearance through competition of the commercial value of the knowledge to the point where it becomes a free good to the world as a whole and can be applied freely in the location with the lowest total factor cost. This may occur through a variety of routes, for example through the incorporation of the knowledge into standard machinery, or even standard complete production plants, supplied competitively with adequate instructions for installation and operation, or through the absorption of originally monopolised and secret scientific knowledge into standard textbooks and instruction courses – that is, through embodiment of the knowledge either in material capital goods or in human capital.

Thus technological exports can be in an embodied or disembodied form. Lall (1982: 11–13) distinguishes three broad groups of technology tradeables:

1. Industrial: includes 'besides manufacturing activity, such sectors as power generation and distribution, desalination, sewage, transportation (but excluding road and airport construction) and communications'. These have four main forms: turn-key projects; direct investments or joint ventures; licensing and consultancy.
2. Civil construction.
3. Other services, 'e.g. hotel management or ownership, financial services, health services, agricultural services'.

With respect to national industrial specialisation and the international division of labour, foreign involvement can result in the transplanting of technologies from advanced to less-developed countries that are 'inappropriate' to the local conditions of the latter. Failure to develop appropriate technologies that take account of local resources can lead to technological dependence that 'crowds out' local entrepreneurial skills, denationalises national industrial strategy, and contributes to a failure to develop local capital goods industries (Rosenberg 1976: 146–7). As F. Stewart has written (1977: 65,82,87,95):

The use of advanced-country technology ... generally requires the use of advanced-country organizations. These organizations are directly imported in the case of foreign investment; in other areas they are imported indirectly via management contracts and/or training managers overseas. Advanced-country technology thus leads to advanced-country techniques of management. It rules out the possibility of local development of local entrepreneurial talent ... [moreover] the introduction of [such] techniques imposes requirements for linked techniques in the rest of the country ... [which] leads to new requirements for imports, or imported techniques and for the type of infrastructural services found in the initiating country ... so that the system becomes self-justifying, generating selection mechanisms which are consistent with it ... the whole thrust of technological development [is] such as to create an entire set of inappropriate techniques, and to leave undeveloped and underdeveloped the techniques which suit the conditions in poor countries.

Thus in poor countries, the capacity to use knowledge in investment and production activities can be externally conditioned (see Lall 1982) for examples of indigenous exports of technological goods). Moreover, even when such countries seek to pursue import-substitution policies, there is a danger of what Marsden calls 'import reproduction' (quoted in F. Stewart 1977: 169), where the exact replication of goods previously imported involves the replication of the technological conditions required to produce them. Thus it is argued by some (Leys 1984) that the technology-in-use in such countries is a manifestation of the 'dominant social relations of production'.

2 Borders, national industrial structures and international trade relations

International economic relations are too frequently viewed as isolated processes unrelated to industrial structure, or at best as phenomena to be superficially explained by descriptions of products and markets or in terms of costs of production and purchasing power. A more comprehensive view is to be obtained by observing the extent to which the foreign trade of a nation and its other external economic relations, as well . . . as many of its domestic economic conditions and problems, are expressions of its organic economic constitution.

Donaldson (1928: 216)

The history of each territory [and its trade] is, in its main features, the history of successes and failures in tension between boundary reduction and boundary accentuation.

Allart and Valen (1981: 31)

Market rules of the game, and the determination of which markets are allowed to operate, are essentially political decisions.

Diaz-Alejandro (1975: 218)

The state – the machinery and power of the state – is a potential resource or threat to every industry. . . With its power to prohibit or compel, to take or give money, the state can and does selectively help or hurt a vast number of industries.

Stigler (1971: 3)

Countries are not homogeneous geographical loci of indeterminate relative size, with economic heritages and economic systems that are unspecified, for which international trade has an equal importance, as implied by many trade theories. Participation by individual states in international trade, the structure of that trade, and the national economic sovereignties exercised by such states with respect to their external economic relations have been crucially shaped by three basic circumstantial macro-structural factors now discussed: country size disparities; government-induced internal and cross-border economic frictions; and the international competitive structure.

COUNTRY-SIZE DISPARITIES

The economic size of a country has consequences for economic policy: it imposes certain constraints and can provide particular opportunities.

Gablis (1984: 36)

The size of one's state is no longer a matter of economic indifference.

Duncan (1950: 935)

Actual country sizes have been determined by political 'territorialisation'. Stojanovic (1978: 240) defines this process as 'the political occupation of tracts of land and their delimitation from other areas occupied in the same way'. While such geographical areas have often been pre-conditioned by natural boundaries such as coasts, mountains or rivers, they have significantly been determined, as Tilly (1975: 637) has written, 'by conquest, alliance, bargaining, argument, and administrative encroachment, until the territory, population, goods and activities claimed by the particular center extend either to the areas classified by other strong centers or to a point where the costs of communication and control exceed the returns from the periphery'. Further, in previously unsettled areas or areas exhibiting no geographical focus, artificial aboriginal geographical 'country' boundaries have been created and imposed by alien forces. This was the case in Africa during the period 1830–80, when that continent was fragmented into fifty-six 'national' entities or 'imperial zones' by individual colonialist European nations, of which the artificially and unsuitable smallness of size Mabogunje (1977: 434) asserts 'constituted a major obstacle not only to their freedom of action in the field of international trade but also to their ability effectively to undertake their own development'.

Once settled, borders, however politically determined, create size disparities that tend naturally to condition the relative significance of trade internally for any economy and, at the absolute level, its external importance for the international trading system as a whole.

(a) Size and the relative internal importance of trade

Kindleberger (1962: 28–32), as a result of his examination of national statistics, has put forward three general propositions with regard to a nation's natural resources and its relative propensity to trade, whatever its achievements in terms of economic development:

(1) *The narrower or more intensive a country's resource base, the more it will need to trade to satisfy its internal multiplicity of wants.* As Stojanovic argues (1978: 240) territorialisation is of crucial significance for it:

> gives rise to a specific kind of contradiction which in the final analysis leads to the essential phenomena out of which international relations emerge [in that it] brings about an interdependence between ... States, since no single given territory can contain all these natural requisites which a country as a whole offers man for the development of material production. [As] it is not possible for all politically bounded territories to offer equal conditions for [such development] ... this disparity ... brought about by territorialization itself ... remains of significance for international relations.

Emphasis here is on the natural resource base provided by geology, geography and climate, the production potential of which can be radically altered by new technologies that may make their primary raw material constituent parts more economically accessible, and may lead to new deposit discoveries that replenish exhaustible resources or diversify the product range. These may extend the geographical range of frontiers as has been the case recently with the exploitation of the resources of the sea bed (see Luard 1977).

(2) *The smaller the economy in geographic area, the narrower its resource base will tend to be, and the higher its foreign trade ratio.* Trade propensity can be

measured either as the ratio of a country's exports to its gross national product or the combined ratio of exports and imports to the latter statistic. While both are only crude measures of a country's trade dependence upon sales in and supplies from external world markets, both are regarded as giving useful approximations of this relationship (Kindleberger 1962; Kuznets 1967b: 301). It must, however, be emphasised here that 'the term "size" is somewhat ambiguous and may refer to either area or population' as 'the concept of "market" has both demand and supply aspects'. A country large in size and in population may, none the less, have low incomes, just as another country small in size but also large in population may equally have low incomes. Thus, the level of per capita income is, or perhaps can be, more important than the size of population or the geographical area (Vakil and Brahmananda 1960: 134).

The definition of small here must be arbitrary with regard to population, although conventionally countries with a population under one million are usually so defined (Kuznets 1960: 1415). As regards economic structure, however, whatever the criterion of country size used, it is the case that small nations are 'typically less diversified than that of larger units because of... the limiting effect [of size] ... on the supply of natural, irreproducible resources'. In the extreme case, some less-developed economies and very small economies such as offshore islands or land-locked mini-states tend to be virtual 'mono-economies', with their export earnings dependent on one or perhaps two primary commodities. Such economies often face greater comparative market instability and suffer if their products have a low income-elasticity of foreign demand; and, in the case of small islands, overall domestic price levels tend to be dominated by movements in the foreign price level of imports.

(3) *Conversely, the larger the economy in geographic area, the more diversified or extensive its resource base is likely to be and the lower its foreign trade ratio.* As regards population, the larger the country in geographic size, the larger the resource base, and *ceteris paribus*, the greater the capacity to have a larger sized population: this was especially important in the settlement by immigration of the United States and Australasia. As regards agriculture, Hicks (1963: 20) has pointed out that:

> one of the reasons who so many 'countries' are so specialised in their agricultural exports is that they are small countries which do have rather uniform climates... But a single country may have more than one such 'patch', and the characteristics of its 'patches' may be different. There is then a natural reason for diversification. Nigeria, for instance, with palm oil and cocoa in the south, can in the north of the country grow cotton. Such combinations are more likely the larger the country is ... It must be emphasised that the effective locational significance of resources is tempered by the qualities and quantities of human and man-made resources available for production purposes. The former includes the personal skill potential of workers, enterprise of managers and societal capacity for cooperative organisation; and the latter the supply of capital set aside and embodied in its combined social and industrial economic infrastructure and superstructure.

In the latter respect, small countries may well have advantages of concentration (Kuznets 1960: 18): 'with population small, labour and other economic resources can be more fully absorbed in a few economic activities'. Large countries, by contrast, may suffer from disadvantages arising from their greater size.

(b) Size and the absolute external importance of trade

As regards the absolute international importance of trade flows, countries which have been able to combine the benefits of large size with advanced economic development are able to exert extra-territorial advantages of international economic sovereignty, which smaller economies find hard to rival unless they act collusively with other states, or unless countervailing international power prevails as through international organisations. Marcy (1960: 269) lists three primary advantages of large countries:

(i) 'By virtue of their geographical size and economic and political power they can exercise domination effects on international markets.' Large countries have a strong bargaining position in international markets as buyers as well as sellers and in international tariff negotiations. They also have the potential to be capital centres which may attract considerable invisible trade, especially if their national currencies are stable.

(ii) 'The size of their domestic markets enables [them] to sell the bulk of their production at home and so to make their economies less sensitive to economic fluctuations originating abroad.'

(iii) 'For the same reason [they] can take full advantage of the economies of scale derived from mass production.' This may place them in a favoured position for technological change and innovation, which they may exploit internationally.

There is a 'conflict between the minimum or optimum scale of plant for some industries, and the limited domestic market of small nations' (Kuznets 1960: 7). Specialisation is limited by the extent of the market. Larger markets mean increased scale of operations which may involve 'scale economies' (see Balassa 1962: part II) such that 'for many types of capital equipment both initial and operating costs increase less rapidly than capacity' (Pratten 1971: 12) and '... longer production runs ... result in lower unit costs because they require less frequent halts in production to set or adjust machinery, less "downtime" to move different models or products through production lines, more specialisation in labour and capital equipment and small inventories of inputs and output' (Grubel and Lloyd 1975: 8). Furthermore, Kravis and Lipsey (1971: 33) have observed that:

> the number of product variants for which economies of scale can be obtained is a continuous function of the size of the economy; in the American market a large volume of production is practicable even for relatively specialized variants of products which have only narrow markets in the smaller economies of U.S. competitors.

It follows that small and medium-size countries must expand into foreign markets if they are to obtain comparable benefits and 'are under a greater handicap than large in the task of economic growth' (Kuznets 1960: 27).

Such a need to overcome the limitations of the domestic market is continually emphasised by the constant advance of production techniques. As Scitovsky (1960: 282) points out:

> Technologically an economy can be too small if its market is too small to provide an adequate outlet for the full-capacity output of the most efficient production plant in a given industry... [but] the minimum size of an economy is generally different for different industries. This would appear to give a technological determinant of the composition of small country trade.

Vaitsos (1976: 124–5) has added two further general propositions about domestic market size and developed countries with respect to investment:

> First, the smaller the domestic market of the home economy the more important the foreign investment operations become. Through the latter, high standards of living can be achieved for the home economy both through returns to capital invested abroad and through the high remuneration of skilled labour, professional or managerial services, research and development activities, etc., all of which are made possible by the sale of goods and services tied to foreign investments and technology sales. The achievement of similar results for an exporting country through simple trade relations is not always attainable in view of market segmentation, specific imperfections in inputs trade, and host government policies on import substitution.
>
> Secondly, the larger the domestic market relative to the country's resources, the more important foreign operations become to assure the availability of inputs as well as their supply at prices which permit rising real incomes at home.

Finally, economic power is a matter of structure as well as magnitude. There are two privileges of power, the ability to inflict situations on others and the ability to limit the actions of others. It tends to be the case that the output of certain key industrial products is unevenly distributed internationally and concentrated in a few states; that countries producing the bulk of raw materials are either unindustrialised or in the early stages of industrialisation and are heavily dependent upon the advanced nations not only as markets but as sources for their capital. Trade dependence will thus clearly be greater if exports and/or imports are concentrated in a few key sectors rather than distributed equally among the full range. What is indisputable, however, is that small countries are more reliant on foreign trade; their economic growth is more trade-dependent; and they tend to have greater problems resulting from commodity concentration of exports. Indeed, at the extreme end of the range, '... satellite relations are likely to emerge [and] their growth [is] so interwoven with that of their large partner[s] that one may question their independence as units for analysis' (Kuznets 1967b: 304).

Table 5 gives an indication of the wide range of the internal and external importance of the trade of 121 countries. Measuring domestic trade ratios as the ratio of national exports and imports averaged to each gross domestic product, and each country's external trade importance by its share of world exports, it is evident that the former lie in the range 5 to 453 per cent, the average for all countries being about 36 per cent; that the latter range is up to 13.2 per cent, the world export market share of most countries being 0.1 per cent or less; and that the country with one of the lowest trade ratios has the largest world export share (the United States), and the

Table 5: *Trade ratios of 121 countries in 1975 as measured by the rounded averaged percentage of their exports and imports to their GDP (a) ranked in ascending order by type of country (b) each country's world export market share, when greater than 0.1 per cent rounded*

Type	a	b	Country	a	b	Country	a	b	Country	a	b	Country
Industrial countries a 24% b 69%	7	(13.2)	United States	19	(4.3)	Italy	22	(0.9)	Austria	29	(0.9)	Norway
	11	(0.9)	Spain	19	(0.3)	New Zealand	24	(2.1)	Sweden	31		Iceland
	13	(1.5)	Australia	20	(11.0)	Germany	24	(1.6)	Switzerland	42	(0.4)	Ireland
	14	(6.8)	Japan	20	(5.4)	United Kingdom	24	(0.7)	Finland	43	(4.3)	Netherlands
	16	(6.5)	France	21	(4.2)	Canada	25	(1.1)	Denmark	47	(3.5)	Belgium
Oil-exporting developing countries a 40% b 13%	21	(1.0)	Nigeria	38	(0.7)	Libya	45	(0.9)	Iraq	50	(0.2)	Oman
	27	(1.1)	Venezuela	39	(0.6)	Algeria	46	(1.1)	Kuwait	52	(0.2)	Qatar
	30	(2.2)	Iran	43	(3.4)	Saudi Arabia	48	(0.7)	United Arab Em.			
Non-oil developing countries a 38% b 15%	5	(0.4)	Mexico	17	(0.1)	Ghana	25	(0.1)	Kenya	42		Barbados
	6	(0.5)	Burma	17		Somalia	25		Togo	43		Grenada
	6	(0.4)	India	17		Sudan	26		Zimbabwe	45	(0.6)	Hungary
	6		Argentina	18	(0.1)	Greece	27		Tunisia	48		Seychelles
	8		Bangladesh	18	(0.3)	Yemen A.R.	28	(0.1)	Nicaragua	49		W. Samoa
	8	(1.1)	Brazil	18		Madagascar	28	(0.1)	Senegal	50		Suriname
	8		Uganda	19	(0.3)	Philippines	30	(0.3)	Korea	51		Jordan
	9		Nepal	19	(0.3)	Thailand	30	(0.3)	Costa Rica	51		Mauritius
	9	(0.2)	Turkey	19	(0.1)	Guatemala	30	(0.1)	Panama	55	(0.2)	Lebanon*
	9	(0.2)	Chile**	19	(0.1)	Cameroon	30	(0.1)	Ivory Coast	55		St. Lucia
	10		Ethiopia	19		Mali	30		Malawi	56		Gambia
	11		Burundi	20	(0.2)	Portugal	32	(0.2)	Fiji	60	(0.2)	Liberia
	11	(0.2)	Colombia	21	(0.5)	Yugoslavia	32	(0.5)	El Salvador	62	(0.2)	Trinidad & Tobago
	12		Rwanda	21	(0.2)	Egypt	32	(0.2)	Honduras	63		Malta
	13		Chad	22		Benin	32		Gabon	70		Guyana
	13		Paraguay	22	(0.1)	Tanzania	33	(0.1)	Israel	73		Yemen P.D. Rep.
	14	(0.1)	Pakistan	23	(0.1)	Syria	34	(0.1)	Cyprus	85	(0.7)	Hong Kong
	14		Haiti	23		Congo	34		Jamaica	115	(0.2)	Bahrain
	14	(0.2)	Peru	23	(0.2)	Morocco	38		Papua N. Guinea	120	(0.7)	Singapore
	14		Upper Volta	23	(1.1)	South Africa	38	(0.2)	Mauritania	320	(0.3)	Bahamas
	15		Cent. Afric. Rep.	23	(0.2)	Zaire	39	(1.1)	Zambia	453	(0.3)	Netherlands Antilles
	15		Niger	24		Sierra Leone	40	(0.2)	Malaysia			
	17	(0.1)	Sri Lanka	25	(0.1)	Dominican Rep.	42	(0.1)	New Caledonia			

* 1974   ** 1972 figures

Source: derived from export and import ratio figures and world export market shares given on pages 52–5 and 105–16 respectively in *International Financial Statistics: Supplement on Trade Statistics, Supplement Series* No. 4. International Monetary Fund. Washington. 1982.

country with the highest trade ratio has a comparatively small world export share (the Netherlands Antilles). The very high trade ratios of the last five listed countries is indicative of their large external sectors that draw their purely domestic economic activities.

GOVERNMENT-INDUCED INTERNAL AND CROSS-BORDER ECONOMIC FRICTIONS

A nation can be defined as an area in which a central government exercises political authority. This . . . means that . . . [it] can be regarded as a unit of action in economic analysis.

Svennilson (1960: 1)

Man-made frictions essentially relate to the preferences exercised by the effective unit of societal control over internal productive resources and their organisation (whether this be a feudal manor, an autonomous city-state or a national government) and its preference for unconditional or conditional exclusivity or inclusivity with regard to its external economic relations or access to extra-area economic activity. Such extra-market action presupposes or requires that borders are sovereign and subject to customs authority monitoring and the areas so circumscribed possess both 'internal legitimacy' (Deutsch 1963: 12) and what Olson (1982: 121) calls 'jurisdictional integration'. In this respect, many less-developed countries have had to overcome certain disadvantages of history that can still threaten their political stability (see Downing 1980). The colonial partition of some continents into artificial imperial zones 'not only caused their subsequent economies to be unsuitably small, but also socially disintegrated without an originating ethnocentrism based on blood ties'. Rejai and Enloe (1969: 140) argue that this geographical ethnocentrism produced 'state-nations' in Asia and Africa as opposed to the 'nation-states' of Europe because in the latter 'authority and sovereignty have run ahead of self-conscious national identity and cultural integration', whereas in the former 'the sense of national identity evolved prior to the crystallization of the structure of political authority'. Their subsequent independence has therefore often been followed by an uncertain period of autonomous nation-building as internal cohesion and political organisation were attempted and asserted. Thus Rustow (1967: 74) argues that 'a low degree of governmental authority remains one of the prime characteristics of the so-called underdeveloped countries'.

Ability to impose economic frictions on non-border economic activity is derived primarily from the internal economic sovereignty exercised by governments as decision-making units in respect of their intra-country internal allocations of resources and control over domestic external entry and internal exit of resources, goods and services. The extent and nature of these frictions indicate the particular orientation of each national economic system with respect to market or planned solutions to the economic problems with which it is faced as well as the international financial viability of its economic relationships with the rest of the world. In the latter respect Svennilson (1960: 2–3) has written:

The international relation which seems to be most fundamental is the fact that international credits are not unlimited, while at the same time for most nations foreign currency reserves are of limited size. In foreign trade each nation has to pay its way. It is therefore faced with an international liquidity problem, corresponding to that of a private firm in a national market. The need to balance its international payments imposes certain restrictions on national policy and creates interrelations between various parts of a national economy; restrictions and interrelations which do not exist, or at least not in the same degree, for a region within a country. This is perhaps the most important discontinuity in economic relations that coincides with national frontiers.

National friction preferences will be expressed within a spectrum, the extremes of which are autarkic 'closed-door' exclusiveness and *laissez-faire* 'open door' free trade, and the interstices of which vary from conditional discriminatory bilateralism to unconditional non-discriminatory multilateralism. The degree of discontinuity imposed on the free inter-country flows of goods, services and economic resources that are mobile, will reflect each country's relative propensity for trade aversion, trade creation and trade diversion, as conditioned by the economic philosophy embodied in the organisation of the economic system as modified by its international financial position. In these ways, states attempt to legitimise certain economic activities and exchanges and delegitimise others with the force of their sovereign laws. Individually and collectively these national friction structures have consequences for the global location pattern of production processes, the international circulation of capital and labour and the size and commodity content of inter-country trade flows. But for these frictions, no special sets of analytical assumptions or special theory for international (as opposed to national) economic relations would be required (Condliffe 1951: 172). Naturally the scope, nature and importance of these change over time, as do other private-sector market imperfections (such as changes in the concentration of business ownership) according to the 'factor policy' (Ohlin 1979: 18) and needs of the internal economic system, the evolution of the international economy and any attempted extra-national assertions of sovereignty. The following list is indicative of the potential areas of national friction incidence and management as they have evolved and become relevant to international business and interstate trade flows:

1. Systemic internal frictions resulting from the general type of economic system pursued (capitalist, mixed, collectivist), its underpinning taxation burden, methods of monetary control, institutions and general economic policy objectives.
2. Selective foreign exchange regulations and capital controls with regard to 'inward' and 'outward' investment in debt instruments, including controls over the ability of economic sectors to switch investments, to disinvest and reinvest the proceeds and the degree of interventionist control applied to the international value of each national currency.
3. Regulations and taxes concerning visible trade (see R.E. Baldwin 1971) including the existence of different selective tariffs, quotas, bounties, and domestic subsidies; anti-dumping regulations, restrictive state-trading policies and discriminatory government and private procurement policies that differentiate between the foreign sector and restrictive foreign competition; patent legislation.

4. Immigration and emigration policies.
5. Company laws relating to incorporation procedures; requirements as to the filing of accounts and disclosure of information; legislation on restrictive business practices; national accountancy principles and standards (see S.J. Gray 1983) etc.
6. Banking laws and other financial regulations (see Griffiths 1975) with regard to industrial entry (branching laws, official overt/covert attitudes to mergers, takeovers etc.) systems of supervision and approaches adopted in respect of liquidity, prudential and solvency control, and the regulation of foreign currency exposure.
7. Other financial regulations including constraints on the issue of foreign and domestic bonds; the admission of securities to capital markets; insurance and reinsurance regulations; and stock exchange listing procedures.
8. Legislation affecting trade unions, wage costs and labour use (see Kitchen 1980: ch.2), this includes factor expenditure levels such as social contributions made by producers, minimum age regulations for employment, equal pay, minimum wages, worker and factory protection, school-leaving age and retirement age legislation.
9. National fiscal protection policies with regard to potentially transferable taxable business and anti-international tax avoidance legislation: this includes the tax treatment of branches and subsidiary companies, the criteria applied to determine the location of management control, and the degree of extraterritorial tax claim asserted by the revenue authority.

Naturally the trade-averting, trade-creating, trade-diverting properties of the national friction structure of the dominant economy in the international trading system will influence the general climate that is prevalent at any particular time. Even with the existence of supranational institutions that seek to impose codes of business conduct internationally, complete general equality of trading opportunity in the sense of equality of access and treatment in each national market is never perfect. Where however, most-favoured-nation treatment applies as a result of a trade treaty, each contracting party is automatically granted any concession subsequently made to a third party and is guaranteed non-discriminatory treatment with respect to tariffs. Even in the latter case, trade can nevertheless be distorted by non-tariff barriers that target particular activities by the selective positive use of incentives or the negative imposition of performance requirements such as minimum export targets; maximum import ceilings; discriminatory taxation, regulation and access to finance; denial of right of establishment; burdensome licensing requirements; requirements on nationality of employees; and limits on the range of services provided. Furthermore, some sectors, such as agriculture, have traditionally remained tightly protected, whereas others, such as defence, transport, financial and other service industries, the media etc., often tend to be closed to foreign investment or have a high degree of domestic protection as compared with other industrial sectors (see Safarian 1983).

Some frictions are designed to counteract market abuses or as embodiments of foreign policy attitudes. Anti-dumping regulations intended to prevent 'the sale of a good abroad at a price which is lower than the selling price of the same good at the same time and in the same circumstances at home' (Haberler 1936: 296) are examples of the former. Dumping is seen as 'unfair' if it materially damages the domestic industry of the focal importing country (Viner (1923); Wilczynski (1969: ch. 9) and Dale (1980)). Strategic embargoes, boycotts and economic sanctions are examples of the manifestations of the latter where economic warfare is being pursued largely for non-economic objectives (see Wilczyski 1969: ch. 12; Doxey 1980 and especially Hufbauer and Schott 1983). While it is true that 'international economic policy straddles . . . [the] two most important objectives of national sovereign nation-states – national security and economic well-being' (S.D. Cohen 1977: 5) – there is a problem of where to draw the line between what is ideally prudent from a national point of view and what is unacceptable from a cosmopolitan viewpoint. Leaving aside the structural abuses that may be imposed in colonial trade relationships (which are not 'international', i.e. trade between areas with autonomous sovereignty and distinctly separate systems of economic control, but intra-empire, enforced bilateral transfers), Hirschman (1980: 14–15) has argued that international (i.e. interstate) trade can be manipulated to achieve two main effects to enhance the power position of a particular country:

A supply effect

'By providing a more plentiful supply of goods or by replacing goods wanted less by goods wanted more (from the power standpoint), foreign trade enhances the potential military force of a country . . . which . . . [it] might bring to bear upon other countries.' As such it is 'an indirect instrument of power, the direct instrument being war or the threat of war'.

An influence effect

It provides 'a method of coercion of its own in the relations between sovereign nations . . . [to secure] relationships of dependence and influence'. This is a manifestation of 'economic aggression'.

Both effects involve a 'politicalisation' of trade, as was practised under national socialism in the inter-world-war period in Germany (see Hirschman 1980: 34–40, ch. 3). Hirschman produced a synoptical table summarising the conditions or policies conducive to increased national power by means of foreign trade based on his discussion of this period, as reproduced in Table 6.

The question of relative internal state power has been discussed by Boli-Bennett in respect of the concept of 'state dominance' which he defines (1980: 77) as 'the degree to which the state controls and regulates economic and social activity'. Since 1945 there has been in most capitalist economies a changed attitude towards internal state regulation of economic activities with the emergence of the mixed economy, the resultant plethora of interventionist objectives and supporting legislation (see Kirschen 1964, 1974) and the direct participation of the state in internal economic activities as is indicated by Table 7. Thus, 'the state [has grown] organizationally, in terms of its taxing power and its bureaucratic control' (Thomas and Meyer 1980: 143). In the latter respect, Kane (1977: 55–6) has

Table 6: *Principles of a power policy using foreign trade as its instrument*

I Policies relying on the *supply effect* of foreign trade and trying to insure its working even in times of war.
   A Concentrate imports on goods needed for the war machine.
   B Accumulate large stocks of strategic minerals.
   C Redirect trade to neighboring politically friendly or subject nations.
   D Secure control of the oceanic trade routes.

II Policies relying on the *influence effect* of foreign trade.
   A Policies designed to make it more difficult for the trading partner to *dispense entirely* with the trade.
      1 Increase the trading partners' gain from trade (without impairing the supply effect).
         a Develop exports in articles enjoying a monopolistic position in other countries and direct trade to such countries.
         b Direct trade toward poorer countries.
      2 Increase the trading partners' adjustment difficulties in case of stoppage of trade.
         a Trade with countries with little mobility of resources.
         b Induce a wide discrepancy betwen the pattern of production for exports and the pattern of production for home consumption.
      3 Create vested interests and tie the interests of existing powerful groups to the trade.
   B Policies designed to make it difficult for the trading partners to *shift* trade to each other or to third countries.
      1 In general: direct trade toward the small trading countries.
      2 With respect to the exports of the trading partners:
         a Import products for which there is little demand in other countries.
         b Drive prices of the export products of the trading partners above world prices:
            i By fostering high-cost production.
            ii By monetary manipulations.
         c Grant to the trading partners' exports advantages not relating to the price of their products.
      3 With respect to the imports of the trading partners:
         a Export highly differentiated goods creating consumption and production habits.
         b Develop trade on a bilateral basis.
      4 Develop transit trade.

Source: Hirschman (1980: 34–5)

argued that a 'regulatory dialectic' tends to develop, whereby regulation of activities accumulates as regulators extend their powers in response to strategic counter adjustments made by firms who seek to avoid/evade such controls: 'in what resembles reflex action, markets rechannel regulatory power, as regulatees short-circuit regulator intentions both by funding and exploiting loopholes [etc.] ... Prototypically, bureaucratic controls and market adaption chase each other round and round, generating additional problems, confrontations, and costs for society at large.'

Table 7: *General government current expenditures on goods services, and transfers as a percentage of GDP for 15 industrial countriess, 1950 and 1977*

	1950	1977
Austria	21.2	39.8
Belgium	19.6	43.5
Canada	19.2	37.0
Denmark	18.0	42.8[c]
Finland	19.7	35.6
France	26.7	40.9
West Germany	28.3	41.3
Italy	20.7[a]	42.5
Japan	14.6[b]	22.3
Netherlands	23.9	52.3
Norway	21.9[a]	46.2
Sweden	23.6	55.6
Switzerland	19.4	30.4
United Kingdom	30.1	40.8
United States	20.0	32.6
Arithmetic average	21.8	42.0

[a] *1951*   [b] *1952*   [c] *1976*
Source: National accounts of OECD countries

Not only has there been a general tendency towards state dominance in many economies, but also a fair degree of convergence in the degree of state dominance among groups of countries, arising from membership of the newly formed common markets or international organisations that impose their own codes of conduct and common regulations. Given that 'some productive agents are trapped behind their nation's boundaries whereas others are geographically free to seek their highest returns' and that 'while trapped productive factors seek the best occupational use for their talents within a country, agents that are footloose in the world market seek locations that are most attractive' (Jones 1980: 257), the above-mentioned frictions have led to concerted attempts by transnational agents to locate economic activities, otherwise constrained by taxes or burdensome prudential or structural regulations, in low-friction, low-tax, free-trade zones and tax havens, and for the latter centres to seek to attract such production transfers by the provision of positively discriminating freedoms for such activities (see Johns 1984; 1983). This has been particularly the case with respect to international finance, where the development of markets such as the Eurodollar market have reduced the ability of regulators to control events and have motivated a certain amount of degregulation in the United States and elsewhere, albeit on a country-by-country reciprocal basis (see Verheirstraeten 1981).

Externally too, as a result of the existence of non-market economies and the emergence of state capitalism, there has been a growth in state-trading – defined as 'when a government or a government-backed agency determines the essential terms (including prices or quantities) on which exports and imports have to take place' (Kostecki 1982a: 6). Such administered trade is estimated to account for at least one-quarter of world trade in general (Ianni 1982: 480) and very high shares in particular products. For example, in the world wheat trade, it was more than 95 per cent in the period 1973–7 (McCalla and Schmitz 1982); at least 28 per cent of OECD agricultural exports and inputs in the mid-1970s was so conducted (Kostecki 1980b); and state trade in metals exports varies from 21 to 31 per cent (Labys 1980). Furthermore, Hufbauer (1983: 328) has demonstrated (see Table 8) that there has been a tendency in recent years for an 'escalating use of subsidies [that] could replace tariffs as the central

Table 8 *Subsidies as a percentage of GDP as shown in the national income accounts of 7 industrial countries*

Countries	1952	1960	1972	1976	1980
Canada	0.41	0.81	0.83	1.73	2.34
United States	0.11	0.25	0.59	0.34	0.43
Japan	0.79	0.34	1.12	1.32	1.32
France	1.71	1.62	1.99	2.68	2.51
Germany	0.65	0.79	1.48	1.49	1.59
Italy	0.89	1.51	2.29	2.60	3.01
United Kingdom	2.68	1.93	1.82	2.78	2.32

Source: Hufbauer (1983: 328, Table 10.1)

distortions of . . . international commerce, and in time dominate other non-tariff barriers'. This has arisen because, as Malmgren (1977: 26) has argued:

> Governments more and more are being called upon to intervene in order to shore up troubled sectors of their economies and promote sectors that are judged politically to have high potential. But as government responsibility has broadened, structural objectives have also multiplied – to the point, in recent years, that structural policies often conflict with, or undercut, international rules and the arrangements which have resulted from international bargaining.

Sometimes trade frictions result from the global competitive deficiencies experienced by particular types of economic system. For example, it has been asserted (Banks 1983: 167) that 'the non-market economies are generally not very successful at marketing their exports and the consumer appeal of many of their manufactured items, in particular, is not all what it could be': because competition is not a prime motivator in the home market, it puts such countries at a disadvantage in international markets. As Holzman and Legvold (1975: 287) have observed: 'to have a comparative disadvantage in selling is much more of a problem than just having, as every nation does, a comparative disadvantage in a particular range of products, since selling affects virtually all manufactured products'. This may make countertrade (barter) attractive to such countries to enable them (Banks 1983: 166–7):

(i) to sell goods which, because of their poor quality, design etc., would ordinarily not get sold in export markets,

(ii) to expand the export-sales volume of other goods, through increased sales in existing markets or access to wider markets, and
(iii) to diversify export composition.

THE INTERNATIONAL COMPETITIVE STRUCTURE

> The relevance of [a] nation . . . is . . . dependent on the *international milieu* in which it is placed, that is to say, on the structure and policy of the nations with which it has its main economic contacts, actual and potential . . . this . . . will decide what parameters of action are at the disposal of national units of action in their international transactions.
>
> Svennilson (1960: 2)

> Core states exhibit a kind of "circulation of elites" in which hegemonic powers rise and fall. Peripheral areas and semi-peripheral areas also move up or down the hierarchical division of labour.
>
> Chase-Dunn (1982a: 22)

The international economic structure can be defined (Lake 1983: 523–4) as 'the number and category of states within the international economy'. Historically, the international competitive structure has not been atomistic, given inter-country differentials created by country size, uneven development and geopolitics, but hierarchical and subject to imperfect market tendencies. In practice it has been orientated by a structural interaction between territorialised, territorialising and unterritorialised areas in a particular historical sequence. As Schmitt (1969: 1–2) has observed, international integration became 'a nuclear process, one in which nuclear regions and social groups gain[ed] ascendancy over others . . . [such that] economic history may . . . best be read, not in terms of equilibratory forces, but rather in terms of shifting patterns of dominance and revolt'. An expanding international economic system emerged in Europe in the sixteenth century and extended from there to the Americas and part of Africa, embracing the rest of the world by the end of the nineteenth century in which various national and colonial economies became related through external trade. This economic interpenetration was essentially Eurocentric both in origin and in continuing global influence. According to Fieldhouse (1982: 178): 'In 1800 Europe and its possessions (including ex-colonies) covered about 55 per cent of the land surface of the world; in 1878, 67 per cent; and in 1914, 84.4 per cent . . . by 1939 the only significant countries which had never been under European rule were Turkey, parts of Arabia, Persia, China, Tibet, Mongolia and Siam.' Three structural aspects of this global economic interpenetration are now outlined:

(i) The creation of an enlarging and geographically shifting competitive inner core of advanced industrialised economies, the constituent parts of which changed in ranking order of importance and world influence.

> This group of economies is distinct from an always less advanced, disproportionally enlarging, and geographically shifting periphery. The whole being characterised by (a) periods of hegemony and rivalry, the latter being when no particular centre dominated the international exchange process; [and] (b) no overarching single state that encompasses the entire arena of economic competition. Rather than a worldstate, there is the *interstate system* of competing

states operating within the world market ... [which] subjects producers to the necessity of increasing productivity in order to maintain or increase their shares of the world [market and] the balance of power (of which) prevents any single state from controlling the world-economy and from imposing a political monopoly [Chase-Dunn 1982: 24–5.]

(ii) A pervasive protogenesis stage of trade development – colonialism – that created patriate world-empire economic unions that distorted many aboriginal trade relationships prior to the commencement of interstate trade when independence was achieved.

(iii) An unprecedented growth in wealth disparities between particular groups of countries.

(a) The development of an industrial elite of advanced nations

Random factors and the chronology of historical events gave certain countries temporary and semi-permanent significance both at the highest and at the lowest level of economic development. Those in the former group possessed, irrespective of their relative size, a superior ability to structure the emerging international system of exchange in their favour, notwithstanding the redistributions of economic power that took place within their elite number.

As an explanation for the initiation of industrial change, clearly the forces already enumerated gave the United Kingdom a leading position that would inevitably be eroded once industrialisation became more generalised. In this connection, S. Pollard (1981: 184) has referred to 'the differential of contemporaneousness', and Myrdal (1956b: 18–46) has evolved a 'theory of cumulative causation' to explain the sustained gap between countries as a result of unequal exchange advantages and their compounded impact over time. At the national level, Wallerstein (1980: 38) has used the concept of a 'hegemonic core power' for the comparatively rare cases where 'the products of a given state are produced so efficiently that they are by and large competitive even in other core states, and therefore the given core state will be the primary beneficiary of a maximally free market'. The basis of hegemony is twofold:

(i) 'Marked superiority in agro-industrial productive efficiency [which] leads to dominance of the spheres of commercial distribution of world trade, with correlative profits accruing both from being the entrepôt of much of world trade and from controlling the "invisibles" – transport, communications, and insurance.'

(ii) Resulting from 'commercial primacy' ... 'control of the financial sectors of banking (exchange, deposit, and credit) and of investment (direct and portfolio)'.

Such states inevitably face a constant trade strategy problem which has to be faced consciously or by default, the nature of which Kindleberger (1968: 54) posed when discussing the erosion of Great Britain's power at the end of the nineteenth century:

To sustain domestic growth and pay for necessary imports [a] country with a long industrial lead faced with rising industrial competition can follow one of several alternative courses. It can withdraw from the market for standardized commodities, in which foreign competition is likely to emerge first, and upgrade its industry to higher quality products. Some of this process is automatic, as the domestic consumer with increased incomes demands an improved product, and manufacturing inexorably alters the composition of output to accommodate this change. A second alternative is to pare costs and attempt to hang on to existing markets. A third is to redirect the identical goods at roughly the same costs to new markets often with the aid of capital exports. To the extent that the third alternative is adopted, it sustains income in the short run by relieving the pressure for technological change, however, and by building up export markets which in turn must crumble before domestic industrialization and third-country competition, it can be said to evade the problem which must be solved for growth to proceed, and in this way to slow down growth.

Moreover, such a position is rarely achieved independently of extra-market behaviour in the political and military sphere. As Baumgartner and Burns (1975: 130) have pointed out:

> International trade does not take place in a social or political vacuum ... The relationship between states and their exchanges of valuables through formal and informal agreements are ... typically characterised by multiplexity ... [also] economic valuables have multiple dimensions. Commodities may entail more than creating or establishing new productive capacity through the process of investment, or possibly the production of new outputs through their use as inputs, or providing consumptive utility. They can equally well be seen as carriers of values belonging to military, cultural, social, and potential spheres.

Thus the commercial and capital penetration of markets, whether inside or outside empires, cannot be seen solely in economic terms. The importance of 'multiplexity' is evident from this extract from Gallagher and Robinson (1953: 3–4):

> Great Britain was in South Africa primarily to safeguard the routes to the East, by preventing foreign powers from acquiring bases on the flank of these routes... By informal means if possible, or by formal annexation when necessary, British paramountcy was steadily upheld ... [in India]. Direct governmental promotion of products required by British industry, government manipulation of tariffs to help British exports, railway construction at high and guaranteed rates of interest to open the continental interior – all of these techniques of direct political control were employed in ways which seem alien to the so-called age of *laissez-faire*.

There was a high degree of multiplexity between visible trade and invisible trade as Mathias (1969: 310) has shown:

> in the new foreign markets being created by British merchants, India, South-east Asia, Australia, Africa, South America, China, most of the enterprise behind the trade, both ways, was British. These countries did not have long-distance merchant shipping fleets of their own, no local discount markets, no powerful insurance brokers, often few indigenous merchant houses who would keep in non-British hands the profits of internal distribution of British exports inland to final customers. Where British merchants organized the cargoes, they insured in London, they discounted in London, they banked in the branches of British banks set up in South America, India, Turkey and Egypt, Hong Kong and else-where. When the grain trade developed round Cape Horn to San Francisco, American insurance companies found to their fury that British merchants and shippers kept their custom firmly with their own nationals. The

same was true of British businessmen using the Bank of London and South America in Argentina. And Lloyd's of London had almost a monopoly of insuring the ships themselves.
The same was true in some of the older, traditional markets.

In respect of the multidimensional aspects of exchange, the export of the industrialisation process involved the export of many cultural British values, ideas and constitutional forms as the ever-extending development of overseas regions took place as Gallagher and Robinson (1953: 5) have indicated:

> Between 1812 and 1914 over 20 million persons emigrated from the British Isles, and nearly 70 per cent of them went outside the Empire. Between 1815 and 1880, it is estimated, £1,187,000,000 in credit had accumulated abroad, but no more than one-sixth was placed in the Empire. Even by 1913, something less than half of the £3,975,000,000 of foreign investment lay inside the Empire. Similarly, in no year of the century did the Empire buy much more than one-third of Britain's exports.

However, as the core became pluralised by the addition of a new generation of newly developing countries, the pre-formed importance of the first generation meant that graduation to that elite could not simply be achieved by the pursuit of policies identical to those of their predecessors. Thus Gerschenkron (1962: 24–5) has argued that 'in every instance of industrialization, imitation of the evolution in advanced countries appears in combination with different indigenously determined elements'. Thus attempts to 'catch-up' are not copy-book repetitions but 'orderly ... graduated deviations'. Pollard (1981: 187) has made the following observations about nineteenth-century conditions.

> Countries that are backward have been more deeply scarred by mercantilism; having a greater gap to overcome when they arrive at the 'take-off' or 'big spurt' point, they then grow faster, they go in more for heavy or high-technology industry, and they are constrained to adopt different methods of finance. Thus in Britain, industry was largely self-financed, while in Germany, as an example of the second generation, only banks could amass large enough sums to finance the big spurt. In Russia and other countries further behind still, it had to be the state. With these different sources of finance, also came different types of control and organizations, the later methods favouring the larger firms. These later alternatives, such as high technology from abroad in place of native skilled labour, and bank or government capital in place of entrepreneurial savings, may be considered to be substitutes by the latecomers for missing factors.

As regards core leadership, Kindleberger (1966, 1973, and 1981) has discussed the pivotal importance and influence of a *dominant* economy and its provision or reluctance to provide as an international collective good, the conditions for a stable but expanding international economy. He argues that a stable international economy will only obtain so long as the single leader is willing to assume responsibilities appropriate to the phase of international economic integration obtaining. Leadership, for Kindleberger, is altruistic, as a stable international economy is produced only at a net physical cost to the country in exchange for the amorphous 'privilege' of leading. The ability of a country to assume responsibility for stabilising the international economy is primarily determined by its position within the international economic structure, which Kindleberger (1981: 249) defines along the single dimension of size: 'small countries have no economic power. At the same time they have no responsibility for the economic system, nor any necessity to exert leadership.' Small states, in other words, are 'free riders'. Middle-sized countries (Kindleberger 1981: 250) are 'big enough to do damage to the system, but not substantial enough to stabilize it . . .'. Since they tend to act as if they were small free riders, middle-sized countries are extremely destabilising and are the 'spoilers' of the system. Only large states have both the capability and responsibility for leading the international economy. On the basis of nineteenth-century history, Kindleberger (1973: 292) asserts that there were three primary aspects of the collective good provision: '(a) maintaining a relatively open market for distress goods; (b) providing countercyclical long-term lending; and (c) discounting in a crisis'. The inter-war experience caused him to add two additional functions (1981: 247): '(d) managing, in some degree, the structure of exchange rates [and] (e) providing a degree of coordination of domestic monetary policies'. He further added (1973: 305) on the basis of that experience that 'for the world economy to be stabilized, there has to be a stabilizer, one stabilizer'. Within the 'first world' such a state can act as the principal 'locomotive' pulling the world economy along behind it (Bronfenbronner 1979).

An important fourth category of international actor, supporters, has been added by Lake (1983: 521–2):

> Supporters are middle-sized countries of high relative productivity; they are not simply smaller or less effective hegemonic leaders. Supporters cannot unilaterally lead the international economy, nor, unlike a hegemonic leader are they willing to accept high short-term costs for long-term gains. Rather, supporters seek to balance their short-term costs and benefits, and prefer to bargain for collective movement toward specified goals. Similarly, while hegemonic leaders forsake protection at home in order to lead the international economy as a whole toward greater openness, supporters are in most cases unwilling to do so. Even the most productive countries possess internationally uncompetitive industries. If a hegemonic leader were to protect such industries, it would undercut its ability to lead the international economy. Indeed, some measure of self-sacrifice in the short run may be necessary for a hegemonic leader to achieve its goal of constructing a liberal international economy. Supporters on the other hand, are not subject to the same constraints of leadership; they will protect their least competitive industries whenever possible.

Lake analyses the international economic structure in relation to two alternative indicators, one for trade share and the other for comparative productivity on the basis of the estimates given in Table 9. He characterises (1983: 524, 520) the evolution of the international trading system as being one where:

> The position of the United Kingdom changed most dramatically between 1870 and 1938, creating three distinct international economic structures. A hegemonic structure under British leadership existed from before 1870 until approximately World War I. Next, a structure of bilateral supportership, in which the United States and the United Kingdom were the key actors, was present from approximately 1913 to the late 1920s. Finally, a structure of unilateral supportership, centering on the United States, existed from 1929 through World War II. . . In the transition between the second and third structures (or very early

Table 9: *The international economic structure, 1870–1977*

	United States		United Kingdom		Germany		France	
	Proportion of world trade	*Relative productivity*	*Proportion of world trade*	*Relative productivity*	*Proportion of world trade*	*Relative productivity*	*Proportion of world trade*	*Relative productivity*
1870	8.8	1.22	24.0	1.63	9.7	.66	10.8	.65
1880	8.8	1.29	19.6	1.50	10.3	.64	11.4	.69
1890	9.7	1.37	18.5	1.45	10.9	.69	10.0	.63
1900	10.2	1.42	17.5	1.30	11.9	.74	8.5	.65
1913	11.1	1.56	14.1	1.15	12.2	.73	7.5	.68
1929	13.9	1.72	13.3	1.04	9.3	.66	6.4	.74
1938	11.3	1.71	14.0	.92	9.0	.69	5.2	.82
1950	18.4	2.77	13.1	1.15	4.5	.66	5.9	.80
1960	15.3	2.28	9.6	.98	9.3	.95	5.7	.87
1970	14.4	1.72	7.2	.86	11.2	1.06	6.4	.96
1977	13.4	1.45	5.9	.77	13.5	1.15	6.5	1.07

Source: Lake (1983: Table 1. p. 525; and Table 3. p. 541)

in the third), the liberal international economy collapsed. The United Kingdom was both unable and unwilling to lead in 1929 and 1930, while the United States was willing but unable to lead alone. It is Britain's transition from supporter to spoiler, in the interpretation presented here, which explains the collapse of the international economy. After World War II, the international economic structure evolved from hegemonic leadership under the United States to bilateral supportership by 1970 with the United States and West Germany as the key actors, and then to multilateral supportership with the addition of France in approximately 1975.

(b) Colonial trade: a protogenesis stage of international trade

An important force in forging aboriginal inter-country specialisation patterns was colonial occupation and resource management. Bergesen and Schoenberg (1980: 235-7) have shown that this occurred in two main historical waves: those of 1415-1825 and 1826-1969, as summarised in Table 10:

Table 10: *The number of colonies established and terminated per year and the net change during the upswings and downswings of the first and second waves of colonialism, 1415-1969*

	First wave, 1415-1825		Second wave, 1826-1969	
	Upswing 1415-1770[a]	Downswing 1775-1825	Upswing 1826-1921[b]	Downswing 1926-1969
Colonies established	.530 (N = 188)	.560 (N = 28)	1.451 (N = 138)	.395 (N = 17)
Colonies terminated	.115 (N = 41)	1.900 (N = 95)	.558 (N = 53)	2.953 (N = 127)
Net change	+415	-1.340	+.894	-2.558

[a] The peak lasted from 1770 through 1774
[b] The peak lasted from 1921 through 1925
Source: Bergesen and Schoenberg (1980: 237, Table 10.1)

The first cycle lasted 410 years (1415-1825), while the second only lasted 143 years (1826-1969). During the upswing of the first cycle, from its beginning in 1415 to the peak in 1770, 188 colonies were established at a rate of 0.530 colonies per year. During the upswing of the second cycle, from the trough of 1826 to the peak of 1921, 138 colonies were established at a rate of 1.452 per year, a little less than three times as fast as during the upswing of the first cycle... The net difference between the number of colonies established and terminated was twice as great during the upswing of the second cycle, when 0.894 colonies per year were being established compared with only 0.415 per year during the upswing of the first cycle. The downswing was also quicker during the second cycle... During the first downswing there was a net loss of 1.340 colonies per year, and an even greater loss of 2.558 colonies per year during the second downswing.

In this way territorial entities were formed, subsumed and given eventual autonomy, with the North American continent gaining independence in the eighteenth century, the South American continent in the nineteenth century and the other main areas after 1945. Sovereignty over global resources was first collectivised under the aegis of empires and then fragmented by the gathering momentum of political independence (see the Appendix on pp. 283–6). As colonial exchange was typically a protogenesis stage of that development, whether in the nineteenth century or before, its general nature must be examined, for it inevitably pre-determined the precise real basis from which international trade gains subsequently evolved, whether in a mutually advantageous manner or unequally once politically independent exchange was inaugurated.

As Bastable (1903: 3) makes clear, 'international trade is . . . as the very name implies, "trade between nations" ' In this connection, Wiles (1968: 4–5) argues that 'the very word "international" ' is misleading and that 'interstate' should be substituted for it. Colonial trade was only foreign in a geographical sense. Colonies were regarded in effect as circumscribed extensions, albeit farflung in most cases, of the resource base of the mother country, and were essentially in quasi-monetary and economic union with their core centres. As Brougham (1803: 148) pointed out at the beginning of the nineteenth century:

> The commerce which a country carries on with its colonies, is, in every respect, a home trade. The stock and the industry engaged in it are employed for the purpose of circulating the surplus produce of the different parts of the same extensive empire, subject to one government, inhabited by the same people, and ruled, in general, by the same system of laws.

Another contemporary writer, Bosanquet (1808: 41), similarly argued: 'The colonies are foreign but in name – the trade is domestic, both ends are British – all the produce appertains to British subjects, and all remains in Great Britain.'

External trade, whether at the micro-plantation/settlement level, or the macro-geographical entity level, was not international but patriate interregional trade in the case of formal colonies, and expatriate interregional trade in the case of informal empires, both types of trade essentially being effectively under the same or similar metropolitan jurisdictional control and set of state imposed economic frictions. They were often subject to special sets of laws that tied trade opportunities to the mother country, and pre-empted exchange with the rest of the world, unless in a re-exported form via the mother country. As Schmitt (1979: 105) comments, 'If colonization and trade became inseparable from the early seventeenth century on, the process can readily been seen as one of vertical integration.' Thus Mill (1909: 685–6) regarded such areas as

> hardly to be looked upon as countries, carrying on an exchange of commodities with other countries, but more properly as outlying agricultural or manufacturing establishments belonging to a larger country . . . [their trade is] hardly to be considered as external trade, but more resembles the traffic between town and country, and is amenable to the principles of the home trade.

He saw the West Indies as 'places where England found it convenient to carry on the production of sugar, coffee, and a few other tropical commodities. All the capital employed is English capital: almost all the industry is carried on for English uses.' A notable aspect of the outflow of direct investment at the time was the concomitant massive movement of labour that went out with it.

Thus it was that the activities of colonies were caught within the mother country's own web of economic activity, the internal demand structure and statecraft of which could very largely decide which products were to be created in relation to the requirements of its expanding home economy, and how they were geographically to be exchanged, whether as purely home trade or foreign trade of a direct or indirect re-exported type. Collectively they formed a world-scale industrial relational production network within the confines of an enforced inter-regional pattern of specialisation. The trade-generic forces in such areas were metropolitan and variously motivated with respect to the trade creation of new low-cost competitive trade to high-cost centres, or trade displacement when competitive goods industries were pre-empted to encourage complementary rather than rival economic development in such peripheries. Fieldhouse (1980: 382–5) lists some six basic exploitative options within the discretion of the colonial power:

(i)   the looting of treasure;
(ii) the transfer of colonial revenues;
(iii) the transfer of money or goods from colony to metropolis as interest on loans, payment for services rendered, the pensions and savings of colonial officials and the profits made by business firms;
(iv) the imposition of 'unfair' terms of trade;
(v)   the pre-emptive local prohibition of competitive rival industries, so holding back indigenous industrial progress; and,
(vi) the exploitation of natural endowments without compensating advantages, as when a colony is robbed of assets which might otherwise have financed the creation of a modern industrial economy.

Furthermore, these patriate and expatriate externally-determined trade relations were not conditioned by the financial disciplines which autonomous balance of payments monitoring might have imposed (see Schmitt 1969: 12; and Greaves 1957: 48, 51). The need for balanced exchange to be satisfied was not present in any rigorous way, so that intra-empire exchanges were uninhibited by balance of payments' adjustment mechanisms and financial constraints, because of their quasi-economic and monetary union relationships with their colonial masters. All sorts of economic distortions were therefore created that became deep-seated over time. Subsequently industrial inertia, an imposed inferior bargaining position and a lack of indigenous reallocative ability made industrial restructuring so much more complex and difficult on independent entry into the evolving international trading system.

Colonial economic union created in effect an empire-extended economy for each mother country and involved, in its purest imperialist form, a metropolitan internalisation via interregional trade of the hypothetical gains from external trade that otherwise would have accrued to the colonial areas if they had had autonomous control of their external economic relations. This 'enforced bilateralism' also enabled the mother country to substitute particular forms of interregional colonial trade for its own existing international trade, whether imports or exports. Colonies were often chosen as sources of supply of raw materials necessary for the mainland production of manufactures and/or sources of foodstuffs that facilitated the process of urbanisation and resource redeployment from agricultural to manufacturing industries in the core. Once the world market became highly competitive and interactionary as industrialisation spread to a group of newly industrialising economies, there was a tendency for mother economies to substitute outward interregional colonial trade for international trade exports. The latter was particularly the case when developing but relatively backward economies sought to catch-up the industrial leaders by effectively extending the size of their home markets, or, when general circumstances of international depression prevailed, as in the inter-war period, and there was a need to find markets sheltered from external competition (Daadler 1962: 141–4).

Historical data (G. Clark 1936) indicate that, in general, while (with the possible exception of Britain) colonial trade represented a comparatively small share of the total external trade of metropolitan economies – in 1913, 27 per cent of the UK, 12 per cent of France, 0.5 per cent of Germany, 0.8 per cent of Italy, 7 per cent of Japan (Daadler) – it nevertheless represented a predominant share of the external trade of those colonial centres.

Flux (1899) has provided a comprehensive picture of trade between the various empires and their metropolitan centres in the second half of the nineteenth century. Table 11 reveals that 74 per cent of the trade of Britain's external empire economy was internalised in the period 1892–6. Flux estimates that the comparable figure for the French, Dutch and Portuguese empires of the time was 60 per cent.

The fact of formal colonial dominion and 'informal' empire naturally led to the realisation that, in the words of Max Sering (quoted and translated from the German in Hirschman (1980: 11): 'It has been wrongly contended that in the economic intercourse of nations the dependence is always a mutual one, that always equal values are exchanged. As between private persons, there exist between national economies relations of exploitation and of subjugation.' The keypoint here is the distinction that needs to be made between situations of 'dependence', which refers to 'external reliance on other actors (Caporaso 1978a: 1) and situations of 'dependency'. which refers to 'the process of incorporation of less-developed countries (LDCs) into the global capitalist system and the 'structural' distortions 'resulting therefrom' (Caporaso 1978b: 18–20). In the latter type of context, countries have been differentiated by some commentators according to their general status within the international trading system. While the arguments for this are reserved for the discussion in Chapter 10, it will suffice to state here that the core-periphery distinction is one now commonly used. In the words of Wallerstein (1979: 97), who adds an intermediate category:

> The core-periphery distinction ... differentiates those zones in which are concentrated high-profit high-technology, high-wage diversified production (the core countries) from those in which are concentrated low-profit, low-technology, low-wage, less diversified production (the peripheral countries) ...

Table 11: *Intra-area British Empire trade as a percentage of total trade, 1892-6*

Empire countries	Imports from	Exports to	Total trade
	Trade with Britain Ave % 1892-6		
India	71.9	33.2	50.0
Australia	71.0	68.7	69.7
New Zealand	64.1	81.1	73.8
Canada	33.0	54.9	44.1
Newfoundland	32.1	24.6	28.5
Cape of Good Hope	78.5	96.4	87.6
Natal	71.3	71.1	71.3
West Indies	44.1	27.1	36.0
West Africa	73.1	53.0	62.8
Straits Settlements	12.9	18.0	15.3
Ceylon	24.9	70.8	46.8
Mauritius	22.4	7.3	15.4
British Guiana	54.6	54.4	54.5
Other countries	22.1	14.1	18.2
Average trade share with Great Britain	55.3	49.0	52.0
Total Colonial intra-empire trade as % of total trade of empire colonies	76	73	74

Source: derived from Flux (1899: 495-8)

the semi-peripheral countries . . . act as a peripheral zone for core countries and in part they act as a core country for some peripheral areas.

This approach posits a world system unified by a single-axial division of labour such that, within the above specified hierarchical order, 'the possibilities open to a given nation for capital accumulation or development are constrained by its structural position within this division of labour and shaped by the cyclical and secular evolution of the world system as a whole' (P. Evans 1979b: 15-16).

The extreme case of subjugation is often referred to as 'marginalisation', where an individual state allegedly faces 'the condition within the world economy, of being condemned to serve others, of being told what to do by the all-commanding international division of labour' (Braudel 1984: 413). Here dependency is so structured that there is 'a lack of capacity to manipulate the operative elements of an economic system . . . [such that it] has no internal dynamic which would enable it to function as an independent, autonomous entity' (Brewster 1973: 91) and that it is 'the structure of the international system – particularly in its economic aspects – that is the key variable to be studied in order to understand the form that development has taken . . .' (T. Smith 1979: 248). Braudel, (op. cit) argues that this was 'the allotted role of Latin America (unlike North America) – both before and after the gaining of political independence'. Such structures are thus not always reversible after decolonisation.

Table 12: *Real GNP per capita trends of major economic regions and of the world and intra-group gaps, 1750–1977 (in 1960 US $)*

	Total GNP (billions)				GNP per capita (dollars)				Gaps between developed countries and Third World		
	Developed countries	Third World	World	Total World	Total (A) developed	Most (B) developed	Total (C) 3rd World	Less developed	A/C	B/C	B/D
1750	35	112	148	187	182	230	188	130	1.0	1.2	1.8
1800	47	137	183	191	198	240	188	130	1.1	1.3	1.8
1830	67	150	218	197	237	360	183	130	1.3	2.0	2.8
1860	118	159	277	220	324	580	174	130	1.9	3.3	4.5
1913	430	217	646	364	662	1,350	192	130	3.4	7.0	10.4
1950	889	335	1,224	490	1,054	2,420	203	135	5.2	11.9	17.9
1960	1,394	514	1,909	633	1,453	2,800	250	140	5.8	11.2	20.0
1970	2,386	800	3,185	868	2,229	3,600	308	140	7.2	11.7	25.7
1977	3,108	1,082	4,190	1,001	2,739	4,220	355	145	7.7	11.9	29.1

Source: Bairoch (1981: 7–8. Tables 1:2 and 1:3)

(c) The unprecedented growth in wealth disparities between particular groups of countries

Bairoch (1981: 20) has shown that (see Table 12):

> in the mid 18th century, the gap between the least developed or poorest country and the richest was in the range 1.0 to 1.6 as a ratio and that the average standard of living of Europe was probably slightly lower than the rest of the world.

However, the initial spread of the industrial revolution to a small but growing number of industrialising countries created significant per capita growth and wealth disparities between such countries and the rest of the world from the 1830s onwards, disparities that became compounded over time. Bairoch establishes that the income gap increased substantially between 1830 and 1876, when the aggregate GNP of developed countries probably exceeded the combined total for those countries that came to constitute the Third World, and that (op. cit) 21–22)

> Around 1972–76, the developed countries, with some 31 per cent of the world population, concentrated 50 per cent of the world's income. This implies that the gap in average incomes was then already in the range of 1.0 to 2.2. This reached 3.4 by about 1913; 5.2 in 1950; 7.2 in 1970 and 7.7 in 1977.

Of greater significance, however, is the observed gap between the most developed countries and the unindustrialised Third World (op. cit: 23–24), between which 'the gap was already of 1.0 to 2.0 in the 1830s . . . of 1.0 to 7.0 in 1913, and [of] 1.0 to 11.9 in 1950'.

ENVOI

Naturally, it is an extremely difficult task (many would claim an impossible one) to create a general theory that could be used to demonstrate, beyond equivocation, that both the origins of the modern world economy and its subsequent evolution were, and are, subject to a single dynamic impulse. Nevertheless, before we examine what Dobb (1963: 29) has called the 'autonomous territory' of theoretical exchange relationships and others have derided as *economism*, economics that excludes the political dimension (Amin 1974: 59) and 'the intimate relation between economic and non-economic factors' (Gardner 1980: 383), it is necessary to attempt a stylised outline of some of the structural and organic elements of the evolutionary process that brought about the trade networks of interdependence that constitute the international economy today. The approach adopted is not that of the economic historian, but eclectic, designed to provide a background against which the foreground of particular trade theories may subsequently be related; the development of international economic thought concerning the impulses surrounding what does/might determine international exchange appraised and in which the parameters governing external exchange are shown to be ever-changing.

3 The changing parameters of external trade: the integration and growth of the international economy in historical perspective

If geography proposes, history disposes.

Braudel (1984: 523)

It is possible to treat the evolution of our modern world as a history of political and economic expansion – a moving frontier of trade, investment, settlement, colonization, and missionary enterprise, preceded by maritime exploration in which trade was a dynamic impulse. The expansion did not cease until the whole world, the unconquered temperate grasslands as well as the ancient civilizations of Asia and Africa, had been brought within the orbit of the dominant western European trading civilization. The political structure and the economic organization of our modern world were created in this vast process of commercial expansion.

Condliffe (1951: 14)

Recognition of the phase phenomenon is important ... because it forces consideration of factors operating for the group as a whole. Each phase is an orbit within which the countries are constrained to move. This does not prevent them from following different trajectories, but it means that their options are different from those they had in earlier orbits. Each phase has its own momentum which it is difficult to break, except by some collective happening. The breaks in trend between phases have in fact been caused mainly by system-shocks rather than by collective planning and foresight.

Maddison (1982: 94)

The development of an interdependent multi-continental, multinational international economy is essentially a post-fifteenth-century phenomenon. Its evolution was temporally patterned, its geographical coverage progressing and broadening from an aboriginal Eurocentric Atlantic economy in the sixteenth century to one that occupied virtually the whole globe by 1914. This achievement was the result:

(a) of a series of country incorporations into an extending oceanic trading system, many of which took place in unequal economic circumstances, and each of which individually lessened the areas external to the system and further advanced the geographical extent of the increasingly world-wide interdependent zone; and,

(b) of three general 'waves' of positive organic integration by trade (as discerned by Haberler (1964) and extended by Maddison (1982)), despite two of relative disintegration, each having its own particular regime outlook.

The processes involved in (a) will be intermittently referred to in the discussion of (b) that now proceeds according to the following periodicity of events:

I   The internal integration of nation states prior to 1870: the early development of the trade of what became of the 'First World' capitalist economies in (a) the period before 1820: the rise and decline of mercantilism; and (b) the period 1820–70: the rise of *laissez-faire* multilateral British trade relations.

II   The First Golden Age of Global Trade 1870–1913: the establishment of world-wide intercontinental trade networks in a largely colonial context; the decline of free trade relations as Britain's competitors industrialised.

III   Trade disintegration and the rise of economic nationalism 1914–1952: beggar-my-neighbour trade policies, and the emergence of a Socialist 'Second World' of command economies.

IV   The First Golden Age of International Trade 1953–1972: decolonisation; the establishment of supranational economic institutions; and the emergence of a politically independent, undeveloped 'Third World' of less developed economies.

V   Relative trade disintegration and the rise of transnational resource allocation 1973–: a period of structural crises and 'managed' trade; the emergence of a 'Fourth World' of newly industrialising countries, 'First-World' post-industrial problems, 'Second World' technological backwardness and 'Third World' problems of debt and continued undevelopment.

Qualitative aspects of each period will be briefly outlined and features highlighted that are considered useful and germane to the theories of trade discussed in Parts II and III.

THE INTERNAL INTEGRATION OF NATION-STATES PRIOR TO 1870

Haberler (1964: 2) considers the first major stage of international integration as that of the internal integration of economies. While a country is *de jure* merely a detached geographical entity on the world map, its bounded demarcation does not *de facto* become an economically integrated area with a national sense of identity until, in effective political terms, common cultural patterns and institutional arrangements support the hegemony of a central government which can exercise political authority and control over the land areas circumscribed by such territorial limits. Once this is achieved, customs and excise arrangements may be effectively imposed on the outward and inward flows of goods, services, capital and people, and control and regulation of internal national resource allocation attempted. Such jurisdictional integration imposes potential frontier discontinuities on the economic relations between geographical areas and permits the state to act as an 'organizng centre' (Braudel 1984: 36) for economic activities. Tilly (1975: 636) has generalised the historical global impact of this process with respect to three time-phases:

(1)   the formation and consolidation of the first great national states in commercial and military competition with each other, accompanied by their economic penetration of the remainder of Europe and of important parts of the world outside of Europe: roughly 1500 to 1700;

(2) the regrouping of the remainder of Europe into a system of states, accompanied by the extension of European political control into most of the non-European world, save those portions already dominated by substantial political organisations (for example, China and Japan): roughly 1650 to 1850;

(3) the extention of the state system to the rest of the world, both through the acquisition of formal independence by colonies and clients, and through the incorporation of existing powers like China and Japan into the system: roughly 1800 to 1850.

The extent of the power of each more or less autonomous political unit and the process of distinct nation-state mapping was concluded as a result of wars, alliances and in some cases a process of federal unification of states; and an extension of the political and economic domination of a small number of successful states from their European base to much of the rest of the world through the creation of client states and colonies, first in the Americas and subsequently in the African, Asian, and Oceanian continents. This state system was only gradually transferred to the entire world and was not finally formally completed until mass decolonisation took place after 1945. Only then did inter-country trade relations become formally pervasively inter-state in their orientation, i.e. strictly 'international'. By this time, some of the first-formed nation-states had been able to secure trade advantages that reflected the organisational weaknesses that obtained in many of the last-formed states. Naturally, during this process, wars and peace treaties brought about major reallocations and extensive reallignments of geographical territory. Several states were created only to be later absorbed or radically redefined, each reorganisation causing a degree of economic dislocation and development discontinuity in the internal integration process. Few countries retained their aboriginal geographical identities over the nineteenth and twentieth centuries. From the Appendix on pp. 283–6, it is clear that, prior to 1800, formal political independence had been gained by some thirty-two countries, including those that became the major industrial powers in Europe and North America; to which number a further twenty-two countries were added in the period 1801–70, many of which were in South America; a further ten in the period 1870–1913, eleven in the period 1914–40, and seventy-nine in the wholesale decolonisation that took place in the period 1945–84 (this excludes mini-states and islands with populations under 200,000).

The process of integration and the transplanting of the state system involved the creation of internal market linkage via inter-regional, intra-continental, and inter-continental trade networks that required the technological conquest of the frictions of time and space that otherwise separate regions and countries. Internally development often had to be effected by the geographical expansion of a frontier of settlement. Eventually a world-system of international interdependence was created from a Eurocentric core of countries that gradually incorporated other countries into its extending peripheries, by reducing the size of what Wallerstein (1974: 301–2) has called the 'external arena': the difference between the periphery and the external arena being that the former contains 'geographical areas' wherein production is primarily of lower-ranking goods but which is an integral part of the overall system of the division of labour because the commodities involved are essential for daily use in the core countries; while the latter encompasses countries that either have no trade relations with the core or 'some kind of trade relationship based primarily on the exchange of preciosities, what was sometimes called the "rich trades" '.

Achievement of internal integration and the formation of national markets were not universally easy to effect: 'at ground level and sea level... the networks of local and regional markets were built up over century after century' (Braudel 1984: 36). Moreover, as Myrdal (1956a: 11) has observed:

> economic integration is at bottom not only, and perhaps not even mainly, an economic problem, but also a problem of political science, sociology, and social psychology... there must be a growing social cohesion and practical solidarity. The members [of the community] must increasingly come to feel that they belong together and have common interests and responsibilities, and they must acquire a willingness to obey rules that apply to the entire community and to share in the cost of common expenditures decided upon by political process.

The significance of the internal integration phase is that (Engels quoted by Stojanovic 1978: 239): 'The old society based on tribal links breaks up in the clash with newly established classes; its place is taken by a new society, the basic units of which are territorial rather than tribal communities.' Economic market forces were an integral part of this territorialisation process. As Lindbeck (1975: 24) points out:

> the emergence and consolidation of the national state... was partly a political adjustment to the economic forces which required larger integrated areas for production, exchange, entrepreneurship and factor mobility. Local regulations, such as those concerning tariffs, transformation fees and laws regarding contracts, production and exchange were replaced by national rules.

While political independence and the internal integration process were largely accomplished by 1870 for what became the major 'First World' twentieth-century industrial nations, two distinctly divergent phases of economic policy attitude towards external trade relations were experienced: the first operative in the period prior to 1820, and the second in the period 1820–70, both of which will now be outlined.

(a) Internal integration and international trade before 1820

Years	Core structure	Core-periphery relations
1500–1820	Multicentric-unstable. A plurality of competing states resulting in commercial rivalries, dynastic struggles and balance of power conflicts within the European state system.	More explicit political regulation: *Colonialism* The first colonial expansion led by Spain and Portugal centered in the Americas. *Trade* Mercantile regulation of colonial trade.

Bergesen and Schoenberg (1980: 241)

Until the nineteenth century, prosperity gained through trade usually involved a considerable beggar-my-neighbour element because of the limited size of the world market and its rather slow growth: national fortunes were largely gained at the expense of ousted rivals. 'A ... high proportion of trade... [was] of an entrepôt character, involving re-exports of tropical products rather than exports of domestic manufacturers. Trade of all the major countries involved monopolistic restrictions' (Maddison 1983: 59). The five centuries preceeding 1800 were marked by the general influence of a broadly mercantilist economic philosophy: aboriginal oceanic trades were developed largely through state approved monopolistic trading companies by those nations possessing superior technology in navigation, shipbuilding and armaments in ways that sought to exploit national state power. At first the main organising centres for inter-country trade were fairs and city-centred economies such as Venice, Genoa, Antwerp and Amsterdam. Subsequently, these functions were subsumed by the constitutional authorities of the surrounding kingdoms. Trans-oceanic links and the territorial penetration of distant lands were achieved following any necessary prior 'voyage of discovery', as a result of a three-stage sequence of events (Moreland 1923: 223): 'First... the "Voyage" – the trading vessel, like a travelling bazaar, peddling its wares on a grand scale; then came the "Factory", a concession operated within a country, or in a trade centre; and the last stage was territorial occupation'. In the case of virgin, unsettled areas all three stages could be almost simultaneous.

In the thirteenth century, there had been a 'hunger for goods'. The commercial policy generally pursued had been a 'policy of provision', emphasising the need to retain and attract basic commodities by hindering or regulating their export, and to facilitate imports by being tolerant of foreign suppliers, especially in the case of foodstuffs, armaments and raw materials. Parochial particularism prevailed, given the existing mosaic of small feudal fiefdoms and poor land communications. This made for economically fragmented kingdoms. Extensions of the domestic system of production, the rise of craft guilds and the break up of the manorial system led to the growth of towns and the commutation of feudal dues and services for money payments. Thenceforth, each town tended to develop its own tolls, customs, coinages, weights and measures, all of which made internal trade excessively friction-bound:

> goods and travellers were held up by customs barriers at about every 6 miles on the best routes – the currency changed with every day's journey ... industrial activity was confined to the handicraftsmen of the locality, and agricultural production was subordinated to the interest of the neighbouring little municipality, and every little community governed as it thought best [Heckscher 1955, *I*: 432.]

These powers intensified as the 'natural economy' was replaced by the 'exchange economy'. Thus, the great roads which joined London to the seaboard were described by Curtler (1920: 41) as 'arteries along which flows money, the most destructive solvent of seignioral power'. Feudal domestic economies were now replaced by provincial 'local urbanism', under which market dues and tolls were levied for the benefit of towns, as collective bodies, in their dealings with the surrounding countryside, on the one hand, and stranger-merchants, on the other. Dobb (1963: 90) describes this development thus:

> Since the municipal authority had the right to make regulations as to who should trade and when they should trade, it possessed a considerable power of timing the balance of all market transactions in favour of the townsmen. If it could limit certain dealings, or at least give priority in dealings, to its own citizens; if it could put minimum prices on goods which townsmen had to sell and maximum prices on things which townsmen wished to buy; if it could narrow the alternative sources of sale or purchase that were available to the surrounding countryside, and limit the right of stranger-merchants to deal with countryfolk direct or with anyone except themselves, then the town manifestly possessed considerable power of influencing the terms of exchange to its own advantage.

Centralising monarchs now sought to secure the above powers within their kingdoms and to replace the system of town policy with an economic order dictated by the interests of the state. Mercantilism now became an important 'agent of unification' of countries. Its aim was (Heckscher 1955, *I*: 22) 'to make the state's purposes decisive in a uniform economic sphere and to make all economic activity subservient to considerations corresponding to the requirements of the state ... [which involved] the total reconstruction of society and its organisation ... [and the regulation of] all commerce and industry, so that the power of [the state] relatively to other nations might be promoted'. Externally, national self-sufficiency was to be emphasised, and a 'policy of power' substituted for the 'policy of plenty'. Imports were to be discouraged and exports encouraged in accordance with a 'balance of trade' approach designed to amass surpluses and national 'treasure'. National security was preferred to abundance. This change of attitude arose from an obsessive static conception of the magnitude of global economic resources (Heckscher 1955, *I*: 25, 31), such that resources 'could be increased in one country only at the expense of another', and a derived belief that 'the position of a particular country could change and was capable of progress, but only through acquisitions from other countries'. While writers like Colbert did allow for the possibility of 'the discovery of new, hitherto unknown, trade', such an eventuality was regarded as 'very uncertain and ... an accident [to be] ruled out'. A 'fear of goods' attitude now made trade policies protectionist, beggar-my-neighbour and, where gains were possible, discriminatory. Economic policy was directed towards the particular ends demanded by political, and more especially military, power: the import of goods necessary for war was allowed and often encouraged, while their export was either forbidden or burdened with dues.

Prior to the late fifteenth century, the centre of world commerce was the Mediterranean, the junction of the Occident and the Orient land trade routes and those from the North and Baltic Seas. The main contents of this commerce were light goods of low bulk relative to their value: the 'rich trades' that included luxuries such as spices, silks, ivory and precious stones; the main distribution centres were the city-states such as Genoa and Venice that were located at the nodal point of East–West interchange. From Italy, these products were distributed via fairs, as at Champagne, to intermediary German Hanseatic cities and thence within a commercial domain that extended in a great semicircle from Novgorod in the east, to Scandinavia and Iceland in the north, England in the west and Lisbon in the south, to the rest of Europe. However, this system was terminated by the rise in the sixteenth century of the Ottoman Empire that interposed itself between Europe and the East. This incipient event, and the power of the Italian city-states induced navigators from other countries to venture forth into unknown and uncharted seas, in search of new routes to the East and elsewhere. The voyages of discovery by Columbus, Vasco da Gama, Cabot, and Magellan, revealed the existence of the Americas in 1492, the Cape route to India in 1498; Newfoundland in 1496; and the route via South America to India in 1520 (Newby 1982). Thence, as Beer (1980: 3) has written, 'the future belonged not to the Mediterranean countries, but to those on or near the Atlantic seaboard' as bases for the penetration of these two important continents.

The period 1500–1700 was characterised by rapidly changing European politico-economic rivalries; competitive penetration of India and the Americas, and the embryonic formation of an international economy within which Britain wrested supremacy from the Dutch in the seventeenth century and the French in the eighteenth century. These main changes will now be outlined in relation to the following time periods, 1470–1590; 1590–1703; 1703–1820.

The period 1470–1590

This was largely an era of Portuguese/Spanish rivalry, terminated by a thirty-year period of decline of both countries. Initially, these countries enjoyed a virtual monopoly of global exploration as a result of the Inter Caetera Papal Bull issued by Pope Alexander VI in 1493, that drew a line of demarcation giving Portugal dominance and exploration rights to the East and Spain to the West of the then known world. Desire for gold and silver treasure strongly motivated the initial voyages of discovery. For this reason, Spain eventually occupied the auriferous and argentiferous soils of Central America, most of South America and first explored the major parts of what is now the southern United States. With the exception of repatriated precious metal treasure, little encouragement was given to indigenous exports from these areas, despite the feudal-like control of production that was imposed in their plantations, haciendas and encomiendas, for, unlike the East Indies, the Americas did not produce articles of great value per unit of weight, such as spices, silks and muslins, suitable for the oceanic trade of the time (Furtado 1970: 11). By contrast, the Portuguese – after the discovery of the Cape of Good Hope by Diaz in 1487 and its use in 1497 by Vasco da Gama to pioneer the sea route to India, then the central part of the crumbling Moghul Empire – established a factory at the Indian part of Calicut in 1500, followed by trading posts both there, on the now accessible east coast of Africa, at Macao and in the Spice Islands. Thus it was that 'the wealth of the Indies poured into Europe through Lisbon' (Condliffe 1951: 54) and Antwerp, having become the entrepôt for North European traders (Walton and Shepherd 1979: 18), was chosen as the new depot for the spice trade.

The mercantilist 'policy of power' encouraged the acquisition of colonies: they were regarded as outposts of the home economy, strengthening the power of its state, their commerce freeing the mother country from a degree of trade dependence on rival nations, their possession providing the potential for gold and silver discoveries. At first they were seen as sources of supply within a self-contained, self-sufficient empire. Tropical possessions in particular were considered ideal, as their natural production embodied a climate different from the European one, the products from which could be a rich source of entrepôt earnings. An important feature of the development of Portuguese trade was the transplanting of sugar cultivation, first to Mediterranean and then to Atlantic islands (Madeira, the Azores and the Canaries), thence across the Atlantic to Brazil and the West Indies in the sixteenth century. As Perkins (1980: 10) has written, 'it is virtually impossible to overemphasize the importance of population growth in explaining the expansion of the colonial economy. Land and natural resources were abundant and already in place waiting for development. Labor was the scarce resource'. Henceforth, until the nineteenth century, labour shortages were solved by a concomitant supportive trade in slaves, that was subsequently supplemented by settlers, indentured labour and convicts in certain areas. The initial origin for the slave trade was West Africa. As early as the 1450s, nearly a thousand slaves per year were being transported for production purposes (Walton and Shepherd 1979: 3). The extent of this 'black ivory' trade over the centuries is shown in Table 13.

Continental religious wars in the sixteenth century made the non-participant Dutch and English the only potential competitors of Spanish and Portuguese colonial expansion, with the English (and to some extent the French) comparative late starters, their initial efforts being 'little more than attempts to side-step Spanish claims and authority ... [their] experimental projects of empire ... directed towards areas far enough away from Spanish territory to avoid armed conflict' (G.S. Graham 1972: 2). The first attempts at American colonies were made by Gilbert (1578) and Raleigh (1584, 1608) as a result of the issuing of Letters Patent. Defeat of the Spanish Armada in 1588 left the sea 'common to all men'; and when Portugal was made subject to Spanish rule from 1580 to 1640, the British took over from the Portuguese in India, and the Dutch secured the East Indies. However, (G.S. Graham 1972: 24)

> by the end of the sixteenth century it was obvious that the wealth of the New World as well as of Asia could be garnered only by those nations which possessed sufficient well-armed ships to transfer it. A new element, scarcely perceptible at first, was about to tilt the scales of the European balance – sea power... Command of the sea became of increasing importance and a department in which the British were to become supreme ... the destiny of North America lay in the hands of that nation which could control the Atlantic with ships of war.

The period 1590–1703

This period was characterised by Dutch supremacy from 1595–1620; Anglo–Dutch rivalry from 1620–1675; the decline of Dutch influences and the rise of the importance of France from 1675–1703. The focus of international trade now firmly moved from the Mediterranean to the Atlantic.

Table 13: *Estimated slave imports into the Americas by importing region, 1451–1870 (000s omitted)*

Region & country	1451–1600	1601–1700	1701–1810	1811–1870	Total
British North America	—	—	348.0	51.0	399.0
Spanish America	75.0	292.5	578.6	606.0	1,552.1
British Caribbean	—	263.7	1,401.3	—	1,665.0
Jamaica	—	85.1	662.4	—	747.5
Barbados	—	134.5	252.5	—	387.0
Leeward Is.	—	44.1	301.9	—	346.0
St. Vincent, St Lucia, Tobago, & Dominica	—	—	70.1	—	70.1
Trinidad	—	—	22.4	—	22.4
Grenada	—	—	67.0	—	67.0
Other BWI	—	—	25.0	—	25.0
French Caribbean	—	155.8	1,348.4	96.0	1,600.2
Saint Dominique	—	74.6	789.7	—	864.3
Martinique	—	66.5	258.3	41.0	365.8
Guadeloupe	—	12.7	237.1	41.0	290.8
Louisiana	—	—	28.3	—	28.3
French Guiana	—	2.0	35.0	14.0	51.0
Dutch Caribbean	—	40.0	460.0	—	500.0
Danish Caribbean	—	4.0	24.0	—	28.0
Brazil	50.0	560.0	1,891.4	1,145.4	3,646.8
Old World	149.9	25.1	—	—	175.0
Europe	48.8	1.2	—	—	50.0
São Thomé	76.1	23.9	—	—	100.0
Atlantic Is.	25.0	—	—	—	25.0
Total	274.9	1,341.1	6,051.7	1,898.4	9,566.1
Annual average	1.8	13.4	55.0	31.6	22.8
Mean annual rate of increase*	—	1.7%	1.8%	−0.1%	

* These figures represent the mean annual rates of increase from 1451–75 to 1601–25, from 1601–25 to 1701–20, and from 1701–20 to 1811–20.
Source: Curtin (1969: 268, Table 77)

During this period, the hegemonic power of Holland was manifested in commercial and financial superiority, and in agriculture, fisheries, shipbuilding and textiles in the period 1625–1675. For example, in 1670 the Dutch owned three times the tonnage of the English and, indeed, more than the totals for England, France, Portugal, Spain and Germany combined (see Wallerstein 1980: 44–47). Their commercial supremacy came from their greater relative 'agro-industrial efficiency', low ship construction costs (40–50 per cent lower than English costs) and, above all, from the marked cosmopolitan importance of Amsterdam, the last city-centred economy. According to Barbour (1963: 13), it was the last time that 'a veritable empire of trade and credit could be held by a city in her own right, unsustained by the forces of a modern state'. The subsequent rise of London as a world trade centre heralded the modern territorial state fully backed by a national economy. Amsterdam became the European entrepôt centre and the Dutch 'the Carryers of the World, the midelle Persons in Trade, the Factors and Brokers of Europe' (Defoe 1728: 192). In the latter case, the invisible earnings of the commission and acceptance trade made it the world centre of banking and international monetary relations (Braudel 1984: 241–8).

The core European states, though continuously subject to economic and military tensions, now completed as a matter of 'conscious mutual imitation or the tactical counter-moves of the chess-board' (Parry 1966: 107), although some Dutch seizures of territory were designed to further the maritime war against Spain. Seventeenth-century rivalry between the English, Dutch and French centered on North America, the Caribbean and India. Thus it was that in the late-sixteenth and early seventeenth centuries, there came into existence what Wallerstein (1974: 15) has called a 'European world-economy':

> a 'world' system, not because it encompassed the whole world, but because it [was] larger than any juridicially-defined political unit. And ... a 'world-*economy*' because the basic linkage between the parts of the system [was] economic although this was reinforced to some extent by cultural links and eventually ... by political arrangements and even confederal structures.

In 1600 the core of this world-economy was located 'in northwest Europe that is Holland and Zealand; in London, the Home counties, and East Anglia; and in northern and western France' (Wallerstein 1980a: 37) and included (1974: 68):

> not only northwest Europe and the Christian Mediterranean (including Iberia) but also Central Europe and the Baltic region . . . certain regions of the Americas: New Spain, the Antilles, Terrafirma, Peru, Chile, Brazil – or rather those parts of these regions which were under effective administrative control of the Spanish or Portuguese . . . Atlantic islands, and perhaps a few enclaves on the African coast . . . but not the Indian Ocean areas nor the Far East . . . not the Ottoman Empire, and not Russia.

Oceanic intercontinental trade was created and largely developed by monopolistic trading companies which were granted privileges under legal charters, amounting to sovereign power. This was the case in respect of the English Muscovy Company in 1555, the Levant Company in 1581, the East India Company in 1600, the Newfoundland Company in 1610, the Virginian Charter in 1609, the Hudson Bay Company in 1670, and the South Sea Company. Stress was put on the exclusion of interlopers, and the importance of developing the long-distance trades. Thomas Mun (1664: 10) emphasised the need 'to esteem and cherish those trades . . . in remote or far countreys, for besides the encrease of Shipping and Mariners thereby, the wares also sent thither and received from thence are far more profitable . . . than . . . trades near at hand'.

Effective British colonisation in North America began in New Plymouth in 1620. By the mid-century, Britain had 'accomplished a vast lateral extension of the sphere of English power and enterprise into the undeveloped coastlands of the Americas' (Farnie 1962: 205–6): her colonies stretched along the entire Atlantic seaboard from Newfoundland to Florida and included the Bermudas and other Caribbean islands such as Jamaica. Adam Smith (1950: *1*: 414) emphasised the importance of the American market thus:

> By opening a new and inexhaustible market to all the commodities of Europe, it gave occasion to new divisions of labour and improvements of art, which, in the narrow circle of the ancient commerce, could never have taken place... The productive powers of labour were improved, and its produce increased in all the different countries of Europe, and together with it the real revenue and wealth of the inhabitants.

Three main export staples became established: tobacco from the 1620s, sugar from the 1650s, and furs from the 1670s, which 'created the basic structure of Atlantic trade in primary produce. Thereby the plantations became dependent on the metropolitan power of England for labour and capital, for markets, manufacturers and naval protection' (Farnie 1962: 206). Such production required significant increases in Atlantic labour migration, much of which was supplied by the slave trade in which the ports of London, Bristol and Liverpool participated from the 1660s, 1690s and 1730s respectively (Farnie 1962: 211).

Pares (1937: 125–6) makes a distinction between 'colonies of exploitation' (the sugar islands with the coastal districts of the Southern colonies) and 'colonies of settlement' ('the colonies north of Maryland within the hinterland of the Southern mainland colonies') within the British mercantilist empire. The former 'alone possessed staple export crops [and] remained until the American Revolution the most important part of the empire in every respect; they employed more shipping, produced more valuable goods, consumed more English manufactures. The latter, he argued 'with few exceptions, theorists and governments disliked... They consumed... a great deal of English manufactures; but they paid for them by somewhat dubious means, such as competing with English fishermen or with English ships in the West India trade, or – worse still – trading to the enemy in war-time'. The same was true of trade with India and the East. Following the formation of the British East India Company, the sites of what became Bombay and Calcutta were acquired in 1639, 1668 and 1686. Despite an earlier settlement, the Dutch developed a station at Cape Town in 1652 via its Dutch East India Company (formed in 1602) to service the route to India. Britain acquired St. Helena as its intermediate stop in 1651. In 1664 the French East and West India company was formed and, in 1674, Pondicherry became its centre until ceded to the British in 1761.

The Dutch were adept at the 'country trade' of Asia –the long-distance coasting trade where one commodity was used to buy another and so on in a series of circuits and networks. This was a coherent system so long as the key products and markets were controlled. The Dutch contrived to secure such a position in spices – mace, nutmeg, cloves and cinnamon. The method of operation is described by Braudel (1984: 218) thus:

> Production was confined to a small island territory, closely controlled and exclusively marketed, while cultivation of the product elsewhere was prevented. Thus Amboyna became the clove island, the Bandas the mace and nutmeg

islands and Ceylon the cinnamon island. Such monoculture rendered these islands almost entirely dependent on regular imports of good and textiles. Meanwhile clove trees growing in the other Molucca islands were systematically uprooted . . .; Macassar in the Celebes was taken by force in 1669, because if . . . left to itself, it would have been a base for free trade in spices; Cochin in India was similarly occupied . . . because this was a way of preventing competition from the production of inferior, but cheaper cinnamon.

The Dutch secured Guiana in South America, Cuba and Curacao in the West Indies and a New Netherlands Colony on mainland North America that they finally lost to the British in 1674. Britain evolved what became known as the 'Old Colonial System', under which colonies were protected, but were expected in return to direct their production along those lines that were considered most advantageous to the mother country and that would not rival the latter's industries. As sea-power was essential, given the transoceanic nature of the empire, a series of protective Navigation Acts had been passed from the thirteenth century onwards, that were made more extensive in the 1650s and 1660s, the general principles of which were:

(a) that all trade within the empire had to be carried in English-built ships, English owned, commanded by an English captain and manned by a crew three-quarters of whom were English (colonists and colonial ships qualified as English);

(b) that colonies could only import European manufactured goods via English ports (with the exceptions of salt for Newfoundland and New England and the wines of Madeira and the Azores);

(c) that bounties were authorised for colonial products desired in the home market; and,

(d) that certain 'enumerated' products could only be exported to England or other British ports, the list being amended and lengthened from time to time but including *inter alia* furs, ship masts, rice, tobacco, sugar, cotton, indigo, ginger and various dyewoods.

These were supplemented by other occasional acts. For example, the export of wool from the colonies and the colonial production of hats were restricted; the Molasses Act of 1733 levied prohibitive duties on molasses imported into the colonies from the French West Indies. Thus, as a proportion of total exports, British 're-exports rose from 3 or 4 per cent in 1640 to 31 per cent around 1700 (Perkins 1980: 72). This was largely due to the importance of empire-produced sugar, tobacco and Indian calicoes that were in demand in Europe and the colonial demand for re-exported goods from Britain that included tea, hemp, German and Russian linens, and various spices and drugs' (Perkins 1980: 72, 84).

As Davis (1966: 316) has shown, the end of the seventeenth century marked a policy change towards greater English industrial self-sufficiency, not only as a result of protected colonial trade, but also as a result of the first explicit use of fiscal protection. Import duties were significantly increased in the period 1690–1704. With the objective of protecting the home woollen industry from Indian and Chinese textile competition, a 20 per cent duty was imposed in 1690 to be followed by complete prohibition in 1701 and prohibitive duties were levied on French goods between 1693 and 1696: the general 5 per cent duty on imports was raised to 10 per cent in 1687 and 15 per cent in 1704–5. According to Davis (1966: 310) 'these measures... provided the foundation, and most of the superstructure... of the tariff wall that nineteenth-century Free Trade demolished' (in 1757, another 5 per cent was added and another in 1759, to be followed by new prohibition in the period 1763–76).

Dutch military failures hastened the end of Holland's period of hegemony, for despite its accumulated wealth, it was too small to carry indefinitely the insupportable burden of military and naval defence its provinces had to bear. The Baltic trade had stagnated and by 1700 Britain had become the country 'with the greatest stake in the Atlantic' (Davis (1974: 314). During the seventeenth century, according to Davis (1974: 45. 80. 85)) '28 new separate units of colonization were established in the Western Hemisphere: 3 Dutch, 8 French and 17 English'. This led to a major colonial re-export trade monopolised by Britain, of which Indian calico and tobacco and sugar from the Americas accounted for two-thirds.

The period 1703–1820

While Franco-British rivalry obtained from 1703 to 1761, Britain emerged thereafter as the leader in sea-power and as the dominant metropolitan economy. Following the Methuen Treaty (1703), she obtained privileged access to the Portuguese colonies in Brazil in return for free Portuguese access to the English market for her wines. As a result of the Treaty of Utrecht (1713), the north-western area of Canada and Acadia (Nova Scotia, New Brunswick and part of the State of Maine) became British and extended 'the network of naval bases which served her transoceanic communications' (G.S. Graham 1972: 27). With the Treaty of Paris (1763), the rest of Canada and the area between the Mississippi and the Atlantic became British. Despite the loss of the American colonies in the 1770s, new colonies were founded in Oceania and an important trade relationship was quickly resumed with the thirteen independent American economies. Command of the sea, and with it the trade routes of the world was further consolidated as a result of the French defeat in the Napoleonic Wars. British territorial gains were of great strategic value for her expanding commercial and industrial power. As G.S. Graham has written (1972: 41, 71):

> Gilbraltar [1704] and Malta [1800] gave Britain tactical command of the western Mediterranean, while a protectorate over the Ionian Islands provided at least an observation post overlooking the Isthmus of Suez and the Red Sea route to India. By taking the Cape of Good Hope [1806] and Ceylon [1802] from the Dutch, and Mauritius [1810] from the French, she was able, with the addition of St. Helena [1673] and Ascension [1815], to service the longer and safer road to the east. The acquisition of Trinidad [1797], Tobago [1763], and St. Lucia [1803] and the former Dutch colonies of Demerara and Essequibo [1814] provided further useful bases in the Caribbean. Fortified by technical revolutions unavailable to nations on a blockaded and war-torn Continent, industrial Britain towered over Europe. Her world position, in the military as well as the economic sense, seemed unassailable ...
>
> All told, within the huge quadrilateral that extended roughly from the Cape of Good Hope to the Red Sea, eastward to the Malay Peninsula [Penang was taken

in 1786, Malacca in 1807 and Singapore in 1819], across the Indonesian Archipelago to the northern shores of Australia, and thence back to the Cape, no European rival threatened British hegemony. Within this landlocked enclosure, Britain had established the nucleus of an informal commercial empire that was already reaching out to South America, China, and the islands of the Pacific . . . Britain was able to exercise an international power far out of proportion to her resources and population. With island bases and mainland trading stations in every sea, a world-wide British empire was held together commercially and strategically . . .

Commercially, Britain had shown great adaptability in this period. The East India Company was reconstituted in 1708, after which, trade with the East more than doubled in the following fifty years, with tea surpassing calico as the most important item of trade in 1760. During the eighteenth century, English trade with Europe declined in importance from 82 per cent of exports in 1700 to 40 per cent in 1722, to be compensated for by a marked expansion of exports to North America and the West Indies. This contributed 42 per cent and 18 per cent to the value of exports over this period (Cain and Hopkins 1980: 480). The north American market share of British exports rose from 10 to 37 per cent during this period. For the first time, non-European markets constituted a major part of the world demand for British exports. Imports of sugar, tobacco, rice and indigo were exchanged for exports of cloth and other manufactures sent to the regions of recent settlement which lacked such industries. British trade became 'Americanized' (Farnie 1962: 214).

Within the American colonies new triangular trade patterns began to emerge before their independence as R.M. Robertson (1973: 83–4) has pointed out (although Walton (1972) and Walton and Shephard (1979: 90, 91) regard this traditional view as an exaggeration):

> The trade of the North, unlike that of the South, involved more than a simple exchange of staple commodities for finished goods that would be put to immediate use. Northern commerce is epitomized in the famous colonial trade triangles, though pentagons and even hexagons of trade were common. Best known of the triangles was one that began as a two-way exchange of fish, timber, livestock and provisions, shipped from the ports of New England, New York, and Pennsylvania, for rum, molasses, and sugar of the West Indies. Molasses were converted into rum by American distilleries, and the dark, heavy liquor, together with rum already imported from the islands, was sent to the African coast to buy slaves. Slaves were in turn brought back to the ports of Richmond and Charleston or to the West Indies. In a second triangle, a ship might take a cargo from Philadelphia, New York or Newport, exchange it at Jamaica or St. Kitts for molasses and sugar, go on to England and trade for textiles and ironware before returning to the home port. A third great triangle started with the shipment of fish, lumber, and wheat products to Spain, Portugal, and the Wine Islands. Salt, fruits, and wine could then be taken to England and exchanged for manufactured goods, which were then returned to America. But the southern European trade could consist of two-way transactions, since the Navigation Acts permitted the direct importation of certain of the commodites obtained there.

The Treaty of Paris of 1763 was a turning point according to Beer (1907: 139), in that 'thereafter greater stress was laid with the emergent industrial revolution on colonies as markets for British produce'. As it was apparent that the population of North America had been doubling every two decades, Britain chose to obtain Canada rather than Guadeloupe and Martinique, and also gained Florida and, in addition to Canada, all French territory to the east of the Mississippi except New Orleans. Rising population in these areas and their enlarged markets, made available new trade goods such as furs and timber from Canada to boost British re-export trade to Europe. Cotton played a leading part in the trade expansion aided by a dramatic increase in the slave trades (see Table 13). The French wars of 1793–1815 disturbed trade conditions with the 'Continental system' of blockade and, together with the effects of the loss of its American colonies in the 1770s – the first substantial decolonisation of a country in the emergent world system – this intensified the British need to discover new markets. Until now the twin arms of European exploration – across the Atlantic to the Americas and round the Cape of Good Hope to Asia – had not met, the intervening expanse of the Pacific Ocean remained unexplored. As a result of Cook's voyages from 1768 onwards, new colonies were founded, chiefly in Australia and New Zealand. 'Trade not dominion' became the objective of this 'second British Empire' (see Harlow 1964). New markets were also sought in South America, the economies of which were beginning to obtain their political independence from the Spanish.

Within Britain, early eighteenth-century industrial changes had taken place that constituted an important prelude to the industrialisation that was to occur after 1780. Separate from the factory, and not necessarily leading to factory industry, was a remarkable rise in rural industry which Mendels (1972) has described as 'proto-industrialisation', from which a new class of merchant entrepreneur emerged. A second stage of factory development and machine industrialisation was facilitated by the growth of road networks and canals, and the linking river systems for specific traffic such as coal. From the 1780s until 1840 the first main phase of the industrial revolution in Britain occurred, wherein the domestic system was replaced by the factory system. Cotton was the 'pacemaker of industrial change' and a process of economic and social transformation occurred at home which centralised industry to a greater extent than heretofore and enabled new technologies to emerge and capital to accumulate. Cotton accounted for 53 per cent of the increase in total export values between 1784–6 and 1814–16. As cheap and abundant supplies of raw cotton were required, for the first time a staple export was dependent on external sources for its manufacture. The loss of the American colonies in 1783 at first gave added importance to the West Indies as 'resource pools' in this regard.

As industrialisation took place the old self-contained colonial system came under pressure, as it was realised that production costs could be reduced by mass production if markets were extended by the establishment of cosmopolitan trading links within the newly independent countries of Latin America. Moreover, Tucker had argued for some time that, in circumstances of free trade, a 'richer manufacturing Nation will maintain its Superiority over the poorer one, notwithstanding this latter may be likewise advancing towards Perfection; such ... superiority might continue, and even grow, so far that no Man can positively define, *when* or where it must *necessarily* stop' (Semmel 1970: 204). However, these unequal implications of free trade were well realised by some independent states, as was made clear as early as 1791 in the former American colonies by Alexander Hamilton in his *Report on Manufactures* (1791: 263)

> the United States cannot exchange with Europe on equal terms; and the want of reciprocity would render them the victim of a system, which would induce them to confine their views to Agriculture, and refrain from Manufactures. A constant and increasing necessity, on their part, for the commodities of Europe, and only a partial and occasional demand for their own, in return, could not but expose them to a state of impoverishment.

Thus protection was instituted to lessen the extent of the 'backwash effect', of superior British goods pre-empting the establishment of indigenous rival industries.

In addition to the new territorial possessions listed, further internal integration took place in India in terms of internal colonisation. Elsewhere, particular countries in the 'external arena' of the world-system continued to adopt a deliberate policy of isolation and self-exclusion from the European world. In such areas some 'administered trade' was conducted either directly through internal prescribed zones of international exchange or what Polanyi (1957: 51–2) has called 'Ports of Trade'; neutral meeting places where trade between 'embedded' (non-market) and 'disembedded' (market) economies took place in accordance with some particular treaty and was administered by officially appointed authorities. A prime example of the latter, was China's lack of interest in international trade relations and sense of 'superiority and exclusiveness', as indicated by the Emperor Chien Lung's response in 1793 when confronted with samples of British manufactures: 'Strange and costly objects do not interest me ... we possess all things. I set no value on strange objects ... and have no use for your country's manufactures' (quoted in Greenberg 1951: 4). Such a superior attitude arose from the self-sufficiency of China's agrarian economy and its plentiful supply of urban handicrafts. A restrictive policy was actively pursued through what was known as 'the Canton System' that became formalised in the period 1755–60: all official foreign trade was confined to Canton, a geographically isolated province in the south-east of the country; all Portuguese trade was exclusively zoned at Macao and Spanish access to the tea from Fulsen province permitted at the port of Amoy; all official trade relations had to be conducted through the aegis of the Cohong company; obstructive administrative barriers were imposed with regard to shipping in the Canton river, the granting of permits, the mandatory use of 'chop-boats' and official linguists; irksome personal restrictions (the 'Eight Regulations') were applied covering conditions of residence, methods of communications and the prohibition of loans; and specific regulations were further imposed on trade in particular products. Some trade nevertheless took place – 'the Old China Trade – but it was one-sided, as there was no effective Chinese demand for British goods. However, a 'Country Trade' developed, whereby exports of cotton and opium from India were used to finance the purchase of Chinese goods for England. Japan maintained an even greater isolationist attitude because of its pathological fear of foreign aggression. From the mid-seventeenth century onwards, all foreigners were excluded, with the exception of the Dutch, who were confined to Dejima, an artificial island within the port area of Nagasaki; and all local inhabitants were forbidden to leave the country.

Within the 'world-system' a division of labour arose, in which certain periphery zones were assigned specific economic roles. Essentially the Americas and particularly the extended Caribbean from north-east Brazil to Maryland became the periphery of the system, their social structures being transformed by the growth of plantations and the intensified, though enforced, international labour mobility engineered by the slave trade. Internally, road improvements and, in some cases, the building of canals brought about a

> move from the regional to the national market, welding together a number of short-range, quasi-autonomous and often highly individualised economies . . . [it] was a form of coherence imposed both by political ambitions – not always realised in the event – and by the capitalist tensions created by trade. As a rule, a measure of expansion in foreign trade *preceded* the laborious unification of the national market [Braudel 1984: 277].

However, consolidation awaited economic growth and superior transport and communication technologies. Nevertheless, globally all continents were experiencing rises in their intercontinental trade relations as shown

Table 14: *A comparison of the extent of intercontinental trade by century, 1500–1800*

Area	Sixteenth century	Seventeenth century	Eighteenth century
Europe	Rising	Constant	Rising
Africa	Constant	Rising	Rising
Temperate America	(Near zero)	Rising	Rising
Tropical America	Rising	Constant	Constant
Asia	Rising	Falling	Falling
World-wide	Rising	Constant	Rising

Source: Wallerstein (1980a: 18, Table 1, adapted from Mauro (1961))

(b) Internal integration and international trade, 1820–70

Years	Core structure	Core-periphery relations
1820–70	Unicentric-stable. One hegemonic power, Britain, and an absence of major conflict among the core powers. A *Pax Britannica*.	Less explicit political regulation: *Colonialism* Decolonisation of Latin America. *Trade* The decline of mercantilism and the rise of free trade.

Bergesen and Schoenberg (1980: 241)

The period 1820–70 saw an unprecedented rise in world output and trade.

Whereas Maddison estimates (1983: 60) that trade and output both grew at 0.9 per cent per annum from 1720 to 1820, his figures for 1820 to 1979 indicate an annual average rise of 3.7 per cent and 2.5 per cent respectively.

During the period under review, what mattered was 'the emergence of rapid technical progress in cotton textiles, iron manufacture, and the use of coal which the UK pioneered' (Maddison 1983: 34). The significance of this industrialisation became crucially related to the greater internal integration of economies made possible by the railways. They overcame the internal natural barrier of geographical distance within countries; opened up the vast as yet untapped resources and often unsettled areas of continents; and, by reducing transport costs dramatically between the areas of actual or potential production and population centres and ports, unified and often created internal markets and the possibilities for external exchange and interdependence on an unprecedented scale – possibilities which the development of marine links by ocean steamships and the universality of telegraphic communications were able to actualise.

There appear to have been three phases of growth before 1900, two of which occurred during the period here reviewed: 'during the first, 1815/1820 – 1845/1847, the volume of European exports grew at rates of 3–4% per year; during the second phase, 1845/1847 – 1873/1875, the annual rate of growth was between 4.5 and 5% per year; during the last phase, 1873/1875 – 1900, the rate was only 2.5% per year' (Hanson 1980: 15) derived from Bairoch (1973) and (1974). Three structural aspects of the first two periods were:

(a) The rise of British free-trade hegemony.
(b) The internal integration of a second generation of industrialising countries that included France, Germany and the United States.
(c) The further extension of the area of the world capitalist system.

(a) The rise of British free-trade hegemony

During most of the nineteenth century, Britain used her sea power for commercial purposes and benefited from her initial trade monopoly position as the first industrialised economy by selling the new products of that revolution and becoming the main agent of its international transmission, and by exporting the necessary investment, expertise and capital goods required for its implementation in a second generation of industrial countries, such that White could later boast (1899: 189) that 'our inventors and scientists have revolutionised the conditions of international intercourse, and have been universal benefactors. The Ocean World has been Anglicised'; and Merival (1861: 137–8) declare that:

> Masters of every sea, and colonists of every shore, there is scarcely a nook which our industry has not rendered accessible, scarcely a region to which the eye can wander in the map, in which we have not some object of national interest – some factory for our trade, some settlement of our citizens. It is a sort of instinctive feeling to us all, that the destiny of our name and nation is not here, in the narrow island which we occupy; that the spirit of England is volatile, not fixed . . .

Historically the economy of Britain was the first to be integrated and unified by the new industrial revolution, which was to radically transform the composition of trade. While France, the United States and other European states, such as Germany and Italy, were to join her in due course, industrial transformation and its attendant social mobilisation occurred in Britain while Germany remained an agricultural state with a semi-feudal organisation and the American States, not yet united, were still an infant economy with a small and widely dispersed population. British prosperity was largely fostered by two main factors:

(1) A series of discoveries and inventions that created the modern factory system displacing the old domestic putting-out system and giving her the advantage of an early start. The concomitant process of urbanisation arising from the establishment of these industrial centres broke down many social ties and created new geographical economic and social mobilities that both redistributed resources and accelerated the process of internal integration.
(2) The presence of mineral deposits such as coal and iron that were essential pre-requisites for the first modern industrial age.

By specialising in a select group of industries such as coal, iron, engineering, textiles and shipbuilding, Britain was able to build up a large export trade, the prosperity of which was based on its virtual monopoly position in foreign markets. Thus, in the 1840s, the share of manufactures in United Kingdom exports was about 80 per cent compared with only 50 per cent in Germany and less than 20 per cent in the United States. At the same time, Britain became a pioneer in the mobilisation and development of the resources of other lands. The height of British hegemony coincided with the second phase of its industrial revolution, 1840–95, based on capital goods industries – coal, iron and steel, and railway construction. At the mid-century, her trade was that of an industrial state with other countries that were still largely agrarian. As the only industrialised economy initially, Britain became an importer of foodstuffs and raw materials, and an exporter of cotton textiles, coal, pig iron, railway materials and steam engines, capital and capital goods. After 1870, competitive rivalry obtained as industrialisation spread and increased the size of the developed country core. It then became easier (Hobsbawm 1968: 121) 'to penetrate further into the underdeveloped world than to break into the more lucrative, but also more resistant and rival, developed markets' (which, at the end of the period, meant the dominions of Canada, Australia, New Zealand and South Africa and the 'informal' empires of Argentina, Chile and Uruguay), given the emergent imperialism and division of the industrially awakening world into an 'economic satellite system' of formal colonies and spheres of influence. Great Britain was forced to exchange 'the informal empire over most of the underdeveloped world for the formal empire of a quarter of it, plus the older satellite economies' (Hobsbawm 1968: 124) as ultimately other countries made the new products for themselves, and competed both in third markets and the British home market.

The international importance of Great Britain in 1860 can be judged by the fact that it was then the major market for the exports of Asia (50 per cent), South America (52 per cent), Egypt (59 per cent), North Africa (51 per

Table 15: *Approximate geographic distribution in 1860 of exports from selected countries (percentage)*

	Asia^a (excl. Japan)	South America (excl. Argentina)	Egypt^c	Algeria^d Barbary States (1840)	South Africa^e (excl. Cape of Good Hope)	Jamaica^f (1850)
United Kingdom	50	52	59	51	35	78
Other West Europe	13	17	25	22	52	
North America	5	20				7
Africa	1					
Asia	30					
South America		6				
Other		5	15	27	13	15

Source: Hanson (1980: a – Table 4.3 p. 61; b – Table 4.5, p. 64; c – Table 4.6, p. 64; d – Table 4.7, p. 65; e – Table 4.8, p. 66; f – Table 4.9, p. 66)

cent), South Africa (35 per cent) and Jamaica (78 per cent) (Hanson 1980) as shown in Table 15. An essential part of this mid-Victorian prosperity and the extension of multilateral world-wide trade relations, was the dismantling of the mercantilist national friction structures that had proliferated in the seventeenth and eighteenth centuries. This was achieved during the period beginning in 1807, when it was made illegal for British subjects to engage in the slave trade, and ending in 1860 with the Cobden–Chevalier Treaty that established a large measure of free trade in Europe. The argument for free trade had the real world developing example of the economic relationship between the United States and Britain representing the first major post-colonial development of interstate trade without political subservience, where, despite the 'backwash' effect of the initial flooding of American markets by the new British goods, and the counter-adoption of tariffs to protect the latter's infant industries by various Acts from 1816 to 1857 (that raised the average tax on dutiable goods to 20 per cent (R.H. Robertson 1973: 259), trade nevertheless proved mutually profitable: in 1836 £12.5 million out of £53 million United Kingdom exports went to the United States, and four-fifths of Lancashire's cotton came from there. Colonies no longer seemed necessary in mercantilist terms. By 1830 free trade with British colonies was extended on a reciprocal basis and all Navigation Act restrictions had been abolished by the 1850s. Slavery was abolished in 1833. The commercial monopolies given to particular companies were now withdrawn, depriving them of their imperial function. For example, the monopoly accorded the East India Company was abolished: over Indian trade in 1813, the 'China monopoly' between India and China in 1834; and the Levant Company monopoly over near eastern trade was abolished in 1825. Preferential duties on empire goods were either abolished (as was the case with cotton in 1845) or were eroded as a result of 'reciprocity treaties' that were concluded with many European states in the period 1823–30. The motivation for this radical change of policy direction came about as a result of the transfer of political power from the landed gentry to the rising commercial and industrial classes that was accomplished by the Reform Bill of 1832 (Kindleberger 1978: 48).

As a result of what Cain and Hopkins (1980: 480) have called 'aggressive trade-cum-diplomacy policy', free trade treaties were pressed upon the North-West Frontier provinces in the 1830s, Turkey in 1838, Egypt and Persia in 1841. Power bases that were also commercial fulcra were secured in Singapore from 1819 and Hong Kong from 1841. Competition in European markets led to a series of commercial invasions, where free trade, overseas investment and resultant invisible income were interlocked and mutually supportive. In the words of Palmerston (quoted by Cain and Hopkins 1980: 481): 'The world is large enough and the wants of the human race ample enough to afford a demand for all we can manufacture; but it is the business of government to open and secure the roads for the merchant.'

Between 1846 and 1860, the previous mercantilist empire made way for a free trade empire, in which informal dominion was wielded by virtue of Britain's industrial position as 'the Workshop of the World' that was to last substantially until 1931. As a result of the unilateral abolition of the Corn Laws and Navigation Acts of the 1840s, and the end of colonial preference for sugar in 1854 and timber in 1860, trade became non-discriminatory and universal. Crouzet (1975: 209) describes the situation that emerged thus:

> Strictly speaking, this empire did not constitute an economic unit. The English market was thrown open and was equally accessible to the goods of any other country, whether a part of the empire or not. Moreover England did not insist on favoured treatment for its own goods in its colonies. From 1859 onwards the self-governing colonies enjoyed complete freedom in tariff policy, which even enabled them to erect protective tariffs against British goods. As for the Crown colonies and India, their customs tariffs had solely fiscal ends and included no preference for goods from the mother country.

Finally, in 1860, the Anglo-French Cobden-Chevalier Treaty was signed, and so began a twenty-year period of free trade, in which, out of some 2,000 items in the tariff schedules of the leading powers, over half were either reduced or abolished entirely.

(b) The internal integration of a second generation of industrialised countries

The advent of the railways freed trade from its dependence on rivers and seacoasts, as in Africa, Asia and Latin America, and accelerated the pace of urbanisation and the growth in heavy industrial sectors. In large countries they 'opened up land for settlement and brought the products of settlement to market' (Platt 1972: 68). The first public railways were opened in 1830 in Britain and the United States; in 1832 in France; in 1835 in Germany and Belgium; in 1837 in Russia; in 1838 in Austria; in 1839 in Italy and Holland; in 1847 in Denmark and Switzerland; in 1868 in Spain; and in 1870 in Japan (S. Pollard 1981: 129). By 1870, Clapham (1928: 339) estimates the following completion of lines in thousand kilometres: United

Table 16: *World railway mileage opened per decade, 1840–80 (to nearest '000 miles)*

Year	United Kingdom	Rest of Europe	America	Rest of world
1840–50	6,000	6,000	7,000	—
1850–60	4,000	13,000	24,000	1,000
1860–70	5,000	26,000	24,000	7,000
1870–80	2,000	37,000	51,000	12,000

Source: derived from Hobsbawm (1968: 93)

Kingdom 24.5; Germany 19.5; France 17.5; Austria-Hungary 10.1; Italy 6.0; Spain 5.5; Belgium 3; Holland and Switzerland 1.4 each. Such building was predominantly in Europe and the United States; very little occurred elsewhere until the 1880s. These transport communications arrived after the industrial revolution in Britain. In inner Europe (and parts of the United States, by contrast, they arrived with the industrial revolution, and formed an integral part of that process. In the regions of recent settlement they arrived ahead of it (S. Pollard 1981: 130, 135):

> In Britain, railways merely boosted an industrialization process in full swing, helping ultimately to export capital, capital goods, and facilities to provide cheap food and raw materials by means of lines laid overseas. In Inner Europe, railways helped to stamp ironworks and coal-mines out of the ground, to provide a major part of the dynamic for industrialization, directly as well as indirectly by their effects on all markets. But in the periphery they had no such effect over many long decades. There iron, rails, locomotives, engineering specialists, as well as capital, were imported. Native industries, far from being stimulated, were swamped by the cheaper foreign imports made possible thereby. The countries fell into debt and had to meet increasing servicing charges, worsening their balance of payments, without necessarily possessing an asset which as yet was yielding a social, let alone a financial, return. For them, railways became a status symbol they could not yet afford and which threatened to ruin them. Ultimately, however, when industrialization began, after varying intervals they would have an economically beneficial effect also. . .
>
> Starting from this base, a mutually reinforcing growth pattern emerged. The striking reductions in transport costs achieved by the railways gave a strong boost to industry, particularly bulky productions, which in turn provided income for railways and incentives to build more. The carriage of coal and iron in particular was cheapened, allowing new markets to be won, and large modern works to be set up depending on wide markets to supplement the antiquated small charcoal plants that had hitherto been protected by distance and transport costs. Among the best markets for iron and engineering products were the railways themselves.

Thus, it was that from 'an "inner" Europe, situated in the north-western corner opposite the British Isles . . . the industrial revolution jumped, as it were, from one industrial region to another, though in a general direction outward . . . while the country in between remained to be industrialized, or at least modernized, much later, if at all' (S. Pollard 1984: 45). An essential part of these trade-related industrialisation processes was what Kojima (1981: 2) has called 'international complementation', i.e. international movements of labour and capital to supplement existent or non-existent indigenous supplies of economic resources. With respect to the latter, a study by the Royal Institute of International Affairs commented (1937: 3):

> International investment was an essential condition of this increasing trade. The development of the new countries required large capital expenditure on the building of railways, the sinking of mines, the draining of marshes, the erection of towns [including the introduction of sanitation, gas and electric supplies]; and the pace of the development would necessarily have been greatly retarded if these countries had had to depend upon their own resources for these purposes. International investment was, of course, not the only necessary condition. A large-scale migration of population was equally essential. In the nineteenth century, indeed, overseas investment, the migration of population, and the growth of international trade were linked together as different aspects of the process of the expansion of economic intercourse between the Old World and the New.

In these ways the core provided both a growing demand for the products of the periphery and a source of finance for the development of the infrastructures they required. The importance of migration is indicated in Table 17.

In the not yet united United States, unification proceeded from the original thirteen states at independence as a result of eight main acquisitions (R.H. Robertson 1975: 106):

1. The Territory of Louisiana, acquired in 1803 by purchase from France.
2. Florida, acquired in 1819 by purchase from Spain. A few years previously the United States had annexed the narrow strip of land that constituted West Florida.
3. The Republic of Texas, annexed as a state in 1845. The Republic of Texas had been established nine years previously after the victory of the American settlers over the Mexicans.
4. The Oregon Country, annexed by treaty with Great Britain in 1846. Spain and Russia were original claimants to this area, but they had long since dropped out. By a treaty of 1818 the United States and Great Britain agreed to a joint occupation of the Oregon Country and British Columbia; the treaty of 1846 set the dividing line at the forty-ninth parallel.
5. The Mexican Cession, acquired by conquest from Mexico in 1848.
6. The Gadsden Purchase, acquired from Mexico in 1853.
7. The Alaskan Purchase, acquired from Russia in 1867.
8. The Hawaiian Annexation, formally ratified in 1898.

Industrial resources such as iron ore and coal were separated by geography and had to be linked. Canals were the main force promoting the growth of commercial farming and international trade between the northern Atlantic seaboard and the West from 1815, beginning with the Erie Canal. Thereafter in the 1840s the railways became the great unifier, and the settlement of immigrants an intimate part of the building of the nation state. A series of development trails now began: the Oregon trail in

Table 17: *World intercontinental migration, 1821–1932*

Emigration, 1846–1932			Immigration, 1821–1932		
Country of emigration	Period covered	Total (thousands)	Country of immigration	Period covered	Total (thousands)
Europe:			America:		
Austria-Hungary	1846–1932	5,196	Argentina	1856–1932	6,405
Belgium	1846–1932	193	Brazil	1821–1932	4,431
British Isles	1846–1932	18,020	British West Indies	1836–1932	1,587
Denmark	1846–1932	387	Canada	1821–1932	5,206
Finland	1871–1932	371	Cuba	1901–1932	857
France	1846–1932	519	Guadeloupe	1856–1924	42
Germany	1846–1932	4,889	Dutch Guiana	1856–1931	69
Italy	1846–1932	10,092	Mexico	1911–1931	226
Malta	1911–1932	63	Newfoundland	1841–1924	20
Holland	1846–1932	224	Paraguay	1881–1931	26
Norway	1846–1932	854	United States	1821–1932	34,244
Poland	1920–1932	642	Uruguay	1836–1932	713
Portugal	1846–1932	1,805			
Russia	1846–1924	2,253	Total America		53,826
Spain	1846–1932	4,653			
Sweden	1846–1932	1,203	Asia:		
Switzerland	1846–1932	332	Philippines	1911–1929	90
Total Europe		51,696	Oceania:		
			Australia	1861–1932	2,913
			Fiji	1881–1926	79
			Hawaii	1911–1931	216
Other countries:			New Caledonia	1896–1932	32
British India	1846–1932	1,194	New Zealand	1851–1932	594
Cape Verde	1901–1927	30			
Japan	1846–1932	518	Africa:		
St. Helena	1896–1924	12	Mauritius	1836–1932	573
			Seychelles	1901–1932	12
Grand total		53,450	South Africa	1881–1932	852
			Grand total		59,187

1843, the Californian trail in 1844. The territory west of the Mississippi became of special migrant interest after the 'Gold Rush' of 1849 which stimulated the extension of the frontier to the coast and commerce in the Pacific Ocean through the subsequent development of transcontinental railways and trans-Pacific steamships. By 1846, the first railroad had spanned the American continent as a result of the building and joining of the Union Pacific and Central Pacific Railroads. Population grew dramatically as a result of the urbanisation process, improvements in public services and the large *ante* and *post bellum* flows of international immigration.

Different unification processes occurred in Germany and Italy. In the former case, the Zollverein set up in 1818 had, by the 1840s, united most of the many German states behind what was originally conceived of as a liberal external tariff. In colonial India, further unification took place following the annexation of the Punjab in 1849, Lower Burma in 1852 and Oudh, the last independent Moslem state in 1856. By 1854, not only had the telegraph network linked Bombay with Calcutta reducing the communication time with England from 35 to 26 days, but uniform postage rates had been introduced between India and England and throughout India. Such changes emphasised the intermediate importance of Egypt and the role played by the P. and O. Company, the activities of which gave

> a character of solidity and compactness to the British empire in the Eastern world... It... linked the most distant countries of the east with the European world... It ... covered the Red Sea with steamers, and converted it into an English lake. [Marshman 1867: 621.]

Elsewhere new corridors of international transport and communications were being formed: from 1848 the first steampacket service was inaugurated between New York and Liverpool; in 1866, the longest steam service in the world from Panama to Sydney was opened by the Panama, New Zealand and Australian Royal Mail Company; and in 1887 the Pacific Mail Steam Ship Company linked San Francisco to Hong Kong, and the P. and O. linked India with Japan.

As had previously been the case in the American colonies in the eighteenth century, great power was initially vested in the hands of foreign shipowners and merchants (due to their contacts and the lack of a domestic entrepreneurial culture) for 'the freighting and marketing of goods... were simply aspects of a single operation, and freights and profits were frequently indistinguishable (Nettles 1934: 70). Given an unprecedented increase in oceanic trade and the distances involved, middlemen were required in the import/export trades to perform vital specialised commercial functions in the establishment of markets and to secure valuable connections with consumers and supplies. Latin America was typical. As Greenhall (1977b: 160) has shown:

> Multiple small commission houses, contracted to merchants and manufacturers at home, dominated Britain's pattern of trading... Working for commissions rather than owning the goods they handled, each merchant firm required little capital and minimised its risks ... Manufacturers preferred to ... retain ... ownership and reap ... the trade and risk profit.

Merchant firms lost their power to determine prices locally after the

Table 18:   *Principal nations participating in world trade in 1820, 1840 and 1860*

1820	1840	1860
EUROPE		
Austria-Hungary	Romania	Bulgaria
Belgium		Finland
Denmark		Greece
France		Servia
Germany		
Italy		
Netherlands		
Norway		
Portugal		
Russia		
Spain		
Sweden		
Switzerland		
Turkey		
United Kingdom		
NORTH AMERICA		
Canada		
United States		
CENTRAL AMERICA		
Cuba		British Honduras
Puerto Rico		Costa Rica
Haiti		Guatemala
Santo Domingo		Nicaragua
British West Indies		San Salvador
French West Indies		Honduras
Mexico		Dutch West Indies
SOUTH AMERICA		
Argentina	Dutch Guiana	Bolivia
Brazil	Peru	Colombia
British Guiana	Uruquay	Ecuador
Chile	Venezuela	
ASIA		
British India	Ceylon	Indochina
China	Straits Settlements	Japan
Dutch East Indies		Persia
Philippines	Turkey in Asia	Siam
AFRICA		
Egypt	Cape of Good Hope	Algeria
Mauritius		Barbary States
		Senegal
		Zanzibar
OCEANIA		
Miscellaneous	Australia	New Zealand
		Hawaii

Source: Hanson (1980: 18–19, Table 2.2)

completion of the world cable network in 1870–2. Prior to this date expatriate businessmen were able to exploit local ignorance.

(c) The growth and consolidation of the international economy

Hanson has shown how the number of nations participating in world trade grew from 1820 until 1860 and that 'entry into the modern network of world trade had nearly been completed by 1860. Tropical Africa was the main . . . addition after that' (1980: 17). While it is indisputable that specialisation processes had changed the trade relationships between countries in a perceptible way, it is nevertheless the case that a degree of coercive economic structuring had taken place. However, the general consumer in industrially advanced countries benefited from these changes in the following tangible ways:

> Until recently, nearly all long distance trade made the greater part of its travel by water: . . . and very few households could show many bulky goods which had not been produced in its near neighbourhood. But now, every British cottager buys tea, sugar, tobacco and other comforts which have come from distant lands: and the greater part even of his clothing is made of material which has travelled some hundreds of miles by land, and some thousands of miles by water. Formerly, nearly all the materials used in construction came from woods, quarries or mines close at hand. But now, Brazilian, Norwegian and other distant forests supply timber for all purposes, and choice woods for tables and other furniture in general use. Even the jobbing carpenter in industrial districts will now select, from many various kinds of pine and deal wood, brought together from different parts of the earth, that which is best for each separate use, taking account of its lightness and its strength, its cheapness, its durability, etc. [Marshall 1923: 103–4]

Elsewhere, however, foreign traders, adventurers, merchants and middlemen had provided initial links between producers and consumers that were not always in the indigenous interests of the countries where they plied their economic services, especially where local enterprise was conspicuously absent. Naturally, the interest in this period lies in the development of interstate trade in Latin America, brought about by the breakup of the Spanish and Portuguese empires during the Napoleonic Wars. Stein and Stein (1970: 126) have posed the following interesting questions:

> Why did two once-colonial areas, the United States and Latin America, develop such markedly contrasting patterns of economic growth after independence? Why did the United States by 1870 emerge as perhaps the second industrial nation of the world in value of manufacturing output, while Latin America still remained primarily a major producer of colonial staples, raw materials, and foodstuffs for the North Atlantic basin?

The answers, they believe, lie in their respective colonial heritages. English investment helped develop the ex-colony's economy. By contrast, the liberated Spanish colonies found neither trade, nor financial or technical assistance in their underdeveloped, erstwhile metropolis. In the United States, the Civil War further opened the way to industrialisation and the industrial power of the Northern States. Whereas:

> the Spanish colonial policy of ruling by dividing . . . left a legacy of sectional and

regional conflict... which remained unresolved for decades... the new nations were torn by conflicts: between those who wished to monopolize all domestic and foreign trade from one national port and those who sought a local distribution monopoly; between those who wished to protect local artisan production, and those who distributed cheaper imports; between those who favored agriculture and those who favored mining or industry... no national unity was readily forged; there was no immediate possibility of a unified, national economic policy, as was created early in the United States... the colonial economic heritage was reinforced by local conditions and, in particular, by the economic presence of Great Britain... Massive imports of British manufactures simply crushed local industry based upon primitive technology. Inevitably... Latin America was drawn to the search for export staples, traditional or new, to pay for imports. They were drawn to external forces of dynamism... utilizing the cheapest available factor of production, the land, and the dependent labor force. [Stein and Stein 1970: 131, 133-5]

Thus many of these countries became part of the 'informal' empire of emergent industrialising capitalist economies that needed cheap raw materials to feed their growing industrial complexes and newly urbanised communities, needed additional markets to consume their rising levels of production and investment outlets to absorb their rapidly accumulating capital. Industrialisation meant mass production but mass production required access to mass markets. As regards British acquisition of territory in this period, the objective became, as Raffles stated (Allen and Donnithorne 1957: 21), 'by the establishment of a free and unrestricted commercial intercourse to draw forth their resources while we improve our own'.

During this period, significant reductions in the 'external arena' came from the further incorporation of China and other Asian countries as a result of 'unequal treaties'. China's isolation was ended by such treaties and a 'treaty-port' system was imposed that served as the vehicle of incorporation and penetration. In 1842, the Treaty of Nankin opened up the ports of Shanghai, Canton, Amoy, Foochow and Ningpo to foreign trade and ceded Hong Kong to the British; in 1858, the Treaty of Tientsin opened up ten new ports and rivers and permitted the penetration of the interior (this increased to sixty-nine by 1920); and, in 1860, the Treaty of Peking ceded Kowloon and legalised Chinese emigration to the rice-fields of Siam and the tin mines of Malaya. Following the steamship link between Shanghai and Hong Kong in 1885, both became centres of international importance, the latter becoming the most significant commercial fulcrum for incorporating China into the international trading system. The treaty-port system evolved to include the granting of extraterritorial powers to Western nations for Shanghai, the administration of certain services; the binding of China to a fixed low *ad valorem* tariff; and the granting of immunity from direct taxation to the western companies that had settled (Vincent 1970: 2).

Other countries now incorporated included Japan, after the Meiji restoration of 1868; Siam, by the Bowning Treaty of 1855; Indo-China (1862-1904); and Burma, by annexation in 1885. Some of these incorporations were by 'unequal treaties' that deprived the countries involved of their tariff autonomy and power to regulate trade in their own interests, forcing them to participate in the international division of labour without protective shelter. In other areas, the metropolitan country continued to organise trade directly, as was the case with the Dutch in Indonesia, 'culturstelsel' or 'cultivation system' was imposed on the local producers of coffee, pepper, chinchona, tobacco and tea in the period 1830–1915. Native growers were required to set aside a fifth of their land in lieu of rent for the production of prescribed crops, which were purchased by the government at a low fixed price, or acquired as taxes in land, then shipped to Holland by the Nederlandse Handel Maatschappig where they were sold at a high profit.

A basic division of the world into exporters of primary products and exporters of manufactures now took shape. The industrial revolution was not transplanted to the former countries because, as Lewis (1978: 10) has written:'the industrial revolution did not create an industrial sector where none had been before. It transformed an industrial sector that already existed by introducing new ways of making the same old things'. In addition, it also depended on a prior or simultaneous agricultural revolution. These two elements were not present in such countries, where the advent of the railways was later than in the core countries and there was a heavy dependence on foreign capital and managerial skills. Whether the latter countries were either as colonies controlled by powers hostile to competitive industrialisation or politically independent (as in most of South America), it was easier to respond to the primary product needs of the industrialising countries, for which anyway there was often a vested indigenous interest, even though this often meant a monocultured or narrowed specialisation bias, as is indicated in Table 19.

Table 19: *Nineteenth-century trade and the less-developed countries*

(a) Percentage of total exports accounted for by the largest product in selected countries in 1860

Country	Largest product % share
Brazil	53
British Guiana	73
Chile	63
Peru	50
Uruguay	50
British India	33
Ceylon	73
China	46
Dutch East Indies	37
Philippines	38
Siam	69
Algeria	17
Egypt	37
Mauritius	94
Reunion	90
Senegal	31
British West Indies	60
Costa Rica	85
French West Indies	84
San Salvador	83

Source: Hanson (1980: 39, Table 3.2)

(b) Selected exports of various countries

Country	Export
Central America	
British Honduras	Dyewood
British West Indies	Sugar, coffee
Costa Rica	Coffee, bananas
Cuba	Sugar, coffee, tobacco
Danish West Indies	Sugar
French West Indies	Sugar
Guatemala	Coffee
Haiti	Coffee, dyewood
Honduras	Coffee
Mexico	Fibres, silver, copper, coffee, lead
Nicaragua	Coffee
Puerto Rico	Sugar, coffee
San Salvador	Coffee, indigo
South America	
Bolivia	Silver, tin, rubber
Brazil	Coffee, rubber, sugar, tobacco
British Guiana	Sugar
Chile	Copper, nitrate of soda
Colombia	Coffee, gold, tobacco
Ecuador	Cocoa
Peru	Guano, sugar, nitrate of soda
Uruguay	Hides, meat
Venezuela	Coffee, cocoa
Asia	
British India	Cotton, rice, tea, hides, skins, opium, jute, assorted seeds, silk, coffee, wheat, indigo, cotton manufactures, jute manufactures
Ceylon	Coffee, tea, plumbago
China	Tea, silk, cotton
Dutch East Indies	Sugar, coffee, tobacco
Indochina	Rice
Philippines	Sugar, hemp
Siam	Rice
Africa	
Algeria	Wine, breadstuffs, animals
Egypt	Cottonseed, cotton, wheat, sugar
Mauritius	Sugar
Reunion	Sugar
Tropical Africa	Nuts, rubber
Miscellanous	
Hawaii	Sugar

Source: Hanson (1980: 47, Table 3.6)

Other areas hitherto not significantly part of the geographical expansion of international production/trade relations became entwined as a result of what has been called 'financial imperialism' (see Blaisdell 1929 and McLean 1976). Thus the Ottoman government signed its first foreign loan agreement in 1854, to be followed by thirteen others and eventual backruptcy in 1875. European-controlled banks were set up in the Middle East such as the Ottoman Bank in 1856, the Anglo-Egyptian Bank 1864. By the mid-1870s, Turkey and Egypt were only two of a long list of nations (and American states) which, at some time or other during the nineteenth century, had been unable to meet their commitments to their foreign creditors: a list which included Austria (five times), Holland, Spain (seven times), Greece (twice), Portugal (four times) and Russia, as well as every country in Latin America and the twelve secessionist states of the United States (Winkler 1933: 314). The path of large-scale borrowing led to backruptcy and increased European control. As Owen (1981: 113) has commented: 'A succession of larger and larger loans led quickly to an increase in the sums required to service the debts well beyond the state's ability to manage'. Financial control often followed. Thus international trade relations became structured by financing considerations:

> Financial interests were entangled in the web of politics and nationalism... Financial force was often used to buy or build political friendship or alliance, was often lent or withheld in accordance with political calculations...
> From this period, the volume of British investment and its cumulative additions remained the greatest, its distribution the widest, its undertakings the most substantial. London was the center of a financial empire, more international, more extensive in its variety, than even the political empire of which it was the capital. In the sphere of financial interest and calculation, distance lost its meaning; along all lines of latitude and longitude British capital worked its way [Feis 1930: xiii, 5.]

Summing up this period, Condliffe (1951: 837-8) has written:

> International trade... In the first half of the nineteenth century... was still an exchange of European manufactures for products of native origin – hides from California, spices from the tropical East, silks and porcelain from China. From about 1860, there was a clearly marked development when western European capital began to be invested in ports, railroads, and plantations all over the world.
> Production was then developed on a large scale for export to Europe. Mining enterprises together with tea, cocoa, coffee, sugar, rubber, jute, and indigo plantations, tin smelters in Malaya, and refrigerated meatworks in the Argentine with transport facilities to match, swelled the volume of world trade. This outpouring of capital equipment and organizing skills raised the totals of both exports and imports, but the colonial world became tributary to and dependent upon the enterprise of western Europe.

THE FIRST GOLDEN AGE OF GLOBAL TRADE: 1870-1913

Years	*Core structure*	*Core-periphery relations*
1870-19[52]	Multicentric-unstable. A plurality of competing states, created by the decline of British hegemony and the rise of Germany, the United States and Japan, and resulting in rivalry, conflict and eventually two world wars.	More explicit political regulation: *Colonialism* The second colonial expansion ... led by Britain and France and centered in Africa, India and Asia (the Age of Imperialism). *Trade* The decline of free trade and the rise of tariffs, protectionism and neo-mercantilism in general.

Bergesen and Schoenberg (1980: 261)

The period 1870–1945 contains two distinct periods, that of 1870–1913, and that of 1914–45 which are separately reviewed, given their different orientations.

The second historical 'wave of integration' described by Haberler (1964), superimposed on the first, begins with the zenith of the free-trade movement in the 1870s and covers the period before 1914, described by A.J. Brown (1965: 47) as 'the golden age of the international economy when international movements both of goods and of factors of production were larger in relation to total output than at any time before or since, and when the world came nearer than at any time to possessing a single monetary system'. Despite the fact that reversal of these relatively liberal commercial policies began in Russia in 1877 and extended to France in 1878, Germany in 1879 and subsequently to the newly formed United States (where the average tariff rate of 20 per cent in 1861 rose to 60 per cent by 1897 and fell to 25 per cent by 1914), the technological revolutions in transport and communications brought about an unprecedented capacity for intercontinental trade; and a mass migration of capital and labour presented significant rapid industrialisation possibilities in 'the regions of recent settlement'. Furthermore, overseas institutional branching of banks and other financial institutions established a net work of multinational trade and payment possibilities. According to Kuznets (1967a: 7) 'a significant network of world trade emerged where there had been little before and major channels of flow and interdependence were established in what was previously a congeries of relatively isolated economic societies'. Kuznets estimates that during the period 1800 to 1913, the proportion of world trade to world output rose from about 3 per cent to 33 per cent. This greater than elevenfold increase was due to two factors:

(a)   The participation of a larger number of nations in world trade. In 1913 the estimated number of such trading areas was about 155, compared with 50 in the early nineteenth century, when areas outside North Africa in Africa, outside India, Burma and Ceylon in Asia and all of Oceania were not yet incorporated in the international trade network. Kuznets estimates that this new entry of countries was responsible for between 133 and 300 per cent of this elevenfold trade increase.

(b)   Technological changes in transport, communications and food preservation had a much greater effect on the rate of growth of trade across boundaries than on the rates of growth of domestic products and resulted in a wider range of goods, especially foodstuffs and manufactures, being made available universally.

Competition between steam and sail, and cost-cutting in ship-building and operation and reductions in voyages to the Indian Ocean and Australia following the opening of the Suez Canal in 1869, brought about a rapid fall in freight rates of bulk commodities such as foodstuffs and raw materials from 1870–3 onwards. For example, the cost of transporting wool from Australia to England fell by 50 per cent between 1873 to 1896 (Farnie 1969: 212–13). A rapid substitution of steam for sail took place as new purpose-built boats were constructed for this new primary transport corridor for international trade that became the principal gateway to the East, and was occupied by Britain in 1882 to ensure through transport, a convention being signed in October 1888 'to guarantee at all times and for all powers the free use of the Suez Maritime Canal'. The number of through transits grew from 486 with a net tonnage of 435,911 in 1870 to 5,085 by 1913 with a tonnage of 20,035,000, by which year national shares of traffic were: Britain 60.2 per cent; Germany 16.7 per cent; Holland 6.4 per cent; France 4.6 per cent; Russia 1.7 per cent; Japan 1.7 per cent and Italy 1.5 per cent. Britain's Mediterranean chain of naval bases that had been the supply chain of her sea power in the days of sail now came into their own as coaling depots, and the supremacy of British shipping was further confirmed by the ready domestic availability of coal and the advanced state of her iron and engineering industries.

This expansion formed the real beginnings of what Ashworth (1952: 163) calls an 'international economy':

> Countries which had previously supplied almost all their own needs and had had only a small surplus production to dispose of abroad, found it advantageous to devote more of their resources to the production, on a scale far beyond the requirements of their own people, of commodities that were in general and growing demand over large areas of the world [because of a rapid increase in population growth and incomes].

By exchange of surpluses it was possible to obtain indirectly through trade products which might have been produced at home but which other countries, because of their more appropriate resource mix, could provide more cheaply. For example, Australia consumed less than one-seventh of the meat she produced, the surplus being exported to pay for manufactures; by 1913, Britain was dependent on overseas suppliers for seven-eighths of its raw materials (excluding coal) and only half of its food. According to Ashworth (1951: 164) 'the great absolute increases in international trade arose from the transactions of the heavily populated industrializing countries ... [and] the diminishing proportion of their productive resources which they devoted to agriculture'. The new internationalisation of relations led to a rise in the external trade coefficient of all industrialising European countries: for example that of Britain from an average of 8.5 per cent in 1805–19 to 29.4 per cent in the period 1910–13. A most important aspect of this trade was its stimulus toward the creation of new production resources. As D.H. Robertson (1938: 5) has observed: 'The specialisations of the nineteenth century were not simply a device for using to the greatest effect the labours of a given number of human beings, they are above all an engine of growth.' Three aspects of change need comment here: (a) the decline of free trade and the different nature of industrialisation in the newly developing countries (b) changes in the core countries (c) colonialism.

(a) The decline of free trade and the industrialisation of newly developing countries

After the 1870s

> governmental actions increasingly came to disrupt the relatively easy and free intercourse of commodities as well as factors of production between nations on which the successful industrialization of Europe had so largely depended.

Two aspects of this change had economic and trade implications:

the rise of nationalism as a political force and the drive towards the conversion of the political unit, the European state, from its dynastic origins to an expression of national unity and popular or democratic control.

A second strand is the growing technical need for state intervention of a new kind in economic matters, and above all a growing technological competence to discharge these functions. Mine inspection and safety at sea, sanitary intervention in the massed proletarian quarters of new cities and protection of children in factories, education for workers' children and police forces to hold them in check, are examples of a whole new apparatus of control developed by central and local authorities in response to the changes brought about by industrialization. [S. Pollard 1981: 252–3.]

Nowhere was this more true than in Germany which consciously used the government as the instigator of trade and industrial revolution in the period 1880–1910. As Laughlin (1918: 28) wrote:

It initiates and supports new enterprises; owning the railways, it grants special traffic rates for exports; it builds canals with public funds, in order that industry may obtain low rates on heavy materials; it stimulates and subsidizes international steamship-lines; it forces the development of colonies; it has helped in establishing banks for foreign operations, and put her banking resources at the service of foreign trade; it bullies other states to gain commercial privileges; it has used its political power to good effect in gaining control of the trade in southeastern Europe and Turkey; it employs its diplomatic body, the prestige of its military power, all the pressure of the government, to control ports, obtain concessions for opening mines and building railways, and to expand its commercial influence in other lands.

The second generation of industrialisers used different means to achieve industrialisation and adopted protectionist policies:

the commercial treaties of the free-trade interlude were renewed but with a rising tendency. Between 1875 and 1895 duties on European manufactured articles were doubled. The eastern emerging countries also opted for high tariffs, Bulgaria instituting high rates in 1883 and raising them in 1897 and 1904, Romania enacted high industrial tariffs in 1893 and 1906, and Serbia raised a tariff against Austria–Hungary, her main trading partner, in 1906. Only Switzerland, Holland, Belgium besides free-trade Britain, still retained moderate, mainly fiscal, customs duties in the last years to 1914. In 1914, average [percentage] levels of tariffs on industrial products [were] ... as follows:

United Kingdom	0
Holland	4
Switzerland, Belgium	9
Germany	13
Denmark	14
Austria–Hungary, Italy	18
France, Sweden	20
[United States[	[25]
Russia	38
Spain	41

Agricultural tariff were particularly high in the larger countries, Germany, France, Austria-Hungary, and Italy. [S. Pollard 1981: 258–9.]

(b) Changes within the core

During this period, Britain played a crucial role as the exporter of the new industrialisation infrastructure. Given the demand, it naturally paid her to meet it, rather than to leave it to be supplied by others, with this profound difference. Previously every time a railway was built abroad, more trade could be expected as an outcome, but every time a machine was exported, less trade would result, the recipient countries equipping for production to satisfy their own demand. Complementary trade relations with particular countries were gradually succeeded by relationships of trade rivalry. As Table 20 shows, North America and most other geographical regions, with the exception of Britain and some European countries, increased their share of world exports in this period.

Table 20: *World exports by geographical region, 1876–1913 (% figures)*

		World export % share	
Geographical region	*1876-80*	*1896-1900*	*1913*
United States & Canada	11.7	14.5	14.8
United Kingdom & Ireland	16.3	14.2	13.1
North-west Europe	31.9	34.4	33.4
Other Europe	16.0	15.2	12.4
Oceania	—	—	2.5 ⎤
Latin America	— ⎤	— ⎤	8.3 ⎥
Africa	— ⎬ 24.1	— ⎬ 21.7	3.7 ⎬ 26.3
Asia	— ⎦	— ⎦	11.8 ⎦

Source: Yates (1959: 32, Table 6)

Despite the erosion of her competitive power, Britain continued to adhere to a free-trade open-port policy. This policy constituted an international public good from which all countries whether developed, developing or undeveloped could benefit. It was essential for the smooth working of the emergent international economy that was replacing previous inter-regional networks and creating a new global form of multilateral trade, no longer based on a series of largely disconnected patterns but 'upon a complex network of activity embracing whole continents or sub-continents, derived from a new world wide division of economic functions' (Saul 1954: 50).

States found it expedient to accept a surplus or deficit in their balance of payments with particular countries, so long as their overall global balance was on average maintained. The balance of payments example of the United Kingdom given by Saul (1954: 61), as shown in Figure 2, is illustrative of the web of activities that resulted. These multinational trade relationships were promoted by London's position as the main world centre of finance and shipping. This symptom of payments grew with remarkable ease, which gave her considerable invisible earnings to fund the growing deficit on her visible trade account, as multicentric core competition occurred within the exchange network. Britain tended to

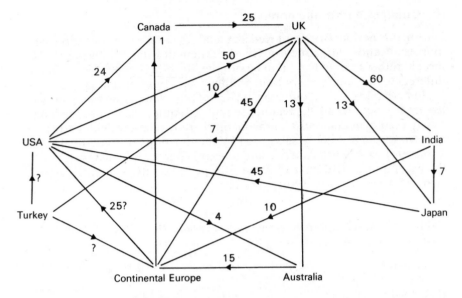

Figure 2: *The multilateral nature of the world trade settlement pattern, 1910*
The arrows point to the debtor of each pair of countries, and the figures show the estimated overall balances outstanding between them in £m.
Source: Saul (1954: 61)

evade visible trade competition by shifting her marketing and production efforts to the countries within her empire, the export share of which rose from about 25 per cent in 1870 to more than a third some thirty years later. The Indian market played a crucial role in this strategy as Fletcher (1958: 571) indicates:

> The key to Britain's whole balance of payments pattern in the decades just prior to the first World War lay in India, which financed more than two-fifths of Britain's total deficits. India could take great quantities of British manufactured goods and make large interest payments and payments for the provision of shipping, banking, and other services, because the Suez Canal provided a means of disposing of ever larger amounts of raw materials and foodstuffs on the Continent. The rapidly industrializing nations of Continental Europe, on the other hand, could expand their purchases of the raw materials and foodstuffs of India because free-trade Britain was at the same time a major importer of their manufactured goods and the most important exporter to India. Thus India provided the most important market for the manufactured goods of England; Continental Europe furnished a market for the raw materials and foodstuffs of India; and Great Britain provided a market for the manufactures of the Continent: the triangle was joined.

New competition and differences of approach also emerged with regard to capital exports. Germany became a capital exporting country from 1883, France from 1885 and the United States from 1890. As regards the global pattern of British investment, the size of which had been expanded from £1,300 million in 1880 to £3,763 million in 1913, the Royal Institute of

Economic Affairs (1937: 117) summarised the principal changes thus:

> In the earlier years of the nineteenth century, British overseas investment was directed mainly towards the continent of Europe, where it hastened the industrial revolution; but with the development of this area, and the increasing opportunities for investments farther afield, the British investor began, after 1870, . . . to pay more and more attention to the undeveloped countries of the world. By 1914 . . . British investments in Europe formed only 6 per cent of the total overseas investments, whereas the great agricultural producing countries, Canada, the United States, Argentina, Australia, New Zealand, and India, . . . absorbed respectively 14 per cent, 20 per cent, 9 per cent, 11 per cent and 10 per cent.

From 1890 to 1913 the whole structure of world trade was in a state of rapid and significant transformation. Whereas the first impetus to the formation of a world-wide inter-country trade network in the period 1870–1900 arose from the rapid growth of European countries and the capital needs of primary producer countries, by 1900 it was the industrialisation of the American economy technologies related to electric power, the internal combustion engine and the use of industrial chemicals and their associated new industries that were beginning to shape a new design. Britain was being surpassed by the many industrialising countries in several of her staple industries and was not at the forefront of the new technologies.

(c) Colonialism

As Cain and Hopkins (1980: 485) have observed:

> After 1870 Britain's relative industrial decline, aggravated by growing competition amongst the great powers for economic and political influence outside Europe, led to a more aggressive search for markets. Exposed to free trade and falling profits, and driven out of Europe and America, industrial interests in Britain shifted, around 1880, into decisive support for the acquisition of new markets in Asia and Africa. In Burma, the Malay States, and China the British government deliberately extended its formal and informal influence in order to create new markets, or to save markets with supposedly high growth potential from absorption by competitors.

The same motivations were at work in West, East and South Africa. G. Clark (1936: 89) has summarised the general shifts in attitude towards colonies in the following terms:

> As in the earlier stages of expansion, the desire for extension of territory was only one of the motives. At least equal in influence, and perhaps more potent even in the three pre-war decades, was the desire for economic opportunities. These might be secured by getting the right to trade at various ports, as in China, or by marking out 'spheres of influence' in which special and partially or wholly exclusive trade and other economic privileges would be enjoyed, as in China or Persia or Turkey, by investments which gave opportunities for developing mineral resources or other profit-making enterprises. Sometimes these opportunities could be secured without taking actual political control. In such circumstances, the expansion remained primarily economic, and did not proceed to the formal establishment of political control.
> But the same two influences were at work that had been earlier, tending to

transform economic penetration, however peacefully intended at first, into political domination.

One was the conviction of the Europeans that they had the right to go where they chose, and to insist that conditions where they went should be satisfactory to them. Unpaid debts, local disturbances, and various such results of local administrative 'inefficiency' or corruption, or of resentment against Western penetration, furnished the excuse for taking control more or less completely. Many of the Westerners were sincerely convinced that such incidents made it necessary to take control. Improvement in living conditions for the common people which sometimes followed the establishment of European control served as further justification for the political expansion.

The other influence working toward the assertion of political claims was the desire to keep some other country from getting the land and whatever trade or raw material or other economic benefits eventually might be secured from it.

Thus the aspiring newly industrialising countries increasingly took the view that their continuous economic development depended on a search for new markets for their products and new sources for their raw material inputs. This led to a series of territorial acquisitions on an unprecedented scale, in which:

England alone added more than three million square miles (all but one-half million in Africa); the French took even more, claiming an additional four million square miles, with most of this area in Africa too. The gains of the other states were less spectacular. Germany, between 1884 and 1890, acquired nearly a million square miles in Africa, as well as scattered possessions in the Pacific, including a part of New Guinea and a leasehold of Kiaochow in China. Italy managed to obtain Eritrea, Italian Somaliland, and Libya – all in Africa. Belgium acquired the nearly million square miles of the Congo Free State (the Belgian Congo) also in Africa. Japan took Korea from China, and the United States raised its flag over the Philippines and Puerto Rico. Russia's expansion, like that of Austria–Hungary but unlike these others, was continental rather than overseas, but its acquisitions were also impressively extensive (see Figure 3). [Hartmann 1973: 131.]

These developments gave enormous impetus to global trade and development, particularly as territory possession avoided the need to obtain local concessions and charters and to negotiate with native regimes. Expedient resort was made of the Protectorate as a constitutional device, on the grounds that there wasn't the

time and opportunity to expand a factory into a colony. Trade can now only develop when modern means of transportation are at its command, and no railway would even be built in an area of which the political control was disputed. Hence the numerous British 'Protectorates' and 'Spheres of Influence', particularly in Africa, which are obviously destined to ripen into important sources of the primary necessities of our natural well being. [A. Pollard 1909: 236.]

A new feature of trading patterns was the inter-dependence between tropical dependencies and temperate zone centres, the one complementing the other as regards natural and manufactured products. White (1899: 94) asserted that 'Vital circulation between them, or the interchange of commodities, is controlled by the universal law of Demand and Supply, flowing along the lines of least resistance'.

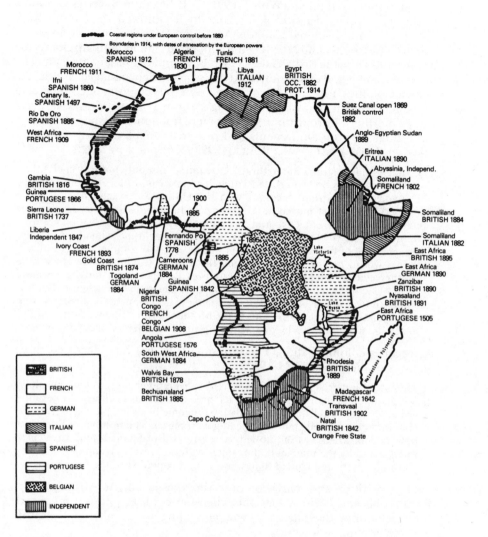

Figure 3: *The pattern of African colonisation*

Source: Foreman-Peck (1983: 113, Map 4.1)

Contemporary thought (White 1899: 93-4) began to have reservations about the relative degrees of freedom to be allowed the 'colonies of settlement' (that included Canada, Australia, New Zealand and to some extent Cape Colony and Natal) in the temperate regions 'built up chiefly by immigrants from the British Isles, which have undergone a natural process of development and expansion'; and the 'tropical dependencies' (India, all Crown Colonies, Protectorates and the numerous emporia or commercial settlements, islands, naval and coaling stations lying within the tropics) where 'Northern Europeans . . . form a mere fraction of the population . . . [and] their superior attainments and resources enable them . . . to act as rulers and task masters'. As White (1899: 95-6) put it in 1899:

> Canada and Australia are naturally gravitating, not only towards each other, but towards every open market in which they can dispose of their products: thus, Canada has important relations with the United States, and Australia has opened up a direct market in Germany. India, too, is likely to develop her relations with the Far East, and to enter into closer competition with British manufactures. It is true, that the aggregate of our trade with the Colonies, representing only a small proportion of our external commerce, has hitherto varied within narrow limits; and that the bulk of Colonial trade is with the Mother country and the Empire: thus proving the connections to be more valuable, commercially speaking, to the Colonies than to ourselves. But our community of interests is so vital, so capable of development in directions that may eventually prove necessitous to the Mother country, that we cannot afford to see the Colonies one by one achieving their commercial independence.

As regards colonialisation, Fieldhouse (1932: 207) has identified three features of the period 1883-1913:

> The rate of imperial expansion increased considerably: more colonial territory was acquired than during the previous three-quarters of a century. Annexation was no longer usually or necessarily the outcome of strong pressures from the circumference on reluctant European governments. The number of European powers concerned was multiplied by the revival of Spanish and Portuguese interest and by the intervention of states with no previous colonial tradition – Germany, Italy, the United States and King Leopold II of the Belgians.

Thus partition and redivision of territory, especially in Africa and the Pacific, became evident as this 'neo-imperialist' phase progressed. Interpretation of these activities vary according to a number of assertions that include the following:

(i)   that tropical colonies were required 'to provide markets for manufacturers, fields for the investment of surplus capital, and an assured source of raw materials' (the Hobson/Lenin/Marxist school), and were needed to compensate for loss of established markets in Europe and America.

(ii) that colonies were needed to demonstrate power and prestige as expressions of European nationalism. Bases were needed in all continents if a country was to be a world power. Supplies of strategic raw materials had to be assured, e.g. copper, iron ore, etc.

(iii) that 'informal' control was no longer feasible and annexation was the alternative to evacuation.

(iv) that the policy attitudes of Germany in its 'bull-like' acquisition of territory in 1884–5 gave it bargaining power and areas within which to assert influence as confirmed by the Berlin Conference of 1884–5.

The period 1883–1892 was consequently one of European expansion by 'Paper Partition' and was followed, 1890–1914, by an uneasy period of effective occupation and small wars (the most notable of which were the Boer War 1899–1902 and the Boxer rising of 1898–1903), and often 'gunboat diplomacy' as some redivision of countries inevitably took place. During this period the United States emerged as an imperial power by annexing Puerto Rico, the Philippines and Guam, and conventions and agreements ratified new situations: the partition of the Pacific was completed in 1906 with an Anglo–French convention; South-east Asia was settled between 1896–1909 as a result of *ententes* and treaties, and Africa by 1914. China was humiliated and subjected to enclave spheres of interest from 1896 onwards after defeat in the Sino–Japanese war rather than partition, 'the cutting up on the melon' (Allen and Donithorne 1954: 24) that involved Britain, Russia, Germany, France, Japan, the United States and Italy.

Imperialism sometimes took an indirect form as in the conditional supply of finance and the provision of transport facilities. As Balogh has shown (1962: 334):

> The provision of cheap facilities for the finance of foreign trade while domestic activity was unable to obtain capital at comparable terms further distorted the productive structure of the colonial area. It accentuated the unfavourable integration of its economy, in which a subsistence agriculture, tribal or feudal, co-existed with a developed market economy. The differential ease with which the international movement of goods could obtain finance at world rates of interest further enhanced the supremacy of the merchandising, mining and plantation operations of large foreign firms, because long-term capital needed for the diversification of the economy and the rise of domestic industry was either not available at all or only on extortionate conditions.

By the late 1890s even Britain adopted a policy of 'constructive imperialism (Saul 1957: 175) with respect to 'several significant departures from the strictest principles of free trade in favour of imperial interests [tariff manipulation in favour of British and Empire interests with respect to Canadian preferences in 1897] . . . [and] a series of measures . . . taken to assist the colonies financially'. As before, the providers of transport often spearheaded the process of internal economic penetration and, by implanting particular staple production and its required transport facilities, predetermined their domestic development specialisations and biased the external articulation. For example, in South America 'the national transport systems served . . . to channel the production of raw materials to the ports for export to the industrialized countries . . . [they were not] designed to link the main population centres with one another within each country (UN 1973: 153) or indeed with contiguous countries and so did not consolidate the national integration process. There was a massive expansion of plantations that involved new areas and new crops. In the latter respect, the newly independent tropical Central and South American republics offered considerable prospects to large-scale United States' interest.

From the 1870s when lands physically suited to banana production on the Caribbean coastlands, generally at altitudes of less than 500 ft., were opened up for cultivation by the development of railways such as that from Puerto Limon to San Jose, the capital of Costa Rica ... the rapid success of the industry ... to supply fruit to the American market ... provided the incentive for further railway construction and for the development of port facilities and other items of infrastructure (e.g. in northern Honduras) [Odell and Preston 1978: 150.]

The importance of these plantations here and in Colombia, Ecuador and elsewhere became linked to the dominance of the United Fruit company 'with access to far greater resources of funds and expertise than any one of the Central American countries' (1978: 152). This company 'besides owning plantations, shipped large quantities of bananas produced by independent growers and, in the absence of other shippers of comparable importance, entirely dictated the terms of sale' (Saul 1957; 180). A similar situation with respect to the development of sugar plantations in Cuba occurred in the late 1890s.

Thus as Odell and Preston (1978: 137) observed, 'the fundamental political change from colony to independent nation had, in most cases, only limited social, economic and geographical effects'. In practice, this meant an extension of beef-rearing (as in Argentina); plantation production of sugar, cocoa, coffee and bananas; and extractive industries, including Chilean nitrates, tin in Bolivia, and copper and lead in Peru. Most such developments were 'enclave-like' and arose from foreign ownership and control.

While the world trading system now encompassed the globe, it is clear that there was inequality in the participation of countries. In 1913, the combined importance of Asia and Africa was only about one quarter of world exports. As Table 21 shows, in each continent one country stood out: in Asia, India accounted for 48.5 per cent of the combined total in 1883 and 36.09 per cent in 1913; and in Africa, South Africa accounted for 5.8 per cent of the 1883 total and 14.7 per cent of the 1913 combined total.

Hanson (1980: 129) has suggested that the countries that were to become the Third World in the twentieth century had in fact deteriorated since 1860 in three important respects from the immediately preceding decades: (1) their rate of growth of exports declined after having risen earlier; (2) Great Britain's share of their exports began to fall; and, most significantly, (3) they now faced increasing competition in many of their specialities from the newly-developed countries. He (1980: 131) argues that, despite certain developments, the rate of growth of the external stimulus to economic development in Asia, Africa and Latin America diminished as the nineteenth century progressed. He believes that Leff's (1973: 692) assessment of Brazil has wider application, i.e. that 'expanding exports, coming concurrently with improved terms of trade, were perhaps the major source of income growth in an otherwise relatively stagnant economy'. Hanson concludes (1980: 132):

> In sum, the expansion of the world economy dating from the early decades of the nineteenth century may have been historic and spectacular, but it was probably insufficient to improve the prospects for most of the millions of people living in Asia, Africa, and Latin America to enjoy the fruits of export-led economic development, even in the absence of exploitative behaviour by

Table 21: *Exports from the undeveloped world, 1883–1913*

	1883 $m	1883 %	1899 $m	1899 %	1913 $m	1913 %
Asia						
Ceylon	13.9	2.0	32.8	3.4	72.7	3.3
India	336.6	48.5	353.9	36.8	792.4	36.0
Malaya	72.7	10.4	102.8	10.7	192.5	8.7
Siam	8.0	1.1	15.2	1.5	43.1	1.9
Dutch East Indies	80.2	11.5	100.9	10.5	249.4	11.3
French Indo-China	15.7	2.2	26.6	2.7	66.9	3.0
China	95.1	13.7	142.9	14.8	294.4	13.3
Asia total	622.2	89.7	775.1	80.7	1,711.4	77.8
Africa						
Nigeria	7.9	1.1	8.5	0.8	33.0	1.5
Gold Coast	1.8	0.2	5.4	0.5	26.4	1.2
Sierra Leone	2.2	0.3	1.6	0.1	6.7	0.3
Gambia	1.0	0.1	1.2	0.1	3.2	0.1
South Africa	40.9	5.8	124.4	12.9	324.6	14.7
Northern Rhodesia	—	—	—	—	1.0	0.0
Southern Rhodesia	0.1	0.0	1.3	0.1	2.0	0.0
Kenya–Uganda	0.3	0.0	0.6	0.0	7.2	0.3
Nyasaland	—	—	0.2	0.0	1.1	0.0
Zanzibar	6.8	0.9	7.4	0.7	3.0	0.1
French West Africa	4.0	0.5	12.4	1.2	24.4	1.1
French Equatorial Africa	—	—	1.6	0.1	7.1	0.3
Togo	0.1	0.0	0.5	0.0	0.6	0.0
Cameroons	0.6	0.0	1.2	0.1	2.9	0.1
South West Africa	—	—	0.2	0.0	17.1	0.7
Tanganyika	0.3	0.0	1.0	0.1	3.9	0.1
Congo	2.2	0.3	7.0	0.7	11.7	0.5
Angola	2.0	0.2	8.6	0.8	5.6	0.2
Mozambique	1.1	0.1	1.5	0.1	5.3	0.2
Africa total	71.3	10.2	184.6	19.2	486.8	22.1
Combined total	693.5		959.7		2,198.2	
£ million	142.4		197.0		451.3	

Source: Latham (1978: 66, Table 8)

advanced nations. Furthermore, international contacts played such a small role in the economic life of many LDCs that exploitation by foreigners through trade can hardly be a complete explanation of how the LDCs came to be impoverished by modern standards. . . . Historically, trade has been more often a handmaiden of growth [to use Kravis's (1972) phrase] and not the engine of growth for most of the non-European world.

This period was a crucial formative phase in which particular industrial countries commanded a dominant share of world secondary industrial activity, became the main global sources for international investment and the export of capital goods, the major import markets for primary product exchange, and the main providers of the concomitant transport and banking services. Thereafter the evolution of technology tended to remain in this nucleus usually linked to the activities of its dominant core economy. On the other hand, as Furtado (1970: 32) has observed, the primary exporters involved in this process tended to fall into three groups, in each of which foreign trade helped to establish a distinctive economic structure having characteristic features which should be borne in mind when studying its subsequent evolution:

(1) Countries exporting temperate agricultural commodities. This included Argentina and Uruguay where

> the very extensiveness of the agriculture practised and the sheer volume of freight involved necessitated the creation of a widespread transportation network which indirectly led to the rapid unification of the domestic market, focusing on the major ports of shipment.

(2) Countries exporting tropical agricultural commodities. This included: Brazil, Colombia, Ecuador, Central America and the Caribbean, as well as certain regions of Mexico and Venezuela. On the whole, these commodities were of little significance as a factor in development, although they did involve the opening up of large areas for settlement [and] . . . since they were produced in areas lacking the capacity to develop new techniques for themselves, tropical products tended to remain within the framework of the traditional economies (1970: 33) [the exception was coffee in Brazil].

(3) Countries exporting mineral products. This included Mexico, Chile, Peru, Bolivia (and Venezuela after 1920):

> The considerable rise in the world demand for non-ferrous metals coincided with major technological progress in production methods which permitted or required the concentration of production in large units. This process of concentration, carried out initially in the major producing country – the United States – soon spread to other areas, where local producers were marginalised by American organisations with heavy financial backing and the technical 'knowhow' required to handle low-grade ores. Thus, the development of the export mining industry entailed not only denationalisation by the establishment of a productive sector which, given its marked technological advance and high capital intensity, tended to become isolated and to behave as a separate economic system, or rather, as part of the economic system in which the decision centre controlling the production unit belonged. Foreign control of a highly capitalised activity, employing a small labour force, meant that the major share of the flow of income generated by this activity was deflected from the domestic economy. [Furtado 1970: 34.]

Similar types of stratification can be discovered in Africa (A.G. Hopkins 1973) and in the Far East (Allen and Donnithorne 1957). Thus, during this period, specific North–South channels of trade, communications, transport and trading arrangements were developed and restrictions were imposed on South–South communication and trade. A concentration of innovation in the North gave North products a great advantage in all markets. The dominance of North products was reinforced by technological linkages – complementary items for inputs or consumption. As new states become incorporated into the capitalist international economy, peripheralisation and trade bias through 'enforced bilateralism' resulted in colonial relationships, as Kleiman (1976) has shown, where typically the colonial periphery country supplied the home metropolitan centre with raw materials and foodstuffs, and provided it with a captive market for its industrial products. Asymmetrical trade relationships necessarily resulted.

TRADE DISINTEGRATION AND THE RISE OF ECONOMIC NATIONALISM: 1914-52

This period includes the equivalent of three disrupted decades: a full decade of two world wars, a decade of depressions and perhaps a third decade absorbed by two postwar recovery periods. It was a period very different from that of 1870-1913. It demonstrated what Haberler (1964) refers to as the first serious 'disintegration' of the world economy, foreshadowed by the rising protectionism and economic nationalism evident from the 1880s, the full effect of which had been dampened by the expansion of external trade following the various transport and techno-logical revolutions. Now, war damage debts, reparations, and trade dislocations brought instabilities to international relations with economic nationalism in their wake, such that the relative freedom of international economic transactions broadly characteristic of the period preceding 1914 was not restored. While precise statistical measurement is impossible for this period, Kuznets (1967a: 8-9) has summarised the important researches of Maddison (1962) and Lamartine Yates (1959) thus:

> There was a sharp break after 1913 in the expansion of world trade. The Maddison estimates of world trade per capita, which include the Communist countries, show a decennial rate of growth for 1913-63 of less than 15 per cent, compared with 33 per cent per decade for 1800-1913, or 35 per cent per decade for 1820-1913. The Lamartine Yates estimates, which exclude the Communist countries after 1913, show a decennial rate of growth in world trade per capita of only 8 per cent for 1913-63 – between a fourth and a fifth of the rates over the preceding century.
>
> Further, this retardation in the rate of growth of world trade was clearly more marked than that in the rate of growth of world product per capita . . . not only [did] the rise in the foreign trade proportion characteristic of the decades before 1913 cease after that date, but the proportion in fact declined [by] about a third by 1963. The average rate of growth in per capita product of these developed countries (which accounted for about a fifth of world population at the beginning of the century) rose slightly from less than 18 per cent per decade for 1880-1913 to 19.5 per cent per decade for 1913-63, whereas the rate of growth in world trade per capita dropped from about 32.5 per cent to about 8 per cent per decade . . . the foreign trade proportion for the non-Communist world declined from 33 per cent in 1913, to 22 per cent in 1963.

The two decades between the wars, when world trade grew at only 0.9 per cent per annum (Lewis 1981: 11), were characterised by two different business climates:

(1) A recovery period of relative boom and free trade, in which the United States emerged in a pre-eminent position as the major international creditor nation, but in which the old multilateral system of trade became increasingly threatened.
(2) The financial crises of 1929-31 in Europe and the United States and their concomitant Great Depression, leading to a disintegration of trade and international monetary relations, such that 'in the 1930s there was fashioned . . . a more systematic economic nationalism than

the mercantilists of the seventeenth and eighteenth centuries had ever been able to achieve' (Condliffe 1951: 497). A 'mania for economic self-sufficiency' (Nadler 1937: 1) prevailed.

As Kindleberger (1966: 230) observed, 'the interwar period was one in which the world centre of economic impulses moved from Europe to the United States both in the mutual relations between the two areas and in their economic impact on third areas'. Prior to 1914, the United States had been a borrower of European savings. Capital had been in short supply and investment opportunities high because of the undeveloped state of its natural resources. During and after the war, however, the United States repaid a large proportion of its accumulated European debt and changed in status from a debtor to a creditor nation. As European postwar import needs to effect industrial reconstruction were not matched by an ability to pay in exports, the 'transfer problem' was financed by American loans which made the American dollar the significant international unit of account, taking precedence over sterling. After 1919, New York rivalled London as the main global centre for long-term loans, and a new pattern of international monetary interdependence was forged. More and more it became true that 'in the field of monetary policy . . . the United States [was] not obliged to respond to changes in Europe; Europe on the contrary [was] required to react, positively or negatively, to changes in the United States' (Kindleberger 1966: 230), the latter now becoming the dominant world economy. The shift of decision-making from the Bank of England to the United States Treasury Department was accomplished slowly and tended to dominate international relations in the period 1925–33, as indeed did monetary questions such as the stabilisation of the European exchanges and the relation of all currencies to gold. This was matched by the relative decline of Europe as a producer: in 1913 it accounted for 43 per cent of world production and 59 per cent of trade; in 1923, 34 per cent and 50 per cent, the main beneficiaries being the United States and Japan.

Four main changes now took place that reorientated the international economy (Furtado 1970: 36–7):

(1) There was a reversal of the upward trend in the external trade coefficient of the industrialised countries: in the United Kingdom it fell from 30 per cent to 25 per cent in the period 1927–9 and to 17 per cent in the 1930s; in the United States, Germany, France and Japan it levelled off in the 1920s and declined in the 1930s.

(2) There was a deterioration in world market prices of primary products relative to manufactures (see Fox 1937). According to Kindleberger (1973: 278–9):

> Prices of European and overseas commodities moved disparately. From 1928 to 1938, European import values as a whole fell from 100 to 73, constituting the trend. Extra-European commodities, such as cocoa beans, sugar, coffee, wool, cotton, fats and oils and silk, fell by more than the trend by percentages clustering around 40 per cent, whereas raw materials of European origin – wood pulp, coal, iron ore, iron and steel, cement – rose relative to trend by 45 to 75 per cent.

(3) There was a change in the composition of world trade away from national products, with the exception of petroleum, and towards

Table 22: *World trade composition, 1913 and 1953*

	% of total	
	1913	1953
Foodstuffs	29	23
Agricultural raw materials	21	14
Minerals	13	20
Manufactures	37	43

Source: Furtado (1969: 38, Table 5.1)

manufactures. Temperate zone exports were relatively less severely affected than tropical products, as is shown by Table 22.

(4) The channelling of trade increasingly into controlled areas, both at the private sector, and at the governmental and inter-governmental levels. As regards the former, there was a distinct rise in the importance of commodity agreements and control schemes set up by governments and international cartels, the latter being:

> voluntary agreements among independent enterprises in a single industry or closely related industries . . . [that] may be either single firms or groups of firms already combined into national cartels . . . with the purpose of exercising a monopolistic control of the market. [UN Department of Economic Affairs 1947: 1.]

Haussmann and Ahearn (1944: 429) concluded that 42 per cent of world trade between 1929 and 1937 was cartelised or influenced by loosely knit associations or conferences, a figure supported by Hexner (1943 and 1945) and including both raw material and industrial cartels. While the phenomenon was not new (see Piotrowski 1933) this intensification resulted (UN 1947: 8–9) 'largely from the establishment and expansion of industries of strategic importance during and after the first world war . . . [and] the duplication of plant after the modification of frontiers and the setting up of new independent states in post-war Europe' and led to the institution of cartel laws in many countries (UN 1947: 10). A number of intergovernmental control schemes for raw materials emerged as a result of war-time experience when it was realised that

> what was created to meet the special and often desperate situations in which primary producers found themselves as the result of the war could be adapted to meet the equally desperate situations with which they often found themselves faced in peace-time, as the result of the vagaries of nature and the weather, or of the trade cycle. [Rowe 1965: 122.]

The diminished importance of international trade was the result of three main factors. Firstly, the number of separate customs units increased from twenty to twenty-seven (Condliffe 1951: 481) following the fragmentation of the former Russian and Austro–Hungarian empires, each with their own customs frontiers. Secondly, the Russian Revolution of 1917 gave rise to prototype socialist command economies, the Second World, where trade between countries was conducted according to autarkic criteria. The third, and perhaps most significant, factor was the move away from multilateralism to bilateralism and the adoption of neo-mercantilist protectionist policies, what Condliffe (1941: 234) has referred to as 'hypertrophic nationalism'. As regards the formation of the Second World of industrial economies, Condliffe has commented (1951: 706, 708):

> The emergence of the USSR and its rise to power introduced a new element into international economic relations. The preceding nationalisms had accepted the competitive principle while controlling and modifying it. The USSR rejected it, just as it rejected the private ownership of the means of production and other fundamental principles of capitalist society. A planned industrial development was projected. This necessarily entailed close regulation of all external economic transactions. New devices of state trading were invented. Former debt obligations were repudiated, foreign enterprise was expelled, domestic monetary policy was divorced from the balance of payments, and international trade was reduced to the vanishing point. Thus was the Russian economy taken out of the world trading system. Thus, whereas the proportion of Russian exports to national income was about 10.4 per cent in 1913, the highest it reached after 1917 was only 3.5 per cent in 1930, the range in the 1950s being around 2 per cent. [Holzman 1963: 290.]

Elsewhere, one result of the 1919 Paris Peace Conference was the creation of a three-tier mandate system, under which certain specific ex-territories of the former Ottoman and German empires were reassigned to particular powers who now became accountable (see Louis 1984):

(i) 'A' peoples, including Iraq, Palestine and Syria, which, it was assumed, would in a relatively short period of time be able 'to stand alone':
(ii) 'B' peoples, including Togo, the Cameroons, Tanganyika, and Ruanda-Urundi which would require an indefinite period of economic and political advancement under European tutelage; and,
(iii) 'C' peoples, including South West Africa, New Guinea, Samoa; and the Marshall, Carolines and Marianas Islands that would probably remain European-run indefinitely.

D.H. Robertson (1938) has identified three phases in what became a relapse into neo-mercantilism, as the world became (Myrdal 1956: 39) 'directed by a monstrously complex network of trade and payments arrangements which has minimised the role of market forces in determining what nations will produce and what they will send to one another'. The interdependent and intercommunicating character of the previously emergent world economy became broken up by bilateralism and the formation of trading blocs; globally markets became increasingly disconnected and separate international relations replaced universal international relations. The 'economic space of each of the participating countries ... [shrank] and the economic significance of political bound-aries increased' (Roepke 1942: 39). World trade became 'hand-to-mouth' in character and 'more hazardous and erratic, a rough-and-tumble of nations vying with each other in their efforts to scrape together by any means whatever exports they can find'. The 'growing "politicalization" of international economic relations' resulted in 'less dependence on the laws of competitive supply and demand ... and more dependence on governmental whims'. The old liberal commercial policy was replaced by planned commercial policy,' "individual" trade was being replaced by the "controlled ... collective trade" of "managed capitalism" ... the real contents of foreign trade, ... while still being conducted by individual firms, became a matter of mutual arrangement between governments' (Roepke 1942: 49, 57, 58). Protectionism became all-pervasive and discontinuities in trade relations resulted from 'the greater changeability of the autonomous commercial policy of the different governments and to the shorter average duration of commercial treaties' (Roepke 1942: 60). The resultant disintergration tendencies within the world economy became cumulative and self-inflammatory. Within economies, vested interests were created which were anti-trade biased. Roepke commented (1942: 204):

> we find ourselves to-day in a vicious circle of economic nationalism, ... policies of nationally contrived stability, more economic nationalism, more international economic disintegration. ... In such a vicious circle the advocates of national economic stabilization may claim with some superficial truth that their policies are only a response to the new situation, but the more fundamental truth is surely that they are trying to argue out of a vicious circle of which their shortsighted reasoning is merely a subjective counterpart.

The trend towards nationalist protectionist policy fed on itself and a vicious circle of retaliation and reaction diminished trade. The world economy became 'disarticulated' and in need of 'international economic disarmament', and 'trade increasingly took place bilaterally, and to the extent it continued to be multilateral, was contained within bloc lines' (Kindleberger 1973: 282).

(i) The first phase detected by D.H. Robertson was 'old-fashioned tariff protection arising out of the war itself ... its chief motive force was the desire of individual industries in numerous countries to perpetuate the natural protection which they had enjoyed, with the end of the submarine and the blockade, during war-time'. The purpose was 'to protect reviving but dislocated domestic industries against the too ready importation of foreign competitive products and to nurture the industries formed or expanded during the abnormal period that they might become permanent gains to the national industrial structure' (1938: 10, 3). Such acts were supported by the dominant nationalistic sentiment engendered by the war, and the complications arising from unstable prices and currencies. Chalmers (1951: 4) distinguishes four types of measures resorted to:

1. Tariff revisions, usually upward, of more or less general scope.
2. Import and export restrictions, in the form of total prohibitions, contingents or government licensing systems.
3. Anti-dumping duties, depreciated currency surtaxes and similar measures to meet abnormal exchange conditions.
4. Revisions of basic treaty relations.

With respect to treaties, the most-favoured-nation clause, present in pre-war treaties to extend automatically to the original parties any benefits conferred by subsequent treaties with other countries, was now abrogated in a new set of treaties in the light of the new trading conditions. Moreover, tariff revisions now were often upward. In some cases, especially Latin American countries and the British Colonies (see F. Meyer 1948), the prime motivation was the need for increased national revenue. In other cases such as Persia, Siam and China, national tariff autonomy was asserted where limitations had previously been externally imposed by 'unequal treaties'.

Between 1913 and 1925, Hartmann (1973: 105) estimates that the average *ad valorem* duty levied by sixteen of the leading industrial states increased by a third, whereafter there was no general downward trend, despite the conversion of the United States to the unconditional form of the 'most-favoured-nation' clause in 1923 and its incorporation in the France–German Commercial Treaty of 1927. The Conference on Import and Export Prohibitions and Restrictions met in Geneva in 1927 to outlaw prohibitions on exports and imports and to subject the use of quantitative restrictions on trade to a common set of international rules. It required the support of a minimum of eighteen nations, but Britain, Germany and France (then responsible for over 50 per cent of world exports of manufactures) could not arrive at an agreed procedure. Shonfield has commented (1976: 33):

> leadership was much less in evidence than the assertion of the hegemonial principle by nations like Britain, Germany and France in their relations with their respective groups of client states [each with a particular geographical domain], [which] no doubt was one factor which explains why the ... international system responded so poorly to crisis.

Emphasis was increasingly put on warfare rather than welfare, divergent rather than convergent policies, discrimination rather than indiscrimination in international economic relations. In the latter respect, withdrawal of the most-favoured-nation clause was:

> a ready-made instrument for setting in motion a downward spiral in the process of bargaining, once nations [began] to adopt an adversary posture towards one another: for a dispute between two countries which leads one of them to withdraw a trade concession originally made as part of a general bargain between them is almost bound to inflict some injury on the trading interests of other countries who happen to be exporters of the products affected. [Shonfield 1976: 48–9.]

Taking 1913 as equal to 100, tariff levels rose as shown in Table 23 between 1927 and 1931.

Considerations of military security and economic independence had engendered a belief in the ideal of a maximum of national self-sufficiency in foodstuffs ('food autarky') which provided a forceful motive for 're-agrarianization' (Roepke 1942: 136) and the protection of domestic agriculture in industrially advanced countries. As Nadler (1937: 4) comments:

> Industrial countries in Europe, finding themselves unable to dispose of their manufactured products abroad and to pay for the necessary foreign raw materials and foodstuffs, devoted all their energies to the production of these materials at home. ... Thus, Italy drained marshes in order to increase its production of wheat and the battle for wheat became as important to Italy's economic nationalism as the battle of the Isonzo River had been during the War. Wheat imports into Italy decreased from 2,300,000 metric tons in 1927 to 465,550 in 1933.

Similar developments took place in Austria, Czecoslovakia, France, Belgium, and particularly Germany. Conversely, in the various agricultural countries of South America (including Argentina, Brazil and Chile) and

Table 23: *Relative changes in average tariff levels in certain European countries, 1927 and 1931 (1913 = 100)*

	1927	1931
Germany	122	244
France	97.5	160
Italy	112	195
Switzerland	160	252
Romania	140	207
Hungary*	131	197
Czechoslovakia*	137	220
Austria*	77	158
Spain	132	185
Bulgaria	296	420

* Comparison is with pre-war Austria–Hungary
Source: S. Pollard (1981: 302, Table 8.4)

continental Europe, new industries sprang up 'stimulated by the inability to obtain goods previously imported' (Nadler 1937: 3) resulting from their decreased export earnings.

(ii) D.H. Robertson's 'second wave' (1938: 10–11) was associated with the depression of 1929 and the final crisis of 1931 and

> extended far beyond mere tariff protection into the jungles of quantitative regulation of imports and control of exchange dealings, [and] was of course associated with the rush for cover from the depression of 1929 and the financial crisis of 1931. In the case of every country the primary and ostensible object of the intensified restrictionism was the protection of its balance of payments, endangered, as the case might be, by the collapse of the market for its exports, by a drying up of the long-term loans on whose continuance it had based its economic life, by a flooding of its market with dumped imports, by a withdrawal of short-term loans which had been incautiously woven into the fabric of its monetary system – or by some combination of these various misfortunes.

What was new about the depression was that it was 'world-wide, whereas many previous depressions were confined to particular countries or, at least were less closely synchronised in different countries' (Fox 1937: 19). This round was dictated as much by the exigencies of national finance as by strictly commercial considerations. The cumulative effect of the depression in 1930 led to a further tightening the subsequent year. There was a revival of the use of licence restrictions and quotas as a means of conserving foreign exchange and protecting currency values; and towards the end of 1931, of the adoption of foreign exchange controls and the coercive use of clearing arrangements (Nadler 1937: 4–6) by most of the continental European countries and those of Latin America. After the Wall Street crash of 1929, the Smoot-Hawley Tariff was enacted in 1930 which raised the general American *ad valorem* level to 41.5 per cent. In the two years that followed, American imports fell by 62.1 per cent substantially because of this. From 1931 onwards, France and Belgium put emphasis on quotas and licences; currencies became 'managed'; and Germany instituted a system of 'blocked' marks valid only for the purchase of certain imports. As Condliffe (1951: 487) comments:

> the great depression of 1929–33 . . . wrecked the European reconstruction effort as completely as a hurricane passing over a temporary housing project erected on inadequate foundations. Out of the wreckage governments fashioned trade into an instrument of economic warfare. Once it had begun, economic warfare became its own justification.

Some, however, felt that political expediency was paramount.

> The greatest of all the difficulties in these negotiations was not that of a real conflict between divergent national interests and national policies, but that there were no genuine national policies conceived as a whole but only a series of national systems devised under pressure. And neither ministers nor officials were effectively masters of the national system so constructed. Always as the negotiations proceeded, one felt that the dominant consideration in the mind of each national representative was not a conception of his nation's interests as a whole, mistaken or not, but a calculation of the pressures to which the national government would be subjected by organized interests in the respective parliaments. [Salter 1936: 39.]

(iii) The 'third wave' involved the inauguration of the Ottawa System of Empire which 'represented the deliberate use of political power for the attainment of exclusive economic advantage' (Hartmann 1973: 105). The majority of the new or increased margins of trade preference to British Empire products was brought about by the imposition of additional duties on the competitive products from non-Empire sources. The tariff schedule ranged from 10 to 33⅓ per cent, with 20 per cent as the most common new rate. Reduced purchasing power became a prime limitation on imports in Latin America. Confusion, experimentation and instability prevailed. Imperial preference was extended to India on 1 January 1933. The British Empire became a close commercial entity. Quotas were extensively used in trade agreements with other countries.

The Import Duties Act of 1932 imposed a general *ad valorem* duty of 10 per cent of all imported goods, although there was a free list. Duties additional to the general tariff could be imposed on 'any goods that were potentially or likely within a reasonable time to be produced in the UK in substantial quantities'. In addition, the Board of Trade could impose retaliatory duties on goods produced in any country that discriminated against the United Kingdom. Imperial Preference was greatly extended by the Ottawa Conference (1932). Under this system preferences were given to members of the Commonwealth giving reciprocal advantages. Thus British exports received a preference as did British imports of raw material from primary producers. The general effect was to reinforce the tendency towards regionalisation of trade and discrimination and almost certainly to reduce the total volume of world trade. Lewis (1949: 85) states that 'Great Britain was not the only country to take unilateral action. But she started it and must bear the blame for setting the fashion.' The policy of developing and expanding inter-empire trade and interdependence was also adopted by France, Italy and Japan. With respect to France: trade with its colonies in 1935 amounted to about 28 per cent of the total foreign trade of France, as compared with about 10 per cent in 1913 and about 12 per cent in 1924. As regards Italy and Japan, Nadler commented at the time (1937: 8–9):

The conquest of Manchuria by Japan and of Ethiopia by Italy was motivated primarily by the desire to become independent of foreign raw materials and foodstuffs. Japan has invested huge sums in Manchuria and since 1932 the trade between Manchuria and Japan has increased by 309 per cent. Not only does Japan hope to obtain most of the needed raw materials in Manchuria and in North China but she also expects that these territories will absorb a greater portion of her manufactured goods and will offer an outlet for her surplus population.

While Japan's aggression in China was at least partly explained on the grounds of military necessity, the conquest of Ethiopia by Italy was motivated almost entirely by economic greed and the desire to decrease her economic dependence on foreign countries. Italy hopes in the not distant future to make herself independent of foreign wheat, coffee, cotton, copper, and a number of other commodities and also to settle hundreds of thousands of Italians in Ethiopia as colonists.

Elsewhere clearing arrangements and compensatory trade arrangements or bilateral balancing were common. Reciprocal trade agreements were often trade-diverting and became dominated by the idea that the value of the trade between each pair of countries should approximate to an annual balance or be adjusted until it did (Chalmers 1953: 123). This weakened and disorganised the network of triangular or multilateral transactions. Quantitative controls dominated in Europe though not in Latin America. Germany indulged in state subsidies and tied sales, whereby foreign earnings from sales in Germany had to be spent exclusively on German products, thereby establishing an equivalent of international barter.

By 1936 some recovery was under way; the United States actively pursued trade arrangements involving reciprocal reductions of excessive trade barriers; the gold bloc countries realigned their currencies in 1936, which allowed more normalised international price relations. The latter was the result of the Reciprocal Trade Agreements Act of 1934 which provided the president with authority to negotiate a reciprocal reduction of tariffs with its trading partners. According to Preeg (1970: 15), such agreements were concluded in the period 1934–46. In the 1930s the most significant were with Canada in 1936 and the United Kingdom in 1938. Apart from distortions caused by currency manipulation, bilateral agreements and economic blocs, it was estimated that the proportions (by value) of imports in 1937 subject to quota restrictions or licences were as shown in Table 24.

Italy, the Soviet Union and Japan pursued self-sufficiency at high cost. Although modest attempts at collective action were made in 1937 by the

Table 24: *Proportions (by value) of imports in 1937 subject to quota restrictions or licences in certain European countries.*

France	58%
Switzerland	52%
Netherlands	26%
Belgium	24%
Ireland	17%
Norway	12%
UK	8%

Source: S. Pollard (1981: 303)

'Oslo Powers' and some return to the use of most-favoured-nation treatment occurred, the closed economy programmes of totalitarian states caused concern and were another restraining influence on the demobilisation of the trade control measures. Furthermore, the manufacturing industries of the United States, Great Britain, Germany and France became national autarkic units, conditions which the arrival of World War II intensified. Shortages of goods and inability to pay meant that normal trade awaited aid in rehabilitation and the Marshall Plan was launched in 1948. Close official regulation continued. Indirect import restrictions were generally subject to the procurement of an official licence or an exchange allocation, or both, and most exports were likewise subject to official control. Trade was often scaled down to avoid gold payments, limited by bilateralism and resistance to 'non-essentials'. The situation obtained until 1950, despite the Bretton Woods Agreement of 1944. Thus at the end of the reconstruction period, Svennilson was able to describe

> a world economy where a few countries, which together dominate world industrial output, provide markets for each other's industrial output only to a very small extent... The five largest industrial countries in the world have almost completely isolated their industrial systems from each other. In this respect, the division of the world into a number of isolated economic blocks is almost a reality. Work on a unified world market is useless if these large countries are not prepared to open up their frontiers to imports of manufactured products... It is to the economic relations between these large countries that the world disintegration can most properly be applied.[Quoted correspondence in Myrdal 1956: 40.]

In these circumstances, Viner (1955: 100) was moved to make the following generalisation about the changed character of trade:

> The elements of governmental operation, of governmental control, and of private monopoly in market operations are now so important that it has become otiose to assume that in most or even many of the national economies the effective prices reflect closely the relative 'real worth' or 'real costs' of the staple goods and services. Given the extent and the character of official control of foreign trade, it has become equally otiose to assume that the course of international trade is dominated by the relations among market determined prices.

THE FIRST GOLDEN AGE OF *INTERNATIONAL* TRADE 1953-72

Years	Core structure	Core-periphery relations
[1953-72]	Unicentric-stable. One hegemonic core state, the United States, and an absence of major conflicts among core powers. A *Pax Americana*.	Less explicit political regulation: *Colonialism* Decolonisation of Africa, India, and Asia *Trade* Lowered tariffs (GATT) and increasing free trade.

Bergesen and Schoenberg (1980: 241)

The third 'wave of global integration' began soon after World War II, gathered momentum at the beginning of the 1950s and thereafter achieved annual rates of trade growth that were unprecedented, even by pre-1914 standards. Briefly summarised the record was as follows:

> During the quarter century between 1948 and 1973, aggregate world production [increased] at an average annual rate of about 5 per cent. Population growth

accounted for about two and productivity gains for about three percentage points, which means that output per person was increasing three times as rapidly as in the earlier period. Production per person in the developing countries during 1948–1973 increased somewhat more rapidly than in the advanced industrial countries, although in absolute terms the gap between the average incomes of the two groups of countries widened. The volume of world trade, which in the earlier period had grown at one-quarter of the growth rate of production, was expanding at an average annual rate of 7 per cent. Between 1948 and 1973 the volume of world trade increased nearly sixfold. [Blackhurst *et al* 1977: 7.]

This historic achievement resulted from, and was propelled by, the spectacular recovery and rapid growth of all industrial nations, and was supported by the first real attempts at supranational interventionist policies. It occurred despite the tendency towards internal state dominance within capitalist economies; an enhanced bi-polar segmentation as between First World advanced economies and Second World command economies; and a further fragmentation of sovereignty within the world trading system brought about by mass decolonisation after 1945.

This period was one in which most First World capitalist economies became more 'mixed' in their economic orientation as a result of the growth of government spending and in the size of their public sectors set beside their private commercial sectors. Furthermore, the latter was increasingly made subject to a plethora of government interventionist objectives, legislation, taxation and regulation. Moreover, in contrast to preceding periods, governments now became more ambitious in their aims of taking on the responsibility for assuring high levels of employment; and regulating and taxing economic activity and wealth.

Within the international economy 'an iron curtain descended from the mid-Baltic to the Adriatic' in the words of Churchill and enlarged the number of the Second World socialist nations. The Cold War divided East and West and severely reduced the transideological international exchange of Second World socialist economies. The East pursued relatively autarkic policies that emphasised international bilateral exchange, conducted via state-trading concerns, in ways that precluded the need for currency convertibility. However, while the East European bloc rejected both the principles and institutions of the multilateral trading system between 1947 and 1955, thereafter, first the principles became recognised and then some change of attitude towards its institutions occurred (Kostecki 1979: 1).

Within the world trading system, international economic sovereignty now became formally more fragmented as a result of the granting of independence to most colonial areas, which now became preoccupied with the need to develop autonomous trade and development strategies, given their new political status and assumed control over domestic resource allocation. Two new features characterised the first truly global existence of international, i.e. interstate, trade relations, following such mass decolonisation after 1945.

(a) Economic harmonisation via supranational institutions.
(b) Regional co-operation via customs unions.

(a) Economic harmonisation via supranational institutions

A new global operational framework for international trade relations was collectively devised during the 1944 Bretton Woods Conference in an attempt to secure a steady expansion of world trade, within a multilateral free trade context, yet subject to common codes of conduct and rules of exchange rate regulation that would be mutually supportive of, or at least neutral with regard to, national economic objectives. It was hoped that the institutions to be set up would hold to account countries whose policies diverged from these objectives and to constrain them within particular limits. By these institutional means, it was hoped that a degree of supranational 'structural engineering' and partial 'management' of the international economy would occur; and that the international division of labour would be rearticulated by co-operative action in three main areas:

(i)   in the trade sphere, the General Agreement of Tariffs and Trade was set up in 1948 to supervise the global reduction of trade restrictions, largely for manufactures;
(ii) in the monetary sphere, the International Monetary Fund was set up *inter alia* to supervise exchange rate arrangements, the convertibility of currencies to overcome the adjustment problem facing countries and to supervise the means of liquidity creation: and,
(iii) in the investment sphere, the International Bank for Reconstruction and Development was set up to maintain world investment flows with its subsequent affiliate organisations, the International Finance Corporation in 1956 and the International Development Association in 1962.

From their inception, the effective policies of the above tended to reflect the considerable international bargaining sovereignty of the United States, the aid programmes and open-ended balance of payments deficit of which largely financed the post-war European reconstruction and the efforts of the Japanese to restore their pre-war economic and political strength. However, achievement of these goals by the early 1960s, highlighted by the formal restoration of gold convertibility at the end of the 1950s, undermined the unquestioned economic strength of the United States, as 'the economic wards of the US quickly matured into strong international competitors' (S.D. Cohen 1978: 274). the period ended with the collapse of the Bretton Woods gold exchange standard in 1971 and a realignment of currencies.

In the trade sphere, the principles of non-discrimination, reciprocity, order and the reduction of trade barriers were insisted on and enshrined in the GATT agreement of 1947. An expanded organisation to be called the International Trade Organisation was proposed by the Havana Charter (1948), which was to include provisions for commodity agreements, the control of restrictive business practices and economic development, but the proposal was not politically acceptable to the participant nations. Nevertheless, the tariff barriers that had accumulated in the preceding decades were appreciably reduced as a result of tariff-bargaining conferences held at Geneva (1947), Annecy (1949) and Geneva (1956), and the 'Dillon Round' of 1960–2, and 'Kennedy Round' of 1963–7, the momentum for which came from American initiatives. For example, the Dillon Round directly arose from the renewal of the United States' Reciprocal Trade Agreements Act of 1958 and reduced tariffs on industrial goods by 20 per cent; the Kennedy Round resulted from the 1962 United

States' Trade Expansion Act, and reduced these tariffs by a further 33 per cent in the period 1967–72. As a result of the two latter rounds of negotiation, the EEC and EFTA country tariff levels were reduced to one-half of their mid-1950s levels and 'prevented a third to a half the anticipated trade diversion resulting from European integration' (Preeg 1970: 220) pre-empting a threatened fragmentation of the global trade structure into a polycentric system of competing trade blocs, although the EEC now emerged as a unified and co-equal bargaining force. Tariffs on dutiable non-agricultural products were reduced to an average of 'only 9.9 percent in the United States, 8.5 percent in the European Community (excluding the United Kingdom, Ireland and Denmark), 10.8 percent in the United Kingdom and 10.7 percent in Japan. Through GATT negotiations and various bilateral agreements during the 1930s, the tariff level on all dutiable United States imports dropped from around 59 percent in 1932 and 25 percent in 1946 to less than 12 percent prior to the Kennedy Round and to 9.9 percent' by the mid-1970s (Baldwin and Kay 1975: 110).

Despite the above, trade trends continued to reveal particular widening inequalities in the distribution of the benefits from trade, especially in the case of developing country exports of primary products. These products were often subject to limited market access as a result of quotas and consumption taxes, so that the developing countries found it difficult to develop secondary processing activities and final consumption goods, particularly textiles and labour-intensive light industrial products and non-tariff barriers. Such problems had been exacerbated by the fact that between 1950 and 1970, primary product world trade growth was only 6 per cent per annum, compared with 9 per cent for manufactures: the volume of world trade in manufactures rose from a base of 100 in 1960 to 278 in 1971, minerals and oils and fuels to 199 and agricultural products to 165. The share of manufactures rose from 50 per cent to 60 per cent. With the publication of the Report of the Commission on International Development ('the Pearson Report'), *Partners in Development*, the widening gap between the developed and developing countries was exposed as a central issue. The problem partly reflected the fact that little attention had been paid to 'fair trade', the maintenance of the rule of non-discrimination, removal of non-tariff barriers and the establishment of the right of ready access to developed country markets for less developed country manufactures. Within the world-system:

> The decolonization of the peripheral areas ... [did] not eliminate the core periphery division of labor, [but] raised the cost of core exploitation of the periphery. And the emergence of the socialist states, although not successful in creating a socialist mode of production ... added constraints to the freedom and manoeuvrability of capital. [Chase-Dunn 1982: 48).]

In the new post-colonial economies, two trends emerged: the delimitation of areas closed to the operations of foreign-owned enterprises, especially in Latin America and an increasing resort to international credit agencies; and a disbelief in the efficiency of (Haq 1976: xii) 'a market system, wholly uncorrected by institutions of justice, sharing, and solidarity, makes the strong stronger and the weak weaker'. Attention was increasingly given to alleged North/South wealth/poverty constraints. Bairoch (1975: 94) has shown that the period under review marked the end of an era in which LDC trade increased as a proportion of world exports, and that the period 1950–62 witnessed a reversal of this historical relationship: 'taking 1950 = 100, exports were 148 in 1962, while the index number of GDP was 174'; that the trade of developed countries had been higher and greater than that of the LDCs and that a problem of a relatively large deficit had appeared, reinforcing the necessity for financial aid. When international trade grew from $108 billion in 1958 to $312 billion in 1970, the relative LDC market share declined from 21.3% to 17.8% (a figure comparable to their share in 1900), though they contained 66% of the world population and produced only 12.5% of the Gross World Product (Commission on International Development 1969: 24). The basis for Bairoch's findings is indicated in Table 25.

Table 25:   *The foreign trade of less developed countries*, 1900–70*

Year	Imports (cif)** in US $m	Exports (fob) (fob)*** in US $m	% World exports	Balance of trade in US $m	% of imports
1900	1,600	1,600	16.0		
1913	5,500	3,800	19.0	+ 300	+ 9
1928	6,500	7,600	23.0	+1,100	+17
1938	5,800	5,900	25.0	+ 100	+ 2
1948	18,600	17,100	29.7	−1,500	− 8
1950	17,500	18,900	31.0	+1,400	+ 8
1953	21,500	21,100	25.5	− 400	− 2
1958	27,800	24,800	22.9	−3,000	−11
1960	30,200	27,300	21.3	−2,900	−10
1963	32,900	31,500	20.4	−1,400	− 4
1965	38,000	36,400	19.5	−1,400	− 4
1968	46,000	44,100	18.4	−2,200	− 5
1970	57,600	55,600	17.8	−2,000	− 4

* excludes communist countries   ** cost, insurance, freight   *** free on board
Source: Bairoch (1975: 93, Table 29)

One of the major reasons for this increasing disparity was that technological changes were increasing the variety of intermediate and final demand goods. This industrial diversification of products played an important part in the expansion of trade (Blackhurst *et al* 1977: 10): 'as the number of products (or versions of products) increas[ed], industrial firms discover[ed] increasing opportunities for specializing in the production of one or a limited number of products'. However, gains from such specialisation could only be reaped by large countries or ones with unfettered access to large markets. The horizontal trade between industrial countries now intensified, relative to their vertical trade with the less-developed countries, and was now significantly based on 'intra-industry' exchange, i.e. a simultaneous export and import of differentiated goods within the same industrial sectors (such as cars), rather than between sectors (such as textiles and machinery). The share of such trade of total manufacture trade (Aquino 1978: 283) was over 70 per cent in respect of France, the United Kingdom, the Netherlands, Sweden, West Germany, Austria, Canada, Italy, Denmark and Belgium; and 57.3 per cent in the case of the United States.

Two additional features of this period noted by Blackhurst *et al* (1977: 15) were: the increasing importance of imported inputs in production (and by implication in exports), and the predominant importance of intra-continental trade. Blackhurst shows how the imported input ratio of production increased for five European countries in the period 1959–70, especially in the case of engineering products (see Table 26). Such trade flows reflected a growth in multinational intra-branch specialisation, foreign processing and international sub-contracting and a decline had taken place in the domestic value added content of exports.

Table 26: *Imported intermediate good content of production and exports, 1959 and 1970 (in percentages)*

	Total production		Production of engineering products	
	1959	*1970*	*1959*	*1970*
France	13	17	10	16
West Germany	15	18	14	16
Italy	16	22	14	23
Netherlands	34	37	33	46
Belgium	34	40	33	50

Source: Blackburst *et al.* (1977: 15, Table 2)

Geographically, the expansion of manufacture trade within Western Europe and within North America, i.e. intra-continental trade, accounted for nearly two-thirds of the total increase between 1955 and 1973. Trade between Western Europe, North America and Japan accounted for a little less than 25%, and the expansion of industrial countries' imports of manufactures from LDCs accounted for only 11% of the increase in total manufacture imports (see Table 27).

Thus, at the global level, there was a general need to reassess policies for reciprocal tariff cuts under the aegis of GATT, in the light of the comparatively lower growth rate of the LDC trade and their poor achievements in industrial diversification into manufactures and processing industries. The significance of this problem intensified from the mid-1960s onwards. The 1964 first United Nations Conference on Trade and Development highlighted this problem, and an additional chapter on Trade and Development was added to the GATT Charter in 1965. UNCTAD, which accepted the need, *inter alia*, for increased access to be given in the developed country home markets to processed and manufactured products of particular interest, or potential interest, to the LDCs (Article XXXVI); and pledged the developed contracting parties to accord

Table 27: *Distribution by area of the increase in industrial countries' trade in manufacture, 1955–73*

	Distribution by area of the increase in:	
	Imports of manufactures	Exports of manufactures
	%	%
(1) Intra-continental trade within North America and within Western Europe	65	52
(2) Mutual trade between North America, Western Europe and Japan	24	19
(3) Trade with the rest of the world*	11	29

* Includes Greece, Portugal, Spain, Turkey and Yugoslavia
Source: Blackhurst *et al.* (1977: 19, Table 4)

high priority to the reduction and elimination of barriers to products of particular interest to the LDCs, including barriers that discriminated unreasonably between such products in their primary and in their processed form (Article XXXVII). Thereafter this remained very much a live issue. UNCTAD IV in 1976 and subsequent discussions about a New International Economic Order all emphasised the need for developing countries to expand processing industries and to develop 'resource-based' industrial strategies, given that primary commodities account for approximately 75 per cent of LDC export earnings (only 40 per cent of total world trade in primary products, whereas the LDC share of manufactures and processed goods is only about 18 per cent), as indicated in Table 28.

(b) Regional co-operation and customs unions

The emergence of customs unions and common markets in Europe, Latin America, Africa and elsewhere required similar investigations concerning the measurement of tariff levels, the economics of integration and the need for, and effects of, common economic policies. Such intra-regional zones of economic activity and decision-taking have been a new force for structural change within the international economy, the progenitor exemplar being the formation in 1957 of the EEC from six countries (France, West Germany, Italy, the Netherlands, Belgium and Luxembourg) and the subsequent addition in 1973 of the United Kingdom, Denmark and Ireland, such that, by the end of the period, it accounted for some 20 per cent of total world exports. Ten other major associations were formed and three loose ones (Baldwin and Kay 1975: 107–8):

1. Latin American Free Trade Association (LAFTA), formed in 1960, comprising Argentina, Brazil, Chile, Mexico, Paraguay, Peru, Uruguay, Colombia, Ecuador, Venezuela and Bolivia;
2. Andean Group, formed in 1969 as a subgrouping of LAFTA and comprising Bolivia, Chile, Colombia, Ecuador, Peru and Venezuela;
3. Central American Common market (CACM), established in 1960,

Table 28: *International trade by commodity groups, 1972*

	Composition of world exports*	Composition of exports from industrial areas	Composition exports from developing areas	Share of developing areas in total world exports
	%	%	%	%
Primary products				
Food	14.3	11.8	22.9	28.8
Raw materials	5.6	4.1	8.6	27.7
Ores and minerals	2.5	1.7	4.5	32.0
Fuel	10.4	3.4	38.6	66.9
Total primary products	32.8	21.0	74.5	40.9
Manufactures				
Non-ferrous metals	2.8	2.4	3.5	22.7
Iron and steel	4.8	5.7	0.9	3.4
Chemicals	7.1	8.8	1.9	4.9
Engineering products	24.6	29.6	4.1	3.0
Road motor vehicles	7.7	10.3	0.1	0.3
Textiles and clothing	6.4	6.4	7.2	20.2
Other manufacturers	11.9	13.9	6.2	9.3
Total manufactures	65.3	77.2	23.9	6.6
Total exports	100.0	100.0	100.0	18.0

* Australasia and South Africa are included in world totals, but not elsewhere
Source: Thoburn (1977: 4)

composed of Costa Rica, El Salvador, Guatemala, Honduras, and Nicaragua;

4. Caribbean Free Trade Association (CARIFTA), formed in 1968, comprising Barbados, Guyana, Jamaica, Trinidad and Tobago, Antigua, Dominica, Grenada, Montserrat, St. Kitts–Nevis–Anguilla, St. Lucia and St. Vincent;

5. East Caribbean Common Market (a subgrouping of CARIFTA), formed in 1968 and comprising Antigua, Dominica, Grenada, Montserrat, St. Kitts–Nevis–Anguilla, St. Lucia and St. Vincent;

6. East African Community (EAC), formed in 1967 and composed of Kenya, Uganda, and Tanzania;

7. Central African Customs and Economic Union (UDEAC), established in 1964, composed of Cameroon, Central Africa Republic, Congo and Gabon;

8. West African Economic Community (CEAC), established in 1972, composed of Dahomey, Ivory Coast, Mali, Mauritania, Niger, Senegal and Upper Volta;

9. Arab Common Market (ACM), formed in 1964, comprising Egypt, Iraq, Jordan, and the Syrian Arab Republic; and,

10. Regional Co-operation for Development (RCD), established in 1964 and composed of Iran, Pakistan and Turkey.

The three loose regional organisations were: the Council of the Entente (Dahomey, Ivory Coast, Niger, Upper Volta and Togo) formed in 1959 in West Africa; the Magreb Group (Algeria, Morocco and Tunisia) formed in 1964 in North Africa; and the Association of South-East Asian Nations,

ASEAN (MAL. PHIL. THAIL. SING. INDO.) 1967

or ASEAN (Malaysia, the Philippines, Thailand, Singapore and Indonesia) formed in 1967.

RELATIVE TRADE DISINTEGRATION AND TRANSNATIONAL RESOURCE ALLOCATION, 1973–

Core structure	*Core-centre relations*
Multicentric-unstable.	More explicit political regulation.
A growing plurality of competitive states created by the decline of American hegemony and the growth of the EEC, Japan and the Soviet Union.	*Newer forms of core domination* Arms dependence creating client states which undermines the non-aligned status of peripheral states.
	Trade Import restrictions and increasing protectionism.

Bergesen and Schoenberg (1980: 241)

Since the early 1960s, it had gradually become apparent that an important structural change was under weigh within the international economy (see Madeuf and Michalet 1978) created by factors that were worldwide in scope, of which two principal features were (a) the emergence of transnational structures; (b) a North/South shift of industrial location and the spread of industrialisation. These features were to be further enhanced by the period of world industrial recession after 1973.

The emergence of transnational structures

Transnational relations have been defined (Nye and Keohane 1972: xi) as 'contacts, coalitions, and interactions across state boundaries that are not controlled by the central ... poly organs of governments'. During this period such structures became increasingly evident in many spheres of activity that included business, banking, technology transfer, behaviour patterns (the demonstration effect) and value systems (westernisation of the Middle East) all of which speeded up the transmission of economic events from one country to another and changed the motivation behind many international exchanges. Nye and Keohane (1972: xviii) outline five main effects of the presence of such forces:

(i)   Attitude change
(ii) International pluralism – the linking of national interest groups in transnational organisations for co-ordination of policy
(iii) Increases in constraints on states through dependence and interdependence
(iv) Increases in the ability of certain governments to influence others
(v)   The emergence of autonomous actors with private extra-national policies that may deliberately oppose or impinge on national state policies

These factors increasingly undermined the state-centric dimension of international relations as the primary focus of economic reality. A network of intersocietal linkages was forged that in principle made economies sensitised to a greater degree to economic forces and made resource allocation increasingly less state-confined and global resource allocation mechanisms more pertinent.

An enumeration of some likely consequences of these phenomena for national economies by Lindbeck (1977: 223–4) indicates that, more than was previously the case, a larger number of important domestic policy variables are increasingly influenced by external forces:

(a) a greater synchronisation (in time) among nations of fluctuations in output and prices, particularly if exchange rates are not very flexible;
(b) a falling profit margin due to increased international competition (and hence flatter demand curves);
(c) a more rapid rate of change in comparative advantage among nations;
(d) a more rapid rate of structural change;
(e) tendencies to increased structural unemployment and possibly also increased wage differentials within countries;
(f) increased geographical dispersion of unemployment, and possibly also of income, within countries;
(g) an increased tendency to mergers because of the fall in the profit margins and the more rapid rate of structural change;
(h) a tendency to weaker investment incentives for private firms;
(i) stronger effects on the domestic economy of decisions by large organisations outside the jurisdiction domain of the individual country – by international organisations, multinational firms and perhaps also interest group organisations;
(j) greater environmental disturbances and demonstration effects from abroad on domicile citizens.

Thus the net impact of the considerable structural transformations within and between the economies of the world has been a series of internationalisation tendencies in the following areas (Lindbeck 1977: 216):

(1) Internationalisation of *markets* for (a) commodities and services, (b) money and credit, (c) labour and human capital, (d) technology and entrepreneurship.
(2) Internationalisation of *institutions*: (a) political, (b) interest groups, (c) market-oriented institutions.
(3) Internationalisation of *externalities*: (a) on the production side (e.g. environmental disturbances), (b) on the consumption side (e.g. taste equalisation).

A North/South shift of industrial location

The emergence of transnational control of production in industries such as textiles, motor cars, electrical and electronic industries, shipbuilding and other industries of a labour-intensive character requiring low levels of specific technological know-how at the assembly stage brought about their 'delocalisation' (Madeuf and Michalet (1978: 255) from advanced countries and relocation in certain developing countries such as South-East Asia, Brazil, Mexico, Argentina and the Magreb. A new style of specialisation was emerging based on the internal needs of transnational firms, a specialisation based on the managerial planning of a transnational private sector and not on national factor endowments and free competition. The industrial production of advanced capitalist economies increasingly overlapped territories and was only partially home-based. Underlying these internationalisation processes was a revolution in telecommunications and data technology which for the first time permitted a global reach. 'The "operation domain" of markets and market-oriented organisations ... more and more exceed[ed] the "jurisdiction domain" of the national state' (Lindbeck 1975: 33). Interpenetration of markets and production structures took place. The value of such 'international production' owned or controlled by parent organisations outside their home countries in the early 1970s was $330m. compared with their world exports of $310m. (Shonfield 1976: 115). Foreign affiliates were responsible for one-third of international trade, over fifty per cent of which was controlled by American-based firms. The United States exported less from its domestic territory than was exported by its enterprises located abroad. The private sectors of national economies were increasingly being integrated into a world economy framework. Galbraith (1973: 31–2) saw the new

> transnational system as an extension of the [corporation's] national planning system, and ... the multinational corporation as the main element in the system ... firms follow their products into ... second countries [and] re-create the firm there ... [and] win the same kind of security in its transnational environment as ... at home. In addition, it can meet competition by going where the cost of labor is lowest and the conditions of production are most efficient ... the multinational corporation is simply the means by which the modern corporation minimized the uncertainties peculiar to international trade.

As a result of a series of industrial invasions abroad, American business became more dependent on its external economic relations:

> Exports as a proportion of total US production of goods (manufactures, raw materials and food) ... increased ... from 9 per cent [in 1950] to a little over 14 per cent in 1971 ... By the latter date ... 60 per cent of all foreign owned business assets in the world were in the hands of American Companies. [Shonfield 1976: 59–60.]

Table 29 compares the scope of the overseas subsidiary networks to a group of the world's largest firms in 1950 and in the 1970s and reveals their dramatic increase.

Table 29: *Networks of foreign manufacturing subsidiaries of 315 multinational companies, 1950 and 1953.*

No. companies with networks including	US-based MNCs		MNCs based in UK & Europe	
	1950	1975	1950	1975
Fewer than 6 countries	138	9	116	31
6 to 20 countries	43	128	16	75
More than 20 countries	0	44	3	29

Source: Harvard Multinational Enterprise Project (quoted in Vernon (1979: 258)

Thus visible trade flows have been progressively transformed through global raw material sourcing, production location and marketing; and invisible trade has been restructured by global deposit sourcing and lender servicing. Both types of international exchange required extensive external production networks which had to be newly created by international capital transfers and institutional migration. A new context for international specialisation was provided,

> the result of managerial planning and no longer simply of national factor endowment or free competition. . . . Increasingly economic internationalization is tending to deprive the concept of nation-State territoriality of all meaning, making it simply an area the structures of which are determined by the interplay of world economic forces . . . the definition of the nation-State as a sealed space of factors of production is belied. [Madeuf and Michalet 1978: 257, 258, 260.]

What matters in the new context is the propensity of countries:

> to attract international business according to their economic *environment* . . ., *systems* . . ., and *policies*. . . . By *environment* is meant the resources, including technology, available to a particular country and the ability of its enterprises to use these to service domestic or foreign markets. By *system* is meant the organizational framework within which the use and allocation of scarce resources is decided. . . By *policy* is meant both the objectives of Governments and the measures taken by them and related institutions to advance their objectives, within the system and environment of which they are part. [Dunning 1982: 357.]

These factors were to play an increasingly important part as the world industrial recession of the 1970s developed.

> Between 1963 and 1973, world output (excluding construction and services) rose by 6 per cent annually, while the volume of world exports increased by 8½ per cent annually. . . During 1974–80 . . . world output growth fell . . . to only 3 per cent . . . [and] world exports . . . to some 4 per cent. By 1981 . . . output grew by only 1 per cent, world trade stagnated. . . the loss of dynamism [was] particularly marked in the case of manufactured products, which account for 55 per cent of world trade and 70 per cent of trade among industrial countries. The growth of world exports of manufactures decelerated from 11 per cent annually during 1963–73 to 5 per cent during 1974–80 and further to 3 per cent in 1981. [Anjaria *et al* 1983: 1, 3.]

Trade disintegration stemmed from a number of factors that included two oil crises and their consequent depressive effects on economic activity; certain structural shifts of competitive power that involved a relative decline in the position of the United States; and the rise in importance of newly industrialising countries such that the number of centres of world economic gravity multiplied and no overarching single country hegemony prevailed. Moreover, given the failure of the gold-exchange international monetary standard in 1971, and a subsequent search for a new exchange pivot for the trading system, no strong consensus emerged concerning the particular policies concerted action might pursue. Flash-points for world depression came with the oil crises of 1973 and 1979 and their attendant balance of payments problems that exacerbated the inflationary problem that had emerged at the end of the 1960s in most advanced economies. Four main features of this period require comment in this context:

(a) the oil crises and industrial recession,
(b) the growth of 'managed' trade,

(c) newly industrialising countries and the spread of industrialisation.
(d) the debt crisis.

(a) The oil crises and industrial recession

Transnational producer control of the world oil market that began with the formation of OPEC in 1972 resulted in two 'shocks' to the international trading system brought about by the sudden large price increases that it effected in 1973/74 and 1979/1980: a quadrupling of price in the first case (the United States' price per barrel of Saudi Arabian crude oil rising from 2.70 to 9.76 US $s); and a more than doubling of the price in the period 1978–80 (the above price rising from its 12.70 US $ level in 1978 to 17.26 US $ in 1979 and 28.67 US $s in 1980 (figures from IMF *International Financial Statistics Yearbook 1984* p. 131). These occurrences caused in their wake an international economic dislocation of historic post-1945 proportions. They had an inflationary impact on the industrial costs of the world economy and a deflationary impact on its growth. World demand was reduced as income was redistributed towards economies with high saving propensities and by the down-turn in demand for cars in particular and in aggregate demand in general, intensified by the concomitant anti-inflationary measures adopted by national governments. This led to intermittent attempts at co-ordinated 'world demand management' by the main industrial nations as a result of a series of economic summits; and an attempt after the 1976 UNCTAD meeting in Nairobi to set up a new Common Fund institution to stabilise certain selected non-oil commodity prices at the world level.

(b) The growth of 'managed' trade

Despite the presence of world economic institutions designed to overcome or regulate international exchange tensions, whether in the trade or monetary areas, 'the continued existence of still mainly nationally based political systems' (Lindbeck 1975; 29) gave rise to 'managed' trade, based on the erection of non-tariff barriers, as a means of coping with the balance of payments to deficits concomitant with the oil crises and their aftermath. Thus, from the mid-1970s, the recessionary climate inspired the adoption of protectionist policies that formed the basis for a 'new mercantilist' era in international economic relations. These particular circumstances also exacerbated the particular problems experienced by what became called by some 'post-industrial' societies (see Gustafsson 1979) that allegedly possessed five central characteristics:

> (1) an *economic sector* based upon a service economy rather than goods production, (2) an *occupational distribution* preeminently based upon a professional and technical class, (3) an *axial principle* that highlights the centrality of theoretical knowledge as the source of innovation and of policy formulation for the society, (4) a *future orientation* emphasizing technology and technological assessment, and (5) *decision-making* based upon the creation of a new 'intellectual technology'. [Targ 1976: 474; c.f. Bell 1973: 14.]

Analysis of the British situation emphasised problems associated with 'de-industrialisation' and an alleged need to use import controls rather than other policy measures such as exchange rate adjustment to restructure the economy and make it once again growth-oriented and internationally competitive. Collectively this approach came to be referred to as the 'New Cambridge View'. The arguments presented in favour of 'managed' trade are systemic, in that they are couched in a macroeconomic context, and relate to an alleged capitalist market failure nationally and internationally. The broad basis of this approach is indicated by the following passage from Singh (1977: 133):

> Liberalisation of trade and free capital movements are not always necessarily beneficial for a country. Because of the uneven development of the world economy and of the productive potential of different regions, there may be many periods when participation in the international economy under such arrangements can lead to disequilibrium and be seriously harmful to a country's economy. The detrimental effects can work in a number of ways – most importantly through the level and structure of demand and through investment. Once the economy is in long-run disequilibrium, for whatever reason, continued participation in international economic relations on the same terms as before may produce a vicious circle of causation. As a consequence, a country in a weak competitive position may have balance-of-payments difficulties, which lead the government to have a lower level of demands, which leads to lower investment and hence lower growth of productivity and continuing balance-of-payments difficulties. There may be no automatic market mechanism to correct the disequilibrium.

Page (1981: 28) summarised the period of the late-1970s thus:

> about 40 per cent of trade by all market countries was controlled before 1974; this has risen to just under a half... Most trade in non-manufactures was already managed in 1974; the rise since then has been small. In manufactures, however, the share has risen from 13 per cent to almost a quarter. For imports by the EC countries, the changes are from 36 per cent to 45 per cent for all goods, and from virtually nothing to 16 per cent for manufactures. For all goods, the share of trade controlled by the European countries is slightly lower than the average for the world, but the increase since 1974 has been rather greater (the high figure for intra-EC trade reflects the high share of steel trade). The differences in levels among EC countries mainly reflect differences in the composition of trade (including differences in trade with the centrally planned economies). There were no large differences in the changes because most of the identifiable trade policies were concerted. Most of the other European countries show similar levels for manufactures with two controlling all their imports.

The country data on which these judgements were made is given in Table 30.
   The industrial sectors prominently affected include textiles, steel, television sets, footwear, ships and automobiles (see Bergsten and Cline 1983). Three main features of this 'new mercantilism' have been the use of voluntary export restraint programmes (VERS) and orderly marketing arrangements (OMAS); 'and, increasingly important, government intervention through subsidies and other means, sometimes aimed at investment decisions rather than trade per se, with indirect but potentially enormous effects on trade' (Cline 1983a: 6). Regarding VERS and OMAS, some analysts (including UNCTAD (1978) have argued that they are particularly damaging for LDCs because of their unique discriminatory qualities: these being

Table 30: *Managed trade by country, 1974 and 1980*

Countries	All goods		Manufactures	
	1974	*1980*	*1974*	*1980*
	%	%	%	%
Belgium/Luxembourg	27.5	34.0	0.7	10.0
Denmark	29.5	43.2	0	21.7
France	32.8	42.7	0	16.2
West Germany	37.3	47.3	0	18.3
Ireland	26.8	34.0	1.5	11.7
Italy	44.1	52.3	0	16.4
Netherlands	32.5	40.1	0	14.8
United Kingdom	38.5	47.9	0.2	17.4
EC (9)	35.8	44.8	0.1	16.1
Australia	17.9	34.8	7.8	30.0
Austria	20.8	30.3	0	13.1
Canada	22.4	18.3	11.4	5.8
Finland	32.9	33.6	3.1	3.5
Greece	100.0	100.0	100.0	100.0
Iceland	20.6	31.2	1.3	15.7
Japan	56.1	59.4	0	4.3
Norway	16.3	33.7	0	24.6
Portugal	25.5	27.5	10.5	11.7
Spain	32.2	52.3	0	37.1
Sweden	24.7	36.3	3.1	19.4
Switzerland	16.9	18.3	2.1	3.4
Turkey	100.0	100.0	100.0	100.0
United States	36.2	45.8	5.6	21.0
OECD (22)	36.3	44.3	4.0	17.4
Other developed (3)	97.5	97.9	97.7	97.8
Oil exporters (15)	51.0	65.3	45.8	59.8
Non-oil developing (81)	49.8	46.9	25.0	22.8
World (122)	40.1	47.8	12.9	23.6

Source: Page (1981: 29, Table 1)

First, they are usually directed at labor-intensive, low-priced goods, products . . . where a developing country has the greatest comparative advantage. Second, they put the burden of implementation on the exporting country. Third, they are negotiated accords. Unlike tariffs and quotas, which are implemented unilaterally, . . . [they] may lead to political tensions as a result of bargaining. Fourth, they involve bilateral negotiations that isolate the weak, developing country in a one-to-one confrontation against a powerful, developed state or the EC. [Yoffie 1981: 572.]

However, Yoffie shows that a number of the NICs have in fact found ways by which to avoid the potentially damaging effects of such import barriers, and have in fact managed to increase their exports during this period (see Table 31) by exploiting particular political and economic weaknesses:

Table 31: *US textile quotas for selected exporters, 1956–76 (in millions of square-yard equivalents)*

Country	1st US VER	1st Multifiber VER	Quantitative increase	% increase
Japan	245	1737	1492	609
Taiwan	56	562	506	903
Korea	26	403	377	1450
Mexico	75	278	203	270
Philippines	45	189	144	320
Pakistan	55	181	126	229
India	79	152	73	92
Colombia	24	91	67	279

Source: Yoffie (1981: 578, Table 1)

recognizing the political basis of trade, and by following two core policies and several supplementary tactics. The essence of a successful exporting strategy is that a NIC give priority to long-term rather than immediate political and economic interests, and that it use the bargaining opportunity created by the new protectionism to negotiate for short run needs... Two bargaining tactics can be employed, separately or in combination, to reduce the restrictiveness of protection and meet an exporter's short-term requirements. The most important of these negotiating policies is trying to foster ambiguity in the agreement as well as bargain for flexibility. To supplement this approach, a NIC may be able to link unrelated issues [e.g. military] to the negotiations at hand ... [to use] leverage from other areas to counterbalance weakness in trade... Cheat [by legal evasion, transhipment and various forms of circumvention], and mobilize transnational and transgovernmental allies. [Yoffie 1981: 572, 574, 582.]

As an example of skilful use of loopholes, and the product of definitions, Yoffie (1981: 584) gives the footwear agreement between OMA, Taiwan and Korea, who 'were careful to limit the restrictions to non-rubber shoes. By adding rubber to footwear soles or making other minor alterations ... exported shoes could be classified as rubber and then legally outside of the quota's jurisdiction'.

(c) Newly industrialising countries and the spread of industrialisation

Chenery (1977: 457) noted that 'the principal reallocation of economic activity in the postwar period had been a shift of manufacturing from the old industrial centres to a group of countries that have been catching up to the industrial leaders'. This latter group he identifies as *'transitional countries'*:

[countries that] have either achieved the income levels and industrial structure of the original group in the past quarter-century or are in a position to do so by the year 2000. From the vantage point of 1976, there are eleven 'newly developed' market economies with a total population of some 250 million and seven centrally planned economies that have nearly completed a similar transformation. Another 30 countries are well advanced in this transition.

The eleven newly developed market economies cited include: Japan, Italy,

Spain, Argentina, Israel, Puerto Rica, Ireland, Greece, Singapore, Hong Kong and Portugal.

The industrial circumstances of the late-1970s, however, gave focal interest to a particular group of such countries that were collectively referred to as the NICs (Newly Industrialising Countries), which, despite the world recession, challenged the competitive abilities of the AICs (Advanced Industrial Countries). Such competitive pressures also led to industrial delocation, much of which was effected under the aegis of multinational companies which channelled parts of their transnational operations to areas in the world where their activities were least frustrated by obstructive interventionist policy, provided the host economies were stable, both politically and fiscally; offered legal situs to external non-resident companies and domestic status to overseas subsidiaries of onshore parent companies for the routing of their globally derived incomes; had institutional facilities for the low-tax reinvestment of earnings and capital accumulation; offered trouble-free locations for tax planning, ease of currency movement and translation and conferred institutional freedom of action with regard to other activities (such as fund flotations, captive insurance, international pension schemes and labour regulations). So it was that there was a shift of invisible production to particular tax haven locations and of visible production to low-friction low-tax economies (see Johns 1984; 1983) or 'investment promotion zones', 'export processing zones' or 'free trade zones' located therein. Ping (1980: 12–14) estimates that such zones proliferated from zero in the early-1960s to more than eighty by 1980, with another forty under construction or being planned, more than half of which are in Asia in the countries fringing the Pacific Basin; whereas Diamond (1977) identified no fewer than 264 such zones in sixty-seven countries, two-thirds of which were in developing countries. The 'first wave' of such industrial invasions concentrated largely on Hong Kong, Singapore, South Korea and Taiwan, but a new phase began in the late-1970s, the main elements of which Ping (ibid.) detects as being:

(a) A relocation of some industries from the above-mentioned original low-labour-cost countries to the sub-continents of South Asia and China, the poorer ASEAN countries like Indonesia and Thailand, and to some small islands in the Pacific and Indian oceans;
(b) The rise of indigenous Asian multinationals as a result of the 'first wave' and their participation in the industrialisation of its 'second wave';
(c) New patterns of activity and refinements in the international division of labour resulting from the micro-electronic technological revolution in which the processing and assembly of component manufactures takes place within a world factory and is undertaken for global rather than initially domestic distribution.

Grubel (1982: 41) estimates that: 'in 1979 about $100 billion of total world trade of $1,300 billion (i.e. 7.7 per cent) went through free trade zones. Forecasts are that by 1985 about $300 billion or 20 per cent of world trade would pass through such free trade zones'.

By the early 1980s, it was possible to identify eight substantial NIC beneficiaries of these developments:

Table 32: *NIC manufactured exports, 1973–9 (in billion US $)*

Country	1973	1979	1979 ÷ 1973
Taiwan	3.8	14.1	3.7
South Korea	2.7	13.4	5.0
Hong Kong	3.6	13.2	5.7
Singapore	1.6	6.4	4.0
Brazil	1.2	5.6	4.7
Mexico	1.5	3.2 (1977)	
Argentina	0.7	1.6 (1978)	
India	1.6	3.4 (1977)	
Global total	17.8		

Source: Bradford (1982: 14, Table 2.2)

By 1976, South Korea, Taiwan, Hong Kong and Singapore accounted for over 90 per cent of the manufactured exports from East Asia; India, 75 per cent of the manufactured exports from South Asia; and Brazil, Mexico and Argentina, 70 per cent of Latin America's industrial exports. Together these eight countries accounted for over three-quarters of the manufactured exports from the developing world in 1971. [Bradford 1982: 10.]

Their growth in exports was as indicated by Table 32.

Some twenty-two countries have been identified as included in a rising 'next tier' of countries (Keesing 1979): in East Asia, these are Malaysia, Thailand, Philippines, Macao, Indonesia; in Latin America, Colombia, Jamaica, Uruguay, Venezuela, Trinidad and Tobago, El Salvador, Guatemala, Chile, Dominican Republic, Costa Rica; in Africa, Tunisia, Morocco, Bahrain, Senegal, Ivory Coast; and in South Asia, Pakistan and Bangladesh.

(d) The debt crisis

The oil price rises and attendant recession intensified the balance of payment difficulties of Third World countries and non-oil exporting countries generally. As a result, non-oil developing countries' debt service payments as a percentage of exports rose from about 15½ per cent in 1973 to about 18 per cent by 1979, the share of bank-financed debt now doubling to around 60 per cent and to 70 per cent after the second oil price shock, with the role of private direct investment and official finance being severely reduced in international importance. Total external debt of these countries rose from under $200 billion in 1973 to $330 billion in 1978, and dramatically to $670 billion in 1983. Over $600 billion of this was accounted for by twenty-five major debtors, the average debt service ratio to exports of which rose to a peak of 32 per cent in 1982. Almost half of the above sum was owned by Mexico, Brazil, Argentina, South Korea and Venezuela (for a full discussion see Cline 1983b; Aramovic 1982; and Nagi 1982). By the end of 1983 Cline (1983b: 9–10) summarised the increasing financial dependence and plight of such borrowing countries thus:

All three of the largest developing-country debtors - Brazil, Mexico, and Argentina - were forced to disrupt normal debt-servicing. Debt-servicing, disruption or formal reschedulings of debt reached approximately two-thirds of bank debt owed by the developing and East European countries. By the end of 1982, 34 countries were in arrears on their debt. The amounts of debt formally rescheduled rose from $2.6 billion in 1981 to ... approximately $90 billion (including amounts being renegotiated) in 1983.

Such problems have intensified the need for a New International Economic Order that had been under constant discussion in the UNCTAD conferences of the 1970s (see Anell and Nygren 1980) that had followed in the wake of the collapse of parts of the Bretton Woods supranationalist model of international political economy and had embodied a number of different North/South perspectives, which Hansen (1979) has summarised according to the following schema, under the two headings: (1) developing country perspectives (the South) and (2) developed country perspectives (the North), recognising that (ibid.):

> The constraints on collective action to manage North–South problems in the emerging global system will be significantly affected by the ways in which those problems are perceived by both sides and by the 'policy space' that mutually compatible Northern and Southern perspectives offer to policy makers in both sets of countries.

The need for an urgent resolution of this problem was underlined by two reports by the Independent Commission on International Development Issues ('The Brandt Commission'): *North–South – A Programme for Survival* (1980); and, *Common Crisis – North–South Co-operation for World Recovery* (1983).

(1)   Developing country perspectives (the South)

The international inequity perspective and the need to redistribute world income
This view stems from the belief that the present unequal international distribution of income and wealth has been sustained in at least five main ways.

(i)   Efforts at international trade liberalisation through GATT have been biased in favour of products of interest to developed country exporters such that LDCs have gained little from the rounds of tariff-cutting.
(ii) The volume and value of foreign aid flowing from the North to the South has been unjustifiably low.
(iii) The North has systematically rejected or stalled over lengthy periods of time *re* reform matters to overuse the availability to the South of scarce foreign exchange needed in the development process.
(iv) Northern multinationals have in general restricted their potential contribution to the Southern development process *inter alia* by (a) limitation of tax liabilities through certain patterns of transfer pricing, (b) limitations on job creation through the use of capital-intensive production methods and artificial limitations on exports, and (c) exaction of monopoly rents on the corporations' technology.
(v)   Adverse terms of trade until the early-1970.

The Southern self-reliance perspective This incorporates two distinct goals:

(i) The creation of an increased capacity for intra-Southern 'self-help' in the development process by *inter alia*, intra-area trade liberalisation; development of Southern multinationals backed by joint governmental co-operation and financial support; joint R and D schemes; joint price stabilisation schemes, etc.
(ii) The political use of enhanced Southern unity to bargain more effectively and forcefully with the North for desired changes in the international economic system (the OPEC example).

The basic-human-needs perspective There is a need to refocus development strategies to meet more rapidly and effectively the minimum needs of the poorest strata of Southern economies and deal with the general problem of world poverty.

(2) Developed country perspectives (the North)

The growing recognition within the North that failure to come to terms with the South would create problems for its own domestic societies and foreign policy goals led to a varied spectrum of views about the need for changed attitudes on its part, five of which merit special consideration (Hansen 1979: 61–80).

The rejectionist perspective There are two distinct rationales for this perspective:

(i) That the present system is highly defensible in both normative and efficiency terms, that the Southern attack aims at total replacement rather than measured reform of the system, so that Northern efforts to 'accommodate' will prove self-defeating in the long run.
(ii) That global politics will be more 'manageable' from a Northern viewpoint without the obstinate presence of a Southern bloc that is consistently politicising issues which the North would prefer to see remain dormant.

The 'bring them into the system' perspective Often subscribed to by those who feel the costs of the rejectionist perspective are too high, this perspective implies a modicum of change which would give a much more prominent role to certain key developing countries, e.g. Iran, Brazil, Mexico and Saudi Arabia. The emphasis is a short-term one on economic-system-maintenance largely on the expedient grounds that 'history has often shown that the greatest dangers to international stability often arise from those nations whose real power is inadequately reflected in both real involvement in the relevant sets of international arrangements and symbols of status therein' (Bergsten *et al* 1976: 9).

The global agenda perspective A need for greater collectivist approaches in decision-taking is felt by some to be essential because of the declining hegemony of the United States and the growing dispersion of influence and power among a broadening number of state and non-state actors in world politics. The continuation of conflict on global agenda problems (e.g. food, environment, population stabilisation, law of the sea) will make optimum outcomes impossible to realise.

The global equity perspective The analogue of the Southern international inequity perspective. This is a 'developmentalist' perspective in that it emphasises increasing growth in LDCs as a result of improved access to Northern markets, capital and technology as a means of closing the North–South gap in aggregate per capita incomes.

The basic-human-needs perspective Holders of this perspective are concerned, above all else, with the development of new international (and national) institutions and norms of behaviour that would assure the provision of a minimum global standard of living within as short a period of time as is deemed feasible (often the year 2000 is given as a target date). Minimum targets are set in terms of per capita standards for food, nutrition, health services and basic education to 'put a floor under global poverty'.

Elsewhere within the system the new resource frontier became that of the oceans and the snowy wastes of the as yet unexploited arctic areas. Within the international trading system a greater degree of interdependence arose between the Eastern and Western blocs (see Levcik and Stankovsky 1979). As Abonyi (1982) has shown, these relationships developed as a result of counterpurchase agreements (the bartering of Soviet products for Western products); compensation agreements (the importation of Western high-technology goods in exchange for long-term payments through a proportion of the output from the imported technology); and transideological joint-ventures. During the 1970s, six East European countries reduced their overall trade with the Soviet Union and increased their trade with developed market economies: export and import trade with the Soviet Union fell from their 1965 levels of 39.9 per cent and 38.4 per cent respectively to 34.2 per cent and 33.7 per cent by 1979, whereas export and import trade with developed market economies rose from 22.7 per cent and 25.1 per cent to 27.8 per cent and 32.3 per cent respectively over the same period (Abonyi 1982: 181). Whether this shift constitutes a reintegration or not within the world trading system is, however, a matter of some controversy (see Szymanski 1982).

ENVOI

The phenomenon of an 'international economy' is of comparatively recent origin and has evolved according to certain systemic pressures and random factors. Its history exhibits one phase of internal integration, three phases of world-wide integraton, the last two phases being followed by a disintegration phase. Within each phase, disparities of country size and international economic sovereignty have characterised events and economic impulses, whether negative or positive. The last phase exhibited an undermining of the state-centric basis for international relations by the rise of transnational actors, the activities of which have not as yet been made subject to effective common policies at the intergovernmental or supranational institutional levels.

The organic process of evolution has been swift. Particular trade structures were established under colonial/imperialist conditions that have not been easy to reverse a century or more later. Growth of world trade resulted from two main components: the rapid expansion of the trade of the First World developed countries, dominated by Great Britain in the second half of the nineteenth century, and by the United States in the twentieth century; and the incorporation of 'new entrants' from Third World developing countries into that trading system. The circumstances of the latter's incorporation were such that they often took place under imperfect 'imperialist' conditions when such states were not, as yet, industrialised, not internally economically integrated, and not autonomous with respect to their internal allocation of indigenous resources. Inevitably the resultant external trade relations tended to be unequal, the exchange patterns exhibiting in many countries:

(a) managed bias in the structure of industrial specialisation;
(b) imposed constraints on the geographical pattern of trade flows; and
(c) development profile proclivities.

Only in the longer run did the costs of interdependence in terms of vulnerable dependency emerge, when the colonial period formally ended for many such countries in the middle of the twentieth century.

Given the complex evolution of an eventually world-scale relational trade and production network from a limited European-dominated Atlantic economy in the sixteenth century, to an Atlantic-North-dominated global economy under threat from countries in the Pacific basin in the late-twentieth century – an evolution that was temporally patterned and subject to variant trade parameters either of a colonial or purely interstate character, the central theoretical task must now be approached, as identified by Ohlin (1933: 325) i.e. 'to explain the character and development of the international division of labour and the exchange of commodities and, above all, to explain short-term and long-term *variations* in trade as well as the production of each country'.

Part II

General theoretical approaches to the explanation of trade flows

An explanation is analogous in many respects to a map. A map records the results of observation, using conventional rules and symbols; it tells us what to expect when certain landmarks are sighted. No map records *everything* in an empirical situation; the map chosen for use should suit the purpose of the user. Maps, like explanations, structure a particular situation from a given point of view. And maps, like explanations, must be altered to include new experience or changes in situation. Given a purpose, and some knowledge of the way in which the map was prepared, some criticism of the adequacy of the map can be made before the map is used. In the end, the value of the map must be tested by use.

Meehan (1968: 98)

Economic theory must be continuously revised in the light of structural and organizational changes in a rapidly evolving economic system. Only thus can it be relevant and of service to society. By revision, I mean a thorough overhauling, even scrapping of many doctrines – not mere qualifications, refinements, or extensions of deeply rooted misconceptions.

Moulton (1946: 52)

In no field of economics has conventional thinking so tight a grip both on Academe and on policy-making as in international trade.

Balogh (1982: 182)

Part I outlined the changing parameters that have conditioned international trade relations and the particular evolution of a world exchange system, without any specific pre-programmed determinist view being presumed about its path of integrative directional change. The system of international trade relations between national economies was shown to have been hierarchically ordered and temporally patterned by unequal economic circumstances, both in colonial and post-colonial politico-economic contexts. It was further revealed that multilateral free trade has been historically exceptional and that the process of global economic evolution has been meaningfully related to international mobility of capital and labour. This background, however, is not one to which successive contemporary orthodox general theories have been directly addressed. On the contrary, international trade models have, until fairly recently, merely provided a general political economy rationale for cosmopolitan trade activity, rather than an empirically based explanation of actual trade flows. Heroic assumptions have been made about universally uniform national market conditions thereby ignoring many historical features of actual inter-country trade relationships. While the nineteenth- and twentieth-century general models are individually discussed in Chapters 5 and 6, an attempt is made in Chapter 4 to indicate the methodological spectrum of choice of different levels of analysis; to outline some common limiting errors of commission and ommission which apply to these theories; and to suggest alternative lines of approach, examples of which are examined in Chapter 7 and the three final chapters contained in Part III.

Publication of Samuelson's articles (1948 and 1949) on the pure theory of international trade and the confusing revelations of Leontief's paradox (1953) led to an important bifurcation in international trade analysis. With respect to the former, Hirschman (1977: 68) argues that, whereas:

> The classical theory of international trade . . . taught that trade could lead to mutual gains for all trading countries . . . Samuelson's results were much stronger and pointed to trade as a potential force toward the equalization of incomes around the world . . . [However] this brilliant theoretical capstone . . . was put into place just as consciousness of the persistent and widening international inequality of incomes was becoming acute in the postwar years . . . as a result, Samuelson's findings – even though they had been put forward with all due warnings about the unrealistic and demanding nature of the assumptions on which they rested – acted as a devastating boomerang for the traditional theory and its claims to usefulness in explaining the problems of the real world.

From the 1950s onwards, the sharp contrast between the theoretical trade benefits of classical and neo-classical theories and the accumulation of contradictory empirical evidence and argument presented by Myrdal (1956a, 1956b), Nurkse (1962) and Prebisch (1959; 1964) among others, led to the emergence and burgeoning of *development economics* as a branch of study in its own right (see Streeten 1979: and Johnson 1969). The latter involved analyses of the relative backwardness of countries and investigation of how it might be overcome. The relationships between trade and development were now examined in the new environment of political independence in former colonial areas in conjunction with the need to transform their less-developed industrial structures, not just the achievement of optimal resource allocation via comparative advantage, however defined. Thus it was that development economics became separated from international economics. It is not intended in the context of this book to review the discussion that emerged from the latter deliberations and the alleged relevance or irrelevance of 'pro-trade', 'outward-looking', 'export-led', strategies as against 'anti-trade', 'inward-looking' 'import-substitution', for which the reader may usefully be referred to etablished development economics' texts (such as Todaro 1982). Chapter 7 will merely report on some of the post-Leontief trade propositions and models that continued to be largely presented in the hypothetical deductive tradition of past international trade theories, some of them extending previous models (neo-factor proportions theories), others offering new insights (Kravis' 'availability' thesis. Linder's theory of trade manufacturers; neo-technology and product cycle explanations); or presenting positive structural disequilibrium models of international trade relations or global and regional trade models. Part III is reserved for the more empirically based theories of recent years, as well as contemporary theories of unequal country development and theories of global development which provide both a new context within which to view international trade relations, and a definite contrast to the orthodox theoretical approach.

4 Methodological aspects of conventional explanations of international trade flows

Economic theorists operate in at least five distinguishable 'universes of discourse', and for some of these universes relevance to reality has no or little relevance

[1] a universe of intellectual play, without other ulterior motives. Rigor and elegance are here the only relevant tests of workmanship, and internal consistency the only test of validity of results . . .
[2] a universe of professional tradition. Here the selection of problems, of assumptions, of techniques of analysis, and perhaps also of pre-established conclusions, is largely determined by inheritance from past teachers or ancient texts . . . Even if the past theorizing was fully relevant for the period of its original blossoming . . . and this should never be taken for granted, it is in the abstract a reasonable presumption that it will have undergone considerable obsolescence with the passage of time . . .
[3] a universe of revolt against professional tradition. The revolt may be in the interest of relevance, and may help to achieve it. It may, on the other hand, be merely prejudiced and blindly negative in its motivation . . .
[4] Economic theorizing may have as its objective merely or primarily a contribution to the understanding of the economic process, without assumption of responsibility for evaluating the social impacts, or of proposing either reforms of or methods of preserving a desired status quo . . .
[5] Finally, economic theorizing may be intended to provide cause-and-effect analysis and guidance as to appropriate objectives for use by economists themselves, by government, or by the public at large, directly or indirectly in solving social problems.

Viner (1955: 107–7)

METHODOLOGICAL CHOICE: TIME HORIZONS, LEVELS OF ENQUIRY, LINES OF APPROACH

With respect to economics in general, the objective of theory (Frisch quoted by Deane 1983: 11) 'is to lay bare the way in which different economic factors act and interact on each other in a highly complex system'. In practice, the economist is motivated by three basic types of discipline need: those of the positive science, those of the normative or regulative science of political economy and those of the art of the subject, where (Keynes 1930: 35) 'the object of a positive science is the establishment of *uniformities*, of a normative science the determinants of *ideals*, of an art the formulation of *precepts*'.

At the positive level, the task is to 'collect the unordered facts available and make them coherent by creative thought' (Einstein and Infield 1938: 33). However, this pursuit is problematical in that the analysis can be conducted according to different time horizons, at different levels of enquiry and along different lines of approach. While each combination of time horizon, level of enquiry and line of approach provides its own social-

130

scientific insight of reality, it also presents its own methodological difficulties and limitations. These basic elements are briefly separately indicated below:

Time horizons: McKewen (1963: 21) maintains that in respect of social-scientific phenomena 'there is a constantly changing temporal process of becoming, rather than a static order of being'. He quotes Whitehead's assertion (1938: 200) that 'there is no nature at an instance ... all the interrelations of matters of fact must involve transition in their essence ... process, activity, and change are the matter of fact'. Thus synchronic/static analysis that describes a particular state at any moment is of limited significance if it is not also related to a diachronically/dynamically defined context.

Level of enquiry: McKewen (1963: 21) in his discussion of the social sciences in general, refers to the central importance of 'reciprocal collective-individual foci' and argues that unless 'the interpenetrating functions of both the collective and the individual aspects of the concrete reality of human action [are recognized] significant channels of inquiry will be closed if the analysis is delimited to one focus'. Both types of analysis therefore need to be attempted. Watkins (1953: 729) calls the two approaches 'methodological holism' and 'methodological individualism'. The former approach seeks to explain processes and events by reference to macroscopic laws which are *sui generis* and which apply to the social system as a whole. The latter approach seeks to explain such outcomes in terms of induced or deduced principles governing the behaviour of the participant actors, and descriptions of their situations.

Traditional orthodox economic theory has, with the exception of Marxist economics, tended consistently to be presented in terms of the narrower rather than the wider framework of reference. According to Heilbroner (1980: 497):

> abandonment of the holistic goal has meant the deliberate constriction of economic theory from a discipline that aspired to the towering stature of a truly social science to the much more modest status of a science that explicates interactions of the economic elements within the social system, without regard to political or social ramifications.

In his view (ibid.):

> *economic systems cannot be conceived merely as 'functional' arrangements for the production and distribution of goods, but must also be seen both as frameworks for the division of social prestige and political power, and as mechanisms for the attainment of some postulated social destination.*

Lines of approach: Methodological choice is exercisable in economics within a spectrum of analytical lines of approach, from apriorism (the most abstract) at one end, to ultra-empiricism (the most world-oriented) at the other, as indicated below (see Blaug 1980: 265–67):

1 *apriorism*: theorising from a few intuitively obvious axioms that are not independently established but taken as given.
2. *conventionalism*: an unquestioning view of theories as merely condensed descriptions of events, neither true nor false in themselves, but simply conventions for storing empirical information.

3. *operationalism*: emphasis on positive relationships arrived at where quantitative values can be assigned to the terms used and verified.
4. *instrumentalism*: emphasis on the predictive power of theories and their use as operative instruments of policy.
5. *ultra-empiricism*: insistence on independent verification of all assumptions by objective data obtained through sense observation.

Dissatisfaction with the above approaches can also lead to an institutionalist approach that puts emphasis on analyses of the evolving goal-directed activities to be discerned in economic systems and in the 'pure logic of the industrial process'.

Whatever the approach pursued, four main points should be borne in mind in any evalution of any theory put forward (Meeham 1968: 115):

(a) The *scope* of the explanation offered, i.e. the range of events that the theory purports to explain.
(b) Its *precision*, i.e. 'the exactness with which the concepts used in explanation are related to empirical indicators, and the precision with which the rules of interaction of the variables . . . are stated [and] measured' (1968: 117).
(c) Its explanatory *power*, i.e. 'the *completeness* of the explanation. An explanation that includes *all* variables known to relate to a given event, and the rules that link them together, is much more powerful . . . than an explanation that [contains only] some of its known variables' (1968: 119).
(d) Its *reliability*: 'Even if the explanation is as exact as we can make it, the problem of uncertainty is still present . . . [if] factors not included in the explanation [can] interfere with the empirical situation that the explanation refers to' (ibid.)

Orthodox theories tend to be the result of the use of the hypothetic-deductive method, i.e. 'a system of pure deductions from a series of postulates derived from inner experience which are themselves not open to verification' (Blaug 1980: 97). Their *a priori* premises are derived from introspection and casual observation, rather than *a posteriori* from actual experience or concrete events. As such the reality to which they refer is only a potential synthetic reality. They are not therefore challengeable on grounds of validity, as the models and their conclusions are true as one aspect of human behaviour by virtue of their assumptions, but on grounds of their applicability:

> they represent not positive but hypothetic truths subject to a ceteris paribus clause that prescribes deviant behaviour . . . the doctrines of Political Economy are to be understood as asserting not what *will* take place, but what *would* or what tends to take place, and in this sense only are they true (Cairnes 1875: 69, 110).

Such theories are in accordance with von Mises' view (1949: 585) that 'the ultimate yardstick of an economic theorem's correctness or incorrectness is solely reason unaided by experience'. Given their prescriptive format, they are not simulations of actual behaviour or even casual laws, but are intended as enumerative statements of the welfare benefits that could be achieved under certain circumstances, having the evangelical property of orienting statements, being intended to convince governments of the need to correct deviant behaviour by structural policy-engineering. They are not to be accepted as statements of invariant mechanical relationships but as statements of tendencies. Moreover, their motivational emphasis on allocative efficiency and production possibility maxima are indicative of target levels of activity which will probably not be precisely realised in practice due to various kinds of real-world inefficiency (see Leibenstein's concept of X-efficiency which allows for such imperfections (1978: 32)). As orthodox theory tends to force economic reality into a rigid, static mould that excludes concern with technological change, non-economic objectives, and internal and external power relationships, some writers (Hutchison 1977: 13) have been moved cynically to state that:

> The model of static equilibrium seemed to be constructed not so much because it was able to contribute to the explanation of reality, but because it was easy to handle diagrammatically or mathematically. Consequently, functional inter-relationships seemed to be assumed, not because they fitted best to elucidate reality, but because they yielded satisfying answers.

While others have stressed the longer-run absurdities of such rationales, for, as McEwen (1965: 368) comments:

> It seems unlikely that any contemporary economist would deny that the change from a dominantly competitive economy to a hybrid economy in which monopoly or oligopoly is more dominant than individual competition, could have occurred, if the only causal conditions had been equilibrating forces.

Despite their apparent lack of realism, however, the use of such theories is upheld by some where:

(a) they have a high instrumental value in generating accurate prediction. The Friedmanite view (1953: 15) is that the only relevant test of a hypothesis is the comparison of predictions with experience, although, in the case of orthodox trade theories that are predicated on perfect market assumptions, they fall foul of the 'Duhem-Quine thesis' that it is not possible to falsify single hypotheses where a conjunction of hypotheses are packaged together because

> if a particular hypothesis is found ... in conflict with some piece of empirical evidence ... We can never be sure that it is not one or more of the auxilliary hypothesis which is responsible for the anomalous ... evidence, rather than the particular hypothesis in which we are most interested [Cross 1982: 320.].

(b) they have not been replaced with something better. In Machlup's view (1978: 498) a theory is never wholly discredited, even in contexts where its fundamental assumptions are known to be false, unless a better theory can be or has been offered. Ohlin (1952: 571) also made the point that 'orthodox theory has enabled a great number of practical problems to be dealt with satisfactorily. A new theory can only justify itself if it can deal equally well with these problems and better with some others.' Thus there is no 'global search-mechanism', no deep study of the contemporary social and economic order or the 'imperial phenomenon'. The paradigm of the scientific method (Heilbroner 1980: 488) 'tends to rule out of bounds those kinds of issues that resist accurate measurement, or that lend themselves only awkwardly or not at all to mathematical representation, or that contain a central and irrepressible value consideration'. As Allen (1976: 13) has said:

> Economists tend . . . when dealing with practical problems, to direct their attention to facets that can be illuminated by the methods of inquiry they find congenial. Their instruments are efficient within a range; but they often choose to ignore what lies outside it . . . so it happens that, on occasions, their inquiries do not penetrate beyond the periphery of fundamental problems.

On the other hand, while Marxist literature does include areas of scientific content such as technological change, class structure and related power relations and the holistic course of economic evolution, many feel that it is 'hampered by the demands of socialist propaganda' (Gruchy 1930a: 86, 87) and has its own 'excessively rigid aprioristic view' and mechanical relationships that have 'not permitted the model to serve as a basis for reliable social prediction or guidance'. Furthermore, as Wiles (1968: 1–2) has pointed out, Marxism

> really has little to say about *international* economics. It is rather about *world* economics, i.e. it purports to analyse and predict the economic and political development of the world. It has almost nothing to say on what a given nation's commercial policy should be and most conspicuously lacks a theory of international values.

GENERAL TRADE THEORIES

Viner (1954: 101) has defined a general theory as

> a comprehensive theory that embraces all the variables recognized as having major significance, which tries to account for all the identified and significant mutual interrelations and dependencies of these variables, which operates with a considerable degree of analytical rigor, and which reaches conclusions that, if true, would be of some consequence.

Any general pure theory of trade must address itself to attempting a comprehensive answer to four fairly basic questions:

1. The causal question *why*? in relation to the motivation behind the process of industrial specialisation for export purposes.
2. The natural compositional question *what*? in relation to the national exercising of choice of domestic production structure in an 'open' economy and the structure of imports.
3. The international specialisation question of *where*? in relation to the aggregate global pattern of international industrial location and division of labour and the consequent stucture of trade flows.
4. The quantitative question of *how much*? in relation to the size of the flows and the price at which trade takes place.

No theory would be a general theory if it did not give answers to these basic questions. It is also necessary to distinguish between the operational importance of positive (empirically based) and normative (political economy based) models of exchange, in order to evaluate the significance of and criticism made of any particular model presented. Unless a theory, or what is regarded as a theory, identifies its *explanandum* (what it is intended to explain), links it to an *explanans* (that which explains) and possess an empirical content capable of proof or falsification, it becomes merely assertion or 'explanation by concept' (Homans 1967: 12). The student should be aware of four quite separate operational contexts in which theoretical contributions may be applied/misapplied, and their differing limitations and appropriateness for each particular purpose:

(a) *Ex post* historical studies of why trade has taken place in the past.
(b) Contemporary studies of why trade is taking place in the present, or very recent past.
(c) From the national interest viewpoint, the operational need for *ex ante* guidelines for trade (and development) strategy objectives and their achievement.
(d) At the supranaturalist level, the need for a paradigm model of international political economy, as a focal point, within which attempted correction of existing trade proclivities, asymmetries and market imperfections may be given a rationale as seen to satisfy some world welfare criterion.

Most textbooks highlight two basic general trade models: *the Classical Model* that embodies the work of Ricardo in the early part of the nineteenth century and Edgeworth and Marshall during the latter part of the same century; and *the Neo-Classical Heckscher-Ohlin Model* of the early twentieth century. Both now appear extremely rarified examples of the economist's art, such that international economics, despite being one of the oldest branches of the subject, has been described as 'the most depraved branch of neoclassical theory' (Galbraith 1973: 32), 'the last refuge of the speculative theorist' (Kenen 1975: xii); its analysis 'a body of theory which is at worst positively misleading, and at best merely vacuous((Balogh 1973: 16); and its achievement (Viner 1954: 11) 'a degree of generality . . . that has . . . not been exceeded in any other branch that has made any real effort to maintain important links with reality'. As Kenen (1975: xii) has observed:

> international trade and finance displayed a stubborn immunity to quantification . . . little was done to verify [its] fundamental propositions. . . . The theory was deemed to be immutably true. The task of the trade theorist . . . was merely to spell out its implication for welfare and policy.

A tradition of thought and belief has grown up around them such that they have become central intellectual stepping stones on which economists perform quite remarkable arabesques of thought when they discuss trade policy. While the two models are conceptually distinct, they each embody the liberal moral philosophy of the eighteenth-century enlightenment in a timeless environment which the fullness of time and the facts of experience have not expunged, i.e. a belief in unfettered *laissez-faire laissez-passer* in circumstances of perfect competition and internal labour mobility, within an analytical structure that is essentially static.

Looking at the 'general theory' problem in the last part of the twentieth century, in the light (or even darkness) of the historical hindsight of the previous 150 years or so of change and development in the world economy, certain observations come to mind concerning (a) the nature of general theories, and (b) their errors of commission and omission.

(a)   The nature of general theories

Viner (1955: 102) correctly points out that:

> A theory that is formally indisputably 'general' may be without relevance for
> any time or any place, because the forces, the variables, it recognises may not be
> the ones that are in fact important and may even be wholly fictitious and
> spurious, or alternatively, because such theory may deal with the really
> significant factors but may attribute them to relative weights or modes of
> operation that are seriously out of accord with the true state of affairs.

A number of points can now be enumerated concerning the general
theories under methodological review.

(1) Their orientation is ahistorical in context and functionalist in content,
emphasising the technically 'efficient' niceties of resource allocation
equilibrium.

The Classical Theory of Ricardo was an *ex ante* theory (essentially a
category not envisaged in purposes (a) to (d) above), which was put forward
at the birth of the international economy in the nineteenth century, when
the universe consisted almost entirely of pristine pre-trade 'closed'
economies, to explain and evaluate the new phenomenon. It was designed
and used to innocently evaluate the cosmopolitan benefits that might arise
from *laissez-faire* international trade relations and to examine the effects
on production, consumption and welare of an 'open' economy and in the
post-trade situation. In the long run, its relevance for any of the purposes
(a) to (d) listed above was clearly going to be limited, given the prior
colonial political setting which necessarily made the development of pre-
industrial, largely internally unintegrated, periphery countries mainly
complementary to that of the centre countries and created trade networks
in circumstances that were not the 'fair' equipoised ones implicitly
supposed by contemporary theorists. The Neo-Classical H-O Theory was
more explicitly put forward as an attempt at explaining the structure of
foreign trade which, when tested (the Leontief Paradox), was controver-
sially found wanting for purposes (a), (b) and (c) above.

The greater degree of necessity for an articulate and enlightened
governmental discussion of national trade strategies from the mid-
twentieth century onwards (especially in newly politically independent
former colonial countries) heightened the need for a theory for purpose (c).
In the circumstances attempts have been made to rehabilitate the Neo-
Classical Theory in the light of those needs and/or to produce new
propositions *re* the cause of particular types of trade flow.

Because of the historical structural transformations within the world
economy previously described, an apparent 'credibility gap' has arisen
between theory and practice such as to give rise to the feeling among some
that the general theories of the past now constitute the very purest form of
social science fiction. The modern international economic scene is
characterized *inter alia* by great disparities in demand structures, levels of
technology, resource endowment, economy size, levels of national
economic development etc. Thus in the view of Viner (1955: 100):

> it would be a mistake to try to rehabilitate [classical theory] in an improved and
> modernized form as a guide to policy in the present-day world [because] the
> world has changed greatly, and is now a world of planned economies, of state

trading, of substantially arbitrary and inflexible national price structures, and of managed instability in exchange rates. The classical (and presumably the neo–classical) theory is not directly relevant for such a world, and it may be that for such a world there is and can be no relevant general theory.

From the policy point-of-view there is the difficulty of generalising to a multi-period time frame from such a theoretic foundation. As Yeats (1979: 15) has stated:

> While production according to comparative advantage may yield optimal results in a single (current) time period, there remains the question of whether some alternative pattern of resource allocation might lead to more advantageous results over the long run. In other words, there is no assurance that current allocation of resources based on comparative advantage will be optimal over time, even though it may be optimal in the current period.

(2) The implicit adoption of a nation state level-of-analysis but in circumstances of free trade severely diminishes the importance of the state and contains certain unrealities that give the exchange process posited 'an environment of rustic simplicity' (Balogh 1982: 185).

The market processes of production, distribution, consumption and exchange are treated in isolation from other motivational and sociocultural factors. Thus the contrived highly homogenised image of the nations of the world abstracts from the entire question of the goals, motivations and purposes of their individual economic systems and national policies. Trade is exemplified as inter-sectoral exchange subject to state manipulation. 'The crucial' intermediary position of states and other economic agents in the international relations of 'production units' (Balogh 1973: 16) is ignored.

The interposition of states

It is implicitly assumed that (F.D. Graham 1948: 158) 'the price of any freely traded good is unaffected by the national origin of sellers or buyers and their less antagonistic sectors'; and that (Whitman 1977: 3) 'the efficiency gains from market integration are maximized by ignoring the boundaries of the nation state'. Wiles (1968: 4) goes further:

> The notion that the relations between states, even merely the economic relation between states, should be subject to the unguided decisions of politically unmotivated individuals seems . . . preposterous. The Western student of international trade sees instinctively an individual merchant or firm or investor operating across a frontier and an exchange rate . . . the whole thing is seen in terms of individual interests. The government's intervention is thought of as a mere canalizer; the micro initiative still rests with the free citizen. And the grounds for the intervention are thought of as individual economic welfare.

In the nineteenth century, List (1916: 141) strongly attacked the Classical School on the basis of 'three major shortcomings' that are pertinent here:

> firstly, from boundless *cosmopolitanism*, which neither recognizes the principle of nationality, nor takes into consideration the satisfaction of its interests; secondly, from a dead *materialism*, which everywhere regards chiefly the mere exchangeable value of things without taking into consideration the mental and

political, the present and the future interests, and the productive powers of the nation; thirdly, from a *disorganizing particularism* and *individualism*, which, ignoring the nature and character of social labour and the operation of the union of powers in their higher consequences, considers private industry only as it would develop itself under a state of free interchange with society (i.e. with the whole human race) were that race not divided into separate national societies.

Between each individual and entire humanity, however, stands the nation, with its special language . . . with its peculiar origin and history, with its special manners and customs, laws and institutions . . . [by means of which] the individual chiefly obtains . . . mental culture, power of production, security and prosperity.

List allows for the possibility that the competitively optimal level of trade may not be that desired by states. In practice, states condition home access to the international trading system and vice versa for both economic and non-economic reasons, and sometimes by default if procedures remain unreformed. Governments may pursue one or more of four major types of non-economic motives (Bhagwati and Srinivasan 1969: 27).

(1) the output level in specific activities may be considered to be of strategic importance and hence may not be allowed to fall below specified magnitudes;
(2) self-sufficiency, that is, the value of imports (or exports under balanced trade), may be considered to be sufficiently strategic to entail that its level not exceed a specified magnitude;
(3) factor employment in certain activities, for example labour in agricultural activities, may be considered vital for defence or 'national character' and hence may not be allowed to fall below specified levels; and finally
(4) domestic availability of certain commodities may be considered to be relevant to 'social policy', requiring that it not exceed certain specified levels, as for example with 'luxury' consumption.

Underlying many of these objectives may be the central one of economic nationalism that, while masquerading under the guise of a domestic collective good, will, according to Breton (1964), seek to restructure the domestic distribution of income, usually for reasons of political necessity to benefit supportive politically organized classes or industries, the non-economic benefits of foregone economic welfare being expediently valued more highly than those of optimum economic welfare, especially when there is a concentration of industrial ownership that co-exists with a dispersion of consumer interests. This can be achieved by nationalisation; by purchasing of foreign-owned assets of by the discriminatory use of tariffs, subsidies and a host of other ploys to disadvantage or pre-empt foreign resident penetration of domestic industries. Such distortions can be created by political patronage or achieved via organised lobbying and thereby circumscribe the impact of free-trade competitive disciplines. In addition particular aspects of capitalist 'market failure' will command different degrees of interventionist activity in different countries, thereby creating inter-country differentials in standards, in ways not allowing for:

(i) The omission of collective wants and the failure of the market to register these. The evolution of particular economic systems may bias resource alloction in this respect. As J. M. Clark has observed (1955: 9), 'in a modern economy it has become impossible to trust an "invisible hand" to turn crude self-interest into an efficient engine of meeting every sound need'.

(ii) The 'goods–bads' problem. Goods are want-satisfying commodities that are marketable and are exchanged in the market and have an identifiable pecuniary importance. However, 'bads' (or negative goods) are not so revealed but are nevertheless of material importance for social welfare and involve the social utilities and disutilities generated by particular activities.

(iii) The 'market mechanism' is seen as 'a want-serving or want-satisfying mechanism'. But neo-institutionalists (Gruchy 1980: 30–1) assert that 'in the modern industrial society the market mechanism is in many cases a wanting-creating mechanism. Consumers do not always freely express what they want through dollar votes. Instead, they buy what the large corporations induce them to buy with the aid of advertising and high-pressure or subtle salesmanship.' Furthermore (Seligman 1980: 263) 'goods and services are not only commodities .. with price tags attached to them but are directions and actions and are significantly related to human actors who control them'.

Whitman (1977: 3) believes that:

> the economic justification for the nation-state must lie in the existence of public or collective goods – including stabilization targets, the distribution of income and the regulatory climate – and of differences in national consumption preferences for such goods … economic openness not only widens the exposure of an economy to external disturbances, it also attenuates … the effectiveness of … domestic policy instruments used to achieve the collective macroeconomic goals … and …the nation's power … to retain … control over economic developments within [its] borders.

In the latter case cultural differences, prestige, and national-building will have their influence, as will the management, the needs of the macro-economic balance of payments. Finally, transnational actors may participate in trade flows based on global institutional advantage rather than national or unicentric firm advantage.

Given these considerations, some would argue that markets must be viewed 'as creatures of social and political systems, not as mechanisms, arising spontaneously and inevitably out of economic necessity' (Diaz-Alejandro 1975: 214), for the latter shows a 'naive disregard of sociopolitical realities and of vested interests' (Hirschman 1971: 28). With respect to administration inertia, it is a common phenomenon for what Bhagwati (1971) calls 'autonomous policy-imposed' distortions to prevail, these being regulations that have prevailed for many years and have no necessary direct relevance to the achievement of current policy objectives but await major policy reform, as distinct from policy-imposed distortions designed for particular short-to-medium policy objectives that are necessarily relatively temporary. Thus the real world consists of (a) m countries, each with its own economic system subject to different degrees of internal friction and interventionist policy; and (b) *n* traded commodities, and therefore approximately *n* industries with their own particular domestic national market structures. Within each structure, the influence of private sector production motivations differ both within industries and between industries with regard to economic and non-economic objectives: profit maximisation may be neither the sole nor the most important objective.

The role of other economic agents in the exchange process

The depiction of production is flawed, even in its own terms. Hobson (1920: 8–9) refers to 'the false presentation [of states] . . . in the capacity of trading firms . . . competition takes place not between America, Britain, Germany, but between a number of separate American, British, German firms'. In this respect the theories that adopt the 'nation-as-actor' approach (Singer 1961: 85) ignore the rivalry which Hobson asserts is closer 'between firms belonging to the same nation and conducting their business upon closely similar conditions' (Hobson 1920: 9). Machlup believes that the embodied concept of the firm is yet another instance of 'the fallacy of misplaced concreteness' being committed by the economist, i.e. his use of a theoretical construct as though it (1978: 399) 'had a direct, observable concrete meaning'. Quoting a statement that 'in economic analysis, the business firm is a postulate in a web of logical connections', Machlup (1978: 400) asserts that:

> The fictitious firm of the model [world of economic micro-theory] is a 'uni-brain', an individual decision-unit that has nothing to do but adjust the output and the prices of one or two imaginary products to very simple imagined changes in data . . . [whereas] we know . . . that there are firms in reality . . . that . . . have boards of directors and senior and junior executives, who do, with reference to hundreds of different products, a great many things – which are entirely irrelevant for the micro-theoretical model.

Thus, while classical theory posits a coincidence of individual interest with the common welfare due to a convergence of consumer and producer interests under perfect competition, such interests historically diverged in the wake of the industrial revolution and the concomitant growth in the size of firms, the development of restrictive business practices and the evolution of producer sovereignty (see Copeland 1942). These structural changes were not, however, embodied in a new international trade theory.

The depiction of the exchange process as one in which 'products are carried to the shore, put on a boat, and sold in second countries for what the market will yield' (Galbraith 1973: 32) ignores the significance of concomitant invisible production factors and that 'firms follow their products into the second countries [and] re-create the firms there' (ibid.). Trade is not a uniorganisational activity, but is polyorganisational and multitiered, involving operational links at the primary, secondary and tertiary level. With respect to the latter, international transport companies, banks and insurance facilities may play a crucial role, as can international capital and labour mobility (precluded by the general theories). Indeed structural changes within the world economy in the first half of the twentieth century changed the importance of trade in at least three ways

which emphasised the importance of the role of 'produced means production' (Steedman 1979: 4).
(i) The increasing trade importance of intermediate (as opposed to final consumption) goods. As Caves (1960: 147) points out:

> The production functions assumed ... are restrictive not only because of [their] special formal properties . . . but also because they telescope a series of production processes into one. Any number of stages of production become combined in a single production function . . . a real difficulty arises if these intermediate goods move in international trade with as much freedom as finished products. At the very least, dealing with this possibility requires describing the production structure of a particular country not in terms of the products created but in terms of the [processing] activities engaged in.

(ii) The importance of capital good trade flows. Here Steedman (1979: 4–5) makes the comment that:

> The traditional concept of capital as opposed to land and labour, in that it consists of, or at the very least is embodied in, *produced* means of production . . .in O-H [it] is ... no such thing. It is simply given in quantity ... and it does not consist of produced means of production, for there is no productive sector to produce [it].

He suggests that this problem may be solved by making one of two assumptions: either that it is 'the traditional factor "land", masquerading under a false name; or that the "capital" endowment has a given sum of *value*'.
(iii) The importance of international finance and its relationship with trade flows. As Steedman (1979: 9) remarks:

> It is a commonplace that international economic relations involve international flows of investment and of profits, as well as trade flows, and that the balance of trade is, consequently, only one component of the balance of payments. Nor are investment and trade flows independent of one another, most obviously because direct foreign investment often leads to changes in exports and imports, in both the country of origin and the country to which the investment flows.

Neither general trade theory makes a contribution to the integration of trade, investment and profit flows, where direct foreign investment is in the form 'of a "package" in which capital, management, and new technology are all combined' (Findlay 1978: 6). The production focus of both theories is one in which production is presented

> as being carried on by the unassisted primary inputs, land and labour, with no role being played by produced means of production, either in the form of intermediates or that of fixed capital goods ... growth, capital accumulation and the role of produced means of production, in both domestic production and world trade are not central issues.[Steedman 1979: 3.]

Moreover, because factor inputs are assumed to be immobile, no foreign involvement can take place and it is thus

> presumed that international production cannot exist and that a foreign country's markets are always supplied by firms producing wholly within, and exporting from, their home countries ... trade reflects *country* or *location* specific endowments rather than any special attributes possessed by the exporting firms, i.e. *ownership* specific endowments. [Dunning and Buckley 1977: 392.]

In addition to transnational factors and international factor mobility

> Little attention is given to *internal* conditions and their influence on international economic relations. These include scale economies, nonfactor costs like taxes and social security payments, risk elements, the mutual interdependence of factor and commodity movements and prices, some aspects of location, agglomeration, and short-term movements in conditions of demand. [Ohlin 1979: 3.]

(iv) Exchange is presented as one of equipoise between its participants. This assertion is countered by objections of the following type that detect a world divison of labour based on dynamic core countries and stagnant peripheral countries [see Chapter 10]:

> The paradigm of non-Marxist international trade theory is the model of . . . [participants] who trade to their mutual benefit under conditions of equality, reciprocity and freedom. But international trade . . . is often based on a division between superior and subordinate rather than a division between equals; and it is anything but peaceful . . . Like the relation of capital to labor, it is based on a division between higher and lower functions: one party does the thinking, planning, organizing, and the other does the work. Because it is unequal in structure and reward it has to be established and maintained by force. [Hymer 1979: 103–4.]

(b) Errors of commission and omission

Orthodox Ricardian and H-O theory contains significant errors of commission and omission, some of which are now outlined.

Both general theories of the nineteenth and twentieth centuries are 'generically anchored' (Archibald, in Krupp 1963: 227) to the perfect competition setting of nineteenth-century thought that was presumed to underpin the circumstances of production and consumption in the real world. Consequently, these theories necessarily incur all the objections that can be levelled at production conditions, which (Johnson 1970: 10) 'are gradually being revealed by further research conducted by specialists on domestic economics as inadequate, and consequently appear . . . increasingly irrelevant, if not downright in error, as a guide to understanding, interpreting, and operating in the real world of experience'. In this 'classical' world of mental constructs derived from idealised heroic abstraction, behavioural and motivational axioms are founded on the laws of supply and demand that are assumed to have 'eternal validity', and 'in which the micro-forces of the market integrate themselves into a macro-state of a stable equilibrium' (Lowe 1965: 102); competition is assumed to be universally atomistic, i.e. there is a large number of small and independent units that buy and sell homogeneous and devisible commodities and services; and economic relationships are impersonal and 'inaccessible to mutual influence' (Lowe 1965: 105), autonomous and independent of any external conditioning. Because of the niceties of the result in terms of an 'efficient' equilibrium, this body of theory did not purport to be (Day 1980: 68) 'a scientific explanation of reality, but . . . the characterization of a state which if achieved would have certain desirable properties'. From a 'pristine context', in which a general conjunction of interests between producers and consumers prevails, was developed 'a set of homilies, rules of thumb, policy recommendations, and criteria that together loosely can be classified as an ideology' (Goldberg 1980;

73). Action was prescribed 'on the basis of dialectical discourse, persuasion, and coercion' (Day 1980: 69), such that the desirable states characterised by the theory could be made to exist if they already did not. Given that the results were deemed 'good', it was a short step thence to regard economic 'laws' 'as regulatory as natural laws' and the competitive market system of exchange 'as an inherent aspect of the total system of nature'. Understandably, therefore, classical economic thought has been criticised because of its 'doctrinaire adherence to the principles of *laissez-faire*', its ideological bias, 'aloof Olympian detachment from ethical issues' and 'irresponsibly speculative' nature (see Deane 1983: 1, 37) on the one hand, and the essentially abstract context of its orientation on the other.

A prime feature of the classical model is the assumption that market prices, and changes therein, act as indicators for resource allocation decisions. In practice, however, they may be defective for a number of reasons that include the following:

(i) Product differentiation may make non-price competition as important as market price as a determinant of competitive abilities.
(ii) Prices may reflect private costs (costs borne by the producer) and not the real social costs (borne by society as a whole), the latter's inclusion being essential from the point of view of community welfare.
(iii) Market prices may reflect pricing policies associated with imperfect market structures in the product and/or factor markets.
(iv) Transnational actors, such as multinationals, may assign non-market prices internationally to their products to promote other objectives, such as the minimisation of global tax payments, etc.
(v) As traders compare domestic and foreign prices through exchange rate conversions, value distortions can occur when these exchange rates are either over or undervalued.
(vi) The general theories of exchange have been based on general equilibrium welfare economics, in which the social welfare criterion is expressed in terms of perfect competition and efficiency in production-mix as between goods; efficiency in resource allocation as between factor inputs; distribution efficiency as between consumers. However, no social welfare criterion is completely value-free. The covert incorporation of such a value system by orthodox trade theories involves a built-in bias in their analysis, in that they implicitly assume that the economic systems of the countries depicted in their models operate according to Pareto-optimal behaviour (i.e. that resources are distributed such that it is impossible to make someone better off by their redistribution without making someone else worse off); and that such behaviour is either desirable, or, at the very least, an 'appropriate' basis on which to construct models. Certain implicit ethical postulates are thereby embodied in the analyses, three of which are:

    (a) That individualism *per se* is a good thing. Individualistic as opposed to collectivist societies are envisaged. Thus the preference of individuals with all their irrationalities and excesses are unconstrained. The importance of consumer sovereignty is emphasised.
    (b) That the distribution of income and property is just and, in the international context of the post-trade situation, remains so and is

not unduly affected by any income redistribution that may take place between factors of production occasioned by the resource reallocation required by the transition from autarky.

(c) Welfare is defined in terms of consumption of goods and services. This is very materialistic and can ignore other values such as the 'quality of life'.

(vii) Conventional trade theories, given their assumption of perfect competition, ignore the importance of monopoly in international trade. Sawhney and Di Pietro (1981: 144) have identified:

> four important dimensions of market power which affect a country's position in international trade. On the positive side, a country can have monopoly power in selling products to the rest of the world or it can have monopoly power in purchasing goods from the rest of the world. On the negative side, a country can face selling power in its imports or face buying power in its exports.

(viii) The differential existence of factor price distortions in national markets, for reasons that include (Magee 1973: 1–4):

1   imperfect knowledge
2   the rural-urban dichotomy
3   racism
4   monopoly power through unionism
5   monopoly power by one or both factors coupled with market power by producers in product markets (bilateral monopoly)
6   the maintenance and spread of union wage increases by 'pattern setting'
7   seniority based on age or education which does not reflect economic superiority
8   differences between the export and import competing sector's access to foreign capital, or differences in ocean freight rates charged to the two sectors
9   discrimination against women or children
10 collusion across industries by a factor which acts as a discriminating monopolist, charging different prices in each industry because of differing elasticities of derived demand for the factor
11 disguised unemployment in agriculture relative to manufacturing
12 differential factor taxation or subsidy
13 factor legislation, social regulation, or policy control for 'prestige-cum-humanitarian' or other normative reasons
14 movements in union/non-union differentials in the business cycle
15 limited mobility with differential product growth

These are additional to other natural differentials that include:

1   age and experience among workers
2   education and skill reflecting a return on human capital
3   regional differentials due to moving costs or other factors
4   factor of preference or disutility associated with particular industries or regions
5   risk aversion

6 regional differences due to geographic concentration of low-wage low-skill industries

The assumption of given resources

As Balogh (1963: 13) has written 'neo-classical theory completely excluded the recognition of the basic importance of the infancy of countries, rather than merely of industries'. In the undeveloped context the crucial question is what type of international regime will maximise growth. The problem is the same as in conventional customs union theory (Dell 1963: 16–7):

> As regards undeveloped countries, the conventional theory simply misses the basic point. Being designed to explore the problem of optimal allocation of given resources, under given conditions of production, within a competitive framework, it cannot illuminate situations . . . where neither resources nor conditions of production can be taken as given and in which immobility of factors of production obstructs the operation of market forces.

What matters in this context is whether there is trade creation, trade diversion or trade displacement. Trade creation takes place when the reallocated pattern of production leads to international specialisation based on efficient low-cost territories; trade diversion takes place when, generally as a result of discriminatory trade controls, trade is diverted from low-cost countries; and trade displacement exists where either specialisation is pre-empted by 'backwash effects and/or specialisation is imposed by external agents without regard to the local relative development cost situation. In addition Kravis (1956: 154) asserts that

> There are important short-run aspects of the country trade pattern of a given moment that cannot be explained by a long-run construct of static economics... [unless] two important sets of conditions [are] satisfied: (1) tastes, resources and techniques remain unchanged so that there is sufficient time to adjust to the supply and demand conditions created by these factors, and (2) there [is] no serious restriction to free competition in foreign or domestic commerce by government or large concentrations of private power. Neither of these conditions is fully met in the real world. The real world is dynamic, so that the long-run implications of a given constellation of tastes, resources and technology never have a chance to work themselves out; a new short-run situation with altered tastes, resources, or technology is continually intervening . . . at any given point in time the export pattern . . . reflects not the influence of a single concatenation of tastes, resources, and technology but rather the impact of a whole sequence of such complex combinations . . .

Twoness

The design of theoretical models in economics necessarily involves a conflict between generality and simplicity. Trade models characterised by two countries, two commodities, and one (Ricardo) or two (Heckscher–Ohlin) production factors constitute the main method of presentation of the present corpus of trade theory. This Noah's Ark method of exposition has three main methodological weaknesses that may be noted:

(1) Such theories may be automatically precluded from displaying compositional features that can emerge in higher dimensional cases.

(2) No room is left for non-traded commodities (ones which by virtue of

high costs of transport are neither imported nor exported) if only 'importables' and 'exportables' are given consideration. They 'differ fundamentally from traded commodities, for which local excess demands or supplies can be accommodated in world markets' because they 'must have their markets cleared locally' (Jones 1974: 121).

Their importance lies in the fact that their output and price structure is part of each national equilibrium situation and, should the price of exportables and/or importables change, domestic substitution to or from this sector will have implications for trade flows (see Hazan *et al* 1981).

(3) *Aggregation Problems* Two-sector models are often defended on the grounds that each sector represents an aggregate of a number of individual commodities. In practice, however, because *inter alia* of diversity among the constituent commodities, cross-substitution effects in production and consumption, and income effects, it is unlikely that all such commodities, whether exportables or importables, will respond in a uniform manner to particular changes in market circumstances. Furthermore, while two-country models are often defended on the grounds that the 'foreign country' represents an aggregate of the rest of the world trading system, interdependent complications that arise in reality from national differentials in country size, bargaining power and market size cannot be subsumed in such two-'country' models. As F. D. Graham (1948: 250) has written:

> It is impossible *by definition* to gather all countries but one into a hypothetically unified 'outside world'. The very *concept* of international trade segregates the several countries, each as a unit, between each of which and each of the others the flow of factors of production is inhibited. To group them is to merge varying cost structures into a single whole which could be attained in fact only if the posited and, in some cases, inevitable immobility of the factors of production were *not* present.

Omission of the technology variable

Most models of international trade focus on the exchange of goods or factors of production. Technology is often assumed to be the same for each country. However, the production of a traded good in a particular country may not reflect differences in factor endowments (central to the H-O models) but differences in technology or 'know-how' between countries (Freeman 1979: 121). The standard H-O model leaves largely unanalysed both the possibility that differences in real (absolute) factor prices resulting from technological differences would promote the diffusion of technology among countries, with consequent changes in comparative advantage and trade patterns; and the possibility that the same influences would promote the international migration of factors of production, with effects on the distribution of factors of production and of economic activity among countries and/or among geographical regions ('brain-drain' etc.) (Johnson 1977b: 314).

ALTERNATIVE APPROACHES

Post–1954 analysis has been more policy-orientated and concerned with structural change within the economy as the chapters in Part III indicate. This chapter has emphasised some of the complexities and difficulties of creating general theories and the ideal of establishing a diachronic-synchronic continuum to which classical economics failed to address itself.

Even if the Classical and Neo-Classical Theories are dismissed for good reasons, together with the attempts at their resuscitation (though some (Willet 1971) would argue that they need not be so dismissed), the past 'tradition' of view constitutes a 'paradigm' that underlies the initial supranationalist Bretton Woods model of international political economy, and is still an essential part of the outlook of many. Accordingly, it is still necessary to examine the niceties or otherwise of its properties: a theory's conclusions do not have to be 'true', i.e. empirically valid, to be of some consequence. In reality, the test of experience shows whether either achievement of the idealised model occurs to any meaningful extent, or if dissatisfaction with ineffectual interventionist attempts to bring it about results in such inequities in international income distribution that a revolution of thought and policy occurs which displaces this system of values.

Given the diversity and complexity of circumstance indicated, it is clearly possible that a 'single factor causality' may not be at work. In such an event, an alternative approach is either to examine particular features of the trading system (such as intra-industry trade, the role of multinational firms, etc.), or to try to present, as Dunning has, an 'eclectic' general theory; or to evolve an inter-disciplinary approach. As regards the latter, however, such attempts have met with condemnation in other branches of social sciences on the following grounds:

> A multiple factor approach is not a theory: it is an abdication of the quest for a theory. It simply asserts that this particular event is 'caused' by this particular combination of circumstances and that particular event by another combination of circumstances [A. K. Cohen 1970: 124].

> The principle of multi-causation may be an honourable heuristic device. But it may also become a powerful force for intellectual inertia. It may point the way to new discoveries. Or it may allow discussions to dodge the necessity of a serious reappraisal of the nature of their object of study [Matza 1964: 22].

As regards an inter-disciplinary approach, while it may be difficult to establish models based on social science fact and inadequate to base them on social science fiction, the aim must be to establish more social science faction. To that end, Phelps Brown (1972: 7) would seek a multidisciplinary approach that is not 'discipline-bound' but 'field-determined'. As Fores (1969: 19) observed: 'if there ever is another great synthetic statement to cover economics . . . then that new statement or theory will not be a general theory of economics alone, it will instead be a general theory of social affairs'. Clearly there is a need to go beyond the purely formal explication of the logical character of the means-ends relationship.

Kindleberger (1951: 47) would add that, particularly in the field of international economics, 'for accurate prediction and policy formation, an adequate theory of the behaviour of large groups (at the national level) and their components, is needed as an adjunct to the analytical tools of the market'. Political factors continually provide a constraint on the effective application of prescriptions and their operational success in two respects: the *de jure* political acceptability of proposals and their *de facto* workability (Lanyi 1969: 31). A proposal will only be acceptable if it can be, or has been, actually adopted by the relevant trading nations whose conduct it seeks to modify. It is workable only if it neither breaks down as a result of failure to resolve the defined problem, nor requires, to avoid a breakdown, excessive sacrifices on the part of the participating nations for which there is no appropriate means of compensation. As politicians do exhibit different behavioural preferences from time to time, such behavioural shifts transform the bias of decision-making processes between the extremes of unilateral action and concerted complete co-operation. Thus trade outcomes can been seen in the light of alternative decision-making mechanisms (see Tinbergen 1978: 224–5). Analysis of the nature and international significance of institutional economics for trade outcomes by Kapp (1976) and others, has led *inter alia* to theoretical explanations of public-good theory and bargaining between large and small countries (S. Brown *et al* 1976); economic theories of mutually advantageous issue linkages in international negotiations (Tollison and Willett 1979); and outline investigations of international sectoral integration policies (Behrman 1972) and industrialisation of the basis of 'agreed specialization' (Kojima 1970). At the national policy level, 'international competitiveness' indicators have been developed (see Chapter 8) and the deteminants of international production investigated (see Chapter 9). The latter approach has necessarily focused on world economics, the same level of analysis as traditional Marxist analysis, which has itself been revised in the light of the new transnational structures, either from a dependencia or a world-system standpoint (see Chapter 10).

5 The classical concept of comparative advantage: the cosmopolitan model of national industrial specialisation and international exchange.

> The impact of the Ricardian . . . model . . . has been predominantly an idealisation which affords a significant clue to the structure of foreign trade.
>
> Bhagwati (1965: 160)

> The traditional approach to international relations, by confining itself to the sterile analysis of trade between (usually two) anonymous countries, has produced a body of theory which is at worst positively misleading, and at best merely vacuous.
>
> Balogh (1973: 16)

> In . . . classical theory there is no path, no process, no movement of any kind. An isolated country is in a stationary equilibrium and hey presto! trade puts it into a new equilibrium with a different composition of output but resources, knowledge and tastes all stay the same. This has cut off the 'pure theory' from any relation to the trade that takes place in real life and has reduced it to an idle toy.
>
> Robinson (1979: 141)

What is now generally referred to as 'the classical theory' of international trade comprises a model, the component parts of which were separately contributed and refined by a series of writers from the end of the eighteenth century to the second decade of the twentieth century, each of which added individual insights and reconditioned the particular limitations of the analysis. In chronological order the list of main contributors includes Smith, Torrens, Ricardo, Mill, Cairnes, Marshall, Edgeworth, Bastable and Taussig.

While the evolution of this model took place during the crucial but varying phases of growth of the international economy, its essential orientation remained within the initial terms of reference declared by Ricardo. It neither addressed the task of understanding the growing phenomenon of imperialism nor that of the description or prediction of actual nineteenth-century trade flows. No allowance for, or anticipation of, unequal trade relationships was made. The model was provided as a reformist guide to statesmen. It presented a picture of international political economy that was intentionally at variance with mercantilist doctrines, the logic of which 'demanded the perpetuation of an international disequilibrium; for, it was impossible collectively for all nations to maintain the required trade surpluses' (Sekine 1973: 263); and which regarded virtually any measure of protection and restriction as deployable to achieve that end, with colonies being prime captive centres whose trade was to be managed in ancilliary support. Whereas Adam Smith and other late eighteenth-century writers were preoccupied with emphasising the real costs of such policies in terms of foregone allocative efficiency and resource use, Ricardo and other writers were eager to demonstrate how a radically different organisation of international trade might bring about both superior national benefits in terms of economic welfare and a mutually beneficial cosmopolitan situation that would lead to harmoniously balanced international economic relations. No attempt was made to try to explain actual trade flows as such, though if the message proved convincing, it was hoped that actual flows might be remoulded in the image of their propounded welfare economics, so that the reality would mirror theory. For these writers, the only *explanandum* was that of the 'optimistic idealism' of a

> dream ... of a great republic of world commerce, in which national boundaries would cease to have any great economic importance and the web of trade would bind all the peoples of the world in prosperity of peace ... [and that] trade should be freed from restraints and governmental interference. [Condliffe 1951: 136, 111.]

As Makler *et al* (1982: 6) have written 'for the classical economists, the international market [was] ... a harmonious summation of a huge number of free transactions among rational economic agents. The market itself was the central – and automatic – integratory mechanism.'

Such was the appeal and persuasiveness of the rationale that it obtained 'almost canonical status' (Chakravarty 1983: 425). International trade theory became an 'almost inviolate section of classical economic theory' (Mason 1926: 63). Its central construct, comparative advantage, was believed to be, despite indications to the contrary, 'undoubtedly the main regulative condition of international exchange' (Bastable 1903: 15). so it was that its 'ideas ... came to be stated as established truths' (Condliffe 1951: 165).

THE DEVELOPMENT OF A *LAISSEZ-FAIRE* RATIONALE AND THE NEED FOR A SUPPORTIVE THEORETICAL TRADE CONSTRUCT

It is convenient to begin our discussion with Adam Smith, not that his thoughts were particularly original, but because of the influence of his vigorous attacks on mercantilist restrictions and his alternative economic premises of *laissez-faire, laissez-passer* free trade; the fact that as a publicist he gave a focus to preceding economic thought by his systemisation and elaboration of its revolutionary principles; and above all, because of his identification of the concept of 'absolute advantage', which provided the foundation stone of what was subsequently developed by others into a law of comparative advantage.

Knorr makes several points about the change of political economy emphasis brought about by Smith's free-trade advocacy. Firstly, it indicated (1963: 158) that trade beyond the national frontier could be dependent on exchange and not dominion: 'territorial expansion and conquest appeared incapable of increasing the gains to be derived from trade. The 'trade empire' was to be based on the free international exchange of goods.' Unless fostered by non-economic objectives, the notion of self-sufficiency lost even the semblance of a national advantage.

Secondly, given the above, it demonstrated that barriers to trade (ibid.):

> would have the effect of limiting international division of labour by impeding and deflecting the natural flow of goods... Utmost competition, unrestricted by national considerations, alone assured the fullest effect of the principle of economy of production... Its ultimate implication was world economic unity based on the most economical distribution of production.

Thirdly, the mercantilist concept of 'a fixed total of foreign trade for the largest comparative share of which the various nations had to struggle' was replaced by the notion of mutual benefit in which any wealth from trade accruing to foreign nations 'only enhanced their capacity as customers and suppliers of goods' (Knorr 1963: 158).

Fourthly, emphasis on national and/or producer power and economic warfare was replaced by an emphasis of individual economic welfare and cheapness of consumer goods. As Smith (1950, 2: 159) wrote:

> Consumption is the sole end and purpose of all production; and the interest of the producer ought to be attended to, only so far as it may be necessary for promoting that of the consumer. The maxim is so perfectly self-evident, that it would be absurd to attempt to prove it. But in the mercantile system, the interest of the consumer is almost constantly sacrificed to that of the producer; and it seems to consider production, and not consumption, as the ultimate end and object of all industry and commerce.

For these reasons, mercantilist organisation was exposed as being disadvantageous to society. Free trade, on the other hand, would terminate the harmful effects on trade brought about by the state-supported monopolies that the latter had created.

Fifthly, the subject of wealth had been isolated for purposes of economic investigation and treated apart from other political and social phenomena. The mercantilists had seen 'wealth' and 'power' as necessarily conjoint phenomena. 'Adam Smith recognised the necessity for state power only for one purpose: that of defence against aggression' (Knorr 1963: 163).

And sixthly, with respect to the colonies, Smith emphasised the costs of administration as a financial drain and maintained that the administered trade imposed on them resulted in benefits that were inferior to those derivable in circumstances of unfettered free trade:

> The exclusive trade of mother countries tends to diminish, or, at least, to keep down below what they would otherwise rise to, both the enjoyments and industry of all those nations in general, and of the American colonies in particular. It is a dead weight upon the action of one of the great springs which puts into motion a great part of the business of mankind. By rendering the colony produce dearer in all countries, it lessens its consumption, and thereby cramps the industry of the colonies, and both the enjoyments and the industry of all other countries which both enjoy less when they pay more for what they enjoy, and produce less when they get less for what they produce. [A. Smith 1950, 2: 93.]

Moreover he further argued (1950: 561):

> England, there are very probable reasons for believing, has not only sacrificed a part of the absolute advantage which she, as well as every other nation, might have derived from that trade, but has subjected herself both to an absolute and

to a relative disadvantage in almost every other branch of trade.

Metropolitan monopolisation of colonial trade was denounced on economic grounds because the outflow of investment from the centre state created an undesirable domestic scarcity of capital that allegedly disadvantaged its economic prospects and because the management of colonial trade prevented the subject states from selling their produce in the dearest market and buying their manufactures and stores in the cheapest market, and on politico-economic grounds because 'colonies are a grand source of wars' (Mill n.d.: 32) and because there was a vicious tendency of colonial expansion to become self-perpetuating – 'every acquisition renders it more necessary for us to extend our conquests' (Nicholls 1922 *I*: 247). so it was, that one protectionist contemporary declared that:

> opinions, the fruit of ages of experience, have been derided as puerile and barbarous; and a section of the people, monopolizing all the wisdom of the United Kingdom, have contrived to set that kingdom in a blaze ... Our colonies are consigned to distruction ... as useless lumber, no longer ministering to the wants of a starving people, because a new principle has been evoked, that a discontented population must be conciliated with preternaturally cheap sugar. Free Trade is the new dodge. Verily it is a perfect Goliath, with a face of brass, and a heart of adamant.[Edinburgh Review 1847: 278.]

Adam Smith saw the main benefits of trade as allocative efficiency gains; increased 'enjoyments' and the stimulus to economic growth provided by widening the extent of the market.

> Allocative efficiency gains are derived because if a foreign country can supply us with a commodity cheaper than we ourselves can make it, better buy it of them with some part of the produce of our own industry, employed in a way in which we have some advantage. The general industry of the country . . . is certainly not employed to the greatest advantage, when it is thus directed towards an object which it can buy cheaper than it can make . . . [and which] could, therefore, have been purchased with a part only of the commodities . . . which the industry would have produced at home, had it been left to follow its natural course [A. Smith 1950, *I*: 422].

Trade was deemed to make possible not only a greater abundance but also a greater variety of goods than would otherwise be possible; 'some for conveniency and use, some for pleasure, and some for ornament (A. Smith 1950, *2*: 92). Smith emphasised one possible function of trade, which was neglected by subsequent writers and not incorporated in the development of classical comparative cost theory (1950, *1*: 413) that trade provided a 'vent-for-surplus' function, whereby a country's 'superfluities' of production could be exchanged 'for something else, which may satisfy a part of [its] wants and increase its enjoyments'. However, no precise reasoning is given as to why such superfluity should arise, unless caused by a bountiful nature. He merely asserts that:

> when the produce of any particular branch of industry exceeds what the demand of the country requires, the surplus must be sent abroad, and exchanged for something for which there is a demand at home. *Without such exportation, a part of the productive labour of the country must cease, and the value of its annual produce diminish.* The land and labour of Great Britain produce generally more corn, woollens, and hard ware, than the demand of the home-

market requires. The surplus part of them, therefore, must be sent abroad, and exchanged for something for which there is a demand at home. It is only by means of such exportation, that this surplus can acquire a value sufficient to compensate the labour and expense of producing it. [1950, *1*: 352.]

Myint (1958: 323, 325) subsequently considered this relevant to a previously isolated country about to enter the international trading system, which possesses surplus productive capacity because of 'an inelastic demand for exportable commodity and/or a considerable degree of internal immobility and specificness of resources' – a condition which would prevail in underdeveloped areas which lack complementary factors to produce other commodities, or where natural resources endowments are extremely narrowly specialized. With respect to a basis for trade which would resolve a country's 'specialization dilemma' he perceived that under free-trade conditions, goods will tend to be produced in those countries where their absolute real costs are lowest. The reasons for cost disparities are seen to be natural ('soil, climate and situation') and acquired, and the basis and commodity composition of trade are implicitly related to the relative abundance of productive factors. Thus:

> Land is still so cheap, and, consequently, labour so dear among them [the American colonies] that they can import from the mother country, almost all the more refined or more advanced manufactures cheaper than they can make them for themselves. Though they had not, therefore, been prohibited from establishing such manufactures, yet in their present state of improvement, a regard to their own interest would, probably, have prevented them from doing so [A. Smith 1950, *2*: 83–4.]

> Agriculture is the proper business of all new colonies; a business which the cheapness of land renders more advantageous than any other. They abound, therefore, in the rude produce of land, and instead of importing it from other countries, they have generally a large surplus to export... The greater part of the manufactures ... they find it cheaper to purchase off other countries than to make for themselves [A. Smith 1950, *2*: 109–10.]

Smith's particular contribution was the exposition of a 'productivity' theory of the virtues of trade: that is specialisation is limited by the size of the market and that in the post-trade situation external trade widens the extent of the market, and results in 'new divisions of labour and improvements of art' (1950, *1*: 414), thereby raising productivity within each trading country and further promoting economies of scale. Little attention was given to labour or capital mobility. He did, however, recognise both the 'natural protection' afforded geographically by transport costs and the importance of the availability and quality of transport facilities and realised that, in the extreme case where transport costs more than outweigh production cost differentials, some goods may not enter into international trade at all. He appreciated the static and dynamic dimensions of trade, and that the gains from trade do not result simply from a once-and-for-all change in resource allocation, but merge thereafter with the gains from growth. He emphasised that the existence of trade *per se* transforms the coefficients of production and induces outward shifts in the production possibilities of each country over time. While other writers acknowledged these effects (as was seen in

Chapter 1) they did not embody them in a trade-cum-development dynamic theory (see Myint 1977) such that J.H. Williams (1926: 196) was later able to reprimand their analysis in the following terms:

> the relation of international trade to the development of new resources and productive forces is a more significant part of the explanation of the present status of nations, incomes, prices, and well-being, than is the cross-section value analysis of the classical economists, with its assumption of given quanta of productive factors, already existent and employed.

Subsequent theorists expounded an essentially static model and concentrated on the nature of the cost oriented basis for trade. Torrens is to be credited as being responsible for sowing the seed of the idea of comparative advantage case which was to be given explicit germination by Ricardo. In his pamphlet *The Economists Refuted* (1807: 14–15), Torrens developed Smith's ideas concerning the advantages of the division of labour between different areas and the resultant 'territorial division of labour' by which 'the productiveness of human industry will be greatly augmented; the things necessary and desirable to man will receive a wonderful increase'. In emphasizing that the gain from trade is the excess of what is obtained indirectly via trade over the amount directly produced domestically by the same quantity of resources, he implicitly suggested that benefit would arise from different domestic cost relationships. However, as Robbins (1958: 23) states, 'it lacked the final emphasis upon the comparison of ratios which is the ultimate essence of the principle'. The main credit for this rests with Ricardo (1939: 153) who was the first economist to advocate a theory of international trade distinct from the theory of intra-national trade because of an alleged condition that labour and capital were immobile between nations while they were free to move within one nation. Ricardo (1951: 133–4) reiterates the generalised benefits to be derived from the territorial division of labour thus:

> Under a system of perfectly free commerce, each country naturally devotes its capital and labour to such employments as are most beneficial to each. This pursuit of individual advantage is admirably connected with the universal good of the whole. By stimulating industry, by rewarding ingenuity, and by using most efficaciously the peculiar powers bestowed by nature, it distributes labour most effectively and most economically: while, by increasing the general mass of productions, it diffuses general benefit, and binds together by one common tie of interest and intercourse, the universal society of nations throughout the civilized world.

His reasoning as summarised by Mill (1948: 2–3) is that:

> It is not a difference in the *absolute* cost of production, which determines . . . interchange, but a difference in the *comparative* cost . . . As often as a country possesses two commodities, one of which it can produce with less labour, comparatively to what it would cost in a foreign country, than the other: so often it is the interest of the country to export the first mentioned commodity and to import the second; even though it might be able to produce both the one and the other at a less expense of labour than the foreign country can produce them, but not less in the same degree; or might be unable to produce either except at a greater expense, but not greater in the same degree.
> On the contrary, if it produces both commodities with greater facility, or both

with greater difficulty, and greater in exactly the same degree, there will be no motive to interchange.

According to J. S. Mill (1909: 576) the low-cost country benefits because 'the commodity received ... would ... cost [it] more'. The latter mentioned equal advantage case in which relative cost differences are equal (even though the absolute figures are different) and there is no incentive to trade, was first illustrated by Torrens in the fourth edition (1827) of his *Essay on the External Corn Trade* (1815) (Robbins 1958: 23-4). In his *Principles*, J. S. Mill (1909: 578-80) expanded on the benefits of trade conducted on this basis thus:

> Setting aside its enabling countries to obtain commodities which they could not themselves produce at all, its advantage consists in a more efficient employment of the productive forces of the world. If two countries which trade together attempted, as far as was physically possible, to produce for themselves what they now import from one another, the labour and capital of the two countries would not be so productive, the two together would not obtain from their industry so great a quantity of commodities, as when each employs itself in producing, both for itself and for the other, the things in which its labour is relatively most efficient. The addition thus made to the produce of the two combined, constitutes the advantage of the trade. It is possible that one of the two countries may be altogether inferior to the other in productive capacities, and that its labour and capital could be employed to greatest advantage by being removed bodily to the other. The labour and capital which have been sunk in rendering Holland habitable would have produced a much greater return if transported to America or Ireland. The produce of the whole world would be greater than it is, if everything were produced where there is the greatest absolute facility for its production. But nations do not, at least in modern times, emigrate *en masse*; and while the labour and capital of a country remain in the country, they are most beneficially employed in producing for foreign markets, as well as for its own, the things in which it lies under the least disadvantage, if there be none in which it possesses an advantage. A country obtains things which it either could not have produced at all, or which it must have produced at a greater expense of capital and labour than the cost of the things which it exports to pay for them. It thus obtains a more ample supply of the commodities it wants, for the same labour and capital; or the same supply, for less labour and capital, leaving the surplus disposable to produce other things ... Commerce is virtually a mode of cheapening production; and . . . the consumer is the person ultimately benefited . . .

Ricardo presented his comparative cost discussion with reference to the domestic relative real labour cost values obtaining in each country in the pre-trade closed economy position. These values are not expressed in terms of money as the common denominator but by reference to the days of unskilled labour [or man-hours] required to produce defined quantities of each of the two products under consideration to which disparate rates are reducible in principle. Thus the relative value of goods is determined by the amount of labour so applied. This 'labour theory of value' requires that capital and labour are employed in the same proportions in the production of all commodities: as Ohlin (1952: 574, 577) comments, 'the relation between capital and labour in production and the relative prices of different categories of labour are treated as fixed and "frozen" ... Different categories of labour are assumed to be paid according to a fixed remuneration scale and ... any day of skilled labour can be converted into so many days of unskilled labour'. As Mason (1926: 74–5) says:

> [either] 'quantities of labour' is an aggregate of homogenous labor units secured by reducing different qualities of labor to a common unit through the equalizing agency of money wages. That is, an hour's labor of a ten-dollar-a-day laborer is called equal to two hours of a five-dollar-a-day laborer . . . or [they] mean quantities of a given grade of labor, bearing so constant a relation to the other factors of production that the values of domestic commodities can be considered to be proportionate to the number of units of this grade involved.

Despite this very narrow approach, Taussig (1928) much later maintained that differences between comparative money costs and comparative labour quantity costs were so slight that the latter could still be considered valid, arguing by means of an alleged 'hierarchy principle' that the hierarchy of labour costs in different industries is likely to be the same in both rank and percentage terms in different countries. Bhagwati (1965: 160) has expressed the above in the following algebraic form:

> If a_1 and a_2 are the output factor ratios for country I and b_1 and b_2 for country II in activities 1 and 2 respectively, country I will export commodity 1 and import commodity 2 if $a_1/a_2 > b_1/b_1$ (as this will imply that commodity 1 will be cheaper, and commodity 2 dearer, in country I than in country II *prior to trade*). The algebraic condition is frequently written as $a_1/b_1 > a_2/b_2$ which states the condition in terms of comparative factor productivities.

The combination of a single factor, labour, with constant returns to scale ensures that neither demand nor the level of factor supply makes any difference to the equilibrium commodity price ration. As regards the flow of international exchange, analysis is simplified to that of barter because as J. S. Mill (1909: 583) states: 'Since all trade is in reality barter, money being a mere instrument for exchanging things against one another . . . international trade . . . [is] in form, what it always is in reality, an actual trucking of one commodity against another.' This assumption neatly evades the complex problems that arise in the context of different national monetary and exchange rate systems.

THE CLASSICAL MODEL

Within the static operational context of a two-nation, two-commodity model, where labour is mobile nationally but immobile internationally, with perfect competition prevailing in all factor and product markets, constant costs of production [no economies or diseconomies of scale], zero transport costs and barter trade, production is measured nationally in terms of its relative domestic real labour costs of production. In comparing national sets of labour costs ratios, a basis for trade is shown to exist where *absolute* and *comparative* advantage persists but not where *equal* advantage exists. At this stage, in the words of J. S. Mill (1909: 585) '[it] is advisable, in these intricate investigations to give distinctions and fixity to the conception of numerical examples'.

Table 33 shows three distinct examples of the possible situations between countries. The real cost ratios are shown as price relatives. In Case A, no trade is possible because no efficiency gain may be made through international specialisation and exchange; Case B is the intuitively

Table 33: *A Ricardian comparative advantage example in terms of the number of labour hours required to produce one unit of cloth and one unit of wine in England and Portugal*

	Case A Equal advantage (Torrens)			Case B Absolute advantage (Adam Smith)			Case C Comparative advantage (Ricardo)		
	Cloth (W)	Wine (C)	W/C Price relative	Cloth (W)	Wine (C)	W/C Price relative	Cloth (W)	Wine (C)	W/C Price relative
England	100	88	0.88	100	60	0.6	100	120	1.2
Portugal	90	80	0.88	90	80	0.88	90	80	0.88

obvious Smithian case of absolute advantage; but the central Ricardian case is Case C, the rationale for which is in the following terms: in England a gallon of wine costs 120 hours of work and a yard of cloth 100 hours of work effort, while in Portugal the cost is 80 and 90 hours respectively for wine and cloth. Portugal thus has an absolute advantage in the production of *both* goods, but a comparatively greater advantage in wine than in cloth. Without trade, a gallon of wine costs only 0.88 (i.e. 80/90) yards of cloth in Portugal, while in England the price is 1.2 (i.e. 120/100). Conversely, cloth is comparatively cheap in England. It is clearly to Portugal's advantge to send wine to England where 1 unit commands 1.2 units of cloth; it is to England's advantage to specialise in cloth if less than 1.2 units of cloth can be given for 1 unit of wine. England produces cloth with 100 manhours and receives 1 unit of wine which would have cost her 120 manhours. Portugal obtains cloth for 80 manhours, which would have cost her 90 manhours of effort to produce. As Cairnes (1874: 312) points out: 'the costs compared, it must be carefully noted, are the costs in each country of the commodities which are the subjects of exchange, not the different costs of the same commodity in the exchanging countries'. Thus as Hirsch (1967: 4) has observed 'competitiveness is predicated upon the difference between the ratios of which various goods can be exchanged domestically and in the international market'. The autarkic price ratios set limits to the willingness of countries to trade and enclose what Angell (1926: 458) calls 'the zone of profitable exchange', in which trade will be mutually advantageous as illustrated in Figure 4. From the reasoning outlined above, it is possible to make five substantive conclusions about what Sir Dennis Robertson (1958: 13) once called 'the verdict of Lord Justice Comparative Cost':

1 *A nation tends to export those commodities which, as compared with their relative (real labour) costs abroad are less abroad in relation to the real labour cost of other commodities. Conversely, the imports of a nation tend to be those of which the comparative real labour costs of production at home are greater at home than abroad.*

2 *The basis for profitable trade is established by intra-country differences in relative (labour) costs: inter-country differences in absolute levels of productivity in all products are no barrier to trade.*

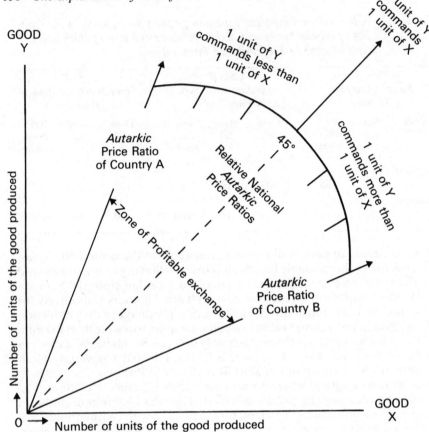

Figure 4: *The zone of profitable international exchange*
This is determined by the pre-trade differential in the relative national labour cost ratios. So long as there is a differential, i.e. that the cost gradients have a different slope from the origin at O, the gap between the gradients – the zone of profitable exchange – indicates a range of different labour cost ratios that are of mutual benefit, to a lesser or greater degree depending on their distance from the original autarkic position. A cost gradient from the origin at O along the 45° line would indicate a one to one relationship between the real costs of producing a defined unit of each commodity. Any gradient to the left of this line indicates a cost situation where the good on the vertical axis commands less than one unit of the good on the horizontal axis. Any gradient to the right of the 45° line indicates a cost situation where the good on the vertical axis commands more than one unit of the horizontal axis good.

3 *The gain to a country consists in getting indirectly through product specialisation and the exchange of the quantities surplus to domestic requirements, more goods, or better quality goods, than could be produced at home by the employment of the same quantity of labour resources (though the possible gain could be used to obtain increased leisure).*
4 *At the global level, the gains from trade will be qualitatively greater, the wider the zone of profitable exchange, and quantitively greater, the larger the volume of the actual trade flows.*
5 *At the national level, the further the ultimate barter terms of exchange from its autarkic cost ratio (and the nearer that ratio is to the partner country's autarkic cost ratio) the larger will be the national share of that country of the given global trade gain.*

In reality, the presumed domestic resource reallocation may not take place because:

> the displaced productive power itself may in large part be lost outright, not merely diverted into other channels. It may be incapable of finding equally remunerative employment in other directions, and the assumed transfer may therefore itself be physically impossible . . . the principle makes little real allowance for the element of growth in economic life, or for the somewhat bewildering phenomena of the transition periods. Price readjustments, for example, are apparently regarded as fundamentally frictionless, and money is at bottom treated as a merely passive transmitter of inter-commodity values. [Angell 1926: 84–5.]

However, this asserted 'law of interchange between nations' is *per se* insufficient to determine the full list of goods, the precise quantities traded, and the precise barter terms of exchange at which trade will be effected. Its theoretic importance is limited as the following observations indicate:

> it is not in general possible to determine *a priori*, from a mere observation of the costs of production in the respective countries before the opening of the trade, which commodities will be imported and which produced at home [Edgeworth 1925: 55.]

> the principle of comparative costs . . . does not define a single ratio of exchange; it simply indicates a zone, within whose limits any ratio whatsoever will be advantageous to the countries concerned [Angell 1933: 82.]

> comparative cost reasoning alone explains very little about international trade. It is indeed nothing more than an abbreviated account of the conditions of supply. It is only when the conditions of demand and of equilibrium are also considered, that one is able to describe what happens [Ohlin 1933: 586.]

J. S. Mill (1909: 584) regarded these questions as being 'in the region of the most complicated questions which political economy affords' – a subject 'which cannot possibly be made elementary'. Assuming no transport costs, he argued (1909: 587), by reference to what is sometimes called a 'principle of international values', sometimes a 'Law of Reciprocal Demand', and sometimes 'the Equation of International Demand', that:

> when two countries trade together in two commodities, the exchange value of these commodities relatively to each other will adjust itself to the inclinations and circumstances of the consumers on both sides, in such manner that the quantities required by each country, of the articles which it imports from its neighbour, shall be exactly sufficient to pay for one another.

In short (1909: 592): 'the produce of a country exchanges for the produce of other countries at such values as are required in order that the whole of her exports may exactly pay for the whole of her imports.'

Mill was unable to assess the precise barter terms of international exchange, arguing that (1909: 587):

> As the inclinations and circumstances of the consumers cannot be reduced to any rule, so neither can the proportions in which the two commodities will be interchanged . . . the limits within which the variations is confined, are the ratio between their costs of production in the other . . . they may exchange for any intermediate number.

And adding (1909: 588) that:

> Trade among any number of countries, and in any number of commodities, must take place on the same essential principles as trade between two countries and in two commodities. Introducing a greater number of agents precisely similar, cannot change the law of their action, no more than putting additional weights into the two scales of a balance alters the law of gravitation. It alters nothing but the numerical results.

Resolution of these problems awaited the contributions of Marshall and Edgeworth which gave the classical model its final integrity, and provided one further substantial conclusion:

6 *The physical rate of exchange is determined by the level of elasticity of demand in each country for each other's exports.*

Marshall's contribution was a general equilibrium analysis in which countries' export goods are measured in terms of a common unit: the 'representative bale'. In its geometrical form, demand was ingeniously depicted by means of 'offer curves', thereby abstracting from the 'money veil . . . on the assumption that the operations of monetary institutions did not in the long run seriously affect the dimension of the "real quantities" or the forms of the "real quantity" functions' (Viner 1955: 112).

An offer curve shows demand for quantities of the imported good not in terms of price, but in terms of the supply of quantities of the exported good the home country would be prepared to offer in exchange at each conceivable level of imports. These curves are constructed for each of two countries for a common origin in a two-dimensional diagram, with one country and its export good together on each axis.

In Figure 5, the Lines *OS* and *OU* represent the terms on which Portugal could obtain cloth [OS] and England wine [OU] in the absence of trade. The pre-trade domestic exchange ratios denote the comparative cost ratios of wine and cloth in the two countries (lines are straight because of a constant cost assumption). Each country's offer curve turns away from its autarkic real cost ray as trade takes place, the rate of change of slope indicating each country's desire to offer increasingly fewer exports for every increment of imports. The point of intersection of the two curves determines the equilibrium terms of exchange *ON*, where the amount of each good reciprocally demanded equals the amount reciprocally supplied.

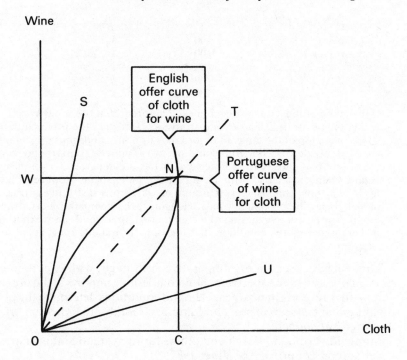

Figure 5: *The determination of the terms of international exchange*
Demand conditions determine the precise terms of international exchange within
the zone of mutually profitable trade, bounded by the pre-trade national relative
labour cost ratios of production for the two products. Each nation's offer curve (or
reciprocal demand curve) shows by its spacial position and changing slope its relative demand for its trading partner's product and decreasing willingness to give up
its exchange product in the form of exports to receive increasing amounts of the
former's exchange good in the form of imports. The two countries are mutually
satisfied at only one rate of exchange, that given by N at the point of intersection of
their offer curves, where OW of wine is exchanged for OC of cloth, on terms of
trade given by the gradient OT.

For the first time, a model of international trade relations had been
provided in which changes in both demand and supply were analysed and
international trade flows were shown to depend not only on comparative
costs, i.e. supply, but on the conditions of demand. Given that the
condition of equilibrium is that the value of imports must equal the value
of exports, it is possible also to indicate in a simple way how, in a multi-
commodity situation, the conditions of demand will determine which
commodities are exported and which imported (Ohlin 1933: 585–6):

Make out a table of the number of days of labour required in country *B* to
produce the quantities of the different commodities (*a*, *b*, *c*, etc.) which
can be produced in country *A* by 100 days of labour. The comparative
cost table then becomes:

	A	B	
a	100	k_1	
b	100	k_2	
c	100	k_3	
d	100	k_4	
e	100	k_5	etc.

If the commodities are arranged in such an order that the series $k_1 k_2 k_3 \ldots$ is rising, then country B has a comparative advantage in the production of the goods at the top of the table. In accordance with the conditions of demand the goods are divided by a horizontal line into two groups; B exports the goods in the upper group, A those in the lower one. B has a comparative advantage with regard to the former, A with regard to the latter. Note, however, that any horizontal line establishes two groups of which this last thing is true, even though B may import certain goods belonging to the 'comparative-disadvantage-group'. The position of the line which separates import goods from export goods is determined by the condition that the value of imports must equal that of exports.

Thus there is a 'chain of comparative advantage', with export commodities at one end of the spectrum, non-competitive imports at the other and competitive imports in between. Demand conditions determine the precise dividing line between exports and imports. Goods are either exported or imported *but not both*.

Mangoldt, Graham, Losch and others further extended this analysis to cover several countries (see Viner 1937).

A GENERAL TECHNICAL CRITIQUE OF THE CLASSICAL MODEL

Perhaps one of the most comprehensive technical critiques of the above model has been given by F. D. Graham (1948) in his book *The Theory of International Values*. Graham's critique is purely at the static level of analysis. Dynamic considerations are ignored. His overall judgement (1948: 308, 75) is that:

> The whole climate of thinking on international trade has been conditioned by classical concepts and the atmosphere is so murky as to have led to highly distorted conclusions ... The classical theory of international values ... is not only useless as an exegesis of equilibrium conditions but, even as an explanation of market phenomena, it is in urgent need of supplement and revision ... Classical theory is at best a theory of exceptional and ephemeral cases rather than a basic explanation of the phenomena of international trade.

The rationale for this wholesale condemnation is largely presented in terms of four aspects of the theory:

(a) Its demand bias as a theory of international values.
(b) The concept of reciprocal *national* demand used.
(c) Its treatment of the determination of exchange ratios.
(d) Its omission of 'commodities produced in common'.

(a) Demand bias

Classical writers, especially Mill, replace the 'supply and demand' explanation of market price in the domestic sphere with 'reciprocal demand' in the international sphere.

> In a barter transaction there is, of course, no conceivable difference between supply and demand. Each of any two bartered commodities may be thought of as having been either supply or demand, or both . . . supply is demand and demand is supply . . . it would . . . have been equally logical to employ the phrase 'reciprocal supply' . . . Mill pronounced this to be an 'anterior' law of values . . . that applies to market values (supplies being given)' [Graham 1948: 271].

Such an assertion essentially ignores the continuing importance of costs. This 'classical vice of thinking in terms of reciprocal demand' (1948: 160) gives rise to an erroneous theory of international values:

> . . . there are no standards set by costs, the influence of demand is exalted, and relative demands for the various demand for each of them, become of overweening presumptive importance . . . market values . . . are held to be definitive, in the sense that they are not subject to correction from changes in relative supply . . . elasticities of demand take on a significance wholly disproportionate to their real influence' [1948: 310].

(b) The concept of reciprocal national demand used

The rate at which the exports of any given nation, taken as a whole, exchange against its imports, taken as a whole, is equated with the concept of 'national demand' (1948: 157) '. . . as if trade . . . were . . . between national entities, in national bales of goods, rather than between individuals buying and selling, as traders nationally undistinguished, individual commodities in a market competitive in every respect except in the mobility of factors of production across national boundaries'.

Furthermore, Graham argues that the repercussions of international trade for domestic transactions, and vice versa, are so numerous and intricate as to make any segregation of the one from the other a logical impossibility (1948: 158, 113):

> All trade is part of a network of world-wide scope . . . The price of any freely traded good is unaffected by the national origin of sellers or buyers (in any freely organised market) and there is, in consequence no occasion for grouping buyers and sellers into more or less antagonistic national sections . . . no adequate theory of *domestic* values can be developed in exclusion of international trade but . . . no valid theory of i ternational values can be developed without regard for the interdependence, in both prices and production, of the various national economies . . . when, instead of discussing the *total* reciprocal demand (supply) for the various products in an integrated trading system, the classicists split demand (supply) into irrelevant national parts . . . they were indulging in pure fantasy . . . there is, in consequence, no such thing as reciprocal *national* demand . . . The demand for almost every product transcends all national lines . . .

(c)   The determination of the exchange ratio of goods between nations

The explanation given to the exchange ratio determination process and changes therein is deficient for a number of reasons, of which three are:

(i)   Insufficient allowance is made for supply (Graham 1948: 272): 'If supply be absolutely invariable, or if, at the moment, there is no way of changing it adequately in response to any shift in demand, there is no definable limit on the movement of the relative values of various goods.'

(ii)   The central locus of the exchange ratio between the national labour cost ratios. Graham maintains here (1948: 31) that:

> the establishment in international trade of any equilibrium other than at one of the extremes of the possible terms of interchange (the national domestic relative labour cost ratios) is dependent upon the *simultaneous* elimination, in each of the trading countries, of the industry which is, to it, of comparative disadvantage. The chance of this happening is negligible; this is the extreme, the barely conceivable, case, not, as Mill alleged, the normal one.

(iii) There is a tendency to confuse and to identify the commodity price ratio (the terms of trade) with the currency price ratio (the exchange rate).

(d)   The commodities produced in common – the 'missing link'

Graham asserts (1948: 252–3) that 'the pre-eminent, the fatal, defect of the classical theory lies in the failure of its authors to recognise the crucial importance, or for the most part even the existence, of commodities produced in common in each of [the] internationally trading countries...' This is a defect because such non-tradeable goods must be part of the overall output determination process as they are (1948: 69, 154): 'vital in the determination of international values... The world integration of prices is also an integration of national relative cost structures ...'

Two further points of criticism were raised by Ohlin (1933):

(i)   'The assumption of an equal relation between capital and the cost of labour in all industries is ... in striking contradiction to reality.

(ii)   There is an inadequate treatment of the laws of increasing and diminishing returns and it ignores changes in the relative combination of factors of production and their prices. Ohlin argues (1933: 574–5) that: 'it is not possible to maintain that the supply of any commodity may be increased or diminished without any effect on the cost of production or on prices (for example, expansion of the export industry in the post-trade situation makes the factors required for that producing more expensive than they were in the pre-trade situation); and that if the classical doctrine is inadequate for the study of price formation within a single market, an examination on the basis of pricing in several exchanging markets cannot be more satisfactory'.

While Ohlin appreciates that (1933: 590) 'the classical theory of international trade has been able to clear up a great many problems' and that 'even a defective tool may yield great results when employed by a master hand' as a result of 'all sorts of modifications which enable (every good economist) to arrive at a fairly correct impression of what is happening', he could not 'find sufficient reason for not attempting to build up a theory, in the framework of which the circumstances necessitating "modifications" are duly considered'.

One final and fundamental objection remains [Chipman 1966: 18] namely, that while 'the classical mode assumed that production relations in different countries differed in a quite arbitrary fashion, no satisfactory way [was] provided for explaining how such production relations differed.

A POLITICAL ECONOMY CRITIQUE OF THE MODEL

The niceties of free trade, the denial of the importance of the state and the harmonious community of interests posited by unfettered comparative advantage did not seem practical at all. The emergent growth in the disparities of national incomes (referred to in Chapter 1) made clear the incipient inequality of trade relations and discrepant development profiles, because (Balogh 1963: 10)

> the units affected by, and acting on, international economic relations, are not [simply] small productive units competing atomistically, but national units in a most important sense competing oligopolistically, unable to disregard the policy of each other... [which] are... *unequal in the sense that there is no similarity in the probability of their initiating new development.*

The doctrines of classical theory seem thus 'instructive more in relation to the ideological than to the actual economic forces which characterised the nineteenth-century expansion of international trade to the underdeveloped countries' (Myint 1958: 319–20). Thus trade between unequal partners is not likely to have a symmetrical impact. As Balogh states (1963: 27), 'trade between countries is inseparable from the determination of the growth of those countries . . . the precise character and shape of [the] so-called 'equilibrium position reached *after readjustment*', is analytically *inseparable from the path of the readjustment*'. Moreover, there is no certainty that actual readjustment will actually take place, for (Balogh 1963: 16–17)

> on the one hand, *in the poor areas* the difficulties and imperfections of effective decision making, the lack of entrepreneurial ability and of capital, vitiate the assumption that potential fields of investment opened up by trade will automatically be exploited... On the other hand, in the wide, progressive areas, there loom the (so-called pecuniary) external economies.

In the latter context 'once the importance of increasing returns (obtained through more production and the development of ancilliary industries) is admitted . . . they will be seen to be largely irreversible and will militate against the weaker less dynamic economies'. The idea that 'political' or *national* economy must be replaced by 'cosmopolitical or world-wide economy' operating under the principle of international free trade only seemed justified to List (1916: 100, 102, 103, 107):

> If . . . we assume a universal union of confederation of all nations as the guarantee for an everlasting peace. . . .

Under the existing conditions of the world, the result of general free trade would not be a universal republic, but, on the contrary, a universal subjection of the less advanced nations to the supremacy of the predominant manufacturing, commercial, and naval power . . . [it] *can only be realised if a large number of nationalities attain to as nearly the same degree as possible of industry and civilisation, political cultivation, and power.* Only with the gradual formation of this union can free trade be developed, only as a result of this union can it confer on all nations the same great advantages . . . In order to allow freedom of trade to operate naturally, the less advanced nations must first be raised by artificial measures to that stage of cultivation to which the English nation has been artificially elevated. . . .

The development of an indigenous industrial base was seen as paramount (List 1916: 130, 145–6, 159):

A nation which exchanges agricultural products for foreign manufactured goods is an individual with one arm, which is supported by a foreign arm. This support may be useful to it, but not so useful as if it possessed two arms itself, and this because its activity is dependent on the caprice of the foreigner. In possession of a manufacturing power of its own, it can produce as much provisions and raw materials as the home manufacturers can consume; but if dependent upon foreign manufacturers, it can merely produce as much surplus as foreign nations do not care to produce for themselves, and which they are obliged to buy from another country . . . A mere agricultural nation can never develop to any considerable extent its home and foreign commerce, its inland means of transport, and its foreign navigation, increase its population in due proportion to their well-being, or make notable progress in its moral, intellectual, social, and political development: it will never acquire important political power, or be placed in a position to influence the cultivation and progress of less advanced nations and to form colonies of its own. A mere agricultural State is an infinitely less perfect institution than an agricultural-manufacturing State. The former is always more or less economically and politically dependent on those foreign nations which take from it agricultural products in exchange for manufactured goods. It cannot determine for itself how much it will produce; it must wait and see how much others will buy from it. These latter, on the contrary (the agricultural manufacturing States), produce for themselves large quantities of raw materials and provisions, and supply merely the deficiency by importation from the purely agricultural nations . . .

Free trade is seen to be in the interests of an advanced industrial nation and can be used to preempt the emergence of competitive industrial rivalry in those lesser-developed areas that are unprotected by indigenous governmental action. The criticism is made that (List 1916: 138):

Nowhere do the advocates of that system care to point out by what means those nations which are now prosperous have raised themselves to that of power and prosperity which we see them maintain, and from what causes others have lost that degree of prosperity and power which they formerly maintained . . .

A state ready for international competition is described in the following terms: (1916: 141)

A nation in its normal state possesses one common language and literature, a territory endowed with manifold natural resources, extensive, and with convenient frontiers and a numerous population. Agriculture, manufactures, commerce and navigation must be all developed in it proportionately; arts and sciences educational establishments, and universal cultivation must stand in it on an equal footing with material production. Its constitution, laws, and institutions must afford to those who belong to it a high degree of security and liberty, and must promote religion, morality, and prosperity; in a word, must have the well-being of its citizens as their object. It must possess sufficient power on land and at sea to defend its independence and to protect its foreign commerce.

In these respects a small state is seen to be at a disadvantage (1916: 142) as it:

can never bring to complete perfection within its territory the various branches of production. In it all protection becomes mere private monopoly. Only through alliances with more powerful nations, by partly sacrificing the advantages of nationality, and by excessive energy, can it maintain with difficulty its independence.

'Territorial deficiencies' will also hamper other states which can only be remedied by union, purchase of land or conquest. These deficiencies arise where (1916: 142-3):

A nation . . . possesses no coasts, mercantile marine, or naval power, or has not under its dominion and control the mouths of its rivers, is in its foreign commerce dependent on other countries. . . . . A nation not bounded by seas and chains of mountains lies open to the attacks of foreign nations, and can only by great sacrifices, and in any case only very imperfectly, establish and maintain a separate tariff system of its own.

Emphasis is placed on state power to effect industrialisation. *Laissez-faire* market-determined comparative costs are therefore to be condemned for their lack of reference to the realities of disparities between countries and the national functions performed by state governments. *Laissez-faire* is regarded as (1916: 272):

at bottom . . . nothing else than a system of the *private economy of all the individual persons in a country, or of the individuals of the whole human race, as that economy would develop and shape itself, under a state of things in which there were no distinct nations, nationalities, or national interests – no distinctive political constitutions or degrees of civilisation – no wars or national animosities*; that it is nothing more than a theory of values; a mere shopkeeper's or individual merchant's theory – not a scientific doctrine, showing how the productive powers of an entire nation can be called into existence, increased, maintained, and preserved – for the special benefit of its civilisation, welfare, might, continuance, and independence.

List's views are consistent with Gershenkron's (1962) view of economic 'backwardness'; Myrdal's (1956b) Law of Cumulative Causation that increases economic disparities between countries; and contemporary core-periphery literature. While a review of this literature is not included here, some consideration is nevertheless given to the relevance of comparative cost doctrine to less-developed countries; colonial trade and the 'graduation problem' and to collectivist international trade relations.

Comparative advantage and less-developed countries

Much of the controversy that surrounds the compatability of the comparative cost doctrine with the development needs of underdeveloped countries has arisen out of an examination of historical data in respect of the trends in the 'vertical' trade between underdeveloped (largely primary producer) nations and developed (largely manufacturing) nations, rather than in the 'horizontal' trade within these two categories of producing countries.

On the basis of historical 'evidence', Myrdal (1956a: 55, 95) and others argue that 'a quite normal result of unhampered trade between two countries of which one is industrial and the other underdeveloped, is the initiation of a cumulative process towards the impoverishment and stagnation of the latter', and that 'market forces tend cumulatively to accentuate international inequalities'. Arguments put forward to support these contentions include:

(a) That on the side of supply, 'manufacturing industry presents, in a sense, a higher stage of production' (Myrdal 1956a: 226) in that 'external dynamic industrial economies' tend to be more important than in primary industry, with important cost-reducing linkage effects for the development of the industrial structure.

(b) That on the side of demand, the demand for primary products is of a higher price and income elasticity than that for secondary products, so that as living standards rise, this type of trade becomes of less relative importance to countries whose incomes per capita are rising.

As a result of (a) and (b), development tends to become stagnant and industrial 'take-off' thwarted. In the short run as the volume and value of primary produce tends to be highly volatile and trade tends to be high as a proportion of national income, development is necessarily a random process. In the long run, the terms of trade tend to move against primary producers *inter alia* due to the Engel Law of Demand (food expenditure falls as a proportion of total expenditure as real incomes rise), and the evolution of synthetic substitutes for natural products. Furthermore, there is a tendency for advanced countries not only to protect home agriculture but also to protect many of their textile and light manufacturing industries which initially tend to suit the factor endowment of LDCs.

(c) That the effect of international factor movements has been to create a highly 'unbalanced' industrial structure in LDCs because: (i) the inflow of foreign capital tends to develop only the natural resource export sector to the neglect of the development needs of the domestic sector. Foreign 'enclaves' are created that bias development; and, (ii) the profits from foreign investment do not benefit the 'exploited' country because they tend to be repatriated and hence a serious income leakage occurs that is not used to finance further development.

(d) That the 'demonstration effect' of advanced consumption standards in rich countries tends to raise the propensity to consume in poorer countries, checking domestic capital accumulation, making faster growth all the more urgent and difficult.

However, the relevant point in the context of this book is not the historical 'truth' or otherwise of such arguments, but that they are based upon a presumption that comparative costs, as measured by factor prices, are necessarily revealed by market forces. If, however, factor prices do not fully reflect long-run opportunity costs (the real social costs of development) because they understate them, then the industrial structure 'revealed' and demonstrated as constituting an inferior specialisation cannot legitimately be used either to dismiss the principle of comparative advantage as an inappropriate one for development planning, or as evidence of incompatibility with the needs of LDCs. In this event government intervention may be required to stimulate industries that give rise to important externalities in production, for (Meir 1963: 130):

> if production costs are lowered for firms in other industries, for technical or pecuniary reasons as the result of an expansion in output of the protected industry, the social cost is less than the private cost of production. In this situation, private profitability understates the social desirability of an expansion of the protected industry.

Thus where industrial specialisation was externally imposed before a proper industrial infrastructure (in the form of roads, postal and transport facilities, marketing and distribution) had been created, and/or trade patterns were made to conform to the external development needs of a dominant, generally colonial, economic power, it is unlikely that 'market forces' reflected such properties. However, the simplicity of the classical concepts is destroyed if market price adjustment has to be made for any of the following (Chenery 1965: 129):

1 Recognition of the possibility of structural disequilibrium in the factor market that may bias the opportunity cost ranking of the alternatives foregone.
2 The inclusion of direct market and non-market effects when any proposed expansion of a given type of production capacity is being evaluated. The quantity and quality of factors of production may change substantially over time, in part as a result of the production process itself (e.g. the skill potential of workers will change) even if there is no change in technological knowledge.
3 As complementarity among commodities is important in both producer and consumer demand (the existence of externalities and industrial linkage effects), planning requires recognition of the interdependence of levels of production in interrelated industrial sectors, as well as consumption, to establish the strategic industrial hierarchy demanded by a rational development process.
4 Allowance for likely variations in the demand for exports over time.

Comparative advantage so calculated could in theory be a respectable criterion for development policy. However, since no well developed body of theory has yet emerged to provide a satisfactory dynamic theory of comparative advantage, the suggestive nature of the above qualifications may lead one to adopt the 'doctrine of balanced growth' for lack of something better, a policy approach that explicitly recognises the horizontal and vertical interdependencies in production referred to, and places a premium on unspecialised growth. Furthermore, the limited ability in practice of policy-makers to foresee changes in demand and supply conditions tends to emphasise the need for flexibility and the keeping open of options in the choice of a development strategy. The implications of either view – balance growth or unbalanced growth conditioned by dynamic comparative cost considerations – lie, however, in protection and import substitution policies (possibly combined with control of primary product prices) to overcome the inherent structural deficiencies of an infant economy. While no clear policy framework emerges, Viner's moral stricture (1958: 62) that 'market price should be made to surrender its judicial role, but not to promiscuous protection' should not be forgotten. It is important to stress that there are two main political economy lacunae in the explanatory structure of the theory: the problem of colonial trade; its incompatibility with collectivist economy resource allocation.

Colonial trade and the 'graduation problem'

Classical trade theory's precommitment to a given set of objectives disregarded the field-relevant facts concerning the existence of colonies and the importance of mother-country allocation of colonial resources in the case of previously settled territories, and exogenous aboriginal allocation of resources in previously unsettled territories. Moreover, the ahistorical context of the theory did not contemplate, let alone address itself to the development continuum of an international economy in embryo. It sought to 'begin at the beginning' as if such structuring of exchange had not already occurred, and thus did not suggest any path of reversibility of extra-market and imperfect market distortions to 'normalize' trade relationships, so as to achieve the mutually advantageous result described in its conclusions, and to solve the 'graduation problem' created by political independence. Yet this was the very setting to which any real-world simulation of the idealised model had initially to relate.

The actual context of the opening-up by trade and development of undeveloped and underdeveloped areas was substantially not one of international exchange, but one of *quasi* economic union (as previously described in Chapter 1). In this protogenesis stage of trade development, trade relationships were often 'artificial' and 'de-indigenised' in the sense that the pattern of exchange was 'managed' either by a mainland governmental authority, by economic agents acting for that authority in an official manner or by patriate individuals still essentially based on the mainland economy.

The advent of such exogenous economic penetration necessarily created a number of trade/developmental effects, the impact of which tended to structure and pre-load the *ex-ante* international trade closed-economy situation in at least three respects: biases in indigenous real-cost ratios: hyperpolic exchange and a substitution of colonial union trade flows for ones with the external international trade arena.

Biased real-cost ratios

Because of colonial union, patriate labour migration and capital mobility from the mother economy (specifically precluded by the assumption set of orthodox trade theory) were either determinants of aboriginal domestic relative cost ratios, or instrumental in altering preexistent indigenous ones. Assuming the classically posed situation of both goods being produceable in both countries, it likely that the terminal situation in a colony at independence will be one where the autarkic price ratio cone has a narrower angle from the origin (previously shown in Figure 3) than would have been the case if colonialism had not preceded international trade entry. The implications of this is that the potential gains from international trade entry will be larger in the case of a country without a colonial past than in the case of a country with such a past; that the narrowing of trade gain potential will be the greater the longer the period of active colonial resource allocation; and that in the case of a virgin unsettled colonised area, where all development has occurred as a result of metropolitan resource transfers, aboriginal cost ratios will be entirely exogenously determined and are likely to be more nearly aligned with the mainland metropolitan country from the beginning, so that international trade entry gains will be even smaller.

In practice the advent of colonialism often pre-dated the completion of the process of internal geographical integration of these areas, such that the potential resources that were theoretically accessible (given contemporary technology) had not yet been activated within the extending internal economic frontier of exploitation. For example, before railways had opened up the interiors of continents, colonies that were parts of continents had not yet been able to develop natural trade relationships with their contiguous neighbours so that external oceanic trade became the expedient engine of growth. The demands of the metropolitan economy often involved the promotion of enclave development of 'non-competitive' industries to the exclusion of rival 'competitive good' development, but supportive of the growth needs of the mainland economy. Such production often took precedence over the interior extension of the frontier of economic exploitation. In these ways colonial resource allocation imposed an industrial bias which might not have proved autonomously justifiable in terms of rational development independently made. All kinds of factor and product price distortions were thereby created that became deep-seated over time.

Hyperpolic trade relations

It is likely that the colony–mother economy trade relationship was one that Wiles (1968: 424–5) describes as 'hyperpoly' or 'over–trading'. This is a situation of economic deviance from free-trade equilibrium, where actual trade flows are in aggregate greater than they would be when 'exports plus net natural long-term capital flows equal imports', and 'all individual agents, in both foreign and domestic trade, are maximizing their profits'. Figure 6 depicts a situation where exogenous control of interregional barter exchange undervalues the export flows from the colony to the metropolitan centre to the benefit of the latter and the disadvantge of the former. The offer curve C_A indicates what the offer situation would be if autonomously determined. The offer curve C_M indicates the 'artificial' but actual situation that obtains when exchange is under the direct exploitatative control of mother country (the offer curve of which is M), such that NN_1 extra trade is extracted. Similar situations partially obtained in 'informal' empire relationships, where lack of effective autonomous control was exploited by foreign traders whose local market power initially went unchallenged by indigenous economic agents, thus enabling them to

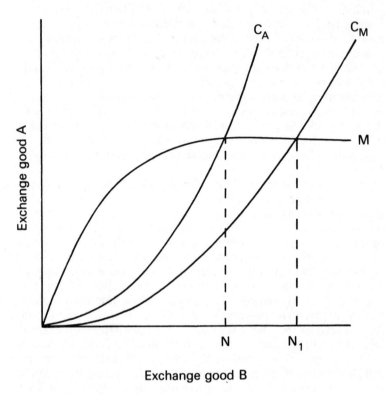

Figure 6: *Hyperpolic exchange*

engineer intercountry profits by undervaluing at source their exports from
the countries of production origin and appropriately marking them up on
their arrival in the consumption countries of destination. Such practices
were the forerunners of contemporary multinational intra-firm 'related
party' trade, with its inherent tendency to embody, for corporate global gain,
transfer-priced valuation rather than open-market, arms' length, valuation
of inter-country trade flows.

Anti-trade biased extra union exchange relations

Colonial economic union involved, in its purest imperialist form, a central
internalisation via interregional trade of the hypothetical gains from
international trade that would have accrued to colonies if they had had
autonomous control of their external economic relations. This 'enforced
bilateralism', apart from suppressing the external trade relations of
colonies, also enabled the mother country to internalise foreign trade
relations by substituting particular forms of interregional colonial trade
for its own existing international trade, whether on the imports or exports
side.

It is perhaps idle to speculate that if colonial trade had been worked into the explanatory structure of orthodox trade theory in the early nineteenth century, the decades of colonial industrial economic structuring that history subsequently imposed might not have been so many, the restructuring problem not now so significant and difficult, the gains from trade not so unequally divided, and the *per capita* income distribution between countries not so extreme. However, the harmonic cosmopolitan ideal might then have been more attainable and so seem less fanciful now. This is not to imply, however, that *per se* interstate trade miraculously makes universal free exchange mutually beneficial for its participants without some international consensus about codes of conduct or degree of supranational interventionism. Manoilesco (1931: 222–3) and other writers would insist that 'it is impossible to regulate distribution among different nations' and that 'international *political* organisation is the indispensable condition for equitable free trade (no conquerors and no conquered)'.

Collectivist economy trade

As the comparative cost approach is essentially relevant to international economic *laissez-faire* conditions, it is incompatible with the *modus operandi* of a centrally planned economy of the Communist type. Wilczynski (1965: 64–6) and (1969: 69–77) gives five main reasons for this:

(a) In such countries the free-market mechanism is not allowed to operate in factor and product markets so that prices in these markets do not reflect real economic costs. Domestic prices are centrally assigned without particular reference to internal or external market pressures.
(b) International exchange is related to the needs of a general economic plan.
(c) Import needs are generally determined first, and exports planned accordingly. Usually self-sufficiency or balanced bilateral trade is emphasised rather than international interdependence; trade-aversion favoured rather than trade creation, autarky rather than polypoly.
(d) Monolithic state control tends to make for bilateral trade relationships which are often concluded in the context of political rather than economic objectives.
(e) Exchange rates are often manipulated for state ends so that foreign and domestic price relationships are highly distorted in relationship to what might otherwise obtain. Exchange control tends to be total.

Soviet writers such as Frumkin tend anyway to dismiss it as 'a pseudo scientific reactionary doctrine ... disseminated by bourgeois economists' (quoted by Wilczynski (1969: 71). Despite this rejection, no comparable doctrine has been evolved so that 'with regard to the problem of the mechanism of foreign exchanges there is "a gap" in the Socialist theory of foreign trade' (Wilczynski (1969: 73).

TESTING THE RICARDIAN APPROACH

A shortcoming of studies that purport to test Ricardian emphasis on differential labour productivity as a monocause of international trade is the international availability of data on labour productivity and that often such data are either not compiled on a consistent basis or are available in a too generalised form for particular comparisons to be properly made on a strictly industrial basis.

Pioneering studies in this field were conducted by MacDougall (1951) and (1962), Stern (1962) and Balassa (1963). The results indicated that something like 60 to 70 per cent of the trade of some twenty to thirty industries accounting variously for around 40 per cent of manufacturing and 40 per cent of exports of the United Kingdom and America could be explained in this way to the satisfaction of their authors. Bhagwati (1965: 171) concluded that: 'these results, limited as they are, cast sufficient doubt on the usefulness of the Ricardian approach ... Contrary ... to the general impression, there is as yet no evidence in favour of the Ricardian hypotheses'.

In addition he (1965: 171–2) pointed out that even if such evidence could be established satisfactorily:

> ultimately the practical utility of the Ricardian hypothesis is somewhat limited. Labour productivity, after all, is not a datum in the sense that production functions are. The reliance of the production on labour productivity is what it is, and how therefore it may be expected to change, restricts the utility of the prediction. Moreover, even if we could forecast changes in labour productivity, we could not tell exclusively, therefrom that the pattern of imports and exports would change in a specified manner; all we could say is that, if the pattern of exports and imports changes in any way, the new pattern will also be characterised by the postulated Ricardian ranking in terms of comparative labour productivities and/or unit wage ratios.

A subsequent review by Stern (1975: 10–11) further concluded that:

> While these various studies offer numerous insights, they are difficult to compare because of intercountry differences in the stage of development, the time periods covered, and the empirical proxies used. Furthermore, these studies offer little guidance in selecting for estimation one production function over another, and, from the standpoint of the international trade models that concern us here, they have not yet been connected systematically with the observed composition and direction of trade. Granted all these limitations, there nevertheless appears to be substantial evidence of intercountry efficiency differences, as posited by the Ricardian-neo-classical model.

As regards countries of different stages of development, Sailors and Bronson (1970) conducted a pioneering study of thirteen countries in relation to some nineteen countries on a roughly comparable basis. Correlation coefficients ranged from a negative result of −0.416 to a positive result of 0.743 in a sample of twenty countries, with eight countries having negative coefficients, 10 between 0 and +0.5 and only 2 between 0.5 and 1.0. Other tests showed a low degree of significance on the whole. The study was therefore unable to provide evidence to verify the Ricardian theory as a basis for trade. The authors concluded that their study indicated: 'that either the theory is invalid, or there are other factors which can explain the generally poor results obtained without bringing the theory itself into doubt.' Sailors and Bronson (1970: 12) did, however, selectively point to a number of implicit assumptions contained in the classical model which :do not necesarily hold true in the real world'. which might have conditioned their results:

(a) The implicit assumption that the exchange rates of the countries involved are at an optimum level, i.e. that trade is balanced and that trade is not distorted by 'unrealistic' exchange rates; that inflation is not proceeding at differential rates in different countries; that there are no artificial distortions created as between exports and imports and good categories within each sector that prevent adjustment to underlying factors such as labour productivity.

(b) An implicit assumption regarding common levels of technology. A technological gap could account for a lack of correlation of trade with labour productivity until such time as the technology became available to all countries, at which time competition could be based on labour productivity differentials and not on accidents of industrial leadership. Not all writers would, however, agree that this assumption was implicit.

(c) The differential imposition of tariff barriers in developed and undeveloped countries. Sailors and Bronson (1970: 15) argue that:

> the 'typical' export of any underdeveloped country to a developed country faces a higher tariff barrier than does the 'typical' export from the developed country to the underdeveloped country. As a consequence of this, the underdeveloped country must have greater relative labor productivity advantages than would otherwise be required to achieve an advantage over the developed country in the production of manufactures. It is open to question how many underdeveloped countries are able to overcome this disadvantage and conduct their trade as would be expected solely from an examination of relative labor productivities.

(d) Imperfections in the market (Sailors and Bronson 1970: 15), 'such as imperfect knowledge of the relatively low cost of products of a distant or very small country. In such a case, the presence of even very substantial differences in labor productivity may have practically no effect on the pattern of international trade'.

(e) The assumption of 'prompt and correct responses to the "signals" of the market place in the allocation of resources'. Linder (1961) has identified a relative lack of 'reallocative ability in less-developed countries as poorly trained workers . . . living at a subsistence level cannot readily be shifted from one industry to another in response to changing domestic and foreign market conditions'. It may therefore be that many underdeveloped countries are not trading in the manner which could be expected from their relative labor productivities due to this (Sailors and Bronson 1970).

The above considerations apart, it would seem that proper testing of this theory awaits the availability of improved, comparable international productivity data (see A. D. Smith *et al* 1982).

ENVOI

It is clear that the classical doctrine of comparative advantage was intended as a refutation of the mercantilist traditions that prevailed at the end of the eighteenth century. It was not, however, mere propaganda to effect the deregulation of international economic relations, but presented as a stylised model for national industrial specialisation and international exchange that abstracted from the economic power of the state, and was directed towards the establishment and ends of transnational cosmopolitan consumer sovereignty. It was intended as a prescriptive model to be followed, given the global long-run benefits it exhibited, in contrast to the supposed benefits of economic warfare and national power emphasised by the mercantilists. Its crucial flaw was that the idealised exchange presented was not linked to a phased picture of how countries that were being incorporated into the world system could proceed towards its objectives, given the accidents of the particular sequence of the impact of industrialisation on countries, country size disparities, and the antecedant dependent history of particular geographical areas. Evidently particular development biases were necessarily created in geographical areas subjected to unequal and dependent colonial exchange relationships, prior to the truly international trade relationships that necessarily followed the gaining of political independence. In the latter areas and those which, while *de jure* independent, were nevertheless 'informal' parts of external foreign commercial empires, the supposed harmony and community of interests and balanced distribution of the benefits from trade were not actualised. Reversibility of the biases referred to once colonial union had been dissolved was made more difficult the longer the period of external economic occupation experienced; the wider the extent of foreign private ownership of many key productive enterprises; and the greater the lack of indigenous reallocative ability to effect such restructuring.

Countries able to unite as a result of the direct territorial integration of small geographical sub-entities, or via regional customs unions, were better placed to reverse actual positions of inferiority both in terms of politics and market power. Myrdal (1970: 230, 229) also stresses other crucial internal factors conditioning economic progress in certain newly-independent countries that obtained especially in South Asia, Africa and Latin America 'not to be understood in moralistic terms ... [but because] ... these countries are as they are not because of any inherent evil of the people but as a result of a long history very different from that of our [Western] countries, where all conditions have interacted in circular causation'. These conditions underlie his concept of the 'soft state', being a state in which there is:

> a general lack of social discipline ... signified by deficiencies in ... legislation and, in particular, in law observance and enforcement, lack of obedience to rules and directives handed down to public officials on various levels, often collusion of these officials with powerful persons or groups of persons whose conduct they should regulate, and, at bottom, a general inclination of people in all strata to resist public controls and their implementation. Within the concept of the soft state belongs also corruption, ...

In this respect Meir would agree (1958: 288-9) believing that 'although traditional theory envisaged foreign trade as an important activator of economic change ... [it] failed to occur in many poor countries ... the lack of "carry-over" [being] attributed to domestic obstacles rather than to any international mechanism of inequality'. This, however, is a much wider issue than can be discussed here and involves the question of the possible role of trade as engine, handmaiden, brake or offspring with regard to the growth of particular economies (see Kravis (1970); Streeten (1982a and b); Henderson (1982); and Balassa (1983)). Reference will be made to some of these aspects in Chapter 10.

Despite the fact that classical trade theory has had its technical defects of omission and comission exposed by generations of critics, embodies 'the excessive optimism of the nineteenth-century's faith in progress (Meir 1958: 288) and raises particular difficulties with regard to its verifiction, its idealised blueprint for the determination of the bases for and content of trade and its identification of the need to emphasise the goal of cosmopolitan economic welfare in international economic relations made it a cultural touchstone that has ensured it longevity and continued importance. Its simplicity, however, is both a strength and weakness for

> the very lack of precision and the unspecified nature of the determinants of comparative advantage in Ricardian analysis proves to be an asset which makes the theory look at least vaguely right. The presence of this asset in the treasury of economic analysis, however, does not leave us any richer. At best, it leaves us with a very unpleasant feeling . . . The classical economists left the principle of comparative costs hanging in the air. [Minhas 1962: 156, 138.]

6 The neo-classical Heckscher-Ohlin theory

> Ohlin will live forever as one of the great innovators in the theory of
> international trade ... [he] endeavoured to make ... trade theory part of a
> general *locational analysis* of *spatial* pricing and good and factor movements.
>
> Samuelson (1981: 147, 151)

> [The factor-endowment analysis of foreign trade] is a monolithic, formal
> structure, rigorous, ... with every deductive nook and cranny of it thoroughly
> explored. If one accepts its restrictive assumptions, a vast number of
> conclusions can be squeezed out of it.
>
> Corden (1965: 30)

> ... the Heckscher-Ohlin Theorem remains woefully restricted in terms of the
> generality of the assumptions needed for its proof ... as a statement about the
> commodity composition of trade, the theorem is valid only in the highly abstract
> environment of the two-factor, two-good, two-country model that has been the
> mainstay of trade theory for half a century.
>
> Deardorff (1982: 683)

Ricardo's classical mutual interdependence theory of comparative
advantage, as reinforced by Mill's reciprocal demand analysis and
extended by Marshall's and Edgeworth's neo-classical graphical presenta-
tions, dominated international economic thought for over a century,
despite continental criticism. It was replaced by a new theory that evolved
as a result of Heckscher's article *Foreign Trade and the Distribution of Income*
(1919), Ohlin's book *International and Interregional Trade* (1933) and
subsequent additions contributed by Samuelson (1948; 1949).

This so-called 'modern' theory came to hold centre-stage in preference
to two other theoretical innovations that evolved at about the same time:
the 'real cost' revisionist theory of Viner and the 'opportunity cost'
'modern' theory of Haberler (1951). The first approach (Viner 1937: 492)
consisted of replacing the discredited Ricardian Labour Theory of Value
with a total 'real cost' concept. This did not attract general support
because:

> In order to vindicate the real cost theory it must be assumed either that all inputs
> involve subjective cost (disutility) and that their prices (remuneration of
> different kinds of labor) are proportional to the disutility involved, or that the
> proportion in which different types of labor and other inputs are used are at
> least approximately the same in different industries. Neither one of these
> alternatives can be regarded as representative of the real world. [Haberler 1961:
> 12.]

Haberler's alternative 'opportunity cost' theory was founded on general
equilibrium economics. With assumptions comparable to what became
the 'modern' model, he asserted that exchange ratios in pre- and post-trade
situations are precisely derived from:

the relative value of the production agents required to produce a unit of each at the margin ... [and that] this relative value of the requisite productive agents is the 'opportunity cost' of a unit of each commodity ... [thus] ... once the costs in two isolated countries have been expressed as values of the productive agents, it is possible to replace two separate series of relative labor costs by two similar series of relative prices which reflect the contributions of many factors (rather than merely labour) at the margin [Ellsworth 1940: 286].

The principle of comparative costs now became reformulated (Haberler 1936: 182) as 'each country [will] specialise in those ... goods where costs were relatively lowest'. However, the more explicit developed and comprehensively presented Heckscher-Ohlin model (henceforth H-O) took the limelight.

Heckscher's initial *explanandum* (1919: 277) was 'to discover the influence of foreign trade upon the prices of the factors of production' and the resultant distribution of income between land, capital and labour as compared with the pre-trade position. His model, like Ricardo's, is a static reallocation model; and, on his own admission (1919: 274), 'changes induced by foreign trade in the nature of the factors of production ('dynamic' changes) are completely disregarded, and so are the disturbing effects resulting from the difficulties of transition from one position to another'. He accepts (1919: 275) the broad, then orthodox, view that 'the law of "comparative costs" operates ... whenever a want is more easily satisfied in an indirect way, through the production of another commodity which can be exchanged for the commodity desired, than by producing the latter directly,' but provides a completely different explanation for the phenomenon as presented by Ricardo. The set of assumptions that condition his findings is long and differs from Ricardo in certain important respects. Bhagwati (1965: 172–3) differentiates its analytical framework thus:

> the Ricardian model assumes one factor, and therewith (through the supporting assumption of constant returns to scale) makes the factor supply irrelevant in determining the trade pattern; on the other hand, ... the H-O model assumes two factors and makes international differences in factor endowments the crucial and sole factor determining comparative advantage. Moreover, whereas the former attributes to international differences in production functions the explanation of comparative advantage, the latter explicitly postulates the international identity of production functions.

In addition, the new theory was considered to be superior to its predecessor because of its explicit attempt to explain the structure of foreign trade *per se*, rather than to establish welfare propositions. Furthermore, it 'provided for the first time, an analysis that was capable of integrating the factor markets into international trade theory in a satisfactory way' (Lancaster 1957: 18), subsuming an analysis of price formation in both the product and factor markets. Although, like Ricardian trade theory, H-O is a 'nonmonetary equilibrium theory of the international division of labor' (Haberler 1954: 544), its analytical framework proved more versatile and applicable to a wider range of problems, though Johnson (1969: 58) argues that 'this characteristic ... [perhaps became] a long-run liability in giving the model an unwarranted monopoly of analytical approaches to trade theory problems'.

The essence of this 'factor endowment' theory of comparative advantage is (a) a factor proportions theorem relating to trade causation, and (b) a factor price equalisation theorem relating to the pricing of factors of production in an open economy. Briefly summarised, the rationale of each part of the theory is as follows:

(a)   The Factor Proportions Theorem: the explanation for comparative advantage. The H-O analysis establishes that *comparative advantage is determined by the absolute distribution of resources as between countries and particularly by the relative factor endowment ratios within countries*. Given, *inter alia* that relative factor endowment ratios differ and that different factor intensities are assumed to underlie the production functions of the traded goods, the conclusion is drawn that *an economy's exports will embody intensively that country's relatively abundant factor and that imports will embody intensively the factor that is domestically relatively scarce*. Trade flows are therefore presumed to be intimately related to inter-country differentials in the relative *composition* of productive resources.

(b)   The Factor Price Equalisation theorem: a price theory explicitly defines the nature of equilibrium in the factor market. *Equilibrium requires* not only that the prices of the commodity outputs be equalized but also, *under certain restrictive assumptions, the international equalisation of factor (input) prices.*

Given the factor proportions theorem as the explanation for trade, the post-trade situation means that:

> Exports decrease the amount of certain factors of production available for production for the domestic market, *i.e.*, those factors used to produce the export commodities. On the other hand, imports which are the payment for exports, make available for domestic markets those factors of production which formerly were used to produce the goods now imported. Foreign trade thus creates, on the one hand, an increased scarcity and, on the other hand, a decreased scarcity of the different factors of production available for domestic-goods production. [Heckscher 1919: 279–80.]

Thus the domestic reallocation of factors brought about by trade will alter relative factor prices. The newly created export industry will raise the relative price of the domestically abundant cheap factor required in its production; imports will reduce the returns to the domestic relatively scarce and expensive factor previously utilised in its home production. The restructuring of national outputs to obtain gains through trade will 'continue to expand until an *equalization of the relative scarcity of the factors of production among countries has occurred*' [ibid: 286]. More important is the conclusion that, with the same technique of production and the same eventual international prices of products, the *absolute* returns to the factors of production must also be equalised.

Given that international trade is exemplified as exchange on the basis of internationally immobile factors of production, the result is identical with that which would obtain with inter-country mobility: trade flows thus seem to substitute for international factor migration.

It has to be borne in mind that both parts of the theory are presented subject to the following two provisos by Heckscher (1919: 280): (i) that 'both the commodity produced domestically and the imported one replacing it are of the same type, *i.e.*, that *no substitution between different kinds of commodities takes place through foreign trade.* The only substitution ... is a replacement of domestic goods with the *same kind* of commodity produced outside the country'. This necessarily excludes many types of international exchange where this is not so; and (ii) that 'when prices of the same factors of production in different countries are compared, the comparison always refers to the prices of the *same qualities* of the given factors'. Samuelson (1948: 181) feels, however, that 'if one is forced ultimately to work with dozens of grades of labor, hundreds of grades of land and innumerable grades of capital equipment, the explanations become rather *ad hoc* and not very hepful'. It is not just that factors differ with regard to their individual type, but that there are many different types not all available everywhere within the system. With respect to labour, for example, Ohlin (1977:40) specified four types of what he called 'subfactors':

> ordinary unskilled labour (OL), skilled labour (SL), managerial and technical labour of lower rank (MTLL), and higher managerial and technical labour (MTLH). Several of the less-developed countries, which belong to the upper half of the LDC group with regard to living standard and industrial development, have a seriously insufficient supply of the MTLL. It has proven easier, for example for some Arab countries as well as India and Pakistan, to train, import and maintain a rapidly growing supply of labour with high technical knowledge (MTLH).

Ohlin later added a further proviso (1977: 31): 'in the usual factor proportion reasoning the quantities of factors used refer to the *total process of production* of each commodity'. But if the analysis is to explain trade where different stages of production are located in different countries, 'it is ... much more realistic to think about costs at *different stages of production.* Under equilibrium conditions the total unit costs is equal to "the value added by manufacture" at a certain stage.'

It is already apparent that this theory is more complex and intricate in its formulation than Ricardo's. It involves explicit reference to and knowledge of much technical language that is otherwise employed in two separate branches of economics: the theory of the firm and welfare economics.

Each part of the theory will now be explained, followed by a critique and brief appraisal of what the attempts to verify the theory seem to indicate.

THE FACTOR PROPORTIONS THEOREM

The model's operational context is the following set of assumptions:

Trade barriers

No transport costs or barriers to international trade in any form: trade is free and costless. Markets are completely accessible except that labour and capital are not mobile internationally. Ohlin's view of factor movements was as follows (1977: 37):

> *The short-run effects* of factor movements on trade can be regarded as minor modifications of the trade that is going on if there are small variations in *domestic* factor supply . . .

The long-run effects of factor movements on development of industry in different countries and on trade between them can, however, be very considerable. Countries with large immigration and borrowing abroad can in a decade expand their trade in a way which is much affected by the changing total supply of productive resources, whether due to domestic variations or international movements. The insufficiency of static trade theory and the need for adding a theory of development to explain international economic relations is obvious.

In less developed areas it must also be questioned as to whether perfect internal factor mobility obtains, given that social infrastructure, including internal communication may be lacking.

National market structures

Perfect competition is assumed both in the factor input (land, labour, capital, enterprise) markets and the commodity (output) markets, i.e. competition is atomistic, between a large number of producers and consumers in the goods markets; and between a large number of producers and a large number of owners of factors of production in the factor service markets – there are no elements of monopoly.

International production conditions

(i) Factor supplies are fixed, identical in every respect and fully employed, though each country is differently endowed. The relative abundance of any two factors of production in each country must not be equal. For example, if the capital/labour ratios of countries X and Y are compared, trade will only take place provided that:

either (i)	*or* (ii)
$$\frac{K_A}{L_A} > \frac{K_B}{L_B}$$	$$\frac{K_A}{L_A} < \frac{K_B}{L_B}$$

where K_A, K_B and L_A, L_B denote the total supplies of capital and labour in the two countries available for production. In case (i) Country A would be the relatively capital-abundant country and Country B the relatively labour-abundant country, in case (ii) the opposite obtains. Such an approach implies that it is possible to find reasonably homogeneous and commensurable factors of production in diverse parts of the world, so that it is meaningful and possible to measure the physical amounts of each productive factor so that such factor-endowment ratios may be constructed and compared.

(ii) Each of the two goods is universally produced according to identical production functions: there are no international differences either in technology or production techniques. The technical coefficients of each respective function require the relatively intensive use of a different factor inputs (as shown in Figure 7) which determines the relative factor intensity ranking of each good and which is presumed to remain constant in the short run, irrespective of changes in output levels and factor prices. One and the same good *always* remains the relatively labour-intensive good, the other good *always* being the relatively capital-intensive good within the operation range of production. There are no factor-intensity reversals (as illustrated in Figure 8) within this range.

In practice, the identification and measurement of factor intensities is not a simple matter. With respect to capital, for example, Ohlin (1977: 30) admitted that three different measures were applicable: 'the quantity of capital *per individual working place*, . . . *per worker*, . . . [or] the percentage share of "*the total unit production costs*" which . . . [are] capital costs [inclusive of] interest and depreciation costs'. Apart from the measurability problem, there are no conclusive research findings concerning the

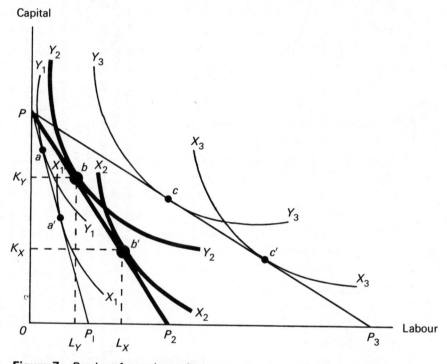

Figure 7: *Product factor intensity*
Relative factor prices are illustrated by linear price lines, along the slope of which a particular price relationship remains constant. With capital on the vertical axis and labour on the horizontal axis, the steeper the slope of such lines the higher will be the price of labour relative to that of capital. The factor intensity ranking of Goods X and Y will be indicated at each price relationship by its point of tangency with the appropriate actual levels of output of each good (as indicated by iso-product curves that depict all the combinations of capital and labour that can yield those particular levels of output).

At the relative factor price levels indicated by PP_2, the comparative factor intensities of Goods X and Y are shown to be OK_X/OL_X and OK_Y/OL_Y respectively. It is evident that Good X is the relative labour-intensive good and Good Y the relative capital-intensive good, because $OK_X/OL_X < OK_Y/OL_Y$. This intensity ranking remains both when the price of labour is lowered (as indicated by the price line PP_3) or raised (as indicated by the price line PP_1) relative to that of capital (the respective tangency points for these two cases of c and a for Good Y are consistently biased towards the capital axis, relative to the tangency points c' and a' for Good X).

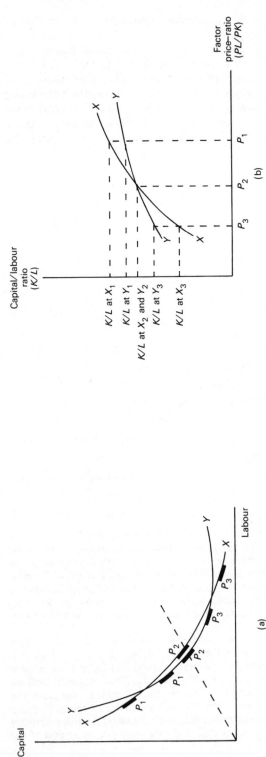

Figure 8: *Factor intensity reversal*

Goods are classified according to their relative factor input intensities. A one-to-one relationship is assumed between factor prices and factor intensity, such that the intensity bias of each good is assumed to remain what it is *irrespective of what factor prices are.* Factor intensity reversal arises when this is not the case, and the factor input intensity bias changes when factor prices change. This will occur when an iso-quant (equal product curve) for one good (X in diagram (a)) intersects twice with one of the other product (Y). It is evident that at different factor-price ratios (p_1, p_2, and p_3 are shown) the relative factor input intensity bias of the two products changes (each price ratio with the same number has an identical slope). At price ratio p_2 both goods use capital and labour in the *same* proportion; all price ratios to the left (p_1 is illustrated) indicate that good X is relatively more capital intensive than good Y (p_1 is tangential higher up the capital axis on X's isoproduct curve than on Y's curve); but all price ratios to the right of p_2 (p_3 is illustrated) indicate that good X becomes the labour intensive good (the point of tangency of p_3 is further along the X isoquant in relation to the labour axis than it is on Y's isoquant).

Diagram (b) illustrates these changes in relation to the changing capital/labour and factor/price ratios. On the vertical axis, the numbers of the capital/labour ratios obtaining for X and Y at the corresponding factor-price ratios p_1, p_2 and p_3.

existence or otherwise of factor-intensity reversals, although Hillman and Hirsch (1979: 280) nevertheless maintain that 'a substantial majority of the developing economies do exhibit factor-intensity reversals... in contrast to that of the developed countries'. The assumption that production functions are the same the world over has been severely criticised. Ignoring questions of technology transfer, even if knowledge were universal as the theory assumes, Samuelson (1948: 1982, 181) argues that

> effective knowledge is even more important than knowledge, and it unfortunately cannot be acquired by reading a book or by editorial exhortation... [and that it] is probably as important a variable in understanding economic history and geography as is specific factor endowment.

Furthermore, the production context outlined lacks the further reality that producers are often faced with a 'choice of techniques', either at given or different levels of output, which range from relative capital-intensive to relative labour-intensive methods, the resolution of which may differ in each country according to different inputs costs, etc., and not necessarily conform to a common method of appraisal. Ohlin (1977: 38) later recognised that five main categories of international technological differences could exist:

(a) Different factor combinations due to the differences in relative factor prices.
(b) The absence in some countries of certain factors – present in others – like managerial and technical labour of high quality ...
(c) The third type is due to the fact that certain technical knowledge may be available in some countries but not in others. Specialist knowledge about production methods may also be kept secret in one or several companies – or be monopolised through patent rights – and not available for others.
(d) The fourth type ... is dependent on social legislation or traditions about the hours of work, the availability of night work and extra hours of work, the number of labour shifts and the rate of additional pay for such 'extra work' ...
(e) A fifth cause is, of course, the utilisation of the economies of scale and specialisation which is affected by the size of the market ... it is easier to build up factories using a modern technique in countries which have very large domestic markets, than it is to do so in those with only a small domestic demand.

(iii) Constant returns to scale obtain in the production of both goods such that if inputs are increased by a given proportion, output will be increased by the same proportion.

The import of all these assumptions, and the new explanation for the basis of international exchange is that of relative differences in national factor endowments. The model is best described in a number of stages.

1 *Each country's production input capacities are displayed by means of an Edgeworth Box* (illustrated in Figure 9).
The dimensions of the box
The vertical and horizontal dimensions of the box indicate the precise amounts of each of the two production factors that are available, the two constituting the country's production resource base. Irrespective of their absolute size, the proportionate shape of the boxes must differ, so as to indicate different relative country distributions of resources if trade is to take place (equal advantage still precludes trade). The vertical or horizontal bias of the shape of an individual country's box will indicate the relative abundance of a particular factor.

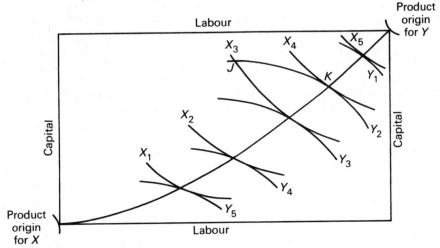

Figure 9: *The Edgeworth box of production*
The production of good *X* is displayed from the origin in the bottom left-hand corner, and that of good *Y* from the origin in the top right-hand corner. Only points on the contract curve of production are 'efficient'. For example, point *J* is inefficient, since a reallocation of capital and labour between the industries is possible, such as to reach point *K* where the same level of *Y* can be produced (Y_2), but with a higher level of output of good *X* (X_4 as opposed to X_3).

The contents of the box
Within the box, representing each economy's total fixed supplies of the two-figure inputs, two production maps are drawn, the production origin of one being in the bottom left-hand corner, with the other diagonally opposite in the top right-hand corner. The production map consist of isoquant (equal product) curves. Each curve depicts a series of combinations of the two factors of production that yield an identical level of output. A series of these curves can be drawn from each production origin, showing increasing levels of output that reaches a maximum in the diagonally opposite corner when all production inputs are exclusively committed to the product in question. Within the box, each product isoquant has a point of tangency with just one of the other product's isoquants. Such points are 'efficiency' points in terms of resource allocation, in that no alternative distribution of resources is possible which can increase the output of one good, without decreasing the output of the other good. When all such points are joined up, an exchange contract curve is formed that indicates a series of maximum output combinations that are possible from the available production inputs.

2 *Each country's production output capacities are displayed by means of a national production possibility curve, the shape of which, given the production functions, is intimately determined by the factor input supplies* (illustrated in Figure 10).
The input coefficients of production link the physical variables of the model, the outputs, to each country's factor endowment. As the assumption is made that production techniques are identical in each country, a

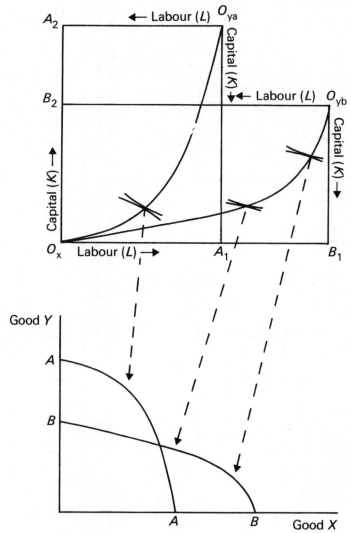

Figure 10: *The derivation of national production possibility curves from national Edgeworth Boxes of production.*
The box $O_xA_1O_{ya}A_2$ represents the total factor endowment of Country A, and the box $O_xB_1O_{yb}B_2$ that of Country B. Comparatively, Country A is shown to be relatively abundant in capital because $K_a/L_a < K_b/L_b$, and Country B to be relatively abundant in labour. Good X is shown to be the labour-intensive good and Good Y the capital-intensive good. The production of Good X is measured from the common origin shared by both countries, and that of Good Y from the two upper right-hand corners. Each position of tangency within each national production box along the respective contract curve provides a given combination of outputs of X and Y, which can be transferred down to the lower diagram to form a series of points that, when joined up, produce a production possibility curve for each country in the way indicated: *AA* for Country A, and *BB* for Country B.

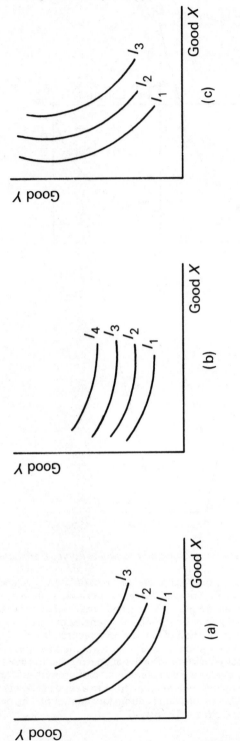

Figure 11: *Community indifference curves*
Demans is depicted in community indifference curves that yield equal levels of community satisfaction. The preference direction of these curves is outward from the origin. A general preference for one good over another will be indicated by a directional bias towards the preferred good's axis: in (b) it is towards the vertical (Y) axis; in (c), towards the horizontal (X) axis.

universal basis for this linkage is established for each of the two goods in the model. By reading off the amounts of each output along the efficiency *loci* of the contract curve previously mentioned, the maximum output combinations established thereon can be translated vertically to form each country's production possibility curve. The vertical or horizontal bias of the production possibility curve for each country will indicate its greater propensity to produce that good which uses intensively its own particular nationally abundant factor of production. The shape of this curve is concave, reflecting the law of increasing opportunity costs, i.e. that as the output of one commodity is expanded, successively larger quantities of the other commodity have to be sacrificed to obtain equal increments of the first commodity.

3 *National demand is displayed by means of community indifference curves* (illustrated in Figure 11).
To illustrate demand at the national level, *community indifference curves* are used that purport to show the preference map of a nation in terms of combinations of consumed levels of output of the two products that yield equal community satisfaction, assuming income distribution effects are of no consequence. The extent to which one product is generally preferred to another will determine whether the preference map is neutral with respect to the origins, or skewed towards the vertical (good *Y*) axis or the horizontal (good *X*) axis.

4 *Exchange equilibrium in the pre-trade situation* (illustrated in Figure 12).
The point of tangency of a community indifference curve with the

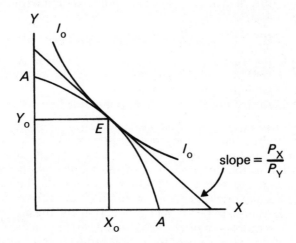

Figure 12: *Closed economy general equilibrium product-mix*
In each closed economy equilibrium obtains where the national production possibility curve (*AA*) is tangential to the highest community indifference curve (*I*$_0$). Equilibrium at *E* shows that *OX*$_0$ of product *X* and *OY*$_0$ of product *Y* will be produced.

production possibility curve establishes an equality in the marginal rates of substitution between national production and national consumption such that welfare is maximised given the national resources available. Through this optimum point a tangential price line can be drawn to indicate the relative prices of the two goods at this point. The point of tangency fulfils the general equilibrium condition that:

$$MRS = P_X/P_Y = MRT$$

where $MRS =$ the marginal rate of substitution of products in consumption (the slope of the community indifference curve);

$P_X/P_Y =$ the price ratio of the two products X and Y

and $MRT =$ the marginal rate of transformation of the products in production (the slope of the production possibility curve).

5 *Exchange equilibrium in the post-trade situation* (illustrated in Figure 12).

With the introduction of trade, a new product price ratio will eventually be established, the slope of which will be tangential to a higher community indifference curve. Thus in Country B the price line becomes more elastic (flatter) than in the pre-trade position, the price of Good X falls relative to Good Y; and in Country A the price line becomes more inelastic (steeper), the price of Good Y falls relative to Good X. Eventually, the common price line is established which is tangential to the production possibility curves of both countries. Given the common slope of the price line and tangency with an identical community indifference curve (for simplification, universal identity of tastes is assumed), an international trade equilibrium is achieved because:

$$MRT_B = MRT_B = P_{XB}/P_{YB} = P_{XI}/P_{YI} = P_{XA}/P_{XB} = MRS_A = MRT_A$$

where the terms used are as above, and the subscripts A and B refer to Countries A and B, and XI and YI refer to the international prices established for the two products X and Y.

The following three effects of trade may be noted:

(a) *welfare*: without any increase in resources or technological change a higher real income is enjoyed than previously.

(b) *production*: industrial specialisation takes place at the national level according to the domestic bias of the relative abundance of factor inputs and a surplus created which is exported. The exported good selected is the one that requires the intensive use of each country's relatively abundant factor in its production and the imported good the one that requires the intensive production use of its scarce factor. In each country, expansion of the export industry and contraction of the industry now partially replaced by imports change the previous (different) national price relations between the two goods until identical national price relationships obtain.

(c) *consumption*: home consumption of the exported product declines and that of the new imported commodity increases compared with the pre-trade consumption pattern. The latter gains more than compensate for the former losses.

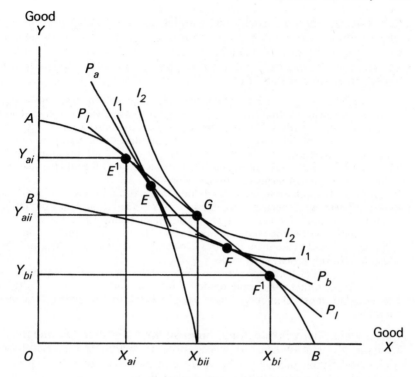

Figure 13: *International trade equilibrium*
In the pre-trade situation, Country A will be in equilibrium at E, producing OY_a of Y
and OX_a of X; and Country B will be in equilibrium at F, producing OY_b of Y and OX_b
of X, The pre-trade product price ratios for A are indicated by the line at P_a for
Country A, and at P_b for Country B. In international equilibrium, a common product
price ratio line is established P_lP_l that is tangential to each national production
possibility curve further along the axis of the good that embodies its particular
abundant factor of production: for Country A, the point of tangency E^1 is above E
(the pre-trade equilibrium) in relation to the Y good axis; for Country B, the point of
tangency F^1 is past F (its pre-trade equilibrium) in relation to the X good axis. Both
countries are better off because the international price line P_lP_l is tangential at G to
a higher community indifference curve I_2 than the one that obtained in their pre-
trade equilibria. Country A now produces OY_{ai} of Y, exporting $Y_{aii}Y_{ai}$ to Country B,
and produces OX_{ai} of X and imports $X_{bii}X_{ai}$ of X from Country B. Country B, on the
other hand, produces OX_{bi} of X, exporting $X_{bi}X_{aii}$ to Country A, and produces OY_{bi}
of Y, importing $Y_{bi}Y_{aii}$ from Country A. As one country's exports are another's
imports it follows that $Y_{ai}Y_{aii}$ equals $Y_{bi}Y_{aii}$; and that $X_{bii}X_{bi}$ equals $X_{ai}X_{bii}$.

The results described and illustrated only obtain if inter-country
differences in factor endowments are not offset by greater differences in
inter-country demand patterns (what Ford (1963: 462) calls 'demand-
counteracting' effects). With this proviso, countries will export goods that
embody their relatively abundant economic resources and import goods
that embody those economic resources that are, domestically, relatively
scarce.

The H-O theory thus provides a 'complete answer' to the question 'what is the minimum difference between countries which would be sufficient to explain the existence of trade?', namely, a difference in the relative endowment of factors between countries. Lancaster (1957: 20–1) also finds it satisfactory on another count:

> A second broad question to which the Heckscher-Ohlin model provides a satisfactory answer is that concerning the 'future of trade' (in the rather abstract sense). In other words, since the ordinary comparative costs approach relied on accidents to explain the difference which initiated trade, accidents such as differences in knowledge or skill, there was a reasonable presumption that international trade could ultimately cease to exist: Portugal could learn to make cloth as cheaply (in terms of wine) as England.
>
> In the H-O model it follows clearly that international trade would continue even if there were perfect transmission of knowledge and techniques and absolute freedom for the costless migration of factors. For the identity of techniques is part of the model in any case, and factor price equalization shows that there would be no incentive for factor endowments to become uniform, so resulting in the cessation of trade.
>
> The H-O model, therefore, deserves a place at the centre of international trade theory. It is, in fact, *the* simple model of international trade when things are reduced to most elemental terms (not necessarily the most elementary terms).

However, simplicity is one thing, simplisticity is another. Despite the fact that its analysis is superior to classical theory, which emphasised labour efficiency differentials as the basis for comparative advantage, it is still subject to at least three fundamental objections.

(i) It has nothing to say about antecedent development in the pre-trade economies. As R. Robinson (1956a: 173–4) has commented:

> Comparative advantage theory, to be of the slightest analytic value ... requires an explanation of when and how production functions come to differ. The problem is to stop the theory from degenerating into a surface explanation, capable of explaining anything *ex post* and nothing *ex ante*.

(ii) Its assumption set makes the basic theory 'exiguous in its reference to reality'. Ford (1963: 470–1) argues that

> (1) a large number of production functions are subject to a condition of increasing returns to scale; (2) production conditions are not everywhere identical; (3) factor-intensities can vary for each and every commodity; and (4) there are international differences in the quality of the productive agents, and conditions of factor ownership and taste.

As regards (4), labour is subdivisible into unskilled, skilled and technical (includes all administrative persons) labour, each of which may be of differing quality in each country. As the actual cost of producing any article depends not only on the prices of factor imports, but also on the efficiency of these imports, 'it could be possible for a country ... to be able to produce a commodity, which in the other country requires a large amount of its abundant and cheap factor, cheaper than the other country by virtue of the immensely superior quality of its factors. [This comes to the same thing as using production techniques.] Moreover, the quality of the goods or commodities to be traded may also vary ... [as] goods that can be classed under a general heading may be of the *same* type but of *different quality and design*' (Ford (1965: 19)). Although these arguments can be avoided by insisting, with respect to labour and product quality differences, that the former constitute different factors and the latter different products, such as refutation is not entirely satisfactory.

(iii) Whilst it provides an explanation for the basis of trade at a particular point in time, it abstracts from the socio-economic forces that will shape subsequent trade patterns, as trade and development interact. In this connection R. Robinson (1956a: 174) makes the point that: 'it is not enough to assert that factor growth analysis belongs in the department of economic development. Any comparative advantage theory, if intended or used to show what happens to a country confronted with trading opportunities, is development theory.' Linder (1961: 12) goes further than this, asserting that: 'this neglect of trade-induced changes in the quarter of factors of production has limited the scope of both its structural analysis and welfare conclusions'.

(iv) Both in terms of the reallocation process described and subsequent growth patterns the theory does not deal with the importance of capital. R. Robinson (1956a: 169) argues that: 'particularly where the factor "capital" is involved, its (H-O) account of the nature of comparative advantage and of international trade is seriously misleading' because (1956b: 348):

> A natural resource becomes a factor only after some measure of preliminary investment work has been done upon it. Investment is the prerequisite to creation of any factor supply. The circumstances under which the factor will be brought into existence, and under which it will or will not continue to be supplied, are governed by the character of this investment work . . .

and that (1956b: 350):

> if by 'capital' is meant a factor capable of furnishing input services of a particular type, it must be recognized that in any of its actual employments, capital is a specialized, *ad hoc* factor. The greater the accumulation of capital and industrial skills, the more complex the equipment used, the more specific capital goods are likely to become. The convenience of an assumption of capital homogeneity hardly justifies its use.

Thus not all capital hitherto employed in the now import-competing industry may be versatile enough to flow to and effect the expansion of the export industry.

Many of these pertinent criticisms are synthesised in Linder's celebrated *Essay on Trade and Transformation* (1961) previously mentioned in Chapter 1. Linder argues (1961: 41) that 'if a country lacks the capacity to respond to the challenge of trade, the effects of trading may not be advantageous'. For this reason, in practice there is likely to be unrealised potential between possible flows of trade and actual flows. Hence countries with superior abilities to reallocate factors of production may be able to overachieve their potential trade gains and accumulate them faster over time, whereas countries with inferior reallocative abilities will underachieve their potential benefits due to various 'factor inflexibilities' (Linder 1961: 12). Because there is no automatism in the realisation of gains from trade, the gains of the former countries are understated and the gains of the latter overstated. The running-down process of de-industrialisation in the home import-competing sector is not necessarily consonant with the building-up process in the expansionary home export sector irrespective of the economy, it may depend on the level of economic development of the economy and the degree of substitution between the particular two industries so changed. As Kindleberger points out (1956: 306–7):

> Good terms of trade come from luck and flexibility, or from capacity to enter new industries and to quit old and to withdraw resources from existing lines ... entry is made easier by a flow of capital formation, by a high level of intelligence in the working population, and by entrepreneurial energy. Innovational capacity makes possible entry into entirely new fields; imitational capacity is next best, and where available in abundance in other countries it limits the extent of the gain in terms of trade of the innovator. Exit is easy in balanced economies, or in those where specialization takes place in market-oriented goods. In highly specialized supply-oriented goods, lack of alternative occupations or the high overhead cost of shifting resources limits capacity for exit and lowers the floor under the terms of trade.

Thus the capacity for structural transformation is not the same in all countries. Moreover, as Kindleberger (ibid.) observes, 'underdeveloped countries may tend to have comparative advantages in land, but capital can substitute land in developed countries to limit the related comparative disadvantage'.

FACTOR PRICE EQUALISATION

The Stolper-Samuelson theorem declares that *trade will equalise the domestic reward a factor in one country earns and what the same foreign factor receives abroad* despite international factor immobility, in circumstances of free trade, identical production input-output coefficients, and the same commodity prices. The rationale for this lies in the fact that a rise in the relative price of a good raises the real reward of the primary factor used more intensively in its production, and lowers the real reward of the other primary factor. A convergence of factor prices takes place from their different pre-trade levels, until in equilibrium a universal factor-price level obtains. A full discussion of the rationale for factor-price equalisation involves knowledge of and reference to general equilibrium welfare economics. Here tradition has emphasized a social welfare criterion in terms of perfect competition and efficiency in production-mix between goods, efficiency in resource allocation between factor inputs and distribution efficiency between consumers. This whole area is not without controversy, as no social welfare criterion is value free. Thus the use of general equilibrium welfare analysis by trade theorists here involves an implicit bias, namely the economic systems depicted, (and 'countries' in these models are just such entities, not mere geographical clearing centres for international exchange) operating according to Pareto optimality behaviour, are assumed either to be desirable or, at the very least, the 'appropriate' basis on which to build trade models. In simple terms, this means that reallocation of economic activity is undesirable, if, by making some people better off, some are made worse off and remain uncompensated for their loss of economic welfare.

Equilibrium in the factor market

Within each now 'open' economy, factors of production are reallocated away from goods that require the intensive use of relatively scarce resources towards goods that require the intensive use of the relatively abundant resource, given that the national pre-trade domestic price ratios between the two factors of production are different i.e. either $PK_A/PL_A >$ PK_B/PL_B or $PK_A/PL_A < PK_B/PL_B$.

The equilibrium implication of the perfect competition assumption made in respect of the factor market is that, within each country, factor mobility ensures that returns to factors are equalised in all industries. Hence:

For Country A $MPL_{Xa} = MPL_{Ya}$ $MPK_{Xa} = MPK_{Ya}$
For Country B $MPL_{Xb} = MPL_{Yb}$ $MPK_{Xb} = MPK_{Xb}$

In each country, each factor is paid according to its marginal value product, i.e. its marginal physical product multiplied by the price of the good of which it is an input. Thus for Countries A and B, the returns to labour and capital must be equalised in Industries X and Y:

i.e. $MVPL_X = MVPL_Y$ $MVPK_X = MVPK_Y$

therefore if $MPPL_X.P_X = MPPL_Y.P_Y$ $MPPK_X.P_X = MPPK_Y.P_Y$

then
$$\frac{MPPL_X}{MPPL_X} = \frac{P_X}{P_Y} \qquad \frac{MPPK_X}{MPPK_Y} = \frac{P_X}{P_Y}$$

As it has already been established that P_Y/P_X has become equalised by trade, it follows that $MPPL_X/MPPL_Y$ and $MPPK_X/MPPK_Y$ must now be identical in both countries. Figure 14 establishes the points at which this obtains. International trade equilibrium on the output side is established at point E^1 for Country A and F^1 For Country B along those countries' production possibility curves. These combinations of Good X and Good Y can now be identified along each country's production contract curve. It has already been established above that, in equilibrium, labour and capital productivities must be equalised as between industries and countries:

i.e. that $MPPL_{Xa} = MPPL_{Ya} = MPPL_{Yb} = MPPL_{Xb}$
$MPPK_{Xa} = MPPK_{Ya} = MPPK_{Yb} = MPPK_{Xb}$

Given the assumption of constant return to scale, the marginal productivities of capital and labour will be constant along any ray from each origin to the contract curve, this being a property of linear, homogenous production functions. For $MPPL$ to equal $MPPK_{Xb}$ (and $MPPK_{Xa}$ to equal $MPPK_{Xb}$), given the common origin O_X, O_XE^2 and O_XF^2 must have the same slope, i.e. E^2 must be a point on the line O_XF^2. For $MPPL_{Ya}$ to equal $MPPL_{Yb}$ (and $MPPK_{Ya}$ to equal $MPPK_{Yb}$), given the different origins O_{ya} and O_{yb}, the rays $O_{ya}E^2$ and $O_{yb}F^2$ must have the same slope, i.e. be parallel. As the points E^2 and F^2 are by definition both on contract curves, the domestic marginal rates of substitution of each factor in the production of both commodities have been equalised, together with the ratios of the marginal products of the factors. Price lines may be drawn through the point of tangency at E^2 and F^2 having parallel slopes to indicate the complete equalisation of the factor-price ratios of the two

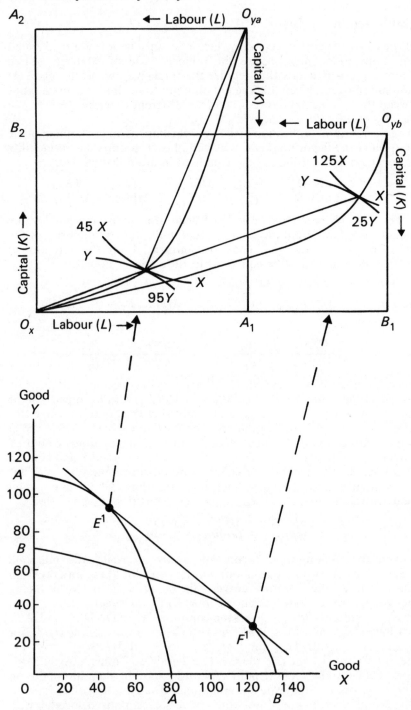

Figure 14: *Factor price equalization*

countries. Thus the post-trade adjusted pattern of national production structures determined by the product market equilibrium output levels is shown to have been brought about by a reallocation of factor inputs and to have resulted in changed factor-price ratios. In Country B, a higher capital-labour price ratio has been established than in the pre-trade equilibrium situation (to the left of F^2 along the contract curve towards O_X) because the slope $O_{yb}F^2$ is steeper – the $MPPC$ has fallen and the $MPPL$ has risen in accordance with the law of variable proportions, more of each input being allocated to Commodity X. In Country A, more of each input is allocated to the production of Commodity Y, as compared to the pre-trade equilibrium position (to the right of E^2 along the contract curve towards O_{Ya}); and the capital/labour price ratio has consequently fallen ($MPPK$ rises relative to labour), i.e. the slope $O_{Ya}E^2$ is not as steep as in the pre-trade situation.

Why factor-price equalisation is partial in the real world

Meade (1955: 348) suggests that there are six main reasons why the assumptions made in the Samuelson theorem are unlikely to be valid in the real world:

(a) *differences in atmosphere*: the physical climate and the social and intellectual atmosphere in which production takes place.
(b) *returns to scale*: where increasing returns are important, it would be only coincidental if the marginal productivity of factors were the same in each country. Here, only if international factor mobility is allowed will factor returns tend towards equality.
(c) *transport costs*: transport of goods is not costless and so these costs will provide a cost differential that will make full equalisation unlikely.
(d) *complete specialisation*: where comparative disadvantage attaches to a small industry, production resource reallocation in the post-trade situation may lead to the elimination of this industry, i.e. complete specialisation on the industry in comparative advantage, before marginal products are equalised between the two countries.
(e) *numbers of products and factors*: these have to be equal for equality in factor rewards.
(f) *factor substitution*: for some commodities considerable possibilities exist for the substitution of one factor for another, thereby making possible factor-intensity reversals.

To this list can be added factor-price rigidities brought about by behavioural, environmental and state-imposed constraints, technologies, differentials in incomplete domestic factor mobility, and non-economic objectives (see Magee (1973) and Chapter 4).

Apart from border obstacles in the form of tariff and non-tariff barriers, Ohlin (1977: 41) cites two other main extra expenditures in industry and trade. If there is an international disparity in the existence or amount of these rates, market prices will be a distortion of 'real' production costs. These are:

'domestic non-factor expenditures' and consist chiefly of internal taxes and social payments. In other cases social conditions, for example, social customs and legislation and pollution aspects, may create a need for factors which would not otherwise exist. This 'extra factor requirement' will raise costs of production and transportation ... These elements make commodity and factor prices differ from what they would otherwise be. Social legislation and labour market agreements may offset not only the demand for but also the supply of factors, such as through a reduction of the number of normal working hours.

Furthermore, he felt that 'differences in factor qualities make the meaning of the expression "international factor-price equalisations" vague'.

In addition to these considerations, two other causes of disparity between real and money costs may arise, as pointed out by Kindleberger and Despres (1952: 338):

> structural disequilibrium at the goods level and structural disequilibrium at the factor level. Disequilibrium at the goods level means that relative goods prices do not reflect the allocation of factors among various industries appropriate to existing factor prices. Disequilibrium at the factor level may arise either because a single factor receives different returns in different uses or because the price relationships among factors are out of line with factor availabilities.

The latter is often true with respect to developing 'dual' economies, where wage rates tend to be higher in the export sector than in the subsistence sector, where often underemployment means that the marginal product is zero. At the dynamic level two further points may be made concerning the operational applicability of this theory:

The relationship between factor costs and innovation patterns

Davidson (1979: 765–6) makes the logical point that

> if innovators are responsive to factor costs, innovative activity will be concentrated in precisely those industries which should be importing sectors according to H-O theory ... Innovative activity will therefore be concentrated in industries which intensively use a nation's relatively expensive factors of production ... and thus may eventually lead to exports and trade patterns that diverge from H-O expectations ... [this may apply both to] process innovations whose sole effect is to lower the cost of manufacturing for an already available product ... and to product innovation, the extreme response to unfavourable production circumstances.

An H-O theorist would no doubt try to get round this difficulty by reference to a 'human capital' factor additional to the factor set of the original theory.

International trade and foreign investment distortions

The relevance of and biases that international capital mobility might impose on trade patterns, particularly of an unequal kind, cannot be ignored. According to Kojima (1975: 12) international investment should be trade-oriented if continuous trade-induced 'up-grading structural adjustment on both sides, resulting in harmonious trade-reorganisation' is to occur. Clearly anti-trade oriented investment will limit the trade exchange potential between countries and therefore the extent of income change obtained by the abundant factors from trade. Kojima (ibid.) thus argues that:

> the most important criterion in undertaking foreign investment should be to take into consideration the present and potential pattern of comparative advantages between investing and host countries and to undertake foreign direct investment from the investing country's comparative disadvantage industry.

In the dynamic context, as Linder (1961: 43) points out, 'there will be a

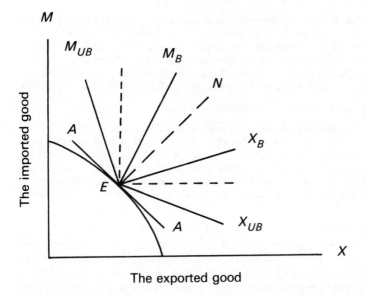

Figure 15: *The dynamic expansion path of the production possibility curve and its trade implications.*

"continued opening-up of trade" in the sense that international prices will be continually changing'. Specialisation implies interdependence which gives rise to vulnerability: because a country has adapted and in some degree shaped its industrial structure to meet the requirements of the export market, its development *ceteris paribus* is necessarily linked to demand and supply changes in that market. A failure to react to these changes will have implications for the balance of payments and growth prospects of the economy. To repeat a point already made, as the gains from trade do not result simply from a once-over change in resource allocation but continually merge with the gains from growth, it is the expansion path of the production possibility frontier, reflecting the growth of factor supplies and their implications for production capabilities that is of crucial significance for the dynamic benefits a country can derive from particular specialisation patterns. While directional changes in that trajectory may be anticipated or planned for as part of a development/trade strategy, this is not within the terms of reference of H-O theory. Some of the long-run possibilities are indicated by Figure 15, although within the constrained parameters of existing specialisation alternatives that omit the possibility of as yet unidentified new industries. From an existing pattern, given by the point of tangency of the international price line AA at E, the direction of production possibility change may be neutral (EN); import-biased M_B); export-biased (X_B); ultra-import-biased (M_{UB}); or ultra-export-biased (X_{UB}). The latter two possibilities involve situations where, in the case of ultra-export bias, imports decline absolutely; and, in the case of ultra-import bias, exports decline absolutely compared with the original position.

The above strictures notwithstanding, Krueger (1977: 2) makes the following point concerning the usefulness or otherwise of the conclusions of H-O theory:

On the one hand, they can be interpreted positively, as predictions about the actual pattern of production, in which case they would constitute a set of hypotheses about the observable production pattern. Alternatively, the factor-proportions model can be interpreted normatively, as predictions about the properties of an efficient production pattern that will provide society with the largest consumption bundle for any given inputs allocated to traded-good production.

In the former area, it has been recognised that:

where the theory is vulnerable is in the realism of its behavioural assumptions of perfect competition and perfect foresight. In an intertemporal context, these assumptions are even less plausible than in static models, but a successful critique of neoclassical theory requires the replacement of these assumptions with a satisfactory treatment of uncertainty, imperfect information and imperfect competition, and to develop such a treatment appears to be no easy task [M. Smith 1979: 248].

The theory remains an indealised description of how resources are allocated and incomes distributed in a competitive capitalist economy, and is not representative of a world where imperfect national market forces and trade at the governmental and transnational levels prevail, although it may have an evangelical purpose with respect to the corrective measures needed to be pursued by national governments and international institutions.

ATTEMPTS AT EMPIRICAL VERIFICATION

The first major attempt at testing the theory was that carried out by Leontief in 1953 (see De Marchi (1976). This study revealed a paradox, that in 1947 the United States imported capital-intensive goods and exported labour-intensive goods. A further study (1956) using 1951 data further

Table 34: *Domestic capital and labour requirements per million dollars of United States' exports and competitive import replacements*

US Production factors	Exports $	Competitive imports $	Ratio of imports to exports
1 1947 production structure and average composition of trade:			
Capital	2,550,780	3,091,339	
Labour	182	170	
Capital per man-year	14,010	18,180	1.30
2 1947 production structure and 1951 average composition of trade:			
Capital	2,256,800	2,303,400	
Labour	174	168	
Capital per man-year	12,977	13,726	1.06
3 1958 production structure and 1962 average composition of trade:			
Capital	1,876,000	2,132,000	
Labour	131	119	
Capital per man-year	14,200	18,000	1.27

Source: Leontief (1956: 392, 397); and Baldwin (1971: 134)

indicated that the United States' trade pattern was still that of a labour-rich country. A re-run of the test made by R. E. Baldwin (1971) again yielded similar results. Other paradoxes were revealed (see Bhagwati (1965) with respect to Japanese, Indian and Canadian trade patterns.

The main results with respect to United States' trade are shown in Table 34. These results indicated to some that 'the Emperor has no clothes', whereas others sought to find out or rationalize why the results might be misleading. Some seven main reasons were advanced in the latter respect (Caves and Jones (1973: 205):

1 The high effectiveness of American labour. Leontief found it three times more productive.
2 The possibility that the United States is a heavy consumer of capital-intensive goods.
3 The high skilled-labour requirements of American exports.
4 The importance of research and development for American exports.
5 The restriction of labour-intensive imports by American tariffs.
6 The influence of scarce natural resources on the capital-labour requirements of traded goods.
7 The possibility that factor-intensity reversals disrupt the test.

Loss of confidence in the theory made researchers turn to other explanations (discussed in the next chapter), each one of which can be seen as containing grains of truth which further qualify or refute neo-classical orthodoxy. Caves and Jones (1973: 204) conclude their review of H-O Theory in the following terms:

> How does it all come out? Is the Leontief paradox lost? when we add up the influence of labor skills, natural-resource scarcities, and United States tariffs excluding labor-intensive imports, they seem to reverse the conclusion that United States trade is *dominated* by the export of the produce of abundant labor and the import of goods that require large quantities of scarce capital. Furthermore, it seems possible to explain away the paradoxical findings for other countries in the same fashion. But in restoring the toppled Heckscher-Ohlin theorem to its throne, we have robbed it of much of its empirical simplicity: two factors of production are not enough, and the absence of factor-intensity reversals between countries cannot be assumed. Perhaps the empirical predictions of the Ricardian model, less rich but less complex, should not be thrust aside lightly.

ENVOI

Clearly the greater explanatory ambitions of the Heckscher-Ohlin model commanded its attention as the centrepiece of trade thought in the period 1919–1954. The integration of factor markets and goods markets created the first general equilibrium attempt to combine what Robinson (1956: 109) calls 'the array of forces which explain export-import patterns under free trade conditions'. As a theory, however, it remained in the classical tradition of ignoring the importance of antecedant development differentials, the adjustment process and country differences in reallocative abilities, etc. Nevertheless, it attracted support for it was clearly a considerable achievement, despite its tendency towards a continued supply bias in the explanation given for comparative cost differentials, emphasising, as it did, the link between the factor content of trade and the commodity compositon of trade. However, explanatory power can only be related to proven verification. Sufficient doubt persisted after the 'Leontief Paradox' about the relevance of H-O theory to inspire a series of quite new approaches. Some of these avoided the traditional omniscient general theory approach to explain particular exchange phenomena. Others were a direct response to the disparities within the international trading system that had been exposed after 1945 and to a realisation (Todarro (1981: 349)) that:

> relative factor endowments and comparative costs . . . are often determined by, rather than determining, the nature and character of international specialization. In the context of unequal trade between rich and poor nations, this means that *any intial state of unequal resource endowments will tend to be reinforced and exacerbated by the very trade which these differing resource endowments were supposed to justify.* Specifically, if rich nations as a result of historical forces are relatively well endowed with the vital resources of capital, entrepreneurial ability, and skilled labor, their continued specialization in products and processes that intensively utilize these resources will create the necessary conditions for their further growth. On the other hand, Third World countries, endowed with abundant supplies of unskilled labor, by specializing in products that intensively utilize unskilled labor, and whose world demand prospects and terms of trade may be very unfavorable, often find themselves locked into a stagnant situation that perpetuates their 'comparative advantage' in unskilled productive activities. This in turn will inhibit the domestic growth of needed capital, entrepreneurship, and technical skills.
>
> A cumulative process is therefore set in motion in which trade exacerbates already unequal trading relationships, distributes the benefits largely to those who already 'have', and perpetuates . . . resource underdevelopment.

It would seem from all the above-mentioned considerations, that Johnson's summary statement (1975: 34) given below accurately reflects the theory's precise but limited usefulness:

> the Heckscher-Ohlin model should probably be thought of, not as explaining actual trade, but as instead asking how far the existence of nation-states would matter to the welfare of citizens of different nations, *if* everyone had equal access to the same world pool of technological knowledge and if countries, though they discriminated against persons of foreign nationalities, did not discriminate against the products produced by foreigners through tariffs, quotas and other departures from free international trade.

7 Post-Leontief orthodox trade explanations and models

What is a 'best theory' of trade? All theories of trade add to our understanding and the best theory is necessarily a composite.

Leamer (1974: 350–1)

The picture which emerges is that of a mosaic of interrelated, overlapping and occasionally conflicting theories and models, each applicable to certain situations. This is a far cry from the imposing unified structure ... developed by neoclassical writers.

Haberler (1977: 10)

Intellectual progress is defined as the gradual loss of certainty, as the slow mapping out of the extent of our ignorance, which was previously hidden by an initial certainty parading as paradigm.

Hirschman (1977: 67)

Technological levels, and differences in them, and changes in the differences, can no longer be taken as exogenous and exogenously changeable, from the viewpoint of international trade theory, in the same way as differences in comparative labour costs were taken in the Ricardian theory of comparative cost, and subsequently differences in national endowments of factors in the Heckscher-Ohlin-Samuelson model of international trade.

Johnson (1967: 322)

The main aim is to add to rather than replace the range of explanations available.

Posner (1961: 323)

The Leontief Paradox proved a watershed in international trade theorising. The apparent malfunctioning of the Heckscher-Ohlin theory caused theorists to be less reverential and inhibited. It was realised that (Clemhout (1964: 13)): 'the admission of cross-country differences in production functions must be supplemented by information about the manner in which differences manifest themselves.' This resulted in much innovative activity and a plethora of more empirically directed propositions concerning the impetus behind particular trade flows and patterns. In general, emphasis was not put on the importance of particular factors that the H-O model had abstracted from in its 'factor abundance' explanation of trade patterns, such as aspects of 'modern' industrial competition (monopolistic competition, scale economies, product differentiation and product cycles); the influence of government intervention in production and trade; and trade aspects of less-developed countries. In addition, newly identified international exchange phenomena such as intra-industry trade and transnational economic production required explanation; and, in the circumstances of world recession in the 1970s, a practical need occurred at the national level to monitor changes in international 'competitiveness'. While the latter elements are given separate consideration in Part III, this chapter will concentrate on an outline examination of theories pertaining to the first-mentioned areas of analysis including, in sequence of consideration, Kravis's availability thesis; Linder's demand theory; neo-technology and product cycle explanations; neo-factor proportions explanations; and balance-of-payments trade models.

THE KRAVIS 'AVAILABILITY' THESIS

Kravis (1956: 133) advanced the idea that a substantial part of international trade was 'an exchange between goods available in one or a few nations but not in others'. With respect to 'availability', he referred to two main types of goods: goods 'not available' in the absolute sense; and goods where for reasons of high domestic inelasticity of supply (1956: 143), 'an increase in output can be achieved only at a high cost'. The former type of exchange involves situations where there is a 'lack of natural resources (relative to the demand)', which he considers to be adequately covered by conventional comparative advantage models; the latter type of exchange involves three principal elements – natural resources; technological progress; and new products and product differentiation.

As regards natural resources, he argues that one reason for the high capital content of American imports is that they are:

> products of natural resources that have become relatively scarce in the US and which American capital has therefore developed abroad... Foreign production of these materials can be profitably expanded at existing market prices, while domestic production cannot be increased, or perhaps even maintained, without large price increases. In short, it is the elasticity of supply abroad and its inelasticity at home that give rise to this trade, not the relative capital or labor requirements of the products. [Kravis 1956: 148, 150.]

With respect to technological progress, availability is paramount because of the stimulus to exports which it provides, this being (1956: 151) 'not confined to cost reduction but also ... the advantages that flow from the possession of the newest products and of the most recent improvements on all kinds of goods'. Benefits materialise from this because Duesenberry's 'demonstration effect' 'may be expected to create an almost instantaneous demand abroad for new products that are popular in the United States'. Thus, a country's export industries are likely to embody higher rates of technical progress than the same industries in its trading-partner countries.

As regards product differentiation, Kravis (1956: 153) refers to 'availability' advantages that are derived from national prestige production differentiation, such as 'English woollens ... German cameras, Belgian lace, Italian silks, and Swedish furniture'.

However, Majumdar (1979: 566–7) later made the following points with respect to a case-study of electronic calculator trade and the relative positions of the United States and Japan (1967–76):

> The 'availability factor' provides an advantage of being first in the market. But a country cannot enjoy this advantage permanently, because cases of absolute 'availability advantage' are few, and also the technology underlying the product

gets transferred abroad through one channel or the other. . . The 'availability advantage' can be absolute or relative. . . In the case of absolute 'availability advantage', the new product cannot be produced elsewhere at all because of the existence of a 'technology gap'. In the relative sense, it means that only a distant or crude substitute can be produced by foreigners. . . As a result, the 'cost factor' comes into the picture . . . the 'cost advantage' refers to the advantage a country may enjoy in the cost of production of the product because of an underlying relative factor supply advantage. . . These two advantages need not accompany each other; a country with the 'availability advantage' may or may not enjoy the 'cost advantage'. If it does not, the 'cost advantage' counteracts the 'availability advantage', and the competitive advantage is determined by the interaction of the two.

A further reason put forward by Kravis (1956: 155) to support his availability explanation of trade flows is that in the real world free trade is abused, as government controls and cartels tend 'to shut out imports that could be produced at home even at a slightly higher cost', with the result that imports may be confined to goods 'unavailable at home or available only at formidable costs'. Consequently, he feels [ibid.] that the quantitative importance of this factor is likely to be considerable in the case of:

the half of world trade that consists of trade between the industrial areas, on the one hand, and primary producing areas, on the other hand. For the other half, which consists of exchanges among primary countries or among industrial countries, further research is required to determine the relative roles of natural endowment, technological progress, product differentiation, and capital-labor ratios in determining international trade flows.

LINDER'S 'DEMAND' THEORY OF TRADE IN MANUFACTURES (1961)

Linder accepts H-O as an explanation of trade in primary products, but rejects it with respect to all other forms of trade, where his basic contention (1961: 87) is that the *'range of exportable products is determined by internal demand. It is a necessary, but not a sufficient, condition that a product be consumed (or invested) in the home country for this product to be a potential export product.'*

Three main reasons are put forward as to why prior 'support of the home market' is deemed so crucial:

(1) It is unlikely that an entrepreneur will ever think of satisfying a need that does not exist at home . . . In a world of imperfect knowledge, entrepreneurs will react to profit opportunities *of which they are aware.* These . . . tend to arise from *domestic* needs.
(2) to the extent that production of a good is based on invention . . . exploitation of the invention will . . . in its first phase, automatically be geared to the home market.
(3) An entrepreneur could not cater for a demand that did not exist at home 'without prohibitive costs being incurred' [Linder 1961: 88, 90.]

Linder's argument is that as:

It is self-evident that *internal demand determines which products may be imported. . . the range of potential exports is identical to, or included in, the range of potential imports . . . The more similar the demand structure of two countries, the more* intensively, potentially, [will be] the trade between [them] ... as a country grows and its per capita income increases, the demand structure of that country will change. As a consequence, the range of potential – and thus also actual – exports will change. This will introduce an element of gradual change in the pattern of specialisation [1961: 94].

In general, he suggests that apart from the constraining and distorting power of 'trade-braking' forces (1961: 197) (distance, transport costs and man-made obstacles), the volume of trade will be greater the larger and similar the per capita income of the trading countries, and the greater the overlap in the commodity composition of the potential export range of any pair or group of countries. Thus 'relative factor proportions, to the extent they influence relative commodity price structures at all, need not be reckoned with in respect to goods outside the overlapping demands (1961: 104). He concedes (1961: 106, 105) that the patterns of trade that this approach would suggest 'are (a) to some extent accidental, (b) not particularly unstable, and (c) gradually changing over time'. However, he does not 'pretend to have a general explanation of the exact pattern of comparative advantages'.

While the rationale provided is not without its weaknesses it does provide an *a priori* reason as to why, in the post-1950 period, horizontal trade between advanced countries grew much faster than that between less-developed countries or the vertical trade between the former and the latter. Leamer (1974: 354) finds that:

> although the theory implies that trade intensity will be related to demand similarity ... it seems to offer no suggestion as to *which* goods will flow in which direction. It is in that sense a non theory, asserting that the commodity composition of trade is effectively a random variable.

However, Johnson (1964: 89) in his review of Linder's book, observed that when the theory was tested:

> in only half of the cases was the computed relationship significant [between the average propensities of other countries to import from a given country on the per capita income differences between them] and only in the case of Western Germany does it account for a substantial proportion [42 per cent] of the variance. Since many of the countries enjoying average incomes comparable to Germany's are also her close neighbours, proximity rather than income similarity may be the true explanation of this result [and some of the others]. It therefore appears that Linder's hypothesis does not possess much explanatory value.

Subsequent empirical tests of the model were conducted by Hufbauer (1970), Fortune (1971; 1979), Sailors *et al* (1973), Hirsch and Lev (1973), Asai and Yorozo (1975) and Hirsch (1977). While some were inconclusive (Hufbauer (1970), Hirsch (1977), Arad and Hirsch (1981)), the remaining studies tended to support Linder's thesis. Linder's theory will be returned to when intra-industry trade is considered in Chapter 9.

Many writers saw the main task of theorists as that of either trying to integrate the technology variable and the comparative advantage concept or devising a technology-based theory of international trade/theory of technology transfer: hence the emergence of neo-technological explanations and neo-factor proportions explanations of comparative advantage. What both sets recognised was that:

technological levels, and differences in them, and changes in the differences, can no longer be taken as exogenous and exogenously changeable, from the viewpoint of international trade theory, in the same way as differences in comparative labour costs were taken in the Ricardian theory of comparative cost, and subsequently differences in national endowments of factors in the Heckscher-Ohlin-Samuelson model of international trade. [Johnson 1977a: 322.]

NEO-TECHNOLOGY AND PRODUCT CYCLE EXPLANATIONS

Posner (1961: 324) argues that

in so far as the process of growth implies continuous technical progress, the effect of economic growth is to develop a cause of trade *sui generis* ... even if new products are not developed, new processes may be, and such new methods will give the country concerned a comparative advantage in some goods.

As these changes do not occur simultaneously in all countries, transient advantages will occur in technically avant garde countries that *per se* are a cause of trade. Both the ability to produce superior products and the possession of superior production technology constitute sources of comparative advantage in trade additional or alternative to that based on relative factor abundance (Johnson (1975b: 35). As a consequence of its proprietorial nature and constrained ubiquity, the market for technology is a highly imperfect one in which information is limited, and monopoly and oligopoly, while sometimes mitigated by intertechnology substitution, is usual. Possession of such information resulting from the pattern of specialised investment selected will undoubtedly confer competitive advantages that through a patent system will be protected, and when selectively relaxed through a licence system may further maximise universal profit possibilities (see Vayrynen (1978).

The standard H-O model leaves largely unanalysed both the possibility that differences in real (absolute) factor prices resulting from technological differences would promote the diffusion of technology among countries, with consequent changes in comparative advantage and trade patterns; and the possibility that the same influences would promote the international migration of factors of production, with effects on the distribution of factors of production and of economic activity among countries and/or among geographical regions ('brain-drains' etc.) (Johnson (1977a: 314). Moreover, such knowledge tends to be privately appropriated and available, if at all, on a conditional basis rather than as a public good. Thus, international profit engineering may result in a 'vicious circle of self-perpetuating dependent technology which, if unconstrained by corrective action, can result in the adoption of 'inappropriate' technology and/or 'inappropriate' products in LDCs.

Ewing (1977: 2–3) asserts that technological dependence is self-perpetuating because:

Whether via direct foreign investment, licensing agreements (disembodied technology), imports of machinery or intermediate goods (embodied technology), the technology goes on being imported and little or nothing is done to generate indigenous technology. In the consumption goods field there is constant product innovation associated with mass advertising and highly skilled marketing; once the train is caught it is impossible to get off.

As for 'inappropriate technology' Helleiner (1976: 306) argues that:

> The vast bulk of technology supplied to the developing countries was not designed with their particular problems in mind ... inappropriateness may be not merely a cause for regret as to the absence of alternatives, but the cause of absolute damage. Distortions in local factor and product prices frequently can render imported technologies privately profitable even though they are socially undesirable. Governments can also be induced by 'marketing' efforts of private firms and aid donors to adopt inefficient or socially undesirable technologies. There can therefore be no presumption of benign national economic effects from technology importing.
>
> The most frequently discussed aspect of inappropriate imported production technology [and by no means all new technologies are inappropriate] is its capital-intensity in circumstances of severe unemployment of underemployment of labor. It is by now agreed that capital-intensity is not undesirable *per se* in any particular activity; in many instances, it is socially efficient. But, in the developing countries' employment circumstances, there is by now virtually agreement that labor-intensive technologies should be employed in those instances where there is a potential choice of technique without sacrifice of efficiency.

Lastly, from a political economy standpoint, the very nature of the imported technology and its supposed beneficiality to particular cultures, societies and types of economic system may need to be questioned, for:

> While 'technological progress' is a necessary condition for economic 'development', because it enables a more 'productive' use of factors and production and ... does increase productivity, and thereby provides better standards of living, this should not be taken at its face value: it is imperative to go behind conventional measures to see *who* benefits, *what* the products actually are, and whether the resultant *structure* of society is in fact conducive to its well-being. [Lall 1976: 24.]

Such national considerations are important in the twentieth century, given that technological conditions permit a potential footloose pattern of production that is not tied to national centres and that can exploit them for temporary gain without regard to the long-term country-specific consequences. As Johnson (1975: 6) has commented:

> technology, unlike the natural climatic conditions of the Ricardo model, can be both moved from one location to another and accumulated or decumulated; and, unlike the material capital of the specified Heckscher-Ohlin-Samuelson model, it can be accumulated fairly rapidly on a massive scale, though [an important point] it cannot be quickly decumulated or transformed from one specific form into another.
>
> To be more precise, the application of known technology to the development of production in new locations, particularly low labour-cost locations can be carried out fairly quickly. This is partly because co-operant requirements of material capital equipment are not all that expensive and are obtainable through international trade in machinery and components on level terms with rival producers, while structures are largely a matter of domestic labour cost; partly because financial capital is fairly mobile internationally, particularly but by no means exclusively as a result of the development of multinational or transnational corporation; and most fundamentally because technology by its nature is capable of being taught to and learned by large numbers of young

adult human beings, in training programmes of specialized types whose cost varies largely with the general level of wages and incomes in the society.

Theoretical discussion of this area consists largely in the presentation of stylised facts and frameworks within which to appreciate what might be happening in the real world, which have come to be referred to as neo-technology hypotheses or 'technological-gap' accounts. The analysis of technological superiority as a source of trade, first put forward by Posner (1961), was followed up by Hufbauer (1965; and 1970) and became entangled with economies-of-scale factors, concomitant with related theories of product-cycle by Vernon (1966), Hirsch (1967: 1974), Magee (1977a; 1977b), and others. Posner's theory was *a priori* in form and needed elaboration, which Hufbauer (1970) later provided. Hufbauer conceptualized a distinction between 'technological gap' trade as the aboriginal source and 'low-wage' trade, which later developed with the gradual international transfer by export or imitation of the new produce/process to countries where they can be applied more cheaply than in their country of origin. However, no explanation was attempted as to why such innovations occur in some countries rather than in others, and the explanation ignored other possible reasons for the diffusion of production from technically advanced to less-developed countries, such as the availability of relatively low capital costs or the need to have access to a large protected market. The gap was partially filled by product-cycle and economies-of-scale models.

Vernon (1961) suggested a three-stage cycle: the new product, the maturing product and the standardised product. He generally supports Linder's view that new products will tend to be produced first within the national economy for which it was designed *inter alia* due to close contact with consumers, and suppliers of inputs, barriers to international trade. He posits an inter-country transfer of specialisation, such that production occurs in the first stage in a developed country and is subsequently transferred to a less-developed country at the third stage. Stage one is centred on a developed country for the reasons already stated and because, on the demand side, high unit labour costs are an incentive for labour-saving investment goods and high incomes involve sophisticated and differentiated consumer products; and on the supply side, the research and development costs of new products is high, and developed countries have a relatively large endowment of the skilled labour required (scientists, engineers, etc.). Stage II gives rise to a transfer to other DCs as the process becomes more standardised. The standardised product in Stage III is ideal for DCs since assembly line production requires fairly unskilled labour.

Vernon was chiefly concerned with American trade. He saw technological transfer as being largely directed to low-wage economies during the 'maturation' period of the innovated product 'as actual or potential competition increased the elasticity of demand facing the producer and makes low cost production costs increasingly important, and as the routinisation of production technique reduces the necessity of close contact with specialist suppliers and consultants' (Johnson 1975b: 38). Thus new and complex products tend to be produced and exported by countries with high per capita incomes because their effectively large domestic markets are more important and certain than potentially cheaper and initially uncertain markets abroad. Moreover, large markets tend to support industries where economies of scale are important. According to Drèze's 'hypothesis of standardization' (1960) moreover, large countries, because of economies of scale, will tend to have a comparative advantage in the export of nationally differentiated products; and small countries, a comparative advantage in the export of 'old', now internationally standardised goods such as intermediate inputs and final consumer goods. This is because the market for internationally standardised products is world-wide, so that here small countries are on the same footing as large ones, whereas only large countries are able to efficiently produce goods having national characteristics that differentiate them from foreign products. In the latter case domestic demand is a pre-requisite for developing an export industry. Thus scale economies are more likely to be of a dominant importance when a product is new and global demand undeveloped, as in the early phase of a product-cycle.

Separate theories of economies of scale were produced by Krugman (1979; 1980) Ethier (1979) and Helpman (1981). As regards product-cycle models, evolutionary explanation scenarios were created in an *a priori* fashion, some being based on a country-by-country analysis (see Hirsch 1967), others being geared more to the process of international technology transfer.

At the country level, recognition is given to the fact that (Rapp 1975: 24) 'the pattern of exports, and industrial production at a particular time is the result of the aggregation of the individual product cycles with each product having its own timing and relative importance according to a country's income levels and factor supplies'. Two types of product-cycle may be distinguished: intra-industry cycles of new products within existing industries, for example cotton to wool to synthetic textiles; and inter-industry cycles of development of new industries, such as textiles to steel to ship-building to autos to computers. Hirsch (1967) was one of the first to develop a three-phased 'probabilistic' H-O oriented trade model in which market sales behave as illustrated in Figure 16: low in the initial 'New' phase, rising sharply during the 'Growth' phase, and flattening out in the 'Mature' phase. Hirsch describes the process of industrialisation of developing ('L') countries [ibid: 16–17]

> as a process of gradually extending the range of local production capabilities by establishing industries which are less mature than those already in existence. As technical experience and management skills are acquired and digested, the establishment of newer industries becomes economically feasible. Graphically, the process may be described as the extension of the range of industrial activities leftwards along the product-cycle curve . . .

His model postulates that as newer industries are established that their factor input intensities as well as their technical and market characteristics will vary in a systematic fashion [ibid. 39-41]:

> The 'L' countries . . . tend . . . to have a comparative advantage in mature products, since, when compared to growth or new products, mature products tend to contain a higher proportion of inputs which are abundant in the 'L' countries, and a lower proportion of scarce inputs. . . Since it is not the rate of input utilization but rather the level of the different inputs weighted by their relative cost which determines comparative production costs, the 'L' countries cannot be regarded as having a comparative advanage in *all* mature products . . .

[Figure 16] shows output of the 'D' countries and the 'A' countries to be normally distributed, whereas the distribution of the 'L' countries is shown to be skewed to emphasise the concentration of these countries on the most mature industries . . .

By focusing on changes in input utilisation rather than on input levels, the model emphasises the dynamic aspects of comparative advantage. It indicates that comparative advantage enjoyed by a particular type of economy, at a given point in time, is liable to disappear as the product in question enters a more mature phase of the cycle. On the other hand, countries which have a disadvantage in certain products, because of their high content of scarce inputs, may find, as the products become more mature, that they are capable of producing them on a competitive basis.

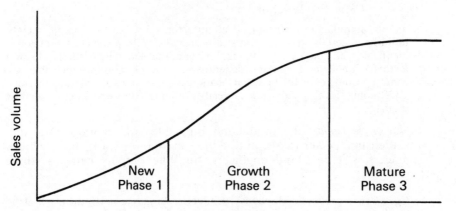

Figure 16: *The product-cycle curve, and the characteristics of its phases*

Characteristics	Cycle Phase		
	Early	*Growth*	*Mature*
Technology	short runs rapidly changing techniques dependence of external economies	mass production methods gradually introduced variations in techniques still frequent	long runs and stable process few innovations of importance
Capital intensity	low	high, due to high obsolescence rate	high, due to large quantity of specialized equipment
Industry structure	entry is know-how determined numerous firms	growing number of firms many casualties and mergers growing integration	market position and financial resources affect entry number of firms declining
Critical human inputs	scientific and engineering	management	unskilled and semi-skilled labour
Demand structure	sellers' market performance and price of substitute determine buyers' expectations	individual producers face growing price-elasticity competition reducing prices product information spreading	buyers' market information easily available

Source: Hirsch (1967)

Hirsch later took the view that (1974a: 65–6) although 'actual trade flows cannot be explained in terms of a simple all-embracing model . . . it is possible to divide the universe of traded goods into a reasonably small number of categories to which existing trade models apply', distinguishing three types of goods within a country's trade structure:

Ricardo Goods: defined as 'minerals, agricultural products and manufactured goods containing a high proportion of domestically available natural resources . . . [when] comparative advantage is largely determined by the natural endowment [includes land and climate] of countries'.

Heckscher-Ohlin Goods defined as:

> mainly manufactures but not all manufactures . . . [and including] metals, building materials, and even transistors . . . [where] the production function is identical in all countries; . . . the real marginal productivity of the production factors – labour and capital – depends only on the ratio in which they are combined and not on their natural location; . . . economies of scale [are absent]; . . . technology is fairly stable and . . . easily available to those wishing to enter the industry

Product-cycle Goods: the production inputs for which are capital (C), unskilled manpower (UM), and skilled manpower (SM) that includes managers, scientists and engineers, and the outputs being of three types:

> *N goods* (new product-cycle goods): 'products . . . largely to satisfy the needs of the markets where the manufacturer resides . . . where design is . . . dependent on specific rather than universal specifications and needs . . . and the production function varies from country to country. Local supplies of SM are essential here.'
> *K-M goods* (capital-intensive mature product-cycle goods).
> *L-M goods* (labour-intensive mature product-cycle goods).

From this, Hirsch (1974a: 70) deduces two main propositions about country trade content:

(a) that developing country exports will be characterised by a high proportion of Ricardo goods and L-M goods. The share of K-M goods and N goods will be small in comparison with that of industrial countries; and,

(b) that industrial country exports will contain a high proportion of N goods and of K-M goods. The proportion of Ricardo goods and L-M goods will be relatively low when compared to the developing countries' exports.

While such structural disaggregation of tradeable goods does not provide a theory that explains total trade flows, including inter-group product exchanges, it is indicative of what might be an appropriate bias for LDC trade strategy because such countries lack supplies of SM goods, the cost of technology transfer is high, and effective demand is locally small. Apart from Ricardo goods 'their advantage lies in LM goods, their capacity for which as industrialization proceeds, will increase'. This (1974a: 79) suggests that the list of goods which developing countries can expect to manufacture on a competitive basis is constantly expanding, and that substantial gains can accrue to countries successful in developing mechanisms which facilitate early identification of suitable new candidates about to pass through the early phases of the cycle.

Magee's 'appropriability' theory (1977a; 1977b) provides a framework with which to interpret discussions of the multinational corporation, direct investment and technology transfer. It is built round one industry technology cycle. Given Nelson's evidence (1970) that patents for a given industry tend to arise in S-curve formation over long periods of time – a major breakthrough in one product causes an initial steep rise due to new component and complementary product activity that eventually declines – he develops his own cycle and view of technology transfer with respect to multinational firms. His industry technology cycle is again three-staged: invention, innovation and standardisation, each described in some detail. He believes that (1977a: 319) 'four traditional types of information are created by private markets in the generation of new products: information required for (1) discovery of new products, (2) development of the products, (3) development of their production function and (4) creation of their markets'. However, each of these is affected by an important fifth type of information: '(5) knowledge of the degree to which creators of information can appropriate to themselves the returns on the new information'.

Multinational firms are thus seen as 'international traders in information' (1977a: 334). He rejects the phrase 'technology gap' as 'a misunderstood catchword equivalent to . . . any situation in which a country is a net importer of a product' and regards 'technology transfer as 'international trade in information' (1977a: 332). With regard to this trade, Magee argues that:

> There are three ways that new products and new ideas can spread from the country developing and discovering them to the rest of the world. Exporting could occur; or, the firm developing the product could produce and market in the host country itself; or it can license the rights to production to a firm in the host country. [Magee 1977b: 306.]

He argues that firms will prefer intra-firm world-wide dissemination for five main reasons which, in his view, explain:

> why new technologies are correlated with concentrated industry structures and why international trade in technology occurs within large MNCs rather than through licensing agreements and why older industries are more competitive and less innovative . . .
>
> Appropriability is the *first* reason why firms which develop new products become large. Innovating firms expand to internalize the externality which new information creates, namely the public goods aspect of new information. *Second*, there is a tendency for new products to be experience goods and for standardized products to be search goods. Optimum firm size is usually larger for domestic retailers of nonbrand name experience goods. By analogy subsidiaries of multinational corportions are more likely than licensing arrangements. *Third*, sales of many high technology products must be accompanied by sales of service information. The firm's optimum size is expanded because of service subsidiaries . . . *Fourth* [because] of product complementarities within . . . and among [each type of information]. *Fifth*, for

new and differentiated products, the spread between the buyer and seller valuation of new information is higher than when the products are older and more standardised [Magee 1977b: 307.]

Thus multinational firms succeed in technology transfer (1977a: 334–5) 'either because they expand to internalize the externality created by the public goods aspect of new information or because they have been in industries with high concentration initially'.

NEO-FACTOR PROPORTIONS EXPLANATIONS

The above neo-technological theories differ from neo-factor proportion theories in that there is some formal introduction (albeit operational) of a time element. Neo-factor theories ignore the costs of developing and adopting different technologies and any potential systematic pattern of inter-country transfer, and aim to relax H-O's limiting costless and universally identical technology assumptions by incorporating an 'intellectual' capital element into an extended definition of capital. Johnson (1970: 14) defines this as 'the capitalist value of productive knowledge created by research and development'. This enables the structure and methodology of the familar neo-classical model to be reatined. The main proponents of this approach include Keesing (1965; 1966; and 1971), Lary (1968), Hufbauer (1970), Kojima (1970) and Lowinger (1971), who found it an appropriate approach to explain trade between developing and developed countries. Keesing (1965: 280) identified five skilled labour classes in his original article:

I   profesional technical and managerial
II   craftsmen and foremen (skilled manual workers)
III clerical, sales and service
IV   operatives (semi-skilled)
V   labourers (unskilled)

Arguing that only the first two classes are particularly difficult to acquire, whether for an individual or a nation, he uses a combined 'skill ratio' of Classes I and II divided by Classes IV and V as a determinant of international patterns of industrial location and trade, thus giving a relative skill endowment ratio for countries. He later argued (1966: 253) that such skill differences may be caused by:

(1) the lingering influence of historical differences in skill supplies, propagated down to the present moment by a need for skilled workers to train skilled workers; (2) cultural (or conceivably, physical) differences leading to contrasts in desire and aptitude for skill-acquisition; (3) unequal incomes, perhaps relating to the skill situation, combined with a functional relationship between income and education and also between material equipment and the learning process; (4) selective migration; and (5) an arbitrary division of labor that is sustained by trade.

Tests by R. E. Baldwin (1971), Branson and Junz (1972), Morall (1972) and Goodman and Ceyhun (1976) mostly of American trade, found that the neo-technology variables such as R and D expenditure, the number of engineers and scientists, economies of scale and product cycles to be more significant. This was confirmed by Hirsch (1974b). On the other hand,

Balassa (1979) and Heller (1976) found that inter-country differences in the structure of countries' exports are in large part explained by differences in physical and human capital endowments, and therefore their structure 'changes with the accumulation of physical and human capital' – what Balassa (1979: 141) calls a 'stages' approach to comparative advantage, when 'the expression stages is used . . . to denote changes over time that occur more or less continuously rather than to discrete, stepwise changes'.

It is fairly evenly balanced as to which is the superior vehicle of verification despite Goodman and Ceyhun's claim (1976: 551) that 'there appears to be a new consensus emerging concerning the power of the neo-technology theory over the new-factor proportions theory'. The generally tentative conclusions of the latter were (ibid.):

> First, it would appear that trade theory to date has been characterized by a fairly general and unwarranted underemphasis of non-price factors. At an earlier point in time, perhaps this could be justified. But with the contemporary revolutions in communications, managerial techniques, marketing institutions, and industry organization, and the rapid transformation of the world economy into a cohesive, tightly interwoven whole, concentration exclusively or even primarily on cost-price factors becomes virtually untenable . . .
>
> Secondly, given the influences mentioned above and the rapid development of multivariate statistical techniques, it becomes difficult to rationalize an approach in terms of a single factor, which is at best incomplete, and at worst may be seriously misleading. A multi-factor approach seems clearly indicated. Future studies should also address themselves systematically to the incorporation of direct investment, trade financing, and government policy into the models.

Other areas of investigation have given emphasis to the importance of information systems and the role of state trading and regulatory activity, and the environment. For example, Pred and Tornqvist (1977) have emphasised the importance of international city-systems and the location of trade in relation to information and communication linkages of multi-locational transnational organisations. Clearly, as state trading accounts for at least one-quarter of world trade, behavioural investigations of how such mechanisms work is necessary, although the intertwining of foreign policy and trade, especially in such areas as military exchange would require a less 'discipline-bound' more 'field-bound' approach. The increasing internal importance of governments as controllers and regulators of economic activity, and the proliferation of such controls, regulations and taxes have led to the emergence of a secondary system of intermediate visible and invisible production based on low-tax low-friction offshore states. Here externally controlled businesses seek to avoid or evade onshore interventionist activity, with the competitive connivance of local governments, the appropriated trade arising from what I (1984: 134) have called 'economic frictioneering':

> the selective appliction of positively discriminatory non-interventionist policies and the provision of low-friction legislative facilities by a host state to promote personal, business or financial sector disintermediation from established location of business registration and financial activity for their mutual net economic gain.

Finally, some have investigated the impact of differential state laws in respect of pollution and the environment as determinants of national production cost differentials (see Walter (1975); and Siefert (1947)).

BALANCE-OF-PAYMENTS TRADE MODELS

In view of the criticism made in Chapter 4 of the classical and neo-classical models' errors of omission and their focus on balance-of-trade questions to the exclusion of other balance-of-payments components which are interrelated thereto, other writers have attempted a more integrated approach at the global, regional, and national levels of analysis.

The global trade model

In view of the greater degree and complexities of interdependence between the constituent members of the world trading system, and the heightened sensitivity of individual economies to exogenous forces, initial attempts have been made to demonstrate, within a global model, how national economies are 'linked' to one another through the exchange of goods, services and capital assets (including international reserve assets). However, as Rhomberg (1973: 9) has observed:

> economic change in any country may, in principle, affect the flows of goods, services and assets among all countries, as well as the prices at which they are exchanged. A full description of the entire interdependent system of the world economy, including all the adjustment mechanisms that are at work, is still beyond present capabilities of model construction and estimation.

Ideally, such a model would be a fusion of global microeconomics and macroeconomics, and, from a policy point of view, would give some precision to any co-ordinated attempts at, for example, world demand management in the light of 'locomotion'-type theories of national economy international linkages (see Bronfenbrenner (1979)). Such theories are highly complex and beyond the level of this introductory text. As an example of such a theory, the reader is referred to Beenstock's 'Transition Theory' (1984) of the evolving relationships between the developed and developing countries.

Regional custom union models

Whereas conventional trade theory implicitly accepts the boundaries of its postulated trading units as given and unchanging, the context of their incorporation in common markets means that national boundaries cease to be parameters, given the integration of previously separate national economies that effectively extends the home market of each country. This will be particularly important where such markets were too small prior to the union to benefit from economies of scale. In this context trade strategy discussions have been widened to include the potential benefits of such economic associations to seek to evaluate their significance at the country, regional and global level.

The evolving theory of customs unions and the associated theory of large markets set out to explain the static and dynamic effects realisable from partial economic integration, the criterion of evaluation being in terms of net welfare gain or loss. Since the publication of Viner's book *The Customs Union Issue* (1950), there has been a gradual evolution of both partial and general equilibrium models at the comparative-static level of abstraction, based on the realloction effects of production, consumption and changes in the terms of trade, the general conclusion of which can be summarised thus:

(1) The higher the initial tariff levels the greater the gains from trade creation.
(2) The more elastic the demand and supply curves for the home country, the greater will be the gains from trade creation.
(3) The losses from trade diversion will be smaller, the smaller the differences in cost between the partner and foreign supply sources.
(4) A union between complementary economies [ones producing similar goods but at different comparative production costs] will give rise to greater gains from trade creation than one between rival economies [ones with similar cost ratios], in accordance with the extent of that differential. The more dissimilar the membership is as a group to the rest of the world, the smaller the post-union trade diversion.
(5) Trade diversion will be smaller the lower the elasticity of union demand for goods imported from outside the union, and the lower the external elasticity of supply of such goods. Also, the more inelastic external demand is for union exports and the more inelastic the supply of foreign exports to the union, the greater will be the terms of trade effect in favour of the union.
(6) The lower the common external tariff imposed after the formation of the union on external imports, as compared with the pre-union tariff, the smaller will be the losses from trade diversion, because it will be less likely under such circumstances that a union producer will displace an outside producer in supplying the union market.
(7) The larger the union, the lower the possibility of trade diversion and the greater the likely gains from reallocating production. Also, the union is more likely to raise economic welfare the lower the proportion of pre-union trade with outside countries.

Interesting as these conclusions are, they must be tempered by dynamic considerations that also have a welfare dimension, namely, the potential and presumed effects of large markets on the rate of technological change, the increased opportunities for innovation, new products, processes, etc., the benefits of internal and external economies of scale. These effects are not, however, easily woven into an integrated analytical framework, as their quantitative significance can only be tentatively gauged.

The above type of analysis raises some dilemmas, two of which are: (1) as Cooper and Massell (1965: 461) point out with respect to custom unions (CUs):

> Except for the terms-of-trade argument, the very grounds on which a CU is said to be superior to non-discriminatory protection are precisely those grounds on which the union is necessarily inferior to free trade. A 'good' CU is one that raises income through trade creation – that is, a move toward free trade. A 'bad' union, on the other hand, reduces income through trade diversion – that is, a

more potectionist. Uf do accept 'good', why not go all the way to free trade?

more protectionist policy. But, if a country accepts a 'good' union as desirable, why does it not move all the way to free trade? And conversely, if a country is willing to reject the full benefits of free trade for the sake of unilateral protection, why should it be willing to give up its sheltered industries for the partial benefit of a CU?

This is a question not answered by 'orthodox reallocation analysis. (2) 'Orthodox' reallocation analysis appeared to rule out customs unions in the 1950s and 1960s for developing countries which typically had a high trade ratio to national income, and traded significantly more with the outside world than with the countries of their surrounding geographical region as shown in Table 35.

Table 35: *Intra-regional trade as a percentage of total trade, 1958*

Region	Intra-regional trade as % of total trade 1958
West Africa	1.0
Middle East	9.4
Latin America	8.4
East Africa	16.6
. . . .	. . . .
EEC	29.7
Continental W. Europe	48.2

Source: Bhambri (1962: 236)

However, in such a development context, dynamic considerations are crucial for the formulation of growth and trade strategies. As Dell (1966:17) observed: 'here the question is whether group protection offers any advantages over national protection in stimulating the rate of growth'.

Consideration of prospective dynamic effects has led to at least three approaches: (i) a theory of agreed specialisation; (ii) an explicitly normative organic concept of integration; and (iii) structural disequilibrium general models.

A theory of 'agreed' specialization

Myrdal (1956: 259, 261) put forward the idea of a 'second-grade international specialization' for less-developed countries in the context of planned development. Harrod later proposed (1962: 14) that:

> The advantages of a larger market should be secured, not *ex post* by some tariff manipulation, but *ex ante* by some previous agreement about the directions into which investment should be channelled in each separate country. Thus, the danger of overlapping and of the production of surpluses in the field of manufactures [e.g. textiles] might be averted. A larger market might be secured for each industry by a more rational direction of investment of resources in the first instance. The nations might authorize each other to specialize, by developing some particular directions, and thus give each the advantage of the large market afforded by the region as a whole.

This suggestion was examined by Kojima (1970), who argued a case for the development of a 'theory of agreed specialization' based on the following observations:

(1) Agreed specialisation is necessary to realise economies of scale in decreasing cost industrial activities.
(2) Countries aiming at agreement should be at the same stage of development, as measured by similarity in their factor proportions, and also of similar size, as measured by the size of their factor endowment and the size and structure of their national markets.
(3) The more similar their productive and consumptive structures the better the prospect for agreed specialisation.
(4) Countries will be more willing to come to some agreement on specialisation if they face competition from non-member countries with superior competitive power. However, such an approach has yet to be rigorously expanded into a theoretical model.

An explicitly normative organic concept of integration

Brewster and Thomas (1969) stress that the potential of an integrated system is greater than that of the summation of the unintegrated component units, and that the criteria for assessing the performance of integrated areas must be related to the whole area (and its potential externalities) as well as to each of its component areas. It is argued that the main advantages result from

> insuring or promoting the integration of the resource base of a region and the consequent possibility this creates for an extension of the production frontier of the region and its member countries . . . [so as to] narrow the gap between the structure of domestic demand and output. [Brewster and Thomas 1969: 115.]

The orthodox approach is rejected for three main reasons:

(1) It is a positive theory. 'Economic integration to have any real meaning must be related to a potential to be maximized, and cannot be defined simply as mechanism for linking existing disconnected units, whether this be by eliminating forms of discrimination, or cooperation in eliminating conflict of aims' (1969: 112).
(2) The almost exclusive preoccupation with the conditions which govern the *exchange* of goods. 'The theory of economic integration must be an integral element of a theory of economic and social transformation and not simply an adjunct of the micro-economics of static location theory' (1969: 113).
(3) A predetermined structure of preference at fixed levels and distributions of income is assumed. 'In any meaningful theory of relevance to over-exploited or structurally dependent economies, one of the explicitly stated normative goals of integration must be to achieve the structural transformation of these economies' (ibid: 115).

Successful transformation requires an explicit collective development strategy in which inter-sectoral dependence in both the regional economy and that of its constituent units is increased. In this process, two criteria are regarded as of primary importance (1969: 122–3).

> Priority should be given to indigenous resource content in all industrial projects. Emphasis should be put upon those resources which are overwhelmingly

used in the production of all final manufacturing output viz. iron and steel, textiles, paper, plastics, rubber, glass, leather, cement, wood, fuel and industrial chemicals. Such a policy should promote backward and forward linkages in economic activity . . .
Industrial maturity is not achieved independently of demand, so that priority should also be given to those items that have a high income-elasticity of demand potential.

Through such a deliberate, planned regional alloction of resources, structural transformation will be achieved by regional import-substitution policies. The nature of export specialisation will be changed from a structure which is externally dependent to one that arises from an internal extension of domestic demand.

In the development context, attempts have been made to extend CU theory to include industrialisation effects and the savings of foreign exchange by import substitution – effects which may be meaningfully brought about by trade diversion.

Structural disequilibrium general models

It will suffice here merely to mention three structural disequilibrium models as an indication of some lines of thinking tht have been put forward to explain trade patterns and changing policy preferences. Linder's model (1967), which is analytical of the balance of trade problems of LDCs, and the systematic observations of Schmitt (1979) and Prebisch (1949) concerning the ways in which the international trading system had tended to work. On the one hand, Schmitt sees a basic contradiction in the competitive interaction of rival economies operating within the world economy that leads mentally to disharmony in the system (contrary to Ricardian assertions). On the other hand, Prebisch sees a long-term secular deterioration in particular countries' fortunes.

Linder's model of structural disequilibrium

A nation's degree of development or underdevelopment is of major importance with respect to the effect of trade on its economy. Linder (1967) posits a world trading system composed of (a) advanced countries (b) developing countries with an acute foreign-exchange gap and (c) backward countries. He notes the possibility of a fourth group (today's NICs?) – developing countries without an acute foreign-exchange gap – but freely disregards them in his analysis. Such a world, therefore, has three types of intra-categories and three different types of inter-category trade to be explained or examined from a policy point of view. At the intra-category level, and the inter-category level (b) to (c), he believes that, with certain modifications, conventional theory gives a reasonable approximation of the effects of trade. His analytical focus is therefore directed at inter-category trade (a) to (b), and (a) to (c).

Linder's argument is that conventional trade theory (the neo-classical realloction theory plus Keynesian amendments) is inapplicable to (a) to (b) and (a) to (c) trade, because its analytical apparatus is geared solely to the question of the welfare and structural effects of the reallocation of given, fully-utilised resources resulting from changes in relative prices in connection with trade, implicitly assuming that internal and external equilibrium can be simultaneously maintained, giving no more attention to their effects on growth than what follows from the presumption that static efficiency in allocation is a precondition for dynamic efficiency in growth. This heroic assumption is invalid in the domestic economy contexts of (b) and (c) countries because:

1 Trade and trade policy cannot be attributed the role of resource alloction optimization as they are supposed to, when post-trade realloction of factors of production may not be possible to the extent required because of extreme internal economic frictions. This situation will be intensified if subsistence incomes were previously being earned in the sector where comparative disadvantage applies, such that the sector cannot be further maintained in the face of the post-trade unfavourable shift in relative prices. Internal equilibrium is not achieved.

2 In (b) or (c) countries, it is usually the case that imports cannot be reduced below a certain level – *the* (required) *import minimum* – without causing internal disequilibrium; and exports cannot be stimulated above a certain level – *the* (constrained) *export maximum*. The latter may be either actually or potentially too low for the former to be covered. The resultant actual or potential foreign-exchange gap will be reflected in an actual or an incipient balance-of-payments deficit. Thus the simultaneous internal/external equilibrium supposed by conventional trade theory is quite unattainable. Moreover, the deficit here does not imply overabsorption of goods and services in the conventional sense, for no matter how much the absorption is reduced, it cannot be removed without substituting internal disequilibrium for external equilibrium.

3 The import minimum level of trade arises because certain imports may be required in certain proportions to achieve the economy's full utilisation of its economic potential – specifically this means three types of capital imports which are necessary collectively to maintain full factor employment and to exploit growth potential. These are (i) *expansion imports* – capital imports without which the growth potential would be frustated; (ii) *reinvestment imports* – required to replace former expansion imports and (iii) *operation imports* – spare parts for imported capital goods and nondomestic primary products. Together (ii) and (iii) constitute *maintenance imports* to avoid underutilisation of existing resources. All three categories constitute *input imports* and are to be distinguished from other capital imports in that substitutability is limited as between domestic factors and these particular input imports. Therefore this import trade is essential if full production capacity use and growth is to be achieved. Its function is not that of improving the allocation of existing fully employed resources, but to create a leverage effect, a superengine of growth. Given that, in order to establish concurrent external/internal balance, import contraction is not viable, the adjustment burden rests with exports.

4 The existence of an export maximum thwarts adjustment, given the import minimum explained above. Exports to (a) countries are constrained because the relative price structure of manufactures is determined by Linder's Theory of Representative Demand which is intimately linked to national per-capita income levels. The large per-capita income differentials that exist between (a) countries and (b) and (c) countries mean that goods in demand in (a) countries are atypical for the economic structure of the latter

countries and so will not be produced there and, moreover, many of the goods that are produced will not be required in (a) countries as a result of this logic. Those goods that may be in demand in (a) countries, however, may be supplied but not in sufficient quantities to offset the import minimum trade level because the general level of absolute productivity in (b) and (c) countries may be too low.

5 For the reasons specified above, the whole edifice of commercial policy built into pure theory is inapplicable in trade relationships between (a) countries and the (b) and (c) countries. Balance-of-payments considerations cannot be omitted from any analysis of trade structure and welfare, especially given the disequilibrium proclivities of underdeveloped countries as outlined.

6 Given the above conclusion, consideration must be given to measures to reduce foreign-exchange expenditure on non-input imports, measures to increase foreign-exchange earnings on current account, and measures to bridge the foreign-exchange-gap through capital account transactions. Recourse to economic integration between (b) and/or (c) countries should also be considered.

Prebisch and the gains from trade

The main body of trade theory does not seek to examine the likely trend of terms of trade between rich and poor countries subsequent to reallocation of economic resources in the post-trade situation, other than to discuss the circumstances of production and demand conditions. Prebisch (1959) and (1964), however, seeks to expose the fact that the division of labour has not been one where the benefits of technical progress have been transferred to all parts of the world community of nations via price falls and/or income increases. On the contrary, industrial nations, while they have increased their productivity, have not lowered their prices as comparative advantage theory would imply, and the gains from trade have accrued in an unbalanced fashion biased against less-developed countries, especially those whose national income depends largely on one or a few primary exports. Two principal reasons are put forward to account for this disparity: the differential existence of organised labour; and an income-elasticity of demand differential between industrial and primary products. His main emphasis is on the first factor and how it affects the wage-price market mechanism.

Prebisch posits that in primary producing economies effective trade union activity tends to be handicapped by the downward pressure on wage rates exerted by surplus labour: wages tend to be constant as productivity rises, export prices falling in the same proportion as productivity increases, this benefit of technical progress appropriated by foreign investors. Whereas, in industrial countries, trade unions ensure that wages increase with productivity so that export prices do not fall. Given that productivity increases have been slower in primary producing countries anyway, this disparity has meant that primary product prices have either increased slowly or even fallen, while manufactured good prices have either increased rapidly or at least stayed the same. Thus the relative rise in manufacture exports compared to primary product exports has created a price trend that has been adverse to the producers of the latter. The second argument reinforces the first in that it is asserted that the demand of the advanced countries for the exports of the LDCs is both price and income inelastic; whereas the demand for LDCs for the exports of the DCs tends to be income elastic. Thus, there is a growth trend with respect to primary products that is anti-trade biased. As a result there is a need for export diversification and industrial development via planning to reverse these tendencies and to bring about a fairer balance in the gains of trade in favour of the LDCs.

Schmitt's view of disequilibrium in the absence of collective codes of conduct

Schmitt (1980: 393) argues that within the trading system as a whole, there is a tendency towards disharmony without a negotiated consensus among governments as to an objective basis for determining what the world's structure of exchange rates should be. This, he argues, has been so since the early 1970s. At the individual country level, he maintains that while a current account surplus is an inducement to technical progress, since all countries cannot run positive current account balances at the same time, yet all have reason to desire them, there is an inherent high degree of underlying turbulence in international trade and monetary relations. Thus, there is a vested interest in mercantilist policies to seek to secure such a balance because [Vines 1980: 379] countries with low exports and high imports 'will find their economies turned inward to the production of non-traded goods, and their capacity for technical progress correspondingly reduced.' Moreover, there may be a welfare gain from such a current account surplus, since technical progress will increase the total availability of goods over time and may bring a benefit large 'enough to warrant a net shipment of goods abroad' (ibid). As a consequence, countries may find it advantageous to artificially achieve a high degree of international competitiveness by maintaining a high price of foreign exchange relative to their domestic money wage levels, in order to both 'protect the domestic market and permit maximum penetration of markets abroad' (ibid). The consequences of this for international economic relations are, therefore, potentially serious.

Vines (1980), however, believes that the pursuit of international competitiveness does not pose a fundamental threat to international harmony provided certain mechanisms are observed. His argument is that:

> Rapid growth of tradeable goods production feeds upon itself by stimulating technical advance, lowering costs, and improving competitiveness. Growth becomes yet more rapid. This sets up a tendency towards excess demand for labour. Capitalists become timid, and contractionary policies are introduced by the fiscal and monetary authorities.
>
> There *is* a fundamental threat to harmony when too many countries at once become cautious and run current account surpluses ... If cautious countries accumulate idle international reserves then there is a failing of effective demand. Deficit currencies come under pressure to depreciate ... or a Keynesian reduction of output sets it in the world economy. It is only if cautious

countries carry out foreign investment, and if this foreign investment is sufficient to sustain world expenditures, that no such depreciation or falls in output need occur [ibid: 384–5].

CONCLUSION

It is evident that the range of explanations for the basis and commodity composition of trade has indeed been extended. The main centres of innovation have been the neo-factor and neo-technological discussions, each type and variant trying to come to terms theoretically with the realities of quality differences, technology differentials and mechanisms of international technology transfer. Realisation of the global context and the structural disequilibrium brought about in a multi-country, multi-product setting has compounded the complexity of explanation, while giving it more reality, whereas important new contributions to the trade strategy debate have been made in the burgeoning subject of development economics. While areas of overlap can be established between many of these aspects of reality, no new theory or spectrum of general theories has, as yet, been created that has held centre-stage, rather the rich diversity of forms of and motivations for international exchange has been more fully appreciated. Empirically-derived structured studies of 'international competitiveness'; the two-way trade of differentiated products; the effects of multinational firms on international exchange and underlying changes in the economic relations between countries have added to the range of investigative approaches and are now outlined in Chapters 8 and 9.

Part III:

The structural transformation of the international trading system and analyses of specific international economic relationships

In the real world, international trade flows depend on a whole host of complex factors and, consequently, cannot be explained by a relationship as simple as that postulated in the conventional theory.

Panic and Rajan (1971:18)

The pattern of trade is increasingly reflecting the mobile ownership advantages of firms, rather than the immobile resource endowments of countries.

Dunning (1982:355)

The problems of underdevelopment are not only, and in most cases, not even primarily problems of national insufficiencies, but relate to the organization and functioning of the world economic system, one in which the rules of the game have been set by the industrialized capitalist countries and stacked in their favour.

Villamil (1979:307)

An explicitly interdisciplinary school does not fit readily into . . . typical unidisciplinary syllabi and research programmes . . . [and] appears to the mainstream economist (and to some extent to the traditional practitioners of other disciplines) to lack 'rigour'. It affronts the aspirations of economists to be genuine 'scientists' like their colleagues in the physical sciences.

Seers (1981:15–16)

Balassa (1965:116–17) was moved to speculate in the following terms after his examination of the reallocation problems that followed the liberalisation of trade barriers in the 1950s:

> [given] the deficiencies of the traditional theories of international trade that attempt to explain international specialisation, and to indicate the gains from specialisation, by the use of a single classifying principle – should this be intercountry differences in factor proportions or in production functions . . . comparative advantages appear to be the outcome of a number of factors, some measurable, others not, some easily pinned down, others less so. One wonders, therefore, whether more could not be gained if, instead of enunciating general principles and trying to apply these to explain actual trade flows, one took the observed pattern of trade as a point of departure, and subsequently attempted to find the main influences that have determined the pattern.

The unprecedented expansion of trade, particularly in the period 1945–73, brought with it a number of structural changes in international economic interaction and penetration that *per se* provided new motivations for trade flows and new bases for international exchange. Most of these new phenomena came to light from the 1960s onwards and provided a new empirical basis for theoretical speculation, four new but separate components of which, not included in the post-Leontief models discussed in Chapter 7, were:

1 The need to widen the production focus of trade models to include the input–output implications of intermediate or middle goods that arise in the series of processes in the production chain from raw material to final consumer product. As Sanyal and Jones (1982:16) point out, 'a few items in international commerce are pure raw materials or primary factors which have not received any value added from other local inputs'. Within the production continuum, a series of tradeable intermediate products become inputs in the production of other tradeable middle products that themselves may be incorporated in a final end-product (Balassa found an average of three such transformation stages with respect to a sample of twenty-two primary products (1968)). Thus the production structure of trade, seen as a series of input-output processes, gives a new analytical dimension to international exchange. Sanyal and Jones (1980:16–17) go so far as to assert that national trade activity is divisible into two types of production activity: *input tier activity*, which combines local primary productive factors/resources to produce middle product outputs for the world market that are never consumed directly as final products; and *output tier activity*, which combines middle products obtainable on the world market with labour to produce final non-traded consumption goods. Presumably a third tier, *intermediate tier activity*, could be added either separately or as a subset of one of the above, when local production factors are combined with middle products obtainable on the world market to produce further middle products for that world market.

2 A realisation that 'very substantial trade flows are not related to any meaningful notion of specialization' (Aquino 1978:275), but an exchange of almost identical commodities. Hence a theory of 'two-way' or intra-industry trade was needed to explain the simultaneous import and export of broadly similar but differentiated products.

3 A recognition that the new forms of international investment are associated with multinational firms motivated by international company advantage, not comparative national advantage, such organisations acting as substitutes for the market as a method of organising international exchange, being 'islands of conscious power in [an] ocean of unconscious co-operation'(D.H. Robertson (1928: 85)).

4 A conscious attempt to fuse the above and other elements and evolve a theory of international exchange based on *international production* rather than specialisation.

This Part examines three different areas of more empirically based approaches and trade explanations that have emerged largely since the 1950s. Chapter 8 will examine some of the statistical approaches that evolved following Balassa's suggestion quoted above to determine the nature of countries' 'revealed' comparative advantages. Chapter 9 outlines some of the new theoretical rationales given for inter- and intra-industry trade and the analysis of international production. By contrast, Chapter 10 examines the approaches put forward to explain the controversial subject of dependent trade relationships as a determinant outcome of international exchange.

Conventional international economics makes the presumption that 'world markets are basically neutral instruments for resource allocation rather than generators of a particular pattern of inter-country income distributions [and] emphasises the efficiency of competitive markets' (Helleiner 1980:27). There are implicit assumptions that the initial intra-country distribution of assets and income is given and already optimal; and that international trade is interstate trade without market imperfections and remains so. Furthermore, 'it is usual to postulate that market relationships are freely and voluntarily entered into and that the market transaction is isolated from other relationships between the transactors' (Helleiner 1980:30). Many of the theories so far considered have been predicated on the presumption of interdependence, mutual responsiveness, co-operation and symmetrical international relations within an international trading system, thereby excluding the analysis of asymmetrical international economic relations. Such a state of affairs did not correspond to the reality facing nations in the period of decolonisation after 1945. As Michalet (1982:37) has written:

> It appears increasingly obvious that the theoretical frameworks of the great English classics, rethought and refined by the neoclassicists, have no relevance to a certain number of phenomena, old and new, that urgently require to be dealt with: whether it is a question of North–South relations, of the development of the multinational activities of companies or of the new rules in operation on the international monetary and financial system. Challenged by these changes in the field of international economy, the observer realizes that the toolbox of theory, which relates to this area of political economy, does not contain the necessary analytical tools.

In practice, as Diaz-Alejandro (1975: 24) asserts, markets are 'creations of social and political systems, not . . . mechanisms arising spontaneously and inevitably out of economic necessity'. Whilst there are many forms of potential/actual world market imperfections (see Helleiner (1980)) and evolved economic systems, what is of concern here is the assertion that the development of capitalism *per se* has international consequences; that the cumulative impact of its various international manifestations inevitably results in a form of 'market failure', the creation of dependent exploitative structured relations between rich and poor countries; and that international trade is the vehicle for its various mechanisms of exploitation.

Whereas it is possible to conduct a non-Marxist or a non-Marxist-related analysis of exploitation as Cooper (1977) has attempted, it is the Marxist and Marxist literature to which reference is made in Chapter 10: the context of unequal trade and exogenous determination of indigenous development, and the structural power of some countries to manipulate the ways in which the international trading system operates. Here the substance of traditionally described international economic relations as being atomistic, decentralised, symmetrical and actor-dependent is replaced by the concept of an evolving global capitalist system that is holistic, centralised, stratified and system-dependent, shaped by a predictable concatenation of circumstances.

The propositions and scenarios of recent writers in the fields of development economics and sociology discussed in Chapter 10 provide a contrasting, in some cases converging, argument to the 'world economics' orientation noted in Chapter 9, and tend to be at variance with the conclusions both of traditional Marxist theory and free trade liberalism, each differently related to nineteenth-century experience. The core of the new discussion is a body of thought that can be subsumed under the headings of *dependencia* and *world system analysis* (there being some degree of interrelation between the two), the range of such analyses provided being within a spectrum of explanatory theories of 'underdevelopment' created by unequal trade relationships on the one hand and increasingly ambitious and more comprehensive, deterministic accounts of the global evolutionary structures of capitalism on the other.

8 International 'competitiveness' and 'revealed' comparative advantage

There is no single measure of competitiveness. At best it is a composite concept, because different measures (price, export share, profitability, unit costs etc.) give different results.

Commission of the European Communities (1982:15)

Competitiveness is essentially a relative concept . . . There can be no single comprehensive index of competitiveness because of the variety of possible contributory factors . . . [in practice] the indicators of competitiveness are restricted by the availability of comparable data for other countries . . .

Doggett and Cresswell (1979:79)

Given a policy need to monitor actual behavioural changes in 'international competitiveness' both in the short and long run, a need that was intensified by the desire to create indicators by which to assess changes in particular countries' international economic performance in the circumstances of the world depression of the 1970s, a series of studies were conducted (see McGeehan 1968), essentially beginning with one by Balassa (1965) which sought to obtain statistical evidence for the 'revealed' comparative advantage of countries in international trade. This chapter seeks to indicate some of the problems that arise in such empirical investigations and to outline some of the general statistical measures so far presented.

THE UNDERLYING CONTEXT AND DETERMINANTS OF COMPETITIVENESS

The annual trade returns of exports and imports of any economy are the result of a whole series of decisions (with lags) taken and made both domestically and in the rest of the world by consumers and producers (public, private, multinational); importers and exporters and departments of state and local government. These decisions are (as was indicated in Chapter 2), to a greater or lesser degree, inhibited or liberated according to the prevalent outlook of the regime of international exchange and the constellation of general world economic conditions, and the particular government-induced and sector-induced economic frictions obtaining nationally. These trade flows inevitably also reflect certain structural features and politico-economic ties historically determined by international politics and the past pattern of international economic development (centre-periphery ties; trading bloc relations; multinational firms etc.). *Per se* these intrusive elements create resource allocation distortions and various forms of x-inefficiency, such that the composition and levels of industrial output are rarely purely determined by technically efficient criteria consistent with comparative advantage (however computed) but often compromised by motivations that are either non-economic or even without rationality. Clearly changes in commercial policy, whether ultimately decided at national governmental level or induced by multi-national agreement at the regional and/or global levels, can alter the context in which market forces operate, thereby making economies more or less open to trade, with implications for their domestic ratios of imports to exports and/or total domestic consumption. This can be achieved, for example, by altering the composition of trade as a result of changes in tariffs, quotas, and subsidies; by altering the direction of trade by changes in preferential treatment given to goods originating in different areas and by altering the exchange rate and affecting the constellation of import and export prices. Furthermore, in the short run the particular level of current home demand may crucially affect the ability and willingness of home manufacturers to export, though the precise order of causation is unclear, since for some a buoyant home market may be a precondition for effective exporting, whereas for others a constrained home demand may provide the capacity and incentive for greater exporting effort. Moreover, in the long run, the economic growth rates achieved may bring about 'vicious' or 'virtuous' cycles of investment and levels of productivity, thereby altering the relative competitiveness differentials between economies. Additionally, private sector industrial competitiveness may be thwarted by particular macro and/or micro economic objectives pursued by different governments. For example, if a domestic budget deficit cannot readily be financed domestically, a reduction in the 'real' rate of exchange will not lead to an improvement in international trade. Rather, inflation will accelerate and trigger further damaging falls in the exchange rate, increases in the external deficit and inflation such that the 'vicious circle' will only be broken by even more severe action on the budgetary and monetary side than would otherwise have been necessary.

The following three commercial facts of life would seem to condition both the circumstances wherein individual producers individually decide on export options and the efficiency of the resultant specialisation pattern of the economy as a whole:

1 Industrial specialisation at the national level is both 'artificially' created and constrained by the existence of national barriers to trade and other restrictive international trade practices

The existence of protective trade barriers and restrictive governmental trade practices in *prima facie* evidence of an inability to compete and leads to the diversion of trade into less efficient, higher cost hands. The removal (partial or whole) of these provides an acid test of competitive ability. Thus in the case of the United Kingdon the reduction of the margins of Commonwealth Preference, the ending of quota restrictions discriminating in her favour (largely at the expense of the United States, West Germany and Japan), and the emergence of the newly independent post-colonial countries with a more general awareness of non-traditional sources of supply inevitably led to structural changes in trade flows that lessoned the artificially competitive position of British goods in these markets. Subsequent membership of EFTA in 1957 and the EEC in 1972 provided further evidence of her ability both to compete and to actualise potential benefits of membership resulting from these effective extensions of her home market.

Private sector imperfections resulting from concentration of industrial ownership, oligopoly, cartels, the use of patents, etc., also constrain the international location of potentially competitive production activities. The existence of multinational firms may involve a transnational allocation of products processes according to company advantage rather than country advantage.

2. At the firm and sectoral industrial levels, within the context set by 1, competitive success is dependent on:

(a) comparative levels and rates of change of export prices,
(b) comparative levels and rates of change of industrial costs,
(c) product non-price competitive elements, and
(d) comparative export trade finance and the provision of credit.

Comparative levels and rates of change of export prices

Export prices largely depend on the pricing policy of exporters. In some countries, exporters tend to 'subsidise' low export price by a higher home price, many of them charging their overheads against home sales and considering exports as 'marginal' production bearing less or none of their general overhead expenses. Some exporters apply a simple cost-plus method in export pricing, which may result in export production being less profitable given the higher marketing costs often incurred. Practices vary from company to company, country to country and commodity to commodity, being dependent *inter alia* on the economic objectives of firms, government subsidies given to exporters and the supply and demand conditions facing their industrial products. Analysis of comparative export prices is, therefore, not easy. Junz and Rhomberg (1964) found that for the period 1953–63, on the basis of eighty-eight observations, 43 per cent of the variation in export shares was attributable to relative export prices, and that a deterioration in price competitiveness by 1 per cent would *ceteris paribus* result in a reduction of exports by almost 3 per cent, though this relationship did vary within the period of their study.

Comparative levels and rates of change of industrial costs

Price is only a proximate influence, costs and their components – productivity and factor prices – are important. Here questions of size of plant; investment policy and industrial relations and the determinants of each in relation to government policy come to the fore. Detailed international comparisons of productivity are, however, few and far between. Import content of exports may be an important cost factor in semi- and final manufactured goods.

Industrial concentration on a limited number of items within the product range may give rise to greater competitiveness if lower costs are significantly brought about by economies of scale. Saunders' study (1978) of the engineering industry used crude measures of the share in total engineering exports of the top ten and fifteen items. This factor, however, was not universally important. Results from this type of analysis may also be dependent on the particular structure of the SITC product classification usually adopted. Multi-product diversification may well be a more important source of economies at the level of the firm, which makes any narrow definition of an 'industry' difficult to apply at a disaggregated level of analysis.

Product non-price competitive elements

As the Commission of the European Communities (1982:9) recently commented: 'Price competitiveness is only a part of overall competitiveness and improvements in this sphere will be neither beneficial nor durable if other factors are leaning in the opposite direction.' Many factors cannot, therefore, be treated quantitatively. A survey of the European Management Forum (1981) used as many as 240 different criteria of competitiveness, many of which were unquantifiable. Non-price factors include design, quality, delivery dates, salesmanship, innovation and marketing. While each may be an important factor in determining foreign demand for an economy's exports and domestic demand for imports as against home production, a NEDC inquiry (1965:28) concluded, on the basis of users' opinions, that technical performance was 'the decisive factor' for most imports of mechanical engineering products, electronic capital goods and scientific instruments, on the practical grounds that 'either a piece of equipment which does a specific job is not available in the UK, or there is a difference in its design characteristics which alters the economics or reliability of operating it'.

Comparative export trade finance and the provision of credit

Lack of provision of insurance for export credits and the finance and the underwriting of any extra risks attaching to international trade may inhibit international exchange. Thus government-backed export guarantees can play a role here, particularly where foreign buyers are offered better credit facilities by the exporters of some countries.

3.   As a result of 1 and 2 above, at the comparative international level, successful specialisation patterns among economies of a similar type depend upon

(i)   the commodity trade pattern – the industrial mix; and
(ii)   the export market pattern – the territorial distribution of products.

The commodity trade pattern

At the industrial level, analysis of an economy's export share of total world trade can be attempted to provide an overview of its general competitive ability. More interesting, however, are inter-country comparative analyses of the relative composition of exports with respect to the various rates of trade growth categories. One such study by Panic and Rajan (1971) categorised commodities into five different growth categories comparing the main developed countries' shares in these categories in the period 1955–68, as reproduced in Table 36.

There is a presumption that if fast growing items form a relatively small share of a country's exports, they are likely to form a relatively large share of the same country's imports.

Table 36: *Distribution of export commodities by growth category, 1955–68*

Commodity growth group	No. of commodities	% Increase 1955–68	% Share 1955	% Share 1968
I Very fast	8	450+	4.75	9.70
II Fast	6	350–449	16.07	22.66
III High average	12	250–349	22.92	28.09
IV Low average	20	150–249	21.58	18.27
V Slow	25	0–149	38.85	21.26

Source: Panic and Rajan (1971: 8, Table 1)

The export market pattern

Clearly, while changes in the commodity composition of trade are an important indicator of changing international competitiveness, effective export sales must also depend upon national abilities to exploit differential per capita income changes in world markets. Sometimes change may be swift, as was the case with the oil-surplus OPEC states after 1973. Thus, flexibility in switching markets and altering global market strategies can be crucial for international success. Analyses of the territorial distribution of products will indicate the extent to which loss of sales competitiveness may be due to a failure to redirect global sales efforts to the growth market areas.

GENERAL STATISTICAL MEASURES OF INTERNATIONAL COMPETITIVENESS

General objections

Clearly the coverage of possible areas of economic differential between countries and change therein do add to our knowledge of the realities of international economic exchange and the sources of international competitiveness, but they do not provide *per se* a model of comparative advantage determination. They are subject to at least four types of general objections, despite the selective 'truths' they reveal: (i) they are theoretically vacuous; (ii) they contain errors of explanatory omission; (iii) they commit certain errors of implicit commission; (iv) they contain inherent statistical deficiencies.

(i) Theoretical vacuity

Statistical measures can purport to describe trade pattens that have taken place but provide no basis for evaluating whether these patterns are 'real' or optimum ones, i.e. they are not the result of 'artificial' manipulation engineered by new government policies. As Donges and Riedel (1977: 69n) argue: 'it is possible to infer what countries can do in the field of industrial expansion, not what they should do on theoretical grounds. The latter prescription can only be made, if at all, on the basis of individual country studies in which particular factor endowments can be taken into account'. Furthermore, it is evident from the points raised in (ii), (iii) and (iv) below, that serious errors can be built-in to the statistical series produced and that the information displayed may suggest a greater homegeneity and stability of context than is the case in reality.

(ii) Errors of explanatory omission

Non-price variables tend to be neglected (quality-differences, goodwill, servicing, the existence of repair facilities, etc.), although as Balassa (1965:102) remarks, they

> all bear influence on the pattern of trade among the industrial countries. Cost consideration will not be sufficient to explain the widespread use of British woollen goods and the success of Volkswagen, for example, and, more generally, a complete expression of comparative advantage could not leave out of consideration the non-price variables.

(iii) Implicit errors of commission

There is an implicit assumption that export prices are the same in all markets of destination, and that imports and exports are symmetrically affected by protective measures, transport costs, taste structure, traditional ties, etc. Exchange rate changes and inflation necessarily affect international comparisons. Even if comparisons are made on a constant price basis, differential exchange rate changes do not always reflect changes in purchasing power. Furthermore, industrial prices will tend to reflect differing accounting conventions and practices.

(iv) Statistical deficiences

While each statistical procedure has its own built-in arbitrariness and limitations, certain main operational difficulties can be noted that need to be sensitively handled if the results obtained are not to mislead:

(a) Index number problems. Index numbers are used to illustrate trends but they are subject to a number of inherent difficulties: the choice of base year may reflect particular cyclical conditions; the weights chosen are not a true reflection of expenditures when prices change; new products and changed quality of products can only be covered by changing the base of the index.

(b) Aggregation problems. As Donges and Riedel (1977:69n) have written: 'The appropriate commodity breakdown is the one in which exports and imports of a specific product category are comparable with each other, i.e. have an elasticity of substitution among each other above zero.' Failure to have precisely matched data will give rise to misleading results if disparities within the group are masked. Furthermore, differences in definition of sectors and product groups will also need to be taken into consideration when indices are constructed as they tend to vary between different countries.

(c) Sampling problems. Some of the data available may have been based on statistical samples, some of which may have been too small because of the difficulties in obtaining certain data.

STATISTICAL INDICATORS OF COMPETITIVENESS

Despite the above problems which are often intractable, a range of different statistical indices have nevertheless been produced that can be grouped under three main headings: (a) general quantity measures; (b) general price and cost measures; (c) sectoral performance indicators. Each group has its own extended family of measures. In general each indicator must be interpreted with common sense, given that international economic development must necessarily lead to a relative statistical decline of existing industrial countries.

(a) General quantity measures

Absolute market shares

Comparative statistics of either total world manufacturing exports and/or world exports of a particular commodity group provide a generalised summary picture of international competitive performances. However, such indices do hide the fact that individual countries are not subject to the same trade barriers in their export markets, or the same degree of domestic protection or export taxes etc. as a result of differentially applied economic frictions.

Relative market shares

Panic and Rajan (1971:25) have applied a measure which seeks to compare a country's relative share in world exports of commodity j to that country's overall share of world exports, i.e.

$$\frac{x_{ij}}{x_{nj}} \Big/ \frac{s_{it}}{x_{nt}} = \frac{x_{ij}}{x_i}$$

where: x = exports of manufactured goods
i = country i
j = commodity
n = all industrial countries together
t = all manufactured goods
x = relative share of exports

$\dfrac{x_{ij}}{x_i}$ is then multiplied by 100 and expressed as an index

The supposition is that if the relative commodity share is greater than the relative share for all manufactured goods, the country will be assumed to have a 'revealed' comparative advantage in that commodity group. If the resultant index figure is less than 100 a comparative disadvantage will be 'revealed'. Such an index if applied over time would therefore monitor shifts in competitiveness and uncompetitiveness but this is only regarded as a 'tentative criterion'.

Export/import ratios

Export/import ratios simply show the net trade balance for a particular commodity or commodity group. Thus an improvement in competitiveness *ceteris paribus* may arise either as a result of a higher growth of exports than of imports, or in a more rapid decline of imports than of exports. A number of basic objections can be made here (Campbell-Boross and Morgan 1974: 79).

(i)   This ratio is only relevant where foreign goods are substitutes or near substitutes for domestic products. The use of these ratios at a highly disaggregated level may further mislead if, for example, exports refer to high-quality products only and imports to low-quality products.

(ii) If the ratio is measured in current values it can tell us nothing about the causes of a change in competitiveness, unless the cause is common to all industries or products compared (there may be differential changes in non-price competitive elements or in rates of growth in demand at home and abroad).

(iii) The ratio may be misleading in certain circumstances. For example, as exports are recorded f.o.b. (free on board) and imports c.i.f. (inclusive of cost of insurance and freight), a rise in freight rates may cause the ratio to fall even though there had been no real change in competitiveness.

An indicator of competitiveness, C, can be calculated from the formula:

$$C = \frac{X_n}{M_n} \div \frac{X_0}{M_0} \; 100$$

where 0 = trade returns in the base year

and n = trade returns in a subsequent year

Panic and Rajan (1971:26) have applied export/import ratio indices to relative market share indices, and, in their view, only when *both* are satisfied (i.e. when $xij / x_i > 100$ *and* the export/import balance is positive) can 'revealed' comparative advantage be established (i.e. $x_{ij} / m_{ij} > 100$). When the two indices were statistically related, the resultant rank correlation coefficients proved high, especially in the case of the smaller economies that had a narrower specialisation pattern, as is shown in Table 37.

Donges and Riedel (1977) carried out a similar type of study.

Advantage utilisation ratios

Having established those commodities which have a positive relative market share index and a positive export/import ratio it is then possible to work out an advantage utilisation ratio which shows simply the proportion of total exports satisfying the joint criterion, as did Panic and Rajan. This would give an indication of the efficiency of the export structure of each country.

Dynamic comparative competitiveness indicators

A more dynamic approach has been discussed by Rothschild (1975: 226–7) to allow for both growth and structural influences by calculating:

Table 37: *Consistency of the relative market share and export/import ratio of comparative advantage*

Country	Rank correlation coefficients between the relative export shares and the export/import ratios	Standard deviations of the relative export shares
Canada	0.916	214.1
Sweden	0.888	88.5
Belgium	0.858	130.3
Switzerland	0.855	287.4
Italy	0.836	110.9
Netherlands	0.833	116.2
Japan	0.831	101.7
West Germany	0.777	42.8
France	0.746	66.0
USA	0.723	54.0
UK	0.526	60.7

Source: Panic and Rajan (1971: 27)

for each country its 'hypothetical exports' by finding out how much its total exports would have risen, if the exports of each commodity group had risen in proportion to world demand ... Dividing actual exports by this hypothetical export figure we obtain an index of export competitiveness, indicating the capacity of a country's firms to over-or under-utilize the exogenous opportunities. Denoting by jX_i^0 the exports of good i by country j in period 0; and by $r_i (= M_i^l / M_i^0)$
the rate of growth of world imports of good i between periods 0 and I, we get the 'hypothetical exports' HX of country j for period I:

$$HX = \Sigma_i (jX_i^0 \cdot r_i) \text{ and the index of competitiveness } (C) \text{ as } C = \frac{jx^l}{\Sigma(jX_i^0 r_i)}$$

Even this is unsatisfactory in that it may not reveal the 'true' picture (Rothschild 1975:229–30): 'In reality apparent changes in the structure of [trade] demand [exports or imports] are partly *ex ante* demand-determined, partly the export result of innovating competitiveness behaviour.' There is clearly a need to distinguish between the 'normal' (imitating) competition of the former and the innovating (pioneering) competition of the latter

where the export effort does not necessarily follow the international demand structure but helps to create it ... The former favours countries with the 'right' export structure ... or who display a high degree of export flexibility, i.e. have the capacity of switching their export structure towards commodities with a higher growth potential – and the separation of structural and competitive elements is analytically a simple matter; in the latter case, a statistical separation would require more factual information on basic trends and innovating successes [ibid. 229–30].

'Required' net trade target indicators

In the context of policy decision-taking and management decision-taking Campbell-Boross and Morgan (1974:79) have produced a modified version of the C indicator above by measuring the excess or shortfall in 'required' net export revenue over time. The word 'required' is set up in relation to the target necessary to satisfy whatever policy is thought to be desirable by the decision-maker.

> Here $N^* =$ the required level of net trade (an 'arbitrary' target figure established at any given level for an industry or group of industries, and for sub-sectors thereof in relation to satisfy a particular objective)
>
> $N_n =$ the actual level of net trade.

The difference between N_n^* *and* N_n measures the excess $(+)$ or shortfall $(-)$ in 'required' net trade. Having fixed N^*, a corresponding 'required' competitiveness indicator C^* may be calculated and subsequently compared with the actual results N and C as they become available. Such indicators may therefore be used as a tool for economic policy management, by which, for example, to monitor the impact of industrial restructuring policies.

(b) General price and cost measures

Price measures

Britain has used three basic measures of price competitiveness: (i) relative export prices, (ii) import price competitiveness, and (iii) relative wholesale prices.

(i)   Relative export prices. This had been defined as the ratio of the export prices of United Kingdom manufactures to a weighted average of the export prices of manufactures of the United Kingdom's main competitors expressed in a common currency. Such an index suffers from a number of limitations: no account is taken of the actual or changing profitability of export trades or of the possibilities of interdependent pricing in world markets; no account is taken of home market competition between imports and domestic production. Both in Britain and the domestic markets abroad, it reflects only the price of goods sold and does not allow for unsuccessful quotations.

(ii) Import price competitiveness. This is defined as the index of United Kingdom wholesale output prices of manufactures (WPI) other than food, drink or tobacco, divided by the unit value of imports of finished manufactures (UVI). This index does not take account of the relative profitability of domestic sales of British forms and British import profitability to foreign exporters. Moreover a problem arose because the weighting patterns used in the two indices were different. Some revision was made in May 1980 and erratic items – 'ships, North Sea installations, aircraft and precious stones' – were excluded either because their prices are notoriously hard to measure (e.g. ships, aircraft) or they feature atypically in British trade (e.g. the considerable entrepôt trade in precious stones).

(iii) Relative wholesale prices. This is defined as the index of United Kingdom wholesale output prices of manufacturers other than food, etc., divided by a weighted average of the indices of competitors' wholesale prices of manufactures, both expressed in a common currency. This compares prices in other countries' domestic markets with the prices with which their exports will be competing in the British market. As the Department of Trade admits, 'although the matching between traded and home-produced commodities carried out to derive the appropriate WPI weighting pattern was made at a fine level of detail, there may still be considerable product differentiation between the "same" traded and home-produced goods, so that they are not real substitutes.'

Cost measures

Cost indicators can more easily cover all manufacturing industries, are not affected by the problem of profit margins mentioned above and are likely to relate better to the coverage of quotations accepted and rejected than a price series. The problem is that it is not possible to cover all costs because of lack of suitable data so that labour costs are usually used as a proxy. Given that the productivity of labour can change it is preferable to use a 'normalised' or 'cyclically adjusted' index. The United Kingdom uses a relative normal unit labour cost index defined as the index of United Kingdom normal labour costs per unit of output divided by a weighted average of competitors' normal unit labour costs, both series being expressed in a common currency and adjusted for variations in productivity about its long-term trends. In addition a relative profitability of exports' index is computed, defined as the index of British wholesale output prices of manufactures other than food, etc., divided by the unit British exports of manufactures.

(c) Sectoral performance indicators

Since October 1977 four ratios have been used to assess the performance of British industries in home and overseas markets. The procedures for these are discussed by J.D. Wells and J.C. Imber (1977). These ratios give somewhat different emphases than those discussed above.

(i) The import penetration ratio: defined as imports/home demand, where home demand = manufacturers' sales + imports − exports. This takes no account of exports, a high level of which might be considered to compensate for a high level of imports.

(ii) The import penetration ratio corrected for export sales: defined as imports/home demand + exports.

(iii) Export sales ratio: defined as export sales/total manufacturers' domestic sales. This ignores imports.
(iv) Export sales ratio corrected for imports: defined as export sales/ manufacturers' domestic sales + imports.
(v) As measures (ii) and (iv) have the same denominator, the difference between the two provides an indicator of the *trade gap* in a particular sector in relation to the size of the sector. This has not been used to the extent of (i)–(v).
(vi) Unit values: a quality of product indicator.

An example of (vi) has been provided by Saunders (1978), who believes that the capacity of countries to produce and sell goods with a high content of value added to their raw material base is a suitable measure of trade competitiveness between industrialised economies. One indicator of this is the relative unit values of goods that are traded (the unit value being the value per physical unit of each product as recorded in official trade statistics, although this measure has a number of defects:

> it is influenced by the degree of detail in which the products are reported, it may be influenced by differences in methods of valuation; and it may reflect monopolistic pricing. But broadly, on the assumption (by no means wholly justified) that in a competitive world the prices of an identical commodity in international trade will be roughly identical, a significant difference in unit values for different trade flows in a given product can be taken ... to represent a difference either in the 'quality' of the product, or in the selection of products of which the reported product group consists ... [Here] 'Quality' must be taken to include a variety of factors other than the product-mix or the technical specification of the product; it may include, for example, punctuality in delivery, efficiency of marketing, after-sales service [ibid: 64].

Saunders also argues that consistency in inter-country differences in unit values would be a *prima facie* indication of where, within the range of 'quality' products, particular countries have a propensity to specialise, i.e. whether it is at the top, middle, or bottom end of the 'quality' product group.

An analysis of the relationship between unit values and market shares indicates that competitive advantages tend to be most marked in the products at the top end of this range of unit values.

CONCLUSION

Balassa's 1957 judgement about the direction in which research about interdependent specialisation changes might be more fruitful has clearly 'revealed' the multi-dimensional character of real world exchange. However, while the statistical approaches outlined here indicate various truths concerning international competitiveness, they do not displace the need to evolve new theories, though they may give pointers towards as yet unexplored areas of investigation that may yield comparative evidence for new trade propositions. They merely provide comparative data on international change differentials and do not *per se* measure whether a particular country was competitive in any absolute sense either at the beginning, middle, or end of the currency of a particular series. All they can show is the level of competitiveness now relative to an earlier period. Thus there is no unique measure of competitiveness but a number of complementary ones, each with certain advantages and disadvantages. This theoretical vacuity is also compounded by errors of omission and commission in their compilation.

9 Modern industrial trade structures and their new orientations for trade theory

> The classic paradigm of international trade as presented by the Heckscher-Ohlin theorem has to be enlarged to accommodate the complexity of ... actual trade and investment flows.
>
> Agmon (1979:49)

> International trade theorists ... must cast their analysis in a framework that includes trade in both outputs and inputs among countries.
>
> R.E. Baldwin (1970:434)

> The existence of two-way trade ... is *prima facie* evidence of the inadequacy of the orthodox factor proportions theory of international trade to provide a realistic framework for analysis of modern trade flows.
>
> H.P. Gray (1973:19)

> The fact of intra-firm trade suggests that transnational corporations might sensibly be added to the traditional nation-states as units of analysis in what might then be better described as 'world economics' rather than 'international economics'.
>
> Helleiner (1981:4)

As has been indicated, classical and neo-classical trade theories ignore the possibility of imperfect competition being present in the trading industries, and concentrate on national cost characteristics allegedly conducive to international exchange on a mutually advantageous basis. Trade is asserted to reflect '*country* or *location* specific endowments rather than any special attributes possessed by ... exporting forms, i.e. *ownership* specific endowments' (Dunning and Buckley (1977: 392). However, studies within the field of industrial organisation, the study of actual product markets, indicate the existence of 'important empirical phenomena [that] have escaped capture' (Caves 1974: 1) by trade theorists (see Johnson 1967). Essentially these consist of the operational importance of imperfect markets, non-price competitive elements such as differentiation of products; and a need to recognise the growth in importance of international production for 'in ... neo-classical theories of trade ... since factor inputs are assumed to be immobile ... it is ... presumed ... that a foreign country's markets are always supplied by firms producing wholly within, and exporting from, their home countries' (Dunning and Buckley (1977); see also Kindleberger (1969)). Three primary areas of empirically based theoretical discussions of trade structure have emerged since the 1950s: intra-industry trade; intra-firm trade; international production and multinational resource allocation.

INTRA-INDUSTRY TRADE

Since the 1930s, periodic observations had been made concerning 'the phenomenon that countries with a relatively high proportion of inter-national trade per head of population export and import what are apparently the same commodities' Frankel (1943:195). The spectacular growth of world trade relative to world production that took place after 1950 contained an evident trade bias that favoured developed rather than developing countries, and manufactures rather than other commodities. Furthermore, during the 1960s, trade liberalisation between industrial countries, whether within customs unions or not, was observed to give rise to national commodity trade patterns that were more rather than less similar. Both trends seemed to be related to the effects of real income growth and per capita similarities and industrial convergence in advanced countries. This led to a speculation by Linder (1961:102) that 'the almost unlimited scope for product differentiation – real or advertised – could, in combination with . . . seemingly unrestricted buyer idiosyncrasies, make possible flourishing trade in what is virtually the same commodity' which was examined by Grubel (1967:287). He observed that 'the availability of a greater variety of styles and brands through the introduction of foreign products permits consumers to satisfy the demands (for different qualities of products), more readily', and initiated a discussion of intra-industry trade or 'trade overlap' as others (Finger 1975) have called it. This was defined (Grubel 1967:374) as: 'a situation where each country simul-taneously produces, exports, and imports products which are very close substitutes for each other in consumption, production, or both'.

Attempts were subsequently made to 'lift intra-industry trade from the role of a nuisance in the data to one of theoretical and policy significance' (Lipsey 1976:312). Main contributions were made by Grubel (1970); Grubel and Lloyd (1971; 1975); and H.P. Gray, who evolved a theory of 'two-way' trade (1973, 1976, etc.), with further elaborations by Barker (1977) under the title of 'the variety theory'. Substantial verification studies were published by Grubel and Lloyd, and among others Hesse (1974), Aquino (1978) and Caves (1981). Nevertheless, problems arose in the empirical identification of the quantitative significance of the phenomenon, and in the establishment of the theoretical underpinnings of the concept, such that even one of its main proponents, H.P. Gray (1979: 102), was moved to write:

> Because of the very large variability of trade patterns within individual commodity groupings and in trade with different partner nations, the topic is not one that lends itself to confirmation or refutation in the scientific sense (although) . . . a substantial amount of intra-industry trade in manufactured goods has been adequately identified. Certainly enough . . . to warrant its consideration as a qualification of the factor-proportions theory narrowly defined.

One of the problems of statistical verification is that (Aquino 1978:276): 'the identification and measurement of the phenomenon heavily depends upon *the degree* and *the kind* of homogeneity of the commodities included in each statistical group'. As Gray (1979:98) says: 'the question breaks down into the two problems of "what level of disaggregation of the data is appropriate to the concept of an industry?" and "how much intra-industry trade exists at that level of disaggregation?" '. Available statistical classifications are not entirely suitable as the basis for grouping commodities acording to their product similarities as they are subject to both upward and downward biases which can lead to quite arbitrary results. Indeed Finger (1975:581) argued that most intra-industry trade can be explained by what H.P. Gray (1979:87) calls 'categorical aggregation' and declares intra-industry trade to be 'valueless'. He maintains that:

> unless one argues that the importation of a product somehow causes the exportation of products with otherwise similar characteristics (or vice versa) the theory of overlapped or intra-industry trade is no more than the 'ordinary' theory of trade combined with the assumption that whatever characteristic determines comparative advantage is not possessed in equal degrees by all the products which have been combined into data categories. [H.P. Gray 1979: 588]

One of the problems of empirical verification is that, in practice, any rigorous analysis of intra-industry trade requires a radical reclassification of product categories, otherwise its existence would merely be a statistical phenomenon or 'an artifact of misspecification of the term industry'. An upward bias will arise where heterogeneous commodities, the 'technology-intensity' of which is not similar, are included in the same United Nations Standard International Trade Classification (SITC) product group. Even where there is a fine level of disaggregation, this difficulty may still exist. For example, SITC Group 7142 contains both the simplest calculating machines and the most sophisticated calculating and accounting systems. On the other hand, a downward bias will arise where commodities that have identical technology-intensities are nevertheless included in different statistical groups, as is the case with textiles (SITC 65) and clothing (SITC 84).

Despite the above-mentioned difficulties, attempts have been made to determine the significance of intra-industry trade. *Prima facie* the evidence obtained would seem to suggest that it constitutes a relatively high proportion of total trade and that its share of total trade has been increasing.

One such study was conducted by Hesse (1974) who compiled a matrix of trade flows between thirteen industrial countries for each of fifty two classes of manufactured goods, excluding all such trade with countries external to the group. Each good was selected because its SITC had remained unchanged between 1953 and 1970. For each individual class of goods, he calculated for 1953, 1961 and 1970 the average percentage to which the imports of that class corresponded to the exports of it in the case of a country with an export surplus balance, and the average percentage to which the exports of that class of commodity corresponded to imports in the case of a country with an import surplus balance. The resulting quotient shares were then related to 1 to obtain a residual to reveal the intra-industry trade coefficient, the value of which can vary between 0 and 1 depending whether bilateral trade is low or high. His results indicated that (1974:43).

> In 1970, 42 of the 52 intra-industry trade coefficients were greater than 50%, 15 even greater than 70% ... 45 of the trade coefficients increased from 1953 to 1961; in 1970, 43 coefficients were greater than in 1981, and 50 were greater than in 1953.

Even when it was possible to narrow the product groups further in some cases, the intra-industry coefficients, while lower, were still remarkably high. A more sophisticated analysis was attempted by Aquino (1978) with respect to a disaggregation of the trade flows of manufactures in 1972 of twenty-five classes of products between twenty-six countries, applying a variety of statistical measures. His main results showed (1978: 285, 287) that intra-industry trade as a proportion of total trade in manufactures ranged from 22.9 per cent for India to 87.4 per cent for France; that 'for most of the leading industrial nations this percentage was greater than 70%: UK 81.9, Netherlands 78.7, Sweden 76.3, West Germany 76.0, Austria 75.0, Canada 73.5, Italy 72.3, Denmark 70.3, Belgium 70.1 (the US was 57.3)' and that 'relatively high values of exports are much more often associated with relatively high than with relatively low values of imports' in relation to industrial countries. The results were also significant at the industry level for office machines, radio receivers, passenger motor cars, and motor vehicle parts. The only significant country exception was Japan; and product category exception, miscellaneous manufactures (excluding instruments). In addition to intra-industry trade in manufactures, Grubel (1978) and Dunning (1981b) have suggested that it is also of significance in international exchange in capital assets and foreign direct investment.

It is important to stress at this juncture that in a wide sense 'intra-industry trade is not one but many phenomena' (Lipsey 1976: 311). It is necessary to distinguish two prime, but analytically separate, types of intra-industry trade and to narrow the definition used. Of central concern here is the simultaneous import and export of 'commodities which are considered as the output of the same industry because either they are close but imperfect substitutes from the consumer's point of view or require very similar inputs, or both' (Grubel 1970:37), *not* the simultaneous trade in 'products which from both the ultimate users' and producers' points of view are perfectly homogeneous' (1970: 36), of which Grubel lists five categories which 'can readily be fitted into the framework of the Heckscher-Ohlin model' (1970: 36-7):

(a) bulky primary products with very high transport costs that might give rise to two-way border trade within industries, as each country is not a point in space but extends over some area so that goods are 'cross-hauled' over a common border.
(b) services in joint production.
(c) entrepôt and re-export trade.
(d) governmentally produced distortions in prices.
(e) seasonal fluctuations in output or demand.

Because of the two dimensions of intra-industry trade mentioned above, Gray (1976:172-73) prefers to use the term 'two-way' trade to apply to the first and to define it as 'the simultaneous exporting and importing of goods which use direct identical mixes of inputs (have closely similar production functions) and which serve very similar purposes'.

Assuming that intra-industry trade is not just a statistical phenomenon arising from 'the aggregation of heterogeneous products, establishments and firms into industries which are far from the single-product, single-process industries of theory, in which industry and product are identical, but is a real phenomenon, can a theory be mounted based on factors such as product differentiation and economies of scale to explain it in a rigorous fashion?' Lipsey 1976:313.

Grubel and Lloyd (1975) identified three separate groups of heterogeneous differentiated products:

Group 1: Commodities that are close substitutes in production (because of their similar input-mix requirements) but not in consumption. Two subsets are identified (1975: 87, 88): (a) 'Products which are distinct but which, as a result of technical pecularities, tend to be manufactured in fixed proportions or proportions which can be altered only at high costs', e.g. petroleum derivations such as tar, gasoline and oils. Here 'joint-product technology combined with international differences in demand (or in derived demand for inputs) which give rise to the intra-industry trade'. (b) 'Commodities such as iron and steel products (i.e. bars, rods, beams, sheets, wires, each of different dimensions and quality) which are made from similar materials and frequently in the same plant and machine'. Here economies of scale may be important. Willmore (1979:186) suggests that intra-industry trade here 'gives rise to the possibility of industry rationalization in that economies of scale may be achievable through a reduction in the variety of goods produced by individual plants and the pursuit of longer production runs' and cites Balassa and others to this effect (see Balassa 1974).

Group 2: Goods that are close substitutes in consumption, but have very different factor input requirements. This group is (Grubel and Lloyd 1975:87) 'analytically . . . the least interesting'. Its appearance as intra-industry trade is the result of statistical aggregation, e.g. furniture may be made of wood, steel, wicker, bamboo and plastic, manufactured by processes with different degrees of factor-intensities. This group is best described in Heckscher-Ohlin terms.

Group 3: Goods that (1975:95) 'have similar input requirements and high substitutability in consumption'. Grubel and Lloyd consider two principal sources of product differentiation: style (product appearance and marginal performance characteristics, often exaggerated by advertising); and quality ('measurable performance characteristics of products', e.g. size, weight, power, durability, etc.). This group consists of goods 'differentiated' in the sense used by industrial economists. Grubel and Lloyd (1975: 96, 99, 100) derive two suggestive propositions here: 'that the pattern of international trade in close-substitute products differentiated by style takes the form of countries exporting styles most popular with its own population while they import styles appealing to minority tastes'; and that 'intra-industry trade in quality-differentiated goods, requiring nearly identical inputs and being subject to increasing returns to scale, is determined by the relationship between countries' income distributions and the elasticity of demand for quality with respect to levels of income' so that 'a high-average-income country should export relatively high-quality and import relatively low-quality products'. The question that arises as to why domestic producers do not satisfy the demand for the variety of goods being imported is answered by Grubel and Lloyd (1975: 189) in terms of the existence of start-up costs and scale economies. Willmore (1978: 189) would add what he considers a more fundamental reason – 'that patent and copyright laws, along with industrial secrecy, prevent a company from producing and marketing a product that is identical to that of a rival firm'.

As regards differentiated capital goods, a similar logic is asserted to apply. Grubel and Lloyd (1975:101) make the further point that as international trade statistics fail to classify goods according to whether they are used as intermediate or final goods it is not possible to identify whether vertical and horizontal intra-industry specialisation takes place. They make the supposition, however, that in relation to intermediate goods:

> Economies of scale due to the length of production run (and those due to the size of plant) indicate the possibility that the specialisation across countries may take the form of what may be called vertical intra-industry specialisation in contrast to the horizontal intra-industry specialisation in different final products, ... [the former] may involve the exchange between countries of certain final products by an industry for intermediate products used by the industry ... [or] two countries may exchange different parts, components or raw materials used in the production of commodities by the industry. They may or may not at the same time also exchange different final products of the industry.

H.P. Gray's analysis (1973:20) is largely in relation to Group 3 above, of which he provides three subsets: *Type A* goods that compete 'in similar differentiated markets both at home and abroad and of which the country of origin has relatively little non-cost impact in away market'; *Type B* goods that reflect 'national tastes and tradition to the point at which the authenticity of [their] designs, as denoted by [their] origin, supplies [their] differentiation and design with intrinsic utility in foreign markets – [such producers] compete more directly with their own domestic competitors in foreign markets than with (foreign) import-substitute producers for a small segment of the total market'; *Type C* goods 'not traded "at arm's length" ' – these are likely to comprise preponderantly intermediate goods and goods that have economics of scale in production, design features, etc.

Gray attempts to estabish what he calls 'theoretical underpinnings' for this trade by reference to the existence of 'reciprocal export price ranges' [as shown in Figure 17], which need to be positive and universally present for two-way trade to occur. In the context of two countries, A and B, and negatively sloped demand curves in each for the other's differentiated product in a single product group, such ranges are determined at one extreme by a price condition – that long-run marginal costs of production need to be covered if exports are to be considered (P_{a1} in A, and P_{b1} in B); and, at the other extreme, the existence of a sales volume constraint to cover selling costs (qa_{min} in A, and qb_{min} in B). Trade is possible, provided at each national level, the price at which the latter can be sold (p_{a2} in A, and p_{b2} in B) is greater than or equal to the supply price (p_{a1}, and p_{b1}). Trade will take place at prices p_{a1} and p_{b1} in quantities q_{a1} and q_{b1}. Thus two-way trade is seen to give consumers access to varieties of goods not domestically produced, and arises (H.P. Gray 1977: 183) because, on the side of supply,

> production of a differentiated good almost inevitably requires industry-specific inputs of human capital and proprietary knowledge as well as the benefits that accrue to 'priority in the field'. These inputs may well earn quasi-rents, at least in

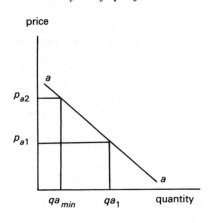

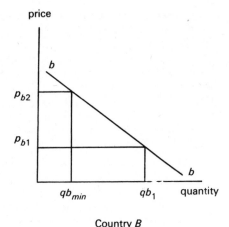

Country A   Country B

Figure 17: *Two-way trade as determined by reciprocal export price ranges*
The demand curve *aa* shows demand in Country *A* for *B*'s differentiated product in terms of *A*'s currency. The demand curve *bb* shows demand in Country *B* for *A*'s differentiated product in terms of *B*'s currency.

the short of medium run . . . [which] can be sacrificed instead of losing
employment of import competition [and, on the side of demand, because] 'the
price-quality-design mix appeals to [consumers] taste'.

In the latter respect, he argues that 'it is very unlikely that two-way trade
would take place in a country in which foreign trade was closely controlled
by the state', and that its significance 'must be limited to developed nations
with predominant manufacturing sectors' (1976:186). He derived a number
of propositions concerning its importance as determined by the probability
of the existence of reciprocal export price ranges (1979:91):

(i) The more differentiated the goods, the steeper the slopes of the
demand curves and the more intense the demand for some quantity of
the imported good. The more intense the demand, the greater the
possible variation in the selling price of the two goods that will permit
them to co-exist in a single market.

(ii) The more similar per capita incomes in the two countries, the more
probable it is that the national tastes will enjoy similar attributes with
respect to quality and post-sophistication.

(iii) The more similar per capita incomes, the greater the probability that
available technology and absolute factor prices will be virtually equal
in the two countries. The more equal the factor prices and available
technology, the closer the costs of production of the competing
differentiated goods are likely to be and the higher the probability of
intra-industry trade being prompted by demand factors.

(iv) Close trading ties and geographic proximity will engender low
impediments to trade between the nations. The lower the impediments
to trade, the greater the probability that intra-industry trade will
exist.

(v) Supply elasticities of both goods must be large to allow the foreign market to be supplied in quantity at a constant price. This is needed to warrant the establishment of a marketing/distribution complex in the foreign market.

Various attempts have been made to verify these and other intra-industry trade propositions. One such by Loertscher and Wolter (1980:289) concluded that their 'explanatory power . . . did not turn out to be impressive'. While finding some comparative evidence, they found 'the role of product differentiation . . . ambiguous', mostly because of 'the difficulties of adequately measuring product differentiation . . . [and obtaining] empirical counterparts for the theoretical constructs. A subsequent study by Caves (1981:220–1) found that:

> [1] The more extensive are scale economies, the less should be the amount of intra-industry trade . . . [2] Intra-industry trade bears a complex relation to product differentiation, being increased by its 'complexity' aspect and reduced by its 'information' aspect . . . [3] Foreign direct investment, which in the long run should be a substitute for trade, also tends to reduce intra-industry trade; but the jointness involved in international trade among affiliated companies is an offsetting factor that increases intra-industry trade . . . [4] Intra-industry trade should increase with transportation costs, which give rise to two-way border trade and limit two-way trade in resource-intensive goods (the statistical evidence is weak). [5] Intra-industry trade should be less, the higher is the variance of countries' tariff rates (weak statistical support); there is no clear theoretical prediction of a long-run relation to the level of tariffs (and no empirical relation was found).

Helleiner, (1981: 5, 7) despite the above, dismisses 'the considerable woolliness of the theoretical under-pinnings', and criticises its relative concentration on trade in final products.

INTRA-FIRM TRADE, INTERNATIONAL PRODUCTION AND MULTINATIONAL RESOURCE ALLOCATION

Dunning (1974: 580) sees the emergence of the multinational firm in the context of a process of 'international spatial diversification': 'The first stage of openness in trade introduced firms of a different nationality of ownership into the market, [i.e. market diversification]: the second stage involves both this *and* the operation of international production units, with all the consequences of branch plant activity [i.e. production facility diversification]'. The advantages of a multi-territorial presence stem from the greater diversity of operations permitted as a result of internationalised production and management decision-taking on a geocentric (or world-oriented) rather than an ethnocentric (or home country-oriented) basis to use Perlmutter's terms (1969: 11). The multinational enterprise can be thought of (Corden 1974:205) as:

> an enclave cutting across national boundaries that is rather like an independent country. This enclave (a) buys and sells factors, (b) buys and sells goods, (c) makes and receives transfers, and (d) creates various external effects . . . that is, effects that by-pass the market – for example through labour and managerial training, and through spreading modern techniques of various kinds, and through pollution.

What is involved here is corporate internalisation of international trade

— intra-firm trade. This phenomenon

> calls into question in a most dramatic fashion two of the most basic premises of
> traditional trade theory: (1) that it is the nation-state which is the appropriate
> basic unit of analysis, within which factors of production are assumed to be
> mobile and between which they are not; (2) that internationally trade
> commodities are exchanged on markets by transactions interacting at arms
> length at prices and volumes established thereon by demand and supply
> considerations. [Helleiner 1981: 3–4.]

Such transactions are not the 'unrelated-party' trade of traditional
theory, where international exchange is implicitly on an open-market,
inter-firm, inter-country basis, but 'related-party' trade, where prices are
not necessarily open-market ones, and exchange is on an intra-firm basis
within a multinational context that includes not just goods and services,
but also capital, management and technology transfers: it is the outcome
(McManus 1972: 66) of 'the process by which productive activities in
different countries come under the control of a single firm . . . the
international extension of managerial control'. What is needed is a theory
of international production to explain the motivation behind the international vertical, horizontal and lateral integration of production
activities across national borders, and why the international corporation
has emerged as an important mechanism of resource allocation in the
new world economy.

Dunning (1979: 271–2) describes the process of the internationalisation of
production in the following terms:

> From investigating overseas primarily to exploit natural resources for export, or
> to supply local markets with a similar product to those produced at home,
> MNCs have increasingly engaged in regional or global process and product
> specialization to take advantage of differential resource endowments, scale
> economies and integrated markets. Sometimes this specialization is *horizontal*,
> where different final products are produced in different locations . . . in other
> cases it is *vertical* . . .

Production thus has become more segmented spacially yet integrated
through the transnational implantation of 'workshop affiliates' (Michalet
(1982: 41). Lall (1980: 98) selects certain factors that he considers relevant to
such intra-firm trade, believing that (1980: 97) 'the conventional theory of
vertical integration provides a number of plausible reasons for the
internationalization of commodity trade' (see Jacquemin and de Jong
(1977); and Howe (1978)). He emphasises three groups of factors: (a)
marketing requirements; (b) factors mostly applicable to intermediate
product exports and the need for backward integration; and, (c) general
operating advantages.

(a) Marketing requirements

Forward integration of tertiary industrial activities is motivated by the
need to control profitable distribution facilities; the need to provide
specialised after-sales services; the need for assimilating and communicat-
ing information to and from consumers *re* their requirements, etc.; the
need to maintain government contacts, monitor or influence policy, or win
large orders ('high' marketing).

(b) Factors mostly applicable to intermediate product exports and the need for backward integration

(i) Specificity of product: The more specific the intermediate input in terms of quality, specifications technology, etc., the more internal supplies will be preferred to external supplies ('high' technology.
(ii) Risk and uncertainty: risks of intermediate input supply (whether specific or non-specific) disruptions, price changes, quality variations will favour internal access to such goods.
(iii) Unexploited capacity and scale economies will be used to supply affiliates rather than let them go to open markets where there exists potential for scale economics or the better utilisation of capacity.
(iv) Divisibility of production processes may lead to their relocation in cheap-labour areas abroad if such areas do not possess indigenous firms capable of undertaking the task, or where MNCs prefer to set up their own affiliates to capitalize on technological advantages.
(v) Home government policy: governments may seek to reduce intra-firm trade by, for example, requiring parent companies to use domestic installed capacity to supply affiliates: or increase it by permitting or even encouraging the transfer of such processes abroad.
(vi) Host government policy can encourage intra-firm trade by seeking to attract foreign investment into highly protected activities or reduce the long-run import content of production by forcing on foreign firms the use of local inputs.

(c) General operating advantages

Increasing the extent of intra-firm activity may increase the scope and potential for using transfer-pricing for purposes of global after-tax profit maximisation, tax and/or regulation avoidance/evasion.

Lall (1979: 139) summarises the importance of the above-mentioned factors in the following terms:

> The greater the significance of these factors for particular industries of TNCs, the greater the benefits of trading within an enterprise than outside it: not only can outside parties not compete with the parent enterprise on price, quality or service, but the enterprise as a whole maximises the profitability of processing special monopolistic advantages by internalising trade. It follows, by the same logic, that in industries and for products which are standardised and so do not afford any monopolistic advantage, open market transactions will tend to predominate over intra-firm transactions.

Helleiner concluded his survey (1979:171) of intra-firm trade thus:

> Using the market involves costs of search and negotiation (transactions costs) and uncertainty. Internalizing what would otherwise be market transactions can reduce and stabilize input costs, reduce uncertainties as to timing and quality of input deliveries, increase and stabilize returns from the sale of both final products and intermediate inputs, and generally increase control over the firm's economic environment.

The importance of the phenomenon is not fully determinable given that there is no systematic collection of statistics in this area. Surveys have been provided by Lall, and Helleiner and Lavergne (1979). According to the latter (1979:298), 1977 statistics of 'related-party' American imports indicate that 48 per cent of all such imports originated with a party related by ownership to the buyer, where this was indicated by a 5 per cent or more control of the voting stock. Of this, just over half was intra-firm importing by American companies from majority-owned foreign affiliates. The 48 per cent figure is an underestimate of the intra-firm import flow because of the existence of licensing agreements, management/marketing contracts, and other forms of subcontracting. Furthermore:

> If these imports are classified according to their broad level of manufacture, we see that related-party trade rises as a proportion of the total as we move from primary goods (excluding petroleum) to semi-manufactured and manufactured ones. While only 23.5 per cent of non-petroleum primary product imports was from related parties, 37.6 per cent of semi-manufactures, and 53.6 per cent of fully manufactured products, were imported in this manner. This general pattern is found for US imports from both the Third World and other OECD members. It is also found in the (relatively less important) imports from centrally planned economies, although, in this case, related-party imports are marginally more important for semi-manufactures than they are for fully manufactured products. Thus, other things being equal, we may expect the role of related-party imports in to the US to rise as industrialization proceeds in Third World countries and manufactured goods assume a larger proportion of their total exports [ibid:298].

On the export side, some 20 per cent of American manufactured exports in 1970 moved from American parent firms to their own majority-owned foreign affiliates. To a considerable extent this was distribution activity: at least half of these flows were for resale without further manufacture, or for lease or rental abroad. The significance of these flows *per se* brings into question whether their pricing is based on real market factors or are set and manipulated on the basis of a firm's own tax or non-market considerations. The analytical point of difference is that:

> in transactions on the open market or between unrelated firms, the buyers and sellers are trying to maximise their profits at *each other's expense*, while in an intra-firm transaction the price is merely an accounting device and the two parties are trying to maximise *joint profits* . . . of *all its operations taken together*. [Lall 1973:113–14.]

Transfer-pricing will tend to occur in a number of circumstances. Lall mentions the following: when losses in a centre can be offset by remitted profits from elsewhere to minimize an overall tax burden; when the existence of taxes, tariffs, quantitative restrictions and subsidies provide an incentive to undervalue or overvalue prices to obtain benefits; when multiple exchange rates discriminate between trade flows; when because of the existence of local shareholders, it is possible for a MNC to overprice imports to increase its own share of the total profits at the expense of local shareholders; or to inflate the initial value of capital equipment contributed by way of equity participation; or, to act in collusion with local partners to provide funds for accumulation abroad or for resale in the black market; and finally to use transfer-pricing as a covert form of exchange rate speculation if exchange rate changes are expected.

Two important results of such activity are, as Lall maintains (1973:129, 128):

(1) Intra-firm trade makes it quite likely that *the benefits of trading are distributed haphazardly between trading partners*, with some countries (the home bases of MNCs in particular) gaining at the expense of others (especially the developing host countries) in such trade.

(2) The existence of transfer-pricing introduces a divergence between the explanation of the *quantities* of goods involved in intra-firm trade as distinct from their stated *values*, and thus renders the existing comparative cost doctrines, of both the traditional Heckscher-Ohlin and the modern technological/oligopolistic types, all of which are couched in terms of market values of trade, inapplicable to such trade.

Given that multinational business acts as a conduit for international capital movements and is intimately involved with the business of technology transfer, in addition to its intra-firm and intra-industry impact on trade flows, it was inevitable that theories of international production should arise to take account of the fact that decisions to export and decisions to manufacture abroad (directly as a result of investment or indirectly via licensing agreements) are real alternatives given the capacity for global reach. Such theories seek to integrate theories of international trade and international investment, given that both activities are subject to a co-ordinated strategy of transnational resource allocation and profit generation. Two of the most significant attempts have been provided by Hirsch (1976) and Dunning (1977; 1979; 1980; 1981, etc.)

Hirsch (1976) divides the variables which influence international direct investment into three groups: comparative input costs; firm-specific revenue producing factors; and information, communication and transaction costs which increase with economic distance. Given that an existing firm in Country A wishes to build a new plant to service markets in Countries A and B, Hirsch argues that the decision to expand in the home market and thereby enhance exports, or to expand abroad and thereby displace export growth, will depend on the following variables:

(1) The relative production costs in A and B, inclusive of capital outlays and purchases of current inputs such as labour, raw materials, and supplies, but exclusive of outlays on R and D, acquisition of know-how, or other expenditures relating to change in technology or product specifications. These costs are P_a and P_b for the two countries respectively.

(2) Firm specific know-how and other intangible income-producing proprietory assets, K. This has resulted from past investment in product or R and D as well as investments in advertising, etc., which enable the firm to create distinct and differentiated products. It provides a barrier to entry by outsiders and gives its owners a temporary monopoly power until rival companies acquire the necessary skills. It has the characteristics of a public good but has to be renewed.

(3) The cost differential (M) between domestic marketing costs (Md) and export marketing costs (Mx) which includes transport, packaging, handling and insurance tariffs imposed in the importing country, i.e. $M = Mx - Md$.

(4) The extra costs (C) involved in controlling and co-ordinating foreign operations (includes cost arising from foreign languages, foreign laws,

taxation systems, labour codes, etc. (*Cx*) as compared with domestic operations (*d*), i.e. $C = Cx - Cd$. They will be lowest in a country as similar culturally and environmentally as the home country.

Hirsch thus concludes that a firm located in Country *A* will invest at home and export to Country *B* if:

$$Pa + M < Pb + K$$
$$\text{and} \quad Pa + M < Pb + C;$$

and will invest abroad in *B* if:

$$Pb + C < Pb + K$$
$$\text{and} \quad Pb + C < Pa + M.$$

Thus international production (investment in a foreign location) will occur when the technological and managerial advantages derived from K outweigh the extra control costs (*C*) associated with subsidiary operations abroad; and, disregarding *K*, such investment will be profitable if the costs of production abroad (*Pb*) and their extra control costs (*C*) are lower than home production costs (*Pa*) + export costs (*M*).

The novelty of this approach is the insertion of the variables *K*, *M* and *C*, without which, the most important conditions of Heckscher-Ohlin theory would be satisfied. However, the variable *K* is seen to be significant and to suggest that direct investment would be most important in technology-based industries or where marketing expertise is at a premium. However, the model is restricted in focus to one product location decisions and does not deal with the intricacies of intermediate production. It does help to explain how the establishment of overseas affiliates often occurs in clusters as an oligopolistic reaction to any marketing advantage one firm might seek to gain from establishing an affiliate organisation abroad. However, a more ambitious and comprehensive approach has been outlined by Dunning which, while it addresses itself to the perplexing variety of variables that may influence international production, has not yet been rigorously formalised.

Dunning (1981a: 32) has developed an 'eclectic' approach towards a general theory of international production. It is eclectic in three respects:

> First, it draws on each of the three main lines of explanation which have emerged over the past twenty or so years [industrial organization, location and market failure theories]; second, it is relevant to all types of foreign direct investment; third, and perhaps of most interest, it embraces the three main vehicles of foreign involvement by enterprises, viz. direct investment, exports and contractual resource transfers, e.g. licensing, technical assistance agreements, management contracts etc.

This 'theory' purports only to provide a framework within which the transnational economic involvement of firms may be determined. Its parameters consist of a list of factors affecting the ownership, location, and internationalisation advantages of enterprises and their degree of country-specificity.

In general, Dunning argues that successful international enterprise requires that firms must either (1982:335):

have access to resource endowments not available to firms in the buying country and not transferable between the two countries, or . . . must possess ownership specific advantages which, although they may reflect the structure of resource endowments of the country from which they originate, are capable of being deployed in another country . . . in . . . the first kind of trade, resources have to be used where they are located, in the second, this is not necessary, and trade will be replaced by foreign production, wherever the location specific endowments (which require to be combined with the ownership advantages of firms) most favour foreign countries.

The resources referred to in the first case (1980:9) are

those which are available, on the same terms, to all firms, whatever their size or nationality, but which are specific in their origin to particular locations and have to be used in that location. These include not only Ricardian type endowments – natural resources, most kinds of labour, and proximity to markets, but also the legal and commercial environment in which the endowments are used – market structure, and government legislation and policies.

The second type of resources (1980:10) are those

which an enterprise may create for itself – certain types of technology and organisational skills – or can purchase from other institutions, but over which, in so doing, it acquires some proprietary right of use. Such . . . inputs may take the form of a legally protected right – patents, brand names, trade marks – or of a commercial monopoly – the acquisition of a particular raw material essential to the production of the product – or of exclusive control over particular market outlets; or they may arise from the size or technical characteristics of firms – economies of large-scale production and surplus entrepreneurial capacity.

The latter ownership advantages are not exclusive to international or multinational firms, but are enhanced by the latter's operation in different location-specific environments and include an

ability to engage in international transfer pricing, to shift liquid assets between currency areas to take advantage of (or protect against) exchange fluctuations, to reduce risks by diversifying their investment portfolios [Rugman (1979)], to reduce the impact of strikes or industrial unrest in one country by operating parallel production capacity in another and by engaging [in] international product or process specifialization. [Dunning 1980: 10.]

Some of the many variables outlined by Dunning as 'OLI characteristics' are summarised in Table 38. It is his contention that (1980:11):

The possession of ownership advantages determines which firms will supply a particular foreign market, whereas the pattern of location endowments explains whether the firm will supply that market by exports (trade) or by local production (non-trade) . . . [and that] the basic incentive of a firm to internalize its ownership endowments is to avoid the disadvantages, or capitalize on the imperfections, of one or the other of the two main external mechanisms of resource allocation – the *market or price system* and the *public authority fiat.*

These matters are discussed at length by Dunning (ibid.). In general he argues that the prosperity to internalise activities will vary between industries, being greatest in technology-intensive sectors and those

Table 38: *OLI characteristics that may vary according to country, industry, and firm-specific considerations*

---

1 *Ownership Specific Advantages* (of enterprises of one nationality (or affiliates of same) over those of another)

  (a) *Which need not arise due to multinationality* – Those due mainly to size and established position, product or process diversification, ability to take advantage of division of labour and specialization; monopoly power, better resource capacity and usage.
Production management, organizational, marketing systems, R & D capacity; 'bank' of human capital and experience. Exclusive or favour access to product markets. Government protection (e.g. control on market entry).

  (b) *Which those branch plants of established enterprises may enjoy over* de novo *firms.*
Access to capacity (administrative, managerial, R & D, marketing etc.) of parent company at favoured prices. Economies of joint supply (not only in production, but in purchasing, marketing, finance etc. arrangements).

  (c) *Which specifically arise because of multinationality.*
Multinationality enhances above advantages by offering wider opportunities. More favoured access to and or better knowledge about information, inputs, markets. Ability to take avantage of international differences in factor endowments, markets. Ability to diversify risks e.g. in different currency areas.

2 *Location Specific Variables*
These may favour home or host countries. Spatial distribution of inputs and markets. Input prices, quality and productivity e.g. labour, energy, materials, components, semi-finished goods. Transport and comm, nication costs. Government intervention. Control on imports (including tariff barriers), tax rates, incentives, climate for investment, political stability etc. Infrastructure (commercial, legal, transportation). Psychic distance (language, cultural, business, customs etc. differences). Economies of R & D production & marketing (e.g. extent to which scale economies make for centralization of production).

3 *Internationalization Incentive Advantages* (i.e. to protect against or exploit market failure).
Avoidance of transaction and negotiating costs. To avoid costs of enforcing property rights. Buyer uncertainty (about nature & value of inputs (e.g. technology) being sold. Where market does not permit discrimination. Need of seller to protect quality of products. To capture economies of interdependent activities (see 1(b) above). To compensate for absence or futures markets. To avoid or exploit Government intervention (e.g. quotas, tariffs, price controls, tax differences etc.). To control supplies and conditions of sale of inputs (including technology). To control market outlets (including those which might be used by competitors). To be able to engage in practices e.g. cross-subsidization, predatory pricing etc. as a competitive (or anti-competitive) strategy.

Source: Dunning (1979: 276, Table 2)

engaging in backward resource integration; and, given the industry, between countries, as government intervention can be country-specific. Where ownership advantages are not marketable and/or transferable across countries, direct investment and exports are the only two routes of international involvement open to an enterprise. Thus Dunning provides a 'tool-kit' with which foreign involvement decisions and the pattern of international production can be 'explained'. He argues (1980: 12) that 'without the advantages of internalization much of direct foreign investment would be replaced by the international transaction of resources on a contractual basis between independent buyers and sellers'. The generalised conclusions of his approach are that (1979:289):

> A country's international economic involvement comprises the sum of the activities by its enterprises in trade in goods, assets and money and in outward direct investment . . . [and that] at any given moment of time, the more a country's enterprises possess ownership specific advantages, relative to enterprises of other nationalities, the greater the incentive they have to internalise rather than externalise their use; and the more they find it in their interest to exploit them from a foreign location, the more they (and the country as a whole) are likely to engage in international production. By the same token, a country is likely to attract investment by foreign enterprises when the reverse conditions apply.

Dunning has also sought to provide a dynamic or developmental version of this theory (1979: 30–1) to suggest 'a systematic relation between the determinants of direct investment flows and the stage and structure of a country's economic development'. In its generalised form, it asserts that:

> changes in the outward or inward investment position of a particular country can be explained in terms of changes in the ownership and internalisation advantages of its enterprises, relative to those of other nationalities and/or changes in its location specific endowments relative to those of other countries, as perceived by its own and foreign enterprises.

While initial testing of this theory has begun, it has yet to be formalised as a model. This approach, being empirically related, does, however, seem to be in the right direction.

Naturally, important national political economy issues arise from the global resource reallocation potential of MNCs and their impact on national industrial structures. While these matters are touched on in Chapter 10, this chapter is not an appropriate context for reviewing such policy discussions. It will suffice merely to indicate the nature of the dilemma as posed by Helleiner and to highlight three main causes for concern as outlined by Mabogunje [but see Nayyar 1978]:

> The less-developed countries must now begin to calculate the potential gains from entry into this new form of manufacturing for export as against those realisable from other types of export, other forms of industrialisation, and other sources of income and employment. In these calculations, account must be taken of the potential for linkage and learning effects, neither of which are in this case likely to be large, and other 'dynamic' influences, both positive and negative. It is quite possible for a country, particularly one at a relative disadvantage with respect to labour and transport costs, to build infrastructure and/or to offer subsidies to attract this particularly 'footloose' type of

manufacturing activity, even on occasions when the social opportunity cost of these outlays exceeds the apparent income gains from the new activity; in such cases, the country is better off without it. Where these calculations do demonstrate the potential for income gains, there may still be legitimate concern about the degree of 'dependence' and/or structural imbalance which too much development of this enclavistic sort may create for the host country. [Helleiner 1973:46–7]

(a) First, these corporations often impose export restrictions on their subsidiaries and affiliates in the developing countries. Such restrictions can take the form of market sharing whereby the subsidiaries are permitted to export to certain countries and precluded from doing so to others; or it may involve the retention by the parent company of the primary responsibility for the multinationals' export activity and an insistence that its prior approval must be obtained for any exports by its subsidiaries. Sometimes, the restriction takes the form of permission to export to or only through special firms . . .
(b) Second, multinational corporations often tie the import of raw material and intermediate goods to sources within the corporation structure. Such tied purchasing arrangements have often frustrated the principle of import substitution since [they prevent] the growth of backward linkage relation involving the development of local sources of raw material . . .
(c) Finally, multinational corporations engage in tremendous surplus creaming through easy movement of funds out of developing countries. Apart from the use of arbitrary transfer pricing, they utilise a variety of other methods to repatriate high profits out of these countries [that expedite or defer payments in the interests of the company, not the country] [Mabogunje 1977:438–9].

CONCLUSION

Postwar trade trends contained a number of structural changes that further undermined the premises on which past orthodox theories were operatively based. The emergence of inter-industry and intra-firm trade flows heralded new determinants of international specialisation and inter-territorial resource allocation. The importance of differentiated products, the simultaneous import and export of such products, the pricing of trade flows acording to transfer-priced and not open-market values, the intra-institutional nature of many trade flows and much international capital mobility required quantitative assessment and qualitative theoretical explanation. However, extremely complex methodological problems beset the precision with which these structural elements could be identified. Consequently the theoretical refinement of their explanation has been low and the degree of controversy attaching to the end products high. Realisation that modern trade theory is required to explain the newly pervasive phenomenon of international multi-process production and that international investment and trade are not necessarily complements but often substitutes led to attempts at integrating their explanations using the motivational xxxx of the multinational firm as the unit of analysis. Trade theoretical propositions are now consequently more empirically directed than in the past, more concerned with what is rather than what could be, but not as yet in a rigorous form. Their orientation lies, however, in the direction of world economics rather than international economics.

10 The analysis of trade-dependent relationships as an outcome of international exchange

To a social scientist brought up in the dominant positive hypothetical-deductive methodology, theories of dependency may seem at best trivial or irrelevant and at worst political slogans wrapped up as a theory.

O'Brien (1975:11)

'Dependencia theory' [is not] ... an ... easily isolated and distinguishable set of arguments. Rather, the label signifies a broad set of contemporary discussions about imperialism, global inequality, and underdevelopment that focus on the economic, social, and political 'distortions' of 'peripheral' societies which result from their incorporation into the global capitalist system.

Duval *et al* (1981:312)

However viewed, world analysis reflects a considerable amount of dissatisfaction with the artificial Balkanization of the study of social, economic, and political interaction and the evident analytical limitations imposed by disciplinary barriers.

Thompson (1983a:10)

The two standard general international trade models, the classical and neo-classical, implicitly assume symmetrical equipoised international trade relationships, being:

based on countries with a very similar economic structure and at an approximately equal stage of development. Their foreign trade [being] chiefly substitutions as they have fundamentally comparable possibilities of production at their disposal ... [However they] hardly provide ... a satisfactory model of explanation for North–South trade ... [relying as they do] on the idea that after a suitable infant-protectionism and internalizing of external effects a 'one World' in the vicinity of the substitution model will be achieved. [Lorenz 1974:83.]

An additional defect is that 'the dominant role of nation-states in the preservation of order and the allocation of values in the world polity is being challenged by other entities and movements – subnational, transnational, and supranational ... [so that] increasingly, the nation-state system operates as a *sub*-system' (S. Brown (1984: 509)). Theories of asymmetrical international trade relations provide explanations both for the conjoint existence of developed and underdeveloped economies; and the role played by the world expansion of capitalism in creating, maintaining or equilibrating these differences via a world economy that allegedly 'integrates the so-called "National economies" in a world market of commodities, capital and even of labour power' (Dos Santos 1970:231). The holistic political economy approach (or more correctly, socio-political economy approach) they adopt seeks to identify the specific forces, motivations and mechanisms behind such alleged structural subjugation and its concomitant unequal, inequalising trade.

Most writers in this area would tend to agree with Palloix that however caused, 'unequal exchange is nothing other than the external manifestation of the problems raised by the internal dynamic' (1969b: 21). Bettelheim (1972: 325) makes the point that:

It is necessary to regard each 'country' as constituting a social formation characterized by a specific structure, and notably by the existence of *classes* with contradictory interests. It is this structure which determines the mode of the insertion of each social formation in the international relations of production ... Relations of exploitation cannot constitute themselves at 'the level of exchanges', they must necessarily be rooted at the level of *production*.

In most of these 'explanations'

foreign factors are seen not as external but as intrinsic to the system, with manifold and sometimes hidden or subtle political, financial, economic, technical and cultural effects inside the underdeveloped country . . . the evolution of capitalism internationally [is linked] to the discriminatory nature of the local process of development . . . Access to the means and benefits of development is selective; rather than spreading them, the process tends to ensure a self-reinforcing accumulation of privilege for special groups as well as the continual existence of a marginal class. [Sunkel 1972: 12.]

In seeking to assess the importance of this view of trade flows as being the interstices of a world development process, one must be aware of the possible methodological traps such ambitious holistic 'explanations' may fall foul of, as have been indicated by T. Smith (1979: 285) in the following terms:

Because this approach is formulistic and reductionist, it is bad historiography. It is formulistic in the sense that it seeks to specify universal laws or processes in blatant disregard of the singular or the idiosyncratic. By the same token it is reductionist, since it forces the particular case to express its identity solely in the terms provided by the general category. The error of this approach is not that it draws attention to the interconnectedness of economic and political processes and events in a global manner, but that it refuses to grant the part *any* autonomy, *any* specificity, *any* particularity independent of its membership in the whole.

Palma (1981) distinguishes three main phases in the development of Marxist thought concerning the capitalist development of backward countries and areas of the world:

1 The aboriginal views of Marx: in which it is asserted that capitalism is progressively transplanted via colonialism, free trade, etc., from advanced countries to backward nations, as a result of which clone-like capitalist societies become established, which, in their post-colonial period, mechanically replicate the evolutionary process of eventual social revolution and the achievement of a 'higher-state' of development.
2 Early-twentieth-century writings on imperialism: in which (1981: 22) 'a far more complex process of interplay between internal and external structures' is outlined, which results in 'a different set of difficulties (particularly of a political nature) hindering the process of post-colonial

industrialisation' not previously envisaged by Marx, but not making the revolutionary transition either easy or indeed quite so inevitable as previously imagined.

3 Mid-twentieth-century views on economic dependency:(ibid.) 'characterised by the acceptance, almost as an axiomatic truth ... that no Third World country can . . . expect to 'break out of a state of economic dependency and advance to an economic position beside the major capitalist industrial powers'.

For reasons of space and extra-economic complexity, the first two above-mentioned phases will be given only a brief outline here (but see A. Brewer (1980); Mommsen (1981); and Williams (1978)), the main discussion being reserved for phase 3 theories.

ABORIGINAL MARXIST VIEWS OF THE WORLD CAPITALIST ECONOMY

The focus of discussion here is the dyadic segmentation of the world into advanced capitalist countries and their relationships and mechanisms of control over the residual less-developed areas. Marx analysed a three-stage historical relationship between the two: plunder; exploitation through trade and taxes and industrial investment. The first two stages are exploitative, with wealth flowing from the latter to the former countries; the third stage involves capitalist industrialisation of the latter as a result of internationally mobile capital. Each stage is an interlinked process of economic development. In the first, the colonial system is seen as a generator of wealth that enabled industrial 'take-off' to occur in Europe. The second involves autonomous capital accumulation in the industrialising capitalist countries and the use of colonised areas primarily as markets for industrial exports. The last 'mature' stage involves international capital transfers and the transplanting of capitalist production to the LDCs and its institutionalisation there, the main momentum for which comes from a declining rate of profit in the former relative to the latter countries. Szymanski (1981: 23) describes the process in the following terms: 'Capital denationalises itself, tending to create a more or less homogeneous world capitalist system . . . [and] the forced capitalist development of the economically less-developed countries ... [establishes] the conditions for their liberation in an eventual socialist revolution'.

Ultimately an international expansion of the capitalist market allegedly incorporates all countries into an international division of labour.

EARLY TWENTIETH CENTURY VIEWS ON IMPERIALISM

Early-twentieth-century writers (the most notable of which were Hobson (1902), Hilferding (1910) and Luxemburg (1913)), with varying emphases, elaborated the above doctrines in greater detail but still essentially within Marx's skeletal outline. Many of their views were synthesised by Lenin in his *Imperialism, the Highest State of Capitalism* (1917). Imperialism was identified as the phenomenon by which exchange relationships were forged with initially non-capitalist economies, and, by means of which, investment opportunities were obtained and safeguarded. The momentum behind such activities was varyingly ascribed to the falling rate of profit, the presence of cheap labour abroad, and an inability to find investment opportunities at home.

Hobson identified 'monopoly capitalism' as the main organisational aegis behind these developments, personified by giant trusts and corporations, that tends to generate profits of a magnitude that cannot be profitably reinvested at home and therefore needs to find profitable investment opportunities abroad. Hilferding gave great emphasis in this to the institutional role of 'financial capitalism', as well as to a progressive concentration of ownership of trusts, that increase the amount of idle capital seeking such externally located investment. Furthermore, Hobson asserts that monopoly capitalism and not capitalism *per se* is 'an inherent result of the capital accumulation process in general . . . [and] there is no possibility of ending or reforming it short of totally abolishing capitalist relations of production'. He argued that capitalism could only continue to grow by being parasitical on non-capitalist economies and foresaw an inexorable progressive capitalist incorporation of external areas as a result of the capital accumulation process [Szymanski (1981: 33]: 'to avoid a cataclysmic economic depression that would be produced by the absence of investment possibilities within the system . . . capitalism is forced to continually expand or die . . . the final economic crisis and collapse of capitalism will occur once there are no more noncapitalist areas into which capitalism can expand'. These needs inevitably lead to inter-imperialist wars (Luxemburg 1913: 446):

> With the high development of the capitalist countries and their increasingly severe competition in acquiring non-capitalist areas, imperialism grows in lawlessness and violence, both in aggression against the non-capitalist world and in ever more serious conflicts among the competing capitalist countries.

Lenin (1913: 790) adopted an eclectic approach with respect to the foregoing authors, and gave great emphasis to the importance of monopoly capitalism as 'the deepest economic foundation of imperialism':

> As long as capitalism remains what it is, surplus capital will be utilized not for the purpose of raising the standard of living of the masses in a given country, for this would mean a decline in profits for the capitalists, but for the purpose of increasing profits by exporting capital abroad to the backward countries.

Financial capital is deemed to exert control over less-developed areas which include:

> formal colonies directly ruled by the advanced capitalist states; semicolonies such as China, Persia, and Thailand, which maintain formal independence but little autonomy; 'commercial colonies', such as Argentina, whose local bourgeoisie are thoroughly dependent on finance capital from the leading capitalist countries; and independent protectorates with a fairly high level of autonomy such as Portugal (in relation to Britain) who have granted favorable economic concessions to their protector in both their own countries and their colonies. [Szymanski; 1981: 38–9).]

The cardinal, underlying idea behind Lenin's theses is (1920: 497) 'the division of the whole world . . . into a large number of oppressed nations and an insignificant number of oppressor nations which . . . command colossal wealth and powerful armed forces'. However, while imperialism was initially seen as promoting both industrialisation and the growth of a revolutionary proletariat in less-developed areas, the Sixth Comitern Congress of 1928 (534–5) came to a rather different view:

> The export of capital to the colonies accelerates the development of capitalist relations there. The part which is invested in production does to some extent accelerate industrial development; but this is not done in ways which promote independence; the intention is rather to strengthen the dependence of the colonial economy on the finance capital of the imperialist country . . .
>
> The favourite form of investment in agriculture is in large plantations, with the object of producing cheap food and monopolizing vast sources of raw material. The transference to the metropolis of the greater part of the surplus value exported from the cheap labour power of the colonial slaves retards the growth of the colonial economy and the development of its productive forces, and is an obstacle to its economic and political emancipation . . .

MID-TWENTIETH-CENTURY VIEW ON ECONOMIC DEPENDENCY IN A GLOBAL CONTEXT

As a background to understanding the evolution of Marxist thought that was contemporary with actual post-colonial experience, it is instructive to outline the initial hopes and strategies adopted in Latin America and their frustration as a predominant motivator of two new visions of international political economy: a general body of discussion loosely referred to as *dependencia theory*, and, what Koo (1984: 36) describes as a 'sister concept', *world-systems analysis*.

Postcolonial dilemmas and hopes for economic independence in Latin America

As Latin America was the major continent to have achieved political independence in the nineteenth century, it was natural that it became a field focus for practical policy and ideological discussions in the post-colonial trade strategy debate and the identification of the parameters that seemingly foreclosed a number of autocentric development options. As early as the 1930s, a number of indigenous writers such as Haya de la Torre (1936) were emphasising the need for states to control the direction of investment as a counterpoise to neo-imperialist tendencies. In search of an 'Indo-american Way', the above-mentioned writer expressed the need for the evolution of an appropriate indigenous economic system (quoted in Hirschman 1961:11) in these terms:

> Why not build into our own reality 'as it really is' the bases of a new economic and political organization which will accomplish the educational and constructive task of industrialism but will be free of its cruel aspects of human exploitation and national vassalage.

A blue-print of such a task awaited the formation of the United Nations Economic Commission for Latin America (henceforth ECLA) in 1948, based in Santiago, which subsequently evolved its own cohesive personality and set of distinctive beliefs, principles and attitudes. The essence of the new ideology was contained in Prebisch's book, *The Economic Development of Latin America and its Principal Problems* (1950), and subsequently evolved as a result of intensive studies of particular Latin American countries and experience with attempts at intra-area economic integration and co-operation. The 'centre-periphery' perspective he discerned highlighted the dilemmas of underdevelopment created and maintained by asymmetrical trade relations between a centre group of advanced countries and a peripheral group of less-developed countries. This asymmetry was allegedly the compound product of an unequal distribution of the gains from trade, an inferior income elasticity of demand for the products of the latter countries and a consequent adverse international bargaining position of these countries. The new emphasis was (Hirschman 1961:16) in terms of: 'the promotion of industrialization through systematic inter-ference with the balance of payments, i.e., through protection and import controls . . . [and the need to] actively . . . plan and accelerate the process of import substitution, since otherwise continued economic development will run into a rigid foreign exchange barrier'.

Such a policy, it was thought, would, if generally resorted to in predominantly raw material-producing developing countries, break the complementary mould and bias in the international division of labour that had been a ninetenth century creation. This aim became declared industrialisation strategy, first in Latin America, then Asia, and sub-sequently in Africa (see Giersch 1974). The policy means by which this was to be achieved was the programming of development as a result of economic forecasting and committed planned rates of growth by indigenous governments. A particular 'structuralist' perspective would be evolved, appropriate to each different national historical situation and economic context. In general, an inward-oriented development path was envisaged based on industrialisation behind high protective barriers, as a result of which, levels of structural unemployment were expected to diminish, underutilisation of capital reversed, and an optimal allocation of resources approached, thereby correcting the alleged 'international market failure'. As a result of greater local control over these economies, the power of traditional oligarchies was expected to diminish and a process of political democratisation ensue, leading to more egalitarian national income distributions, the integration of rural masses into modern societies, and a more progressively conscious pursuit of national independence. It is to be noted that this analysis was intentionally at variance with the contemporary 'modernization perspective' that assumed that:

> the values, institutions and patterns of action of traditional society are both an expression and cause of underdevelopment and constitute the main obstacle in the way of modernization . . . [and that] the national society is the basic unit of analysis, while the writer in a dependence framework considers the global system and its various forms of interaction with national societies as the primary object of inquiry. For the dependency perspective, the time dimension is the crucial aspect of what is fundamentally a historical model . . . Individual societies cannot be presumed to be able to replicate the evolution of other societies because the very transformation of an interrelated world system may preclude such an option. [Valenzuela 1979: 35,52.]

Similar policy reconsiderations were going on in other parts of the world, including the West Indies, for which Demas (1965) developed a concept of 'economic transformation' as a way of identifying a schema of corrective policies, and McIntyre (1961: 166) tried to distinguish between:

> *structural dependence* – the dependence that arises because of the size and structure of the economy and cannot be helped, and *functional dependence* – the dependence that arises as a result of the particular policies chosen and can therefore be avoided if alternative policies are pursued.

The Latin American presumptions made by ECLA, as summarised by Dos Santos (1973: 65,67), were that:

> As the economy turned 'towards the interior' a national centre of decision-making would emerge . . . [resulting in] the establishment of an independent national society, and of an independent State machine which, though interventionist rather than liberal in character, would nevertheless respect private initiative . . . [and] was expected to lead to greater independence in foreign trade, and to transfer the centre of decision-making to the local economy.

However, lack of commitment to those policies and/or their only partial success, when implemented vitiated the credibility of this approach:

> By the 1960s, it had become obvious that this model was in crisis. Import substitution industrialization had not lessened dependence. Income distribution seemed to be growing more unequal, and a large segment of the population remained marginal . . . Latin American societies still continued to be divided and unstable. National policies and industrialization had succumbed to the multi-national corporations, and industrialization in Latin America was primarily being undertaken by foreign investors [O'Brien 1975: 11.]

Given these circumstances, new approaches were evolved, some in the pure Marxist tradition, others in the context of theories of dependence or 'dependencia', in an attempt to explain the apparent impasse and to suggest different policy escape routes by which to achieve higher levels of effective indigenous economic independence.

Neo-Marxist views of dependency

When it was evident that early-twentieth-century Marxist thought had been made 'largely out of date because of the profound internal changes which both developed and underdeveloped countries [had] experienced, and the radical transformations which . . . [took] place in their relations with one another' (Sunkel 1969: 24), revision of some of its assertions seemed necessary. Whereas the traditional view had been that lack of development in countries was a result of imperialist blocks on the development of capitalism, a new body of neo-Marxist and Marxist-related thought emerged, centred on what was increasingly referred to as 'peripheral capitalism', that argued that on the contrary,

> because of the structural blocking of industrialisation by the economic policies of the transnational corporations and the states they dominate . . . capitalism, rather than being a progressive force that stimulated economic development, is seen as a regressive force that 'underdevelops' backward countries. [Szymanski 1981: 70–1.]

Given this general vision, Palma (1981:42) discerns three major aproaches not mutually exclusive, under the general portmanteau term 'dependency analysis';

(a) The 'theory of underdevelopment' approach: this includes important and sometimes mutually inconsistent contributions by Frank, Dos Santos, Emmanuel, Magdoff and Amin.

(b) The critique of the obstacles to 'national development' approach: adopted by Sunkel, Furtado and others in an attempt to reformulate the previously discredited ECLA analyses of development.

(c) An *ad hoc* 'concrete situations of dependency' approach: this eschews a mechanico-formal theory of dependency in favour of case-study analyses of the dilemmas facing individual countries.

The theory of underdevelopment approach

This approach essentially stems from the cumulative writings of Baran in the 1950s, Frank in the late 1960s and 1970s, with important contributions being made by Dos Santos, Emmanuel and Amin among others in the 1970s. Baran (1957: 28, 142–3,184) perceived that the economic development of underdeveloped countries is 'profoundly inimical to the dominant interests in the advanced capitalist countries' and that the 'intrusion' of Western capitalists in such areas gave rise to 'the removal of a large share of [their] . . . previously accumulated and currently generated surplus', they being 'determined to extract the largest possible gains from the host countries . . . [engaging] in outright plunder or in plunder thinly veiled as trade, seizing and removing tremendous wealth from the places of their penetrations', particularly in the form of interest and dividends from their investments. Baran argues (1957: 197) that the termination of colonial rule made little difference to these processes and that:

> the contemporary form of imperialism . . . is now directed not solely towards the rapid extraction of large sporadic gains from the objects of its domination, it is no longer content with merely assuring a more or less steady flow of those gains over a somewhat extended period. Propelled by well-organised, rationally conducted monopolistic enterprise, it seeks today to rationalise the flow of these receipts so as to be able to count on it in perpetuity.

Monopoly capital is still seen as the *deus ex machina* but with rather different results. Despite political independence, continued imperialist activity is ensured by domestic reproduction of socio-economic and political structures in accordance with the interest of the rich, formerly metropolitan, powers. For this reason, the development of capitalism in such areas does not replicate that experienced by advanced countries in an earlier period of history, and, contrary to classical Marxist views, does not lead to a uniformity of production methods and standards of living of the bulk of the world's population. The gulf between these different countries widens not narrows.

Baran's approach was developed, with varying emphases, by writers such as Frank, Magdoff, and Amin, seeking to further identify and clarify the areas and mechanisms of international market failure via such themes as the 'development of underdevelopment', 'contemporary monopoly capitalism', 'unequal exchange' and 'dependency'.

Frank's influential book *Capitalism and Underdevelopment in Latin America* (1967) has as a central theme the view that (1967:9-10)

> economic development and underdevelopment are relational and qualitative, in that each is structurally different from, yet caused by its relation with, the other... One and the same historical process of the expansion and development of capitalism throughout the world has simultaneously generated [them].

This relationship arises from a metropolitan-controlled monopoly structure of the world market exerted via a system of world-wide exchange links. Underdevelopment is regarded as the product of this trade structure. As Lind (1978: 675) has observed, here ' "Underdevelop" is an active verb; "underdevelopment" is what one actor *does to another actor*'. Underdevelopment is not an original state (the term underdevelopment is reserved for that), but one effected through an evolving expropriation/appropriation *chain* of metropolis–satellite relations:

> At each step along the way the relatively few capitalists exercise monopoly power over the many below, expropriating some or all of their economic surplus, and to the extent that they are not expropriated in turn by the still fewer above, appropriating it for their own use ... at each point, the international, national and local capitalist system governs economic development for the few and underdevelopment for the many. [Frank 1967: 78.]

In short, (Palma 1981: 44), 'the only alternative becomes that of breaking completely with the metropolis–satellite network through socialist revolution or continuing to "underdevelop" within it'.

Frank's general approach spawned a plethora of subsequent writing by Magdoff, Dos Santos, Emmanuel and Amin, among others, that sets out particular aspects of his discussion in more detail, often with conflicting variants. In contrast to classical Marxism, new rationales were suggested for international monopoly activity, the primary motive force behind which was deemed to be wider than the mere export of capital motivated by an alleged declining rate of profit:

> some combination of the need to control sources of cheap raw materials, the need to find protected export markets, the drive to make profits to repatriate to the advanced countries, and the need to justify an expensive (and profitable) military establishment [Szymanski 1981: 78.]

Moreover, contrary to what Lenin and Luxemburg had asserted, it was now argued that 'the process of capital accumulation in the metropolitan countries is actually *facilitated* and *sped up* by international capital flows'. The latter are seen as the consequences of monopoly situations

> due to cost advantages of Big Business, exclusive patents, superior technology, or preferred market demand stimulated by establishment of desired brands via sales promotion ... and an alleged "urge to dominate", and a need to eliminate as much risk as possible ... in a world of tough antagonists by geographical global sourcing and market servicing. [Magdoff 1969: 37.]

Hymer (1972: 113-14) argued that the multinational firm is both a product of and a medium for two 'laws of development': 'the Law of Increasing Firm Size ... a tendency [since the beginning of the Industrial Revolution] for the representative firm to increase in size from the *workshop* to the *factory* to the national corporation to the *multi-divisional corporation* . . . to the *multinational corporation*'; and 'the Law of Uneven Development . . . the tendency of the system to produce poverty as well as wealth, underdevelopment as well as development'. As a result of these asserted laws, he discerns a global tendency for:

> a regime of North Atlantic Multinational Corporations . . . to produce a hierarchical division of labor within the firm . . . to centralize high-level decision-making occupations in a few key cities in the advanced countries, surrounded by a number of regional sub-capitals, and confine the rest of the world to lower levels of activity and income, i.e. to the status of towns and villages in a new Imperial system. Income, status, authority, and consumption patterns would radiate out from these centers along a declining curve, and the existing pattern of inequality and dependency would be perpetrated. The pattern would be complex, just as the structure of the corporation is complex, but the basic relationship between different countries would be one of superior and subordinate, head office and branch office. [Hymer 1972: 114.]

Dos Santos's contribution was an examination of the nature of 'dependence' (1970: 231) as

> a situation in which the economy of certain countries is conditioned by the development and expansion of another economy to which the former is subjected. The relation of interdependence between two or more economies, and between these and world trade, assumes the form of dependence when some countries (the dominant ones) can expand and can be self-sustaining, while other countries (the dependent ones) can do this only as a reflection of that expansion, which can have either a positive or a negative effect on their immediate development.

Three forms of historical dependence are distinguished, each generating mutual but unequal relations between the two types of economies.

(1) Colonial dependence, trade export in nature, in which commercial and financial capital in alliance with the colonialist state dominated the economic relations of the Europeans and the colonies, by means of a trade monopoly complemented by a colonial monopoly of land, mines, and manpower (serf or slave) in the colonized countries.

(2) Financial-industrial dependence which consolidated itself at the end of the nineteenth century, characterized by the domination of big capital in the hegemonic centers, and its expansion abroad through investment in the production of raw materials and agricultural products for consumption in the hegemonic centers. A productive structure [of 'foreign-oriented development'] grew up in the dependent countries devoted to the export of these products.

(3) Technological-industrial dependence. In the post-1945 period, a new type of dependence has been consolidated, based on multinational corporations which began to invest in industries geared to the internal market of underdeveloped countries. [Dos Santos 1970: 232.]

It is perhaps useful for clarity to confine the use of the word 'dependency' exclusively to the structuralist paradigm of the process of incorporation of LDCs into the global capitalist system and the 'structural distortions' resulting therefrom, and to reserve the word 'dependence' for the lesser context of 'external reliance on other actors'.

Other writers identify important non-economic characteristics of dependence, such as its socio-political aspects. For example, Senghaas (1974:162–3) asserts that:

[the] political structure of foreign rule still exists today though the accents are set differently, *and it still mirrors the profound penetration of the dependent areas by the outside centres*. This asymmetrical penetration of the dominating centres took place . . . in all the essential social fields. This was done by controlling the socialization processed in the widest sense of the word (*cultural imperialism*); by controlling the media of communication (*communication imperialism*), as well as political, military and legal systems (*political imperialism*) . . . A history of the political and social structures of the third world can be seen as a function of this external penetration.

As a result of the above types of analysis, a number of dependencia propositions were put forward with respect to the operation of multi-national firms. Summarised by Moran (1978: 80, 85, 93) these include:

1. [that] the benefits of foreign investment are 'poorly' (or 'unfairly' or 'unequally') distributed between the multinational and the host, or the country pays 'too high' a price for what it gets, or the company siphons off an economic 'surplus' that could otherwise be used to finance internal development . . .
2. [that] multinational corporations create distortions within the local economy . . . first, [they] . . . 'preempt' the development of an indigenous economic base by squeezing out local entrepreneurs in the most 'dynamic' sectors of the host country economy; second, [they] . . . employ 'inappropriate' capital-intensive technologies when they move in, adding to host country unemployment; third, [they] worsen the distribution of income in the host country or even produce an absolute loss for the lower 40 per cent; fourth, [they] alter consumer tastes and undermine the culture of the host country . . .
3. [that] foreign investors pervert or subvert host country political processes (a) by co-opting the local elites; and/or (b) by using their influence in their home countries to bring pressure to keep host governments 'in line'; and/or (c) by structuring the internal system to respond to their multinational needs to the detriment of host authorities.

Tangential to the above, but in contrast to both classical Marxist thought and classical economic theory, came Emmanuel's *Unequal-Exchange: A Study of the Imperialism of Trade* (1972), in which the explanation of the basic problem of economic inequality between nations is addressed. He believes that unequal exchange can exist in two forms that have different operational conditions:

(a) 'the narrow sense': this arises when wage rates are identical but the organic composition of capital in developed and less-developed countries differs.
(b) 'the broad sense': when unequal exchange arises from international differences in wage rates.

Making the assumption that capital is mobile internationally and that labour is not, Emmanuel argues that international capital flows respond to inter-country wage differentials and seek to equalise profit rates internationally. Wage-rates, he argues, are not determined by productivity but by institutional factors that include trade union pressure. Thus any autonomous increase in wage rates in rich countries, brought about by their greater and stronger indigenous trade union activity, will tend to reduce domestic profit rates relative to those in poor ones, and the mechanism of international profit rate equalisation will depress the prices of the latter countries' exports in relation to those of the former. Thus it follows that:

> Exchange is 'unequal' because the low-wage country has to pay more for its imports than it would if wages were the same in both countries, without getting higher prices for its own exports. It thus has to export more to get a given amount of imports. Correspondingly, the high-wage country gets more imports in return for a given amount of exports. Whether the actual amounts traded would stay the same regardless of prices is another matter; the argument is concerned only with the terms of trade [A. Brewer 1980: 212].

Absolute costs, not comparative costs, determine the specialisation pattern. Two basic injustices are alleged to underlie the differential market conditions in the two types of countries: at the sectoral labour market level (assuming labour to be of universal equal quality), the labour of the poor country is rewarded much less than comparable labour in rich countries for identical tasks; and, at the economy level, 'because poor countries have relatively low wage-levels, the prices at which they trade reflect those wage levels and, input for input, are therefore low compared with those of rich countries' (Ross 1976: 42). In unfettered conditions of international trade an inferior bargaining position results. Once established, unequal exchange is deemed to be the basis for a continuous process of unequal development and profit extraction and to provide a determinant of international prices:

> Unequal exchange is the *elementary* transfer mechanism and that, as such, it enables the advanced countries to begin and regularly give new impetus to that *unevenness of development* that sets in motion all the other mechanisms of exploitation and fully explains the way that wealth is distributed. [Emmanuel 1972: 265]

However, A. Brewer (1980: 227) makes a major objection that no convincing answers are given to two basic questions that are central to the above model, namely 'why should the high-wage, high-price products go on being produced in the high-wage countries? *Given free mobility of capital between countries why should any investment go to the high-wage countries at all?*' Furthermore, Bettleheim (1972: 284) argues that Emmanuel's treatment of wage determination 'gives rise to the impression that to "correct" the "inequality of exchanges" it would be sufficient to change wage levels', and yet he argues against this on the grounds that

> a sudden levelling up of their wage levels to those of the advanced countries being, of course, out of the question *a priori*, they can only seek means to keep for themselves and prevent from leaking abroad the excess surplus value that they extract from their own workers [Bettleheim 1972: 267].

As an alternative to autarky as a means by which to impede any further transfer of value via unequal exchange, which is deemed to require a socialist revolution, attempts at diversification into high-skill/high-wage capital-intensive sectors are suggested. An intermediate solution is given in terms of a world export-tax on each primary commodity exported by poor countries, so that, in low-wage countries, export prices are raised relative to import prices and the surplus value drain overseas lessened. However, the asserted benefits are by no means inevitable but reliant on the relative home and foreign elasticities of demand and supply for the products concerned (see Ross 1976:52–3).

Trace elements of the above discussions of the 'development of underdevelopment', 'monopoly capitalism' and 'unequal exchange' are to be found in Amin's eclectic attempt at analytic synthesis (1974;1976;1978). He argues (1974: 3) that:

> Whenever the capitalist mode of production enters into relations with precapitalist modes of production and subjects these to itself, transfers of value take place from the precapitalist to the capitalist formations as a result of the mechanisms of primitive accumulation. These mechanisms do not belong only to the prehistory of capitalism; they are contemporary as well. It is these forms of primitive accumulation, modified but persistent, to the advantage of the center, that form the domain of the theory of accumulation on a world scale.

Like Emmanuel, he argues (1974:134) that 'unequal exchange' between metropolitan countries is the primary mechanism by which value is transferred and accumulated on a world scale and whereby unequal specialisation is effected. A. Brewer summarises his views thus (1980: 234):

> The process of accumulation, of development, must be analysed as a single process on a world scale . . . in a world divided . . . into two categories: those of the centre and those of the periphery . . . Accumulation at the centre is 'autocentric' . . . governed by its own internal dynamic, as analysed by Marx. In the periphery, by contrast, accumulation is dependent . . . , constrained by the centre-periphery relation . . . the development of capitalism in the periphery is blocked by the superior competitive strength of the industries at the centre.

The mechanism of subjugation is summarised by Amin (1976:200) thus:

> The distortion towards export activities (extraversion), which is the decisive one, does not result from 'inadequacy of the home market', but from the superior productivity of the centre in all fields, which compels the periphery to confine itself to the role of complementary supplier of products for the production of which it possesses a natural advantage: exotic agricultural products and minerals. When, as a result of this distortion, the level of wages in the periphery has become lower, for the same productivity, than at the centre, a limited development of industries focussed on the home market of the periphery will have become possible, while at the same time exchange will have become unequal. The subsequent pattern of industrialization through import-substitution, together with the (as yet embryonic) effects of the new international division of labour inside the transnational firm, do not alter the essential conditions of extraversion, even if they alter the forms that is takes.

International specialisation is again seen to arise from absolute cost levels, in contrast to Ricardian comparative advantage. Once the centre countries establish an historical productivity lead, they are able, initially via imperialism, to generate and subsequently maintain a pattern of unequal specialisation, and thereby structure peripheral economic development in ways that suppress the level of wages and result in unequal exchange as analysed by Emmanuel, although wages are not seen by Amin purely as independent variables institutionally determined. Inequality is thus a self-perpetuating process and is explained both historically and theoretically. Further features of Amin's analysis of 'peripheral capitalism' include the following types of distortion [T. Smith 1979: 18]:

the abnormal enlargement (hypertrophy) of the tertiary sector, which reflects (a) the difficulties of realising surplus value at the centre and (b) limitations of peripheral development – inadequate industrialisation and rising unemployment . . . [and a] distortion towards light branches of activity and the use of modern production techniques . . . Underdevelopment is . . . manifested in . . . certain characteristic structural features that 'oblige us not to confuse the UDC with the now-advanced countries as they were at an earlier stage of their development'. [Amin 1976:201]. These features are: extreme unevenness in the distribution of productivities and in the system of prices transmitted from the centre; disarticulation, because of the adjustment of the economy to the needs of the centre; and economic domination by the centre. As economic growth proceeds, features of underdevelopment are accentuated; autocentric growth is impossible, whatever output per capita is achieved.

Amin denies the importance of national economies as units of analysis, given his 'world accumulation' scenario, and comes to a series of pessimistic conclusions about industrial state action:

1   There is no real freedom of manoeuvre for LDCs in relation to world capitalism. In general, peripheral economic policy is doomed to be ineffective because:

So long as [an] underdeveloped country continues to be integrated in the world market, it remains helpless . . . the possibilities of local accumulation are nil . . . The creation of a national currency confers on the local authorities no power of effective control so long as a country's inclusion in the world market is not challenged: even control of the exchange and of transfer does not prevent transmission to the periphery of fluctuations in the value of the dominant currencies of the centre, nor does it prevent transmission to the periphery of the centre's price structure. Money here constitutes the outward form of an essential relation of dominance but is not responsible for this relation . . . [Amin 1974: 131;483.]

2   As economic growth in the periphery occurs, so underdevelopment develops. Autonomous and self-sustained growth is impossible, whatever the level of production per capita that may be attained. Since no 'development' is possible, only a radical and complete break with the world capitalist system – de-linking – will provide the necessary conditions for genuine development.

3   The internationalisation of capital means that capital can no longer be valued on a national basis corresponding to the exercise of the sovereignty of the state.

The critique of the obstacles to 'national development' approach

The structuralist paradigm of a vicious circle of underdevelopment that was supposedly reversible by an import-substitution approach to industrial diversification and economic growth did not, however, appear in practice to give rise to the intended result of a diminution of dependency in extra Latin American trade relationships. At the end of the 1960s, Sunkel (1969: 37) identified four main areas of dependence that still persisted despite all attempts to the contrary:

(1) 'the traditional agrarian structure had largely been preserved, seriously limiting modernization and technological improvement of rural production' . . .

(2) [the] 'structure of foreign trade . . . still relies principally on the export of a handful of primary commodities . . . the degree of concentration of exports has in fact slightly increased . . .'

(3) 'industrialization has not produced all the expected benefits, in particular, it has not resulted in a lessening of foreign dependence which . . . was one of its basic objectives'. He sees the root cause of the central failing of import substitution policies as being the following, that had made countries 'more dependent, more vulnerable and more unstable':

> *The import of capital and intermediate goods necessary to produce consumer goods has been substituted for the import of consumer goods themselves. The structure of manufacturing production is now organized basically to produce for the consumer and the traditional export sector has been left to 'produce' the investment goods.*

(4) An inherent financial problem arising from the above, in conjunction with two contrary tendencies derived from the new importance of the state:

> On the one hand, there is an insatiable thirst for appropriating resources in order to use them in programmes of industrialization and infrastructure and especially in the area of social services. On the other hand, the goose which lays the golden eggs – the export sector – has remained relatively stagnant, due partly to heavy taxation but mainly to policies and technological developments in the world's developed industrial economies, over which the Latin American countries have little influence. Therefore, once the principal base of the taxation system stagnated and tax rates reached a certain level, revenues no longer grew at a rhythm commensurate with the rapidly increasing necessities of the public sector. [ibid: 30].

Greater external dependence is generated by the following four features:

> the vulnerability and structural deficit of the balance of payments, the type of industrialization and the form of exploitation of the export sector which have not permitted our countries – with a few exceptions – to acquire the ability to adapt and create their own technology; the fact that an important and probably growing part of industry and of the export activities are either foreign owned or depend on licences and foreign technical assistance, all of which weighs heavily on the availability of foreign exchange; and the fact that both the fiscal sector and the balance of payments persistently tend to deficit, which leads to the necessity of foreign financing. In certain conditions this foreign financing can mean the accumulation of such considerable debts and such a structure of maturities that the very servicing of the debt requires resort to additional foreign financing – a genuine vicious circle. It is this aspect – the overbearing and implacable necessity to obtain foreign financing – which finally sums up the situation of dependence; this is the crucial point in the mechanism of dependence. [Sunkel 1969: 31]

Furtado (1973: 10–11) makes an additional point, stressing demand and not production as a dynamic element in the system of preference/values adopted: 'dependence is permanently reinforced through the introduction of new products whose production requires the use of more sophisticated techniques and higher levels of capital accumulation'. These products become desired and the consumption-pattern distorted as a result of the international demonstration effect. Sunkel and Paz (1970), quoted by Cardoso (1982: 146–7, 148) emphasise that:

> Development and underdevelopment . . . can be understood as partial but interdependent structures which make up a single system. The principal characteristic which differentiates the two structures is that the developed one, owing to its endogenous capacity for growth, is dominant, while the underdeveloped one, given the induced nature of its dynamics, is dependent: and this applies as much between countries as within a single country.

and that:

> this way of seeing development puts the emphasis on action, on the instruments of political power and on the power structure themselves and, in the last instance, it is these that explain the orientation, efficacy, intensity and nature of the internal and external social manipulation of culture, productive resources, technology and socio-political groups . . .

There is a presupposition (Cardoso 1982: 147) that 'it is possible and desirable to generalize what has already been achieved in terms of development in the industrial advanced countries'. Emphasis is put on:

1 the necessity of reinforcing the decision-making centers, which could articulate the 'deliberate will' to alter a situation diagnosed as unfavorable;
2 the necessity of absorbing technical progress, initially through the investment of foreign capital, in order to assure industrialization;
3 [and] the necessity of expanding domestic markets, in order to displace the axis of the main orientation of the economic system from outside to inside the country; to which end some redistributive measures should be supported. [Cardoso 1982: 148.]

It is assumed that obstacles to development could be overcome by appropriate strategies.

Subsequent discussions (Palma 1981:55) were related to the three central characteristics of the peripheral economy: unemployment, external disequilibrium and a deterioration in terms of trade but, unlike the approaches outlined in the 'theory of underdevelopment' above, they did 'not touch on relations of production, nor, as a result, on the manner in which the two interact'. Sunkel and Fuenzalida (1979:68,70) emphasise the importance of the transnational process, making the point that 'national development policies have tended to underestimate the influence and strength of transnational capitalism', which is described as 'a system' of 'interdependent parts, acting and reacting as an integrated whole'; 'techno-industrial' (a 'close structural interrelationship between scientific and applied research and development and mass production and marketing); 'oligopolistic' ('most economic activity is highly concentrated in a few very large enterprises, which occupy a dominant position') and 'global' (world-wide geographical coverage, i.e. widening of capitalism in a horizontal and vertical (deepening) manner).

The trend is away from the reliance on the functioning of markets as the means of relating independent production and consumption units, to an organization of these different units within a single enterprise and decision making structure, where planning for the entire organization replaces markets (ibid.).

Sunkel and Fuenzalida (1979: 77–8) argue that: 'contemporary trans-national capitalist growth has produced cumulative and increasing polarization, which in turn has affected relations between the nation state and transnational capitalism'; and see three main effects of transnationali-sation in underdeveloped societies (1979: 83–4):

(a) *Transnational integration*: the emergence of a dependent nucleus of the global system in the underdeveloped society with its own institutions, culture and community, that differentiates itself sharply from the rest of the society, and that controls to a large extent the machinery of an increasingly repressive state.

(b) *National disintegration*: the creation of a mass of unemployed or under-employed people that, having very precarious and unstable sources of income, are forced to survive in conditions of extreme poverty, whereas at the same time they are stimulated to aspire to the level of living enjoyed by the people in the dependent nucleus of the global system. This state of affairs is the direct consequence of the destruction, displacement and or stagnation of the traditional socio-economic institutions that offered them jobs, income and goods and services – however poor and primitive – by the more efficient ones brought in by the global system.

Attempts at reintegration: the accentuation of the authoritarian and repressive character of the state as the hegemonic social groups became increasingly threatened. But there are also other types of responses that attempt to deal with the casual forces rather than with its consequences. These are attempts at severing the links of the society with the global system and at reorganizing it internally in a less polarized way, both in terms of social action and in social thinking.

Given such a scenario, attempts have been made to clarify and develop a concept of 'collective self-reliance' which Oteiza (1979: 290; 301) asserts:

implies and incorporates at least some elements of earlier ideas such as autarky, self-generated and self-sustained development, new forms of intra Third World integration and association, and independence. It does not imply breaking up the world into isolated, xenographic states . . . [but] on delinking from traditional dependency connections with the international system . . . [and] the autonomous definition of development and life styles.

Such an orientation needs, in Oteiza's view, the development of 'criteria which could provide a clear-cut orientation as to when to delink and when and how to relink' (interestingly delinking was also at this time being put forward as a means of overcoming the 'de-industrialization' problems of the 'post-industrial' countries, as noted in Chapter 3). Some of the aspects of planning for self-reliant growth and the development of an 'appropriate technology' are outlined by Villamil (1979).

The 'concrete situations of dependency' approach

This approach essentially stems from Cardoso's work. This has been characterised by Palma (1981:60) as a belief that, with regard to peripheral countries, 'the options which lie open to them are limited by the development of the [world capitalist] system at the centre ... [and that] *the analysis therefore requires primarily an understanding of the contemporary characteristics of the world capitalist system*'. Essentially, this means an examination by case-study of 'dependent development' engendered by the multinational firms in conjunction with an extended analysis of the internal determinants of that development in each society, so as (Palma 1981: 61) 'to avoid losing the specificity of history in a welter of vague abstract concepts' – what Chase-Dunn (1982: 122) calls 'the singulariza-tion of national societies'. The merit of this approach is that it abstracts from the 'structural-mechanistic' view of cross-national global determinism and allows for national difficulties, even though a dialectical approach tends to be adopted, albeit at a national level. As Cardoso and Faletto (1979: 10–11) emphasise, it is:

> the diversity of domestic conditions, local class structure, state organizations, and of the timing and mode of insertion into the global system that has created different situations of dependency in peripheral countries ... the relationship between external and internal forces ... form[s] a complex whole whose structural links are not based on mere external forms of exploitation and coercion, but are rooted in coincidences of interests between local dominant classes and international ones, and, on the other side, are challenged by local dominated groups and classes.

Palma (1981: 61) evaluates this approach in the following terms:

> The system of 'external domination' reappears as an 'internal' phenomenon through the social practices of local groups and classes, who share its interests and values. Other internal groups and forces oppose this domination, and in the concrete development of these contradictions the specific dynamic of the society is generated. It is not a case of seeing one part of the world capitalist system as 'developing' and another as 'under-developing', or of seeing imperialism and dependency as two sides of the same coin with the underdeveloped or dependent world reduced to a passive role determined by the other ...

P. Evans (1979a) has provided one such case-study of Brazil.

WORLD-SYSTEM ANALYSIS

This analysis, sometimes merely referred to as a 'perspective', has been described (Chase-Dunn 1981: 19) as 'a reinterpretation of the theory of capitalist development inspired by dependency theory'; and as 'an orienting perspective ... used to interpret history toward a new, or renewed, theory of the underlying laws of development' (Chase-Dunn 1983:55). It arose as a reaction to the developmentalist viewpoint. The main source of this approach has been the writings of Wallerstein, the central themes of which are dealt with in his book, *The Modern World System* Vol. 1 (1974) and Vol. 2 (1980), and a series of important journal articles collected together under the general title *The Capitalist World-Economy* (1979); and a series of 'world-system studies' spawned therefrom, the major contributions to which have tended to be collected since 1978 in Sage Publications' series of *Political Economy of the World-System Annuals* and a number of volumes in the Academic Press's *Social Discontinuity and Change* series. At present, 'this perspective has not been formalized as a theory of capitalist development because its methodological approach seems to assume that the world-system . . . only loosely conforms to a systematic dynamic, and thus overly formalistic theory-building is thought to be inappropriate' (Chase-Dunn 1983: 55).

The general essence of the approach is again the adoption of a global rather than a national level of analysis from which to examine international economic relations, given a belief that: 'national states are *not* societies that have separate, parallel histories, but parts of a whole reflecting that whole . . . [and that to] understand the internal class contradictions and political struggles of a particular state, we must first situate it in the World-economy' (Wallerstein 1979: 53).

Wallerstein distinguishes between a socioeconomic system in which the economic division of labour is incorporated without a single overarching state apparatus – a world empire; and one in which an economic division of labour is overlaid by a multicentre system of states – a world system. He argues (1979: 4–5) that:

> the defining characteristic of a social system [is] the existence within it of a division of labour, such that the various sectors or areas within are dependent upon economic exchange with others for the smooth and continuous provisioning of the needs of the area . . . the total totalities that exist or have historically existed (e.g. the Arabs, Ottomans, Chinese, medieval Europe) are minisystems and world systems [but] in the nineteenth and twentieth centuries there has been only one world system in existence, the capitalist world economy.

His perspective is in terms of the historical evolution of a world-system, driven by capitalist accumulation, that has a development continuum that started in Europe in the fifteenth century and gradually enveloped most countries within its capitalist web of activities as it became global in its reach. Wallerstein recognises (1979: 14) that not all countries are locked in to its activities (these collectively form 'the external arena') and that it is possible for countries to leave and even re-enter the system. He differentiates incorporation on the basis of exchange that involves 'substantial interdependence' not mere 'luxury' or 'non-essential exchange' that is of very limited significance. He is concerned to describe how the capitalist world-system has expanded geographically and evolved functionally and yet has maintained within its structures a strong element of continuity. Thompson (1983a: 11) detects three central processes: 'the historical development of a core-periphery division of labour, the episodic rise and fall of hegemonic powers, and the gradual geographic expansion, coupled with the periodic growth and stagnation, of the world economy'.

Wallerstein's analysis is synchronically expressed in terms of linked economic processes, and stresses the eventual independent significance of the world capitalist system and its impact on the socioeconomic processes of all nations, including the socialist countries. A multinational structure of capitalist relations is presented within a three-level stratification that is united by a number of processes that (Hopkins and Wallerstein 1981: 233) 'work through a massive world-scale complex of relational networks or social structure, which the processes produced, continually reproduce, and also continually modify'. The three tiers of states are those of the core, the semi-periphery and the periphery, the essential difference being the differential economic power of states. The latter two categories are seen as integrated essential parts of the system and conduits of surplus transfer for the core-states. Wallerstein (1979:13) argues that historically this segmentation arose because:

> given slightly different starting points, the interests of various local groups converged in northwest Europe, leading to the development of strong state mechanisms, and diverged sharply in the peripheral areas leading to very weak ones. *Once we get a difference in the strength of these state machineries, we get the operation of 'unequal exchange'* which is enforced by the strong states on weak ones, by core states on peripheral areas.

Unequal exchange differentially benefits core over periphery to produce an inter-group hierarchical division of labour. Trade is seen as a metabolic process, the world economy's primary social relation. The world capitalist economy is integrated through markets, rather than tribute extraction (as in world empires), and:

> such a system . . . is *necessary* for the expansion of a world market if the primary consideration is *profit*. Without *unequal* exchange, it would not be *profitable* to expand the size of the division of labour, and without such expansion, it would not be profitable to maintain a capital world-economy, which would then either disintegrate or revert to the form of a redistributive world-empire. [Wallerstein 1979: 71.]

Within the system there is scope for vertical mobility up and down the hierarchy. Chase-Dunn (1981:29) characterises the situation thus:

> In the competitive state system it is impossible for any single state to monopolize the entire world market, and to maintain hegemony indefinitely. Hegemonic core powers . . . in the long run [lose] their relative domination to more efficient producers . . . success . . . is based on a combination of effective state power and competitive advantage in production. The extraction of surplus product is based on two legs: the ability to use political power for the appropriation of surplus products; and the ability to produce efficiently for the competitive world market. This is not the state-centric system which some analysts describe, because states cannot escape, for long, the competitive forces of the world economy. States that attempt to cut themselves off or who overtax their domestic producers condemn themselves to marginality. On the other hand, the system is not simply a free world market of competing producers. The interaction between political power and competitive advantage is a delicate balance.

Unlike Marx, Wallerstein perceives that states are often involved in the international accumulation process and that (Chase-Dunn 1982a: 24) 'market forces are either supported or distorted, depending on the position of the classes controlling a particular state' in the interactive context of their relationships.

Within Wallerstein's triadic hierarchy of states, his innovation is the introduction of the 'semi-periphery', which he regards (1974: 349) as 'a necessary structural element in the world economy'. Descriptively it contains:

> the economically stronger countries of Latin America: Brazil, Mexico, Argentina, Venezuela, possibly Chile and Cuba. It includes the whole outer rim of Europe: the southern tier of Portugal, Spain, Italy and Greece; most of Eastern Europe; parts of the Northern tier such as Norway and Finland. It includes a series of

Arab states: Algeria, Egypt, Saudi Arabia and also Israel. It includes in Africa at least Nigeria and Zaire and in Asia, Turkey, Iran, India, Indonesia, China, Korea and Vietnam. And it includes the old white Commonwealth: Canada, Australia, South Africa, possibly New Zealand. [Wallerstein 1979:100.]

These states are conduits, within which individual capitalists shift their capital 'to survive the effects of cyclical shifts in the loci of the leading sectors'. By trading with both core and peripheral countries, semi-peripheral countries have a different rationale in three respects:

[Firstly] . . . Whereas, at any given moment the more balanced trade a core country or a peripheral country can engage in, the better off it is in absolute terms, it is often in the interest of a semi-peripheral country to reduce external trade.

[Secondly] . . . The direct and immediate interest of the state as a political machinery in control of the market (internal and international) is greater than in either the core or the peripheral states since the semi-peripheral states can never depend on the market to maximise, in the short run their profit margins . . .

[Finally] . . . In a expanding world-economy, semi-peripheral countries are beggars, seeking to obtain a part of the world market against other semi-peripheral countries . . . However, when world contraction comes . . . semi-peripheral countries may be courted as the outlets for core products get relatively rarer. [Wallerstein 1973: 4,3,16.]

Since the publication of Wallerstein's *World-Economy* Vol. 1 (1974), further interpretations of the international history of the world have been provided by Frank (1978a), Amin (1974) and Braudel (1984); and research studies have been conducted to classify and extend world-system assertions, to provide variants thereof and to evolve alternative macro-structural studies.

With respect to the extension of Wallerstein's analysis, important areas of further discussion have included contemporary world capitalism and multinational firms; the importance of international banking and its facilitative role in the extension of world capitalism; an outline of 'metacapitalism' by Borrego and a debate about the degree of exclusive integrity possessed by socialist states as a group within the world-system.

Borrego (1982: 114) has speculatively suggested that a new phase of transformation has been reached, wherein the system is being 'refined into a worldwide matrix of isolated enclaves and regions located within the various groups of nation-states controlled by . . . [a] metanational network . . .'. This is a new social formation which has 'as its foundation social forms that are both transnational and transideological' (1982: 111). This is perceived as Phase III of a 'transformation process', the previous stages being Phase I – 'the pre-1900s "Wallersteinian system" of core, semi-periphery, periphery, and external areas'; which was replaced by 'a world system composed of an expanded capitalist core, an extensive network of socialist societies, an enlarged semi-periphery and some residual peri-pheral societies – Phase II'. His rationale for this new phase of world accumulation is as follows:

the more successful a nation becomes as a social-economic unit, the less successful it becomes as a profitable unit of production within the world capitalist system. As nations reach this economic tipping point, metanational capital migrates to more profitable national and regional locations. In a world system in which some core nations are being developed while former peripheral countries are developing, the old meaning of core-periphery is lost. The core becomes a 'floating entity', while the metanational corporations continue to have geographical bases for the legal purposes of doing business, such bases become less significant. Metanational corporations operate from any *place* they choose to incorporate . . . they control the resources (a denationalized capital and technology) migrating *out* of a declining core and semi-peripheral nations, and they also control the relocation of those resources *into* the expanding semi-peripheral and modernizing socialist countries. [Borrego 1982: 114,116,117.]

The essence of the new metanational formation (1982:122) is 'one of integrating (and exploiting) the masses from the expanding semi-periphery and modernising, socialist societies into world capitalist accumulation.' This alleged reintegration of previously apparently anti-systemic socialist economies is, however, denied by Szymanski (1982), among others. Other writers, who reject Wallerstein's world-system analysis, have nevertheless put forward alternative world-level lines of approach. Some reject altogether the assumption that the world-system is dominated by economic processes and accentuate other dimensions such as leadership (Modeleski 1983), war (Thompson 1983b), and political power (Doran 1983). Others have produced a series of 'world-order' studies/scenarios concerned with the construction of possible and/or preferred world futures, the general framework of which involves a three-level approach:

(i)   a diagnostic/prognostic task of describing present world order conditions and trends,
(ii) a modelling task of designing preferred futures, and
(iii) a prescriptive task of mapping a step-by-step transition process, and an overall strategy.

Such attempts have not had a common orientation: some are system-diminishing; some system-maintaining; some system-reforming; and some system-transforming, each 'holding up a mirror to the deficiencies of the existing order and [suggesting] what life could or should be like if human potential or aspiration were to be fully realigned' (Falk and Kim 1983: 225).

Ideally, if a consensus of opinion were to emerge on the precise areas and mechanisms of global international market failure and the lines along which such distortions might be jointly corrected, it might yet be possible to effect a restructuring of international economic relationships via existing or a new set of supranational economic institutions, according to some new model of international political economy.

GENERAL CRITIQUE

It is evident that the main merit of the interrelated but distinct schools of approach outlined in this chapter is that they greatly extend the range of factors to be considered as determinants of the long-run outcomes of international exchange, as compared with mainstream economics; and that they make a more ambitious attempt to unravel the mysteries of the dynamics of the world economy and to address the problem of explaining revealed asymmetrical international economic relations, phenomena neither predicted nor allowed for in conventional classical and neo-classical analyses. While these approaches tend to raise 'the right questions – much more relevant ones than those derived from neo-classical economics' (Seers 1984: 15–16) with respect to phenomena that lie outside the limited scope of the latter, and attempt to achieve a more 'field-bound' and less 'discipline-bound' social-scientific approach, it must be borne in mind that (Cairnes 1875: 138): 'in Political Economy, as in all the positive sciences, classification, definition, nomenclature, *is* scaffolding and *not* foundation'. Theories must have general explanatory power if they are to be distinguished from mere histories, on the one hand, or prophesies of what might happen, on the other. The problem with both dependencia theories and world-system analyses is that by insisting on emphasising particular processes in a globally defined historical context they may:

> substantially overestimate the power of the international system . . . and systematically . . . either overlook the function of the state entirely, or dismiss it as historically insignificant, or recognise its importance only to reduce it forthwith to a product of the international system. [T. Smith 1979: 249,262.]

There is an implicit assumption that the subsumed sociological, political and economic elements will provide a new unidisciplinary approach separate from, and superior to, a multidisciplinary combination of those elements of the separate disciplines that seem relevant in this field of studies. However, many of the concepts used, such as 'core' and 'periphery' and 'dependence' 'carry with them a raft of meaning and connotations' (P. Evans 1979b: 16), lack rigorous definition and are unduly mechanico-formal. A. Brewer (1980: 167) criticises the general lack of rigor in Wallerstein's writings thus:

> Overall . . . what he offers . . . seems . . . to amount to little more than a series of definitions and phrases together with a mass of detailed material that often seems to have little connection with his overall generalizations. What is lacking is a level of theory that would connect the two. A formidable apparatus of scholarship . . . and a fondness for obscure jargon . . . are no substitute.

Yet other writers find an insufficiently wide focus in his discussion:

> The emphasis on capitalism and capital accumulation narrows the system's motors of change to a version of the profit motive. Non-economic forces and processes frequently are relegated to subordinate or residual categories of analysis. To adopt the framework, one must accept this initial choice of model reductionism. [Thompson 1983a: 14.]

Zolberg (1981: 25) argues that there is a systematic neglect of politics and political processes. Other writers, such as Brenner (1977), argue that Wallerstein's particular world-system implies 'a circulationist theory of capitalism in which market exchange is central and production relations (class relations) to not much matter' (Chase-Dunn 1982a: 12). Navarro

(1982: 87,91) accuses him of 'limited awareness . . . of the major categories of historical materialism [which] limit significantly his understanding of socialism and the transition from Capitalism'. On the other hand, Bergesen (1980: 9–10) insists that 'there are . . . class relations on a world-scale between core and periphery as a whole', and argues that:

> The final paradigm revolution will come when we invert the parts-to-whole framework of the world-system outlook and move to a distinctly whole-to-parts paradigm which posits a priori world social relations of production which in turn determine the core-periphery relations of trade and exchange.

He believes that Wallerstein has not gone far enough in his analysis:

> By focusing upon unequal exchange as the world economy's primary social relation, the world-system perspective looks at only the outcome, or by-product, of the much more fundamental social relation which precedes exchange and makes its very existence possible. That is, the world class relation of owning-controlling the world means of production, a relation which can only be understood when we conceptualize the world economy as a singular mode of production, with its own distinctive world class relations.

Others would emphasise the neglect of areas of national autonomy. Seers (1981b: 141), for instance, argues that 'size is perhaps the most important determinant of the room to manoeuvre', and that superficial treatment is given to natural resources as determinants of a government's bargaining power, a country's physical location in relation to other countries, military preparedness, etc. On the positive side, Palma (1981: 62) states, with respect to dependency theory, that he

> [does] not have any illusions that [its] findings could explain every detail of our past history, or should be capable of predicting the exact course of future events . . . [and] can take out from history all its ambiguities, uncertainties, contradictions and surprises. As it has done so often in the past, history will undoubtedly continue to astonish us with unexpected revelations.

Seers (1981b: 146) cautiously refers to the very real possibility 'that human reality is so constructed that no model can be devised for its analysis (especially a dynamic one) which is both realistic and simple enough to provide a universal development ideology that could be applied with safety in any nation'. He believes that perhaps the safest way to proceed is to tailor 'new theory from the material of country studies, rather than trying on the old Marxist clothes handed down from Europe'.

However, the integrative international framework has now been so firmly established in the literature, that even Zolberg (1981: 281), who is very critical of these approaches, makes the comment that:

> There are indeed many good reasons to adopt a sceptical stance toward the possibility of ever devising an elegant theory encompassing the origins of the modern world and its subsequent evolution. Our efforts might more fruitfully be directed toward the elaboration of theories concerning various aspects of the transformation, unified not by a belief in the possibility of delineating a system moved by a singular dynamic, but rather by a shared sense of the fundamental interconnectedness among the disparate strands of human experience and history. However lacking in overall elegance, such disparate efforts do not constitute a waste of time: they can lead to more precise knowledge of some aspects of the transformation and thereby result in a somewhat more coherent understanding of the whole.

Appendix

The fragmentation of sovereignty: countries of the world by region, year of independence, and size of population*

Independent before 1775

		Population mid-1981 in millions	Area in 000 km²
Europe			
	Austria	7.5	84
	Denmark	5.1	43
	France	54.0	547
	Germany: East ⎤ 1945	16.7	108
	West ⎦	61.7	249
	Italy	56.2	301
	Netherlands	14.2	37
	Portugal	9.8	92
	Spain	38.0	505
	Sweden	8.3	450
	Switzerland	6.5	41
	United Kingdom	56.0	244
	USSR	268.0	22,402
East & South Asia			
	China (mainland)	991.3	9,593
	Japan	117.6	372
	Thailand	48.0	514
	Nepal	15.0	141
	Bhutan	1.3	47
Middle East & North Africa			
	Afghanistan	16.3	648
	Ethiopia	31.8	1,222
	Iran	40.0	1,648
	Muscat & Oman	0.9	212
	Turkey	45.5	781

Independent between 1776 and 1943

		Population mid-1981 in millions	Area in 000 km²
Europe			
1830	Greece	9.7	132
1831	Belgium	9.9	31
1878	Romania	22.5	238
	Yugoslavia	22.3	256
1890	Luxembourg	0.4	3
1905	Norway	4.1	324
1908	Bulgaria	8.9	111
1912	Albania	2.8	29
1918	Czechoslovakia	15.3	128
	Finland	4.8	337

		Population mid-1981 in millions	Area in 000 km²
1918	Hungary	10.7	93
	Iceland	0.2	103
	Poland	35.9	313
1921	Ireland	3.4	70
North America & Oceania			
1776	United States	229.8	9,363
1867	Canada	24.2	9,976
1901	Australia	14.9	7,687
1907	New Zealand	3.3	269
East and South Asia			
1921	Mongolia	1.7	1,567
Middle East & North Africa			
1918	Yemen: [North 1967]	7.3	195
	[South	2.0	333
1922	Egypt	43.3	1,001
1925	Saudi Arabia	9.3	2,150
1932	Iraq	13.5	435
1943	Lebanon	2.7	10
	Syria	9.3	185
Tropical & Southern Africa			
1847	Liberia	1.9	111
1910	South Africa	29.5	1,221
Middle & South America			
1811	Paraguay	3.1	407
1813	Guatemala	7.5	109
1816	Argentina	28.2	2,767
1818	Chile	11.3	757
1819	Colombia	26.4	1,139
1820	Mexico	71.2	1,973
1821	Peru	17.0	1,285
1822	Brazil	102.5	8,512
1825	Bolivia	5.7	1,099
1828	Uruguay	2.9	176
1830	Ecuador	8.6	284
	Venezuela	15.4	912
1838	Costa Rica	2.3	51
	El Salvador	4.7	21
	Honduras	3.8	112
	Nicaragua	2.8	130
1840	Haiti	5.1	28
1844	Dominican Republic	5.6	49
1901	Cuba	9.7	115
1903	Panama	1.9	77

Independent between 1944 and 1984

Europe			
1964	Malta	0.4	0.4

		Population *mid-1981* *in millions*	*Area* *in 000* *km²*
East & South Asia			
1945	Korea: North	18.7	121
	South	38.9	98
1946	Philippines	49.6	300
1947	India	690.2	3,288
	Pakistan	84.5	804
	Sri Lanka (Ceylon)	15.0	66
1948	Burma	34.1	677
1949	Indonesia	149.5	1,904
	Taiwan	18.3	36
1954	Kampuchea (Cambodia)	7.1	181
	Laos	3.5	237
	Vietnam	55.7	330
1957	Malaysia	14.2	330
1965	Singapore	2.4	0.6
	Maldive Islands	0.2	0.3
1972	Bangladesh	90.7	144
1984	Brunei	0.2	6
Middle East & Northern Africa			
1946	Jordan	3.4	98
1948	Israel	4.0	21
1951	Libya	3.1	1,760
1956	Morocco	20.9	447
	Sudan	19.2	2,506
	Tunisia	6.5	164
1960	Cyprus	0.6	9
	Mauritania	1.6	1,031
	Somalia	4.4	638
1961	Kuwait	1.5	18
1962	Algeria	19.6	2,382
1971	Bahrain	0.4	0.6
	Qatar	0.2	11
	United Arab Emirates	1.1	87
1977	Djibouti	0.4	22
Tropical & Southern Africa			
1957	Ghana	11.8	239
1958	Guinea	5.6	246
1960	Benin	3.6	113
	Cameroon	8.7	475
	Central African Republic	2.4	623
	Chad	4.5	1,284
	Congo	1.7	342
	Gabon	0.7	268
	Ivory Coast	8.5	322
	Madagascar	9.0	587
	Mali	6.9	1,240
	Niger	5.7	1,267
	Nigeria	87.6	925
	Senegal	5.9	196

		Population mid-1981 in millions	Area in 000 km²
	Togo	2.7	56
	Upper Volta	6.3	274
1961	Tanzania	48.0	514
	Sierra Leone	3.6	72
1962	Burundi	4.2	28
	Rwanda	5.3	26
	Uganda	13.0	236
1963	Kenya	17.4	583
1964	Malawi	6.2	118
	Zambia	5.8	753
1965	Gambia	0.6	11
	Zimbabwe (Rhodesia)	7.2	391
1966	Botswana	0.9	600
	Lesotho	1.4	30
1968	Mauritius	1.0	2
	Swaziland	0.6	17
1974	Guinea-Bissau	0.8	36
1975	Angola	7.8	1,247
	Cape Verde	0.3	4
	Comeros	0.4	2
	Mozambique	12.5	783
Middle & South America			
1962	Jamaica	2.2	11
	Trinidad & Tobago	1.2	5
1966	Barbados	0.3	0.4
	Guyana	0.8	215
1973	Bahamas	0.2	14
1975	Surinam	0.4	163
Oceania			
1968	Equatorial Guinea	0.3	28
1970	Fiji	0.6	18
1975	Papua New Guinea	3.1	462
1978	Solomon Isles	0.2	28

Still dependent in 1984		
Hong Kong	5.2	1
Martinique	0.3	1
Namibia	1.0	824
Puerto Rico	3.7	9
Reunion	0.5	3
Western Sahara	n.a.	267.8

* This table only includes countries with populations over 200,000, thereby excluding a large number of mini-states and islands, both independent and dependent.
Source: derived from Rustow (1967: 292–3) and Kidron and Segal (1984)

Bibliography

Abonyi, A. (1982), 'Eastern Europe's Reintegration', ch.9 of *Socialist States in the World System*, C.K. Chase-Dunn (ed.), Beverly Hills, Ca., Sage Publications.

Adams, F.V. (1914), *Conquest of the Tropics: the Story of the Creative Enterprises Conducted by the United Fruit Company*, Garden City, NY, Doubleday, Page and Co.

Agmon, T. (1979), 'Direct Investment and Intra-Industry Trade: Substitutes or Complements?', *On the Economics of Intra-Industry Trade*, International Symposium 1978, H. Giersch (ed.), Tuebingen, J.C.B. Mohr (Paul Siebeck).

Allart, E. and Valen, H. (1981), 'Stein Rokham: An Intellectual Profile', *Mobilization, Centre–Periphery Structures and Nation-Building* P. Torsvik (ed.), Bergen, Universitetsforlaget.

Allen, G.C. (1976), *The British Disease*, London, Institute of Economic Affairs.

—— and Donnithorne, A.G. (1954), *Western Enterprise in Far Eastern Economic Development: China and Japan*, London, Allen and Unwin.

—— and —— (1957), *Western Enterprise in Indonesia and Malaya: A Study in Economic Development*, London, Allen and Unwin.

Amin, S. (1974), *Accumulation on a World Scale: A Critique of the Theory of Underdevelopment*, New York, Monthly Review Press.

—— (1976), *Unequal Development: An Essay on the Social Formations of Peripheral Capitalism*, Hassocks, Sussex, Harvester Press.

Anell, L. and Nygren, B. (1980), *The Developing Countries and the World Economic Order*, London, Frances Pinter.

Angell, J.W. (1926), *The Theory of International Prices*, Cambridge, Mass., Harvard University Press.

Anjaria, S.J., Iqbal, Z., Kirmani, N., and Perez, L.L. (1983), *Developments in International Trade Policy*, revised ed. July, IMF Occasional Paper No.19, Washington, DC, International Monetary Fund.

Aquino, A. (1978), 'Intra-Industry Trade and Inter-Industry Specialization as Concurrent Sources of International Trade in Manufactures', *Weltwirtschafliches Archiv* 114, pp. 275–96.

Arad, R.W. and Hirsch, (1981), 'Determination of Trade Flows and Choice of Trade Partners: Reconciling the H.O. and the B. Linder Models of International Trade', *Weltwirtschafliches Archiv*, 117, pp. 276–97.

Asai, I. and Yorozo, I. (1975), 'An Alternative Testing of Linder's Trade Thesis', *KSU Economic and Business Review* No.2, pp. 61–78.

Ashworth, W. (1952), *A Short History of the International Economy, 1850–1950*, London, Longmans.

Avramovic, D. (1982), 'The Developing Countries after Cancun: the Financial Problem and Related Issues', *Journal of World Trade Law* 16, pp. 3–26.

Bacha, E.L. (1978), 'An Interpretation of Unequal Exchange from Prebisch-Singer to Emmanuel', *Journal of Development Economics* 5 pp. 319–30.

Bairoch, P. (1973), 'European Foreign Trade in the XIX Century: The Development of the Value and Volume of Exports', *Journal of European Economic History* 2, pp. 5–36.

—— (1974), 'Geographical Structure and Trade Balance of European Foreign Trade from 1800 to 1970', *Journal of European Economic History* 3, pp. 557–608.

────── (1975), 'Foreign Trade', ch.5, *The Economic Development of the Third World Since 1900*, C. Postan (trans.), London, Methuen.

────── (1981), 'The Main Trends in National Economic Economic Disparities Since the Industrial Revolution', ch.1, *Disparities in Economic Development Since the Industrial Revolution*, P. Bairoch and M. Lévy-Leboyer (eds.), London, Macmillan.

Balassa, B. (1962), *The Theory of Economic Integration*, London, Allen and Unwin.

────── (1983), 'An Empirical Demonstration of Classical Comparative Cost Theory', *Review of Economics and Statistics* **45**, pp. 231-8.

────── (1965), 'Trade Liberalization and "Revealed" Comparative Advantage', *The Manchester School* **33**, pp. 99-124.

────── (1968), 'Tariff Protection in Industrial Countries and Its Effects on the Exports of Processed Goods from Developing Countries', *Canadian Journal of Economics* **1**, pp. 583-94.

────── (1974), 'Trade Creation and Trade Diversion in the European Common Market: An Appraisal of the Evidence', *The Manchester School* **42**, pp. 93-135.

────── (1979), 'A "Stages Approach" to Comparative Advantage', ch.11, *Economic Growth and Resources*, Vol.4, National and International Policies, I. Adelman (ed.), London, Macmillan.

────── (1983), 'Outward versus Inward Orientation Once Again', *World Economy* **6**, pp. 215-18.

Baldwin, D.A. (1980), 'Interdependence and Power: A Conceptual Analysis', *International Organization* **34** pp. 471-506.

Baldwin, R.E. (1970), 'International Trade in Inputs and Outputs', *American Economic Review* **60**, pp. 430-40.

────── (1971a), *Non-Tariff Trade Distortions of International Trade*, London, Allen and Unwin.

────── (1971b), 'Determinants of the Commodity Structure of U.S. Trade', *American Economic Review: Papers and Proceedings* **61**, No.2, pp. 126-46.

────── and Kay, D.A. (1975), 'International Trade and International Relations', *International Organization* **29**, pp. 99-131.

Balogh, T. (1962), 'The Mechanism of Neo-Imperialism: the Economic Impact of Monetary and Commercial Institutions in Africa', *Bulletin of the Institute of Statistics, Oxford* **24**, pp. 331-46.

────── (1962), *Unequal Partners* Vol.1 - The Theoretical Framework, Oxford, Blackwell.

────── (1973), *Fact and Fancy in International Relations*, Oxford, Pergamon Press.

────── (1982), *The Irrelevance of Conventional Economics*, London, Weidenfeld and Nicholson.

Banks, G. (1983), 'The Economics and Politics of Countertrade', *World Economy* **6**, pp. 159-82.

Baran, P.A. (1952), 'On the Political Economy of Backwardness', *The Manchester School* **20**, pp. 66-84.

────── (1957), *The Political Economy of Growth*, New York, Monthly Review Press.

Baranson, J. (1970), 'Technology Transfer Through the International Firm', *American Economic Review Papers and Proceedings* **60**, No.2, pp. 435-40.

Barber, J. (1975), *British Economic Thought and India 1600 - 1858: A Study in the History of Development Economics*, Oxford, Clarendon Press.

Barbour, V. (1963), *Capitalism in Amsterdam in the Seventeenth Century*, Ann Arbor, Mich., University of Michigan Press.

Barker, T. (1977), 'International Trade and Economic Growth: An Alternative to the Neoclassical Approach' *Cambridge Journal of Economics* **1**, pp. 153-72.

Bastable, C.F. (1903), *The Theory of International Trade with Some of Its Applications to Economic Policy*, 4th ed. revised, London, Macmillan.

Baumgartner, T. and Burns, T.R. (1975), 'The Structuring of International Economic Relations', *International Studies Quarterly* 19, pp. 126–59.

Beenstock, M. (1984). *The World Economy in Transition*, 2nd. ed., London, Allen and Unwin.

Beer, G.L. (1907), *British Colonial Policy*, Macmillan.

——— (1908), *The Origins of the British Colonial System 1578–1660*, London, Macmillan.

Behrman, J.N. (1972), 'International Sectoral Integration: An Alternative Approach to Freer Trade', *Journal of World Trade Law* 6, pp. 269–83.

Bell, D. (1973), *The Coming of Post-Industrial Society*, New York, Basic Books.

Bergesen, A. (1980), 'From Utilitarianism to Globology: the Shift from the Individual to the World as a Whole as the Primordial Unit of Analysis', ch.1, *Studies of the Modern World-System*, A. Bergesen (ed.), London, Academic Press.

——— and Schoenberg, R. (1980), 'Long Waves of Colonial Expansion and Contraction, 1415–1969', ch.10, *Studies of the Modern World-System*, A. Bergesen (ed.), London, Academic Press.

Bergsten, C.F. (1976), *The Reform of International Institutions*, New York, The International Commission.

——— and Cline, W.R. (1983), 'Trade Policy in the 1980s: An Overview', *Trade Policy in the 1980s* W.R. Cline (ed.), Washington DC, Institute for International Economics.

Bettelheim, C. (1972), 'Theoretical Comments' (Appendix I) and 'Preface to the French Edition (Appendix III), A. Emmanuel, *Unequal Exchange: A Study of the Imperialism of Trade*, London, Monthly Review Press.

Bhagwati, J. (1965), 'The Pure Theory of International Trade: A Survey', *Surveys of Economic Theory: Growth and Development*, Royal Economics Association, London, Macmillan.

——— (1971), 'The Generalised Theory of Distortions and Welfare', ch.4 *Trade, Balance of Payments and Growth*, J.N. Bhagwati *et al* (eds.), Amsterdam, North Holland Press.

——— and Srinivasan, T.N. (1969), 'Optimal Intervention to Achieve Non-Economic Objectives', *Review of Economic Studies* 36, pp. 27–38.

Bhambri, R.S. (1962), 'Customs Unions and Underdeveloped Countries', *Economia Internazionale* 15, pp. 235–58.

Blackhurst, R., Marian, N., and Tumlir, J. (1977) *Trade Liberalization, Protectionism and Interdependence*, GATT Studies in International Trade No.5, Geneva, GATT.

Blaisdell, D.C. (1929), *European Financial Control in the Ottoman Empire*, New York, Columbia University Press.

Blaug, M. (1980), *The Methodology of Economics, Or How Economists Explain*, Cambridge, Cambridge University Press.

Bloomfield, A.I. (1975), 'Adam Smith and the Theory of International Trade', ch.10, *Essays on Adam Smith*, A.S. Skinner and T. Wilson (eds.), Oxford, Clarendon Press.

Boli-Bennet, J. (1980), 'Global Integration and the Universal Increase of State Dominance, 1910–1970', ch. 5, *Studies of the Modern World-System*, A. Bergesen (ed.), London, Academic Press.

Bolton, G.C. (1966), 'The Founding of the Second British Empire', *Economic History Review, Second Series* 19, pp. 195–200.

Booth, D. (1975), 'Andre Gunder Frank: An Introduction and Appreciation', ch.4, *Beyond the Sociology of Development*, I. Oxaal, T. Barnett, and D. Booth (eds.), London, Routledge and Kegan Paul.

Borkakoti, J. (1975), 'Some Welfare Implications of the Neo-Technology Hypothesis of the Pattern of International Trade', *Oxford Economic Papers* 27, pp. 383–99.

Borrego, J. (1982), 'Metanational Capitalist Accumulation', ch.6, *Socialist States in the World-System*, C.K. Chase-Dunn (ed.), London, Sage Publications.

Bosenquet, C. (1808), *Thoughts on the Value to Great Britain of Commerce in General*, London, S. and C. McDowall.

Bradford, C.I. (1982), 'Rise of the NICs as Exporters on a Global Scale', *The Newly Industrializing Countries: Trade and Adjustment* L. Turner and N. McMullen (eds.), London, Allen and Unwin.

Branson, W.H. and Junz, H. (1971), 'Trends in U.S. Comparative Advantage', *Brookings Papers on Economic Activity* 2, Washington DC, Brookings Institution.

Braudel, F. (1984), *Civilization and Capitalism: Fifteenth to the Eighteenth Centuries* Vol.3 – The Perspective of the World, S. Reynolds (trans.), London, Collins.

Brenner, R. (1977), 'The Origins of Capitalist Development: A Critique of Neo-Smithian Marxism', *New Left Review* No.104, pp. 25–87.

Breton, A. (1964), 'The Economics of Nationalism', *Journal of Political Economy* Vol.72, pp. 376–86.

Brewer, A. (1980), *Marxist Theories of Imperialism: A Critical Survey*, London, Routledge and Kegan Paul.

Brewer, T.L. (1982), 'International Regulation of Restrictive Business Practices', *Journal of World Trade Law* 16, pp. 108–18.

Brewster, H. (1973), 'Economic Dependence: A Quantitative Interpretation', *Social and Economic Studies* 22, pp. 90–5.

———— and Thomas, C.Y. (1969), 'Aspects of the Theory of Economic Integration', *Journal of Common Market Studies* 8, pp. 110–32.

Bronfenbrenner, M. (1979), 'On the Locomotive Theory in International Macro-economics', *Weltwirtschafliches Archiv* 115, pp. 38–50.

Brougham, H.P. (1803), *An Inquiry into the Colonial Policy of the European Powers*, Edinburgh, Balfour, Manners and Miller.

Brown, A.J. (1965), 'Britain and the World Economy', *Yorkshire Bulletin of Economic and Social Research* 17, pp. 46–50.

Brown, E.H.P. (1972), 'The Underdevelopment of Economics', *Economic Journal* 82, pp. 1–10.

Brown, S. (1984), 'The World Polity and the Nation-State System', *International Journal* 34 pp. 509–28.

———— , Price, D., and Raichur, S. (1976), 'Public-Good Theory and Bargaining Between Large and Small Countries', *International Studies Quarterly* 20, pp. 393–414.

Byé, M. (1959), *Relations Economiques Internationales*, Paris, Dalloz.

Cain, P.J. and Hopkins, A.G. (1980), 'The Political Economy of British Expansion Overseas 1750–1914', *Economic History Review, Second Series* 33, pp. 463–90.

Cairnes, J.E. (1874), *Some Leading Principles of Political Economy Newly Expounded*, London, MacMillan.

———— (1875), *The Character and Logical Method of Political Economy*, 2nd. and enlarged ed., London, Macmillan.

Campbell-Boross, L.F. and Morgan, A.D. (1974), 'Net Trade: A Note on Measuring Changes in the Competitiveness of British Industry in Foreign Trade', *National Institute Economic Review* No.68, pp. 77–85.

Caporaso, J. (1978a), 'Introduction', Special Issue on Dependence and Dependency in the Global System, *International Organization* 32, pp. 1–12.

———— (1978b), 'Dependence, Dependency and Power in the Global System: A Structural and Behavioural Analysis', *International Organization* 32, pp. 13–43.

———— (1980), 'Dependency Theory: Continuities and Discontinuities in Development Studies', *International Organization* 34, pp. 605–28.

—— (1981), 'Industrialization in the Periphery: the Evolving Global Division of Labor', *International Studies Quarterly* 25, pp. 347–84.

Cardoso, F.H. (1982), 'Development Under Fire', ch.6, *The New International Economy*, H. Makler, A. Martinelli, and N. Smelser (eds.), London, Sage Publications.

—— and Faletto, E. (1979), *Dependency and Development in Latin America*, M.M. Urquidi (trans.), London, University of California Press.

Carr-Saunders, A.H. (1936), *World Population: Past Growth and Present Trends*, London, Oxford University Press.

Caves, R.E. (1974), 'International Trade, International Investment, and Imperfect Markets', *Special Papers in International Economics* No.10, Princeton, NJ, Princeton University.

—— (1981), 'Intra-Industry Trade and Market Structure in the Industrial Countries', *Oxford Economic Papers* 33, pp. 203–23.

—— and Jones, R.W. (1973), *World Trade and Payments: An Introduction*, Boston, Mass., Little, Brown and Co.

Chakravarty, S. (1983), 'Trade and Development: Some Basic Issues', *International Social Science Journal* 35, pp. 425–40.

Chalmers, H. (1953), *World Trade Policies: the Changing Panorama, 1920–1953*, Berkeley, Ca., University of California Press.

Chase-Dunn, C.K. (1975), 'The Effects of International Economic Dependence on Development and Inequality: A Cross-National Study', *American Sociology Review* 40, pp. 720–38.

—— (1981), 'Interstate System and Capitalist World-Economy: One Logic or Two?', *International Studies Quarterly* 25, pp. 19–42.

—— (1982a), 'Socialist States in the Capitalist World-Economy', ch.1, *Socialist States in the World-System*, C.K. Chase-Dunn (ed.), London, Sage Publications.

—— (1982b), 'The Uses of Formal Comparative Research on Dependency Theory and the World-System Perspective', ch.5, *The New International Economy*, H. Makler, A. Martinelli, and N. Smelser (eds.), London, Sage Publications.

—— (1983), 'The Kernel of the Capitalist World-Economy: Three Approaches', ch. 3 *Contending Approaches to World System Analysis*, W.R. Thompson (ed.), London, Sage Publications.

Chenery, H.B. (1965), 'Comparative Advantage and Development Policy', *Surveys of Economic Theory* Vol.2, American Economic Association, London, Macmillan.

—— (1977), 'Transitional Growth and World Industrialization', ch.14, *The International Allocation of Economic Activity*, B. Ohlin, P-O. Hesselborn, and P.M. Wijkman (eds.), London, Macmillan.

Chipman, J.S. (1966), 'A Survey of the Theory of International Trade: Part 3', *Econometrica*, 34, pp. 18–76.

Clapham, J.H. (1928), *The Economic Development of France and Germany, 1815–1914*, Cambridge, Cambridge University Press.

Clark, G. (1936), *The Balance Sheets of Imperialism: Facts and Figures on Colonies*, New York, Columbia University Press.

Clark, J.M. (1955), *The Ethical Basis of Economic Freedom*, Westport, Conn., the Calvin K. Kazanjian Economics Foundation, Inc.

Clemhout, S. (1964), 'Efficiency, the H.O. Theorem and Patterns of International Trade as Exemplified by the Leontief Paradox', *Economia Internazionale* 17, pp. 1–16.

Cline, W.R. (1983a), 'Introduction and Summary', *Trade Policy in the 1980s*, W.R. Cline (ed.), Washington DC, Institute for International Economics.

—— (1983b), 'International Debt and the Stability of the World Economy', *Policy Analyses in International Economics* No.4, Washington DC, Institute for International Economics.

Coats, A.W. (1964), 'Value Judgments in Economics', *Yorkshire Bulletin* 16, pp. 53–67.

Cohen, A.K. (1970), 'Multiple Factor Approaches', *The Sociology of Crime and*

Cohen, A.K., (*continued*) Delinquency, H.E. Wolfgang, K. Savitz, and N. Johnston (eds.), 2nd. ed., New York, Wiley and Sons.

Cohen, M.R. (1953), 'Reason in Social Science', *Readings in the Philosophy of Science* H. Feigl and M. Brodbeck (eds.), New York, Appleton-Century-Crofts, Inc.

Cohen, S.D. (1977), *The Making of U.S. International Economic Policy: Principles, Problems, and Proposals for Reform*, New York, Praeger.

―――― (1978), 'Changes in the International Economy: Old Realities and New Myths', *Journal of World Trade Law* 12, pp. 273–88.

Commission of the European Communities (1982), *The Competitiveness of the Community Industry*, Brussels, EEC.

Commission on International Development (1969), *Partners in Development* ('The Pearson Report'), London, Pall Mall Press.

Communist International (1928), 'The Programme of the Communist International: Theses on the Revolutionary Movement in the Colonial and Semi-Colonial Countries', *The Communist International 1919–1943: Documents* Vol.2 - 1923–1928, J. Degras (ed.) (1960), London, Oxford University Press.

Condliffe, J.B. (1941), *The Reconstruction of World Trade: A Survey of International Economic Relations*, London, Allen and Unwin.

―――― (1951), *The Commerce of Nations*, London, Allen and Unwin.

Cooper, C.A. and Massell, B.F. (1965), 'Toward A General Theory of Customs Unions for Developing Countries', *Journal of Political Economy* 73, pp. 461–76.

―――― and Sereovich, F. (1970), *The Channels and Mechanisms for the Transfer of Technology from Developed to Developing Countries*, Paper TD/D/AC. 11/5, Geneva, UNCTAD.

Cooper, R.N. (1968), *The Economics of Interdependence: Economic Policy in the Atlantic Community*, London, McGraw Hill Book Company.

―――― (1977), 'A New International Economic Order for Mutual Gain', *Foreign Policy No.26, pp. 66–120.*

Copeland, M.A. (1924), 'Communities of Economic Interest and the Price System', *The Trend of Economics* R.G. Tugwell (ed.), New York, A.A. Knopf.

Corden, W.M. (1965), *Recent Developments in the Theory of International Trade*, Princeton, NJ, International Finance Section, Princeton University.

―――― (1974), 'The Theory of International Trade', ch.7, *Economic Analysis and the Multinational Enterprise*, J.H. Dunning (ed.), London, Allen and Unwin.

Cross, R. (1982), 'The Duhem-Quine Thesis, Lakatos and the Appraisal of Theories in Macroeconomics', *The Economic Journal* 92, pp. 320–40.

Crouzet, F. (1975), 'Trade and Empire: the British Experience from the Establishment of Free Trade until the First World War', ch.9, *Great Britain and Her World 1750–1914*, Essays in Honour of W.O. Henderson, B.M. Ratcliffe (ed.), Manchester, Manchester University Press.

Curtin, P.D. (1969), *The Atlantic Slave Trade*, Madison, Wisconsin, The University of Wisconsin Press.

Curtler, W.H.R. (1920), *The Enclosure and Redistribution of Our Land*, Oxford, The Clarendon Press.

Daadler, H. (1962), 'Capitalism, Colonialism, and the Underdeveloped Areas: The Political Economy of (Anti-)Imperialism', ch. 6, *Essays on Unbalanced Growth*, E. De Vries (ed.), 'S-Gravenhage, Mouton and Co.

Dale, R. (1980), *Anti-Dumping Law in a Liberal Trade Order*, London, Macmillan.

Davidson, W.H. (1979), 'Factor Endowment, Innovation and International Trade', *Kyklos* 32, pp. 764–74.

Davies, K.G. (1974), *The North Atlantic World in the Seventeenth Century*, Minneapolis, Minn., University of Minnesota Press.

Davies, R. (1977), 'Two-Way International Trade: A Comment', *Weltwirtschafliches Archiv* 113, pp. 179–81.

Davis, R. (1966), 'The Rise of Protection in England, 1689–1786', *Economic History Review, Second Series* 19, pp. 306–17.

Day, R.H. (1980), 'Orthodox Economics and Existential Economics', *The Methodology of Economic Thought,* W.J. Samuels (ed.), New Brunswick NJ, Transaction Books.

Deakin, B.M. and Seward, T. (1973), *Shipping Conferences: A Study of Their Origin, Development and Economic Practices,* University of Cambridge Department of Applied Economics Occasional Paper No.37, Cambridge, Cambridge University Press.

Deane, P. (1983), 'The Scope and Method of Economic Science', *The Economic Journal* 93, pp. 1–12.

Deardorff, A.V. (1982), 'The General Validity of the Heckscher-Ohlin Theorem' *American Economic Review* 72, pp. 683–94.

Defoe, D. (1728), *A Plan of the English Commerce,* London, C. Rivington.

Dell, S. (1966), *A Latin American Common Market?,* London, Oxford University Press.

De Marchi, N. (1976), 'Anomaly and the Development of Economics: the Case of the Leontief Paradox', *Method and Appraisal in Economics,* S.J. Latsis (ed.), Cambridge, Cambridge University Press.

Demas, W. (1965), *The Economics of Development in Small Countries with Special Reference to the Caribbean,* Montreal, McGill University Press.

Deutsch, K.W. (1963), 'Nation-Building and National Development: An Introduction', *Nation-Building,* K.W. Deutsch and W.J. Foltz (eds.), New York, Atherton Press.

———— (1981), 'On Nationalism, World Regions and the Nature of the West', *Mobilization, Center-Periphery Structures and Nation-Building,* P. Torsvik ed., Bergen, Universitetsforlaget.

Diamond, W.H. (1977), 'Free Trade Zones Offer Worldwide Opportunities', *Area Development Studies,* Miami, Fla, University of Miami.

Diaz-Alejandro, C.F. (1975), 'North-South Relations: the Economic Component', *World Politics and International Economics,* C.F. Bergsten and L.B. Krause (eds.), Washington DC, The Brookings Institution.

Dobb, M. (1963), *Studies in the Development of Capitalism,* revised ed., London, Routledge and Kegan Paul.

Doggett, E.A. and Cresswell, J.C. (1978), 'Aspects of U.K. Trade Competitiveness', *Economic Trends* No.304, pp. 79–64.

Donaldson, J. (1928), *International Economic Relations,* London, Longmans.

Donges, J.B. and Riedel, J. (1977), 'The Expansion of Manufactured Exports in Developing Countries: An Empirical Assessment of Supply and Demand Issues', *Weltwirtschaftliches Archiv* 113, pp. 58–87.

Doran, C.F. (1983), 'Power Cycle Theory and the Contemporary State System', ch.7, *Contending Approaches to World System Analysis,* W.R. Thompson (ed.), London, Sage Publications.

Dos Santos, T. (1970), 'The Structure of Dependence', *American Economic Review* 60, pp. 231–36.

———— (1973), 'The Crisis of Development Theory and the Problem of Dependence in Latin America', ch.3, *Underdevelopment and Development,* H. Bernstein (ed.), London, Penguin.

Downing, D. (1980), *An Atlas of Territorial and Border Disputes,* London, New English Library Ltd.

Downs, A. (1957), 'An Economic Theory of Political Action in a Democracy', *Journal of Political Economy* 65, pp. 135–150.

Doxey, M.P. (1980), *Economic Sanctions and International Enforcement,* 2nd. ed., London, Macmillan.

Drèze, S.J. (1960), 'Quelques Réflexions Sereins sur l'Adaptation de l'Industrie

Drèze, S.J. (*continued*)   Belge au Marché Commun', *Comptes Rendues des Travaux de la Société Royale d'Economie Politique de Belgique* No. 275.

Duncan, G.A. (1950), 'The Small State and International Economic Equilibrium', *Economia Internatzionale*, 3, pp. 933–51.

Dunning J.H. (1973), 'The Determinants of International Production', *Oxford Economic Papers* 25, pp. 289–336.

——— (1974), 'Multinational Enterprises, Market Structure, Economic Power and Industrial Policy', *Journal of World Trade Law* 8, pp. 575–613.

——— (1977), 'Trade, Location of Economic Activity and the MNE: A Search for an Eclectic Approach', ch.12, *The International Allocation of Economic Activity*, B. Ohlin, P-O. Hesselborn, and P.M. Wijkman (eds.), London, Macmillan.

——— (1979), 'Explaining Changing Patterns of International Production: In Defence of the Eclectic Theory', *Oxford Bulletin of Economics and Statistics* 41, pp. 269–95.

——— (1980), 'Toward an Eclectic Theory of International Production: Some Empirical Tests', *Journal of International Business Studies* 11, pp. 9–31.

——— (1981a) 'Explaining the International Direct Investment Position of Countries: Towards a Dynamic or Developmental Approach', *Weltwirtschaftliches Archiv* 117, pp. 30–64.

——— (1981b), 'A Note on Intra-Industry Foreign Direct Investment', *Banca Nazionale del Lavoro Quarterly Review* 34, pp. 427–38.

——— (1982), 'International Business in a Changing World Environment', *Banca Nazionale de Lavoro Quarterly Review* 35, pp. 351–74.

——— and Buckley, P.J. (1977), 'International Production and Alternative Models of Trade', *The Manchester School* 45, pp. 392–403.

Duvall, R., Jackson, S., Russett, B.M. *et al* (1981), 'A Formal Model of "Dependencia Theory": Structure and Measurement', ch.13, *From National Development to Global Community*, R.L. Merritt and B.M. Russett (eds.), London, Allen and Unwin.

Eckaus, R.S. (1955), 'The Factor-Proportions Problem in Underdeveloped Areas', *American Economic Review* 45, pp. 539–65.

Edgeworth, F.W. (1925), *Papers Relating to Political Economy* Vol.II, London, Macmillan.

Edwards, C.D. (1960), 'Size of Markets, Scale of Firms, and the Character of Competition', ch.7, *Economic Consequences of the Size of Nations* E.A.G. Robinson (ed.), London, Macmillan.

Einstein, A. and Infeld, L. (1938), *The Evolution of Physics*, New York, Simon and Schuster.

Ellsworth, P.T. (1940), 'A Comparison of International Trade Theories', *American Economic Review* 30, pp. 285–89.

Emmanuel, A. (1972), *Unequal Exchange: A Study of the Imperialism of Trade*, B. Pearce (trans.), London, Monthly Review Press.

Ethier, W. (1979), 'Internationally Decreasing Costs and World Trade', *Journal of International Economics* 9, pp. 1–24.

European Management Forum (1981), *Report on Industrial Competitiveness*, Geneva.

Evans, H.D. (1981), 'Trade, Production and Self-Reliance', ch.5, *Dependency Theory: A Critical Reassessment*, D. Seers (ed.), London, Frances Pinter.

Evans, P. (1979a), *Dependent Development: The Alliance of Multinational, State, and Local Capital in Brazil*, Princeton, NJ, Princeton University Press.

——— (1979b), 'Beyond Center and Periphery: A Comment on the Contribution of the World System Approach to the Study of Development', *Sociological Inquiry* 49, pp. 15-20.

Ewing, A.F. (1977), 'Transfer and Development of Technology: the Problems of Developing Countries in Perspective', *Journal of World Trade Law* Vol.11, pp. 1–16.

Falk, R. and Kim, S.S. (1983), 'World Order Studies and the World System', ch.9, *Contending Approaches to World System Analysis*, W.R. Thompson (ed.), London, Sage Publications.

Farnie, D.A. (1962), 'The Commercial Empire of the Atlantic, 1607-1783', *Economic History Review, Second Series* 15, pp. 205-18.

——— (1969), *East and West of Suez: The Suez Canal in History, 1854-1956*, Oxford, Clarendon Press.

Feis, H. (1930), *Europe the World's Banker, 1870-1914*, New Haven, Conn, Yale University Press.

Fieldhouse, D.K. (1973), *Economics and Empire, 1830-1914*, London, Weidenfeld and Nicolson.

——— (1981), *Colonialism 1870-1945: An Introduction*, London, Weidenfeld and Nicolson.

——— (1982), *The Colonial Empires: A Comparative Survey from the Eighteenth Century*, 2nd ed., London, Macmillan.

Findlay, R. (1978), 'Relative Backwardness, Direct Foreign Investment and the Transfer of Technology: A Simple Dynamic Model', *Quarterly Journal of Economics* 92, pp. 1-16.

Finger, J.M. (1975), 'Trade Overlap and Intra-Industry Trade', *Economic Inquiry* 13, pp. 581-9.

Fletcher, M.E. (1958), 'The Suez Canal and World Shipping, 1869-1914', *Journal of Economic History* 18, pp. 556-73.

Flux, A.W. (1899), 'The Flag and Trade: A Summary Review of the Trade of the Chief Colonial Empires', *Journal of the Royal Statistical Society* pp. 489-522.

Ford, J.L. (1963), 'The Ohlin-Heckscher Theory of the Basis of Commodity Trade', *The Economic Journal* 73, pp. 458-76.

——— (1965), *The Ohlin-Heckscher Theory of the Basis and Effects of Commodity Trade*, Asia Monographs No.6, London, Asia Publishing House.

Foreman-Peck, J. (1983), *A History of the World Economy: International Economic Relations Since 1850*, Brighton, Wheatsheaf Books.

Fores, M.J. (1969), 'No More General Theories?', *The Economic Journal* 79, pp. 11-22.

Fortune, J.N. (1979), 'Income Distribution and Linder's Thesis', *The Southern Economic Journal* 46, pp. 158-67.

——— (1971), 'Some Determinants of Trade in Finished Manufactures', *The Swedish Journal of Economics* 73, pp. 311-17.

Foster-Carter, A. (1974), 'Neo-Marxist Approaches to Development and Under-development', *Sociology and Development*, E. de Kadt and G. Williams (eds.), London, Tavistock Publications.

Fox, A.M. (1937), 'Quantitative and Qualitative Changes in International Trade During the Depression', *American Economic Review* 27, pp. 12-28.

Frank, A.G. (1966), 'The Development of Underdevelopment', *Monthly Review* 18 pp. 17-31.

——— (1967), *Capitalism and Underdevelopment in Latin America*, New York, Monthly Review Press.

——— (1978a), *World Accumulation, 1492-1789*, London, Macmillan.

——— (1978b), *Dependent Accumulation and Underdevelopment*, London, Macmillan.

Frankel H. (1943), 'Industrialization of Agricultural Countries and the Possibilities of a New International Division of Labour', *The Economic Journal* 53, pp. 188-201.

Fransman, M. (1984), 'Technological Capability in the Third World: An Overview and Introduction', *Technological Capability in the Third World* M. Fransman and K. King (eds.), London, Macmillan.

Freeman, C. (1979), 'Technical Innovation and British Trade Performance', ch.3, *De-Industrialization*, NIESR Economic Policy Papers No.2, F. Blackaby (ed.), London, Heinemann.

Friedman, H. and Wayne, J. (1977), 'Dependency Theory: A Critique', *Canadian Journal of Sociology* 2, pp. 399–416.
Furtado, C. (1970), *Economic Development of Latin America: A Survey from Colonial Times to the Cuban Revolution*, Cambridge, Cambridge University Press.
———— (1973), 'Underdevelopment and Dependence: the Fundamental Connections', paper presented to the Faculty Seminar on Latin American Studies, Cambridge University, quoted by Lall (1975:805).
Gablis, V. (1984), 'Ministate Economics: Underlying Characteristics and Macroeconomic Policies', *Finance and Development* 21, No.2, pp. 36–8.
Galbraith, J.K. (1973), 'Conversation with an Inconvenient Economist', *Challenge* 16, pp. 28–37.
Gallaher, J. and Robinson, R.E. (1953), 'The Imperialism of Free Trade', *Economic History Review, Second Series* 6, pp. 1–15.
Gardner, R.N. (1980), *Sterling-Dollar Diplomacy in Current Perspective: the Origins and the Prospects of Our International Economic Order*, new expanded ed., New York, Columbia University Press.
Gerschenkron, A. (1962), 'Economic Backwardness in Historical Perspective', ch.1, *Backwardness in Historical Perspective: A Book of Essays*, Cambridge, Mass., Harvard University Press.
Ghosh, R.N. (1964), 'The Colonization Controversy: R.J. Wilmot-Horton and the Classical Economists', *Economica* 31, pp. 385–400.
Giersch, H. (ed.) (1974), 'Conditions for the Success of Import Substitution and Export Diversification as Development Strategies in Latin America, Southeast Asia and Africa', Part IV, *The International Division of Labour: Problems and Perspectives*, International Symposium, Tuebingen, J.C.B. Mohr (Paul Siebeck).
Goldberg, V.P. (1980), 'Remarks on the State of Orthodoxy', *The Methodology of Economic Thought*, W.J. Samuels (ed.), New Brunswick, N.J. Transaction Books.
Goodman, B. and Ceyhun, F. (1976), 'U.S. Export Performance in Manufacturing Industries: An Empirical Investigation', *Weltwirtschaftliches Archiv* 112, pp. 525–55.
Gordon, D.F. (1955), 'Operational Propositions in Economic Theory', *Journal of Political Economy*, 62, pp. 150–61.
Graham, F.D. (1923), 'The Theory of International Values Re-examined', *Quarterly Journal of Economics*, 28, pp. 54–86.
———— (1948), *The Theory of International Values*, Princeton, N.J., Princeton University Press.
Graham, G.S. (1972), *Tides of Empire: Discussions on the Expansion of Britain Overseas*, Montreal, McGill – Queen's University Press.
———— and Humphreys R.A. (eds.) (1962), *The Navy and South America 1807–1823: Correspondence of the Commanders-in-Chief on the South American Station*, London, Navy Records Society.
Gray, H.P. (1973), 'Two-Way International trade in Manufactures: A Theoretical Underpinning', *Weltwirtschaftliches Archiv* 109, pp. 19–39.
———— (1976), *A Generalized Theory of International Trade*, London, Macmillan.
———— (1977), 'Two-Way International Trade: Reply', *Weltwirtschaftliches Archiv* 113, pp. 182–4.
———— (1979a), 'Intra-Industry Trade: The Effects of Different Levels of Data Aggregation', *On the Economics of Intra-Industry Trade*, International Symposium 1978, H. Giersch (ed.), Tuebingen, J.C.B. Mohr (Paul Siebeck).
———— (1979b), *International Trade, Investment and Payments*, Boston, Houghton Mifflin Co.
———— (1980), 'The Theory of International Trade Among Industrial Nations', *Weltwirtschaftliches Archiv* 116, pp. 447–70.
———— and Martin, J.P. (1980), 'The Meaning and Measurement of Product

Differentiation in International Trade', *Weltwirtschafliches Archiv* 116, pp. 322–9.

Gray, S.J. (ed.) (1983), *International Accounting and Transnational Decisions*, London, Butterworth.

Greaves, I. (1957), 'Colonial Trade and Payments', *Economica* 24, pp. 47–58.

Greenberg, M. (1951), *British Trade and the Opening of China, 1800–1842*, Cambridge, Cambridge University Press.

Greenhill, R. (1977a), 'Shipping, 1850–1914', ch.4, *Business Imperialism 1840–1930*, D.C.M. Platt (ed.), Oxford, Clarendon Press.

——— (1977b), 'Merchants and the Latin American Trades', ch.5, *Business Imperialism 1840–1930*, D.C.M. Platt (ed.), Oxford, Clarendon Press.

Griffin, K. (1974), 'The International Transmission of Inequality', *World Development* 2, pp. 3–15.

Griffiths, B.N. (1975), *Invisible Barriers to Invisible Trade*, London, Macmillan.

Grubel, H.G. (1967), 'Intra-Industry Specialization and the Pattern of Trade', *Canadian Journal of Economics and Political Science* 33, pp. 374–88.

——— (1970), 'The Theory of Intra-Industry Trade', ch.3, *Studies in International Economics*, Monash Conference Papers, I.A. McDougall and R.H. Snape (eds.), Amsterdam, North-Holland Publishing Co.

——— (1979), 'Towards a Theory of Two-Way Trade in Capital Assets', *On the Economics of Intra-Industry Trade*, International Symposium 1978, H. Giersch (ed.), Tuebingen, J.C.B. Mohr (Paul Siebeck).

——— (1982), 'Towards a Theory of Free Economic Zones', *Weltwirtschafliches Archiv* 118, pp. 39–61.

——— and Lloyd, P.J. (1971), 'The Empirical Measurement of Intra-Industry Trade', *Economic Record* 47, pp. 494–513.

——— and——— (1975), *Intra-Industry Trade: The Theory and Measurement of International Trade in Differentiated Products*, London, Macmillan.

Gruchy, A.G. (1980), 'Review of B. Ward's *What's Wrong with Economics?*' and 'Neo-institutionalism and the Economics of Dissent', *The Methodology of Economic Thought*, W.J. Samuels (ed.), New Brunswick N.J., Transaction Books.

Gustafsson, B. (1979), *Post-Industrial Society: Proceedings of an International Symposium*, London, Croom Helm.

Haberler, G. (1936), *The Theory of International Trade with Its Applications to Commercial Policy*, London, W. Hodge and Co. Ltd.

——— (1951), 'Real Cost, Money Cost and Comparative Advantage', *International Social Science Bulletin*, Vol.3, pp. 54–8.

——— (1954), 'The Relevance of the Classical Theory Under Modern Conditions', *American Economic Review* 44, pp. 543–51.

——— (1959), *International Trade and Economic Development*, National Bank of Egypt 50th Anniversary Commemoration Lectures, Cairo.

——— (1961), *A Survey of International Trade Theory*, revised and enlarged ed., Special Papers in International Economics No.1, New Jersey, International Finance Section, Department of Economics, Princeton University.

——— (1964), 'Integration and Growth of the World Economy in Historical Perspective', *American Economic Journal* 54, pp. 1–24.

——— (1977), 'Survey of Circumstances Affecting the Location of Production and International Trade as Analysed in the Theoretical Literature, *The International Allocation of Economic Activity*, B. Ohlin, P-O. Hesselborn, and P.M. Wijkman (eds.), London, Macmillan.

Hallberg, C.W. (1931), *The Suez Canal: Its History and Diplomatic Importance*, New York, Columbia University Press.

Hamilton, A. (1791), *Report on the Subject of Manufactures*, Philadelphia, 5 Dec., *The Papers of Alexander Hamilton* Vol.10, (1966) H.C. Syrett and J.E. Cooke (eds.), New York, Columbia University Press.

Hamilton, F.E.I. and Linge, G.J.R. (1979), 'Industrial Systems', ch.1, *Spatial Analysis, Industry and the Industrial Environment* Vol.I – Industrial Systems, F.E.I. Hamilton and G.J.R. Linge (eds.), Chichester, John Wiley and Sons.

Hansen, R.D. (1979), *Beyond the North–South Stalemate*, New York, McGraw-Hill.

Hanson, J.R. (1980), *Trade in Transition: Exports from the Third World, 1840–1900*, New York, Academic Press.

Haq, M. ul (1976), *The Poverty Curtain: Choices for the Third World*, New York, Columbia University Press.

Harley, C.K. (1971), 'The Shift from Sailing Ships to Steamships, 1850–1890: A Study in Technological Change and Its Diffusion', ch.6, *Essays on a Mature Economy: Britain After 1840*, D.N. McCloskey (ed.), London, Methuen and Co. Ltd.

Harlow, V.T. (1964), *The Founding of the Second British Empire, 1763–1793* Vol.II – New Continents and Changing Values, London, Longmans, Green and Co.

Hartmann, F.H. (1973), *The Relations of Nations*, 4th ed., New York, Macmillan.

Harrod, Sir R. (1962), 'Economic Development and Asian Regional Co-operation', *Pakistan Development Review* 2, pp. 1–22.

Haussmann, F. and Ahearn, D. (1944), 'International Cartels and World Trade', *Thought*, Fordham University Quarterly – September.

Hazari, B.R., Sgro, P.M. and Suh, D.C. (1981), *Non-traded and Intermediate Goods and the Pure Theory of International Trade*, London, Croom Helm.

Heckscher, E. (1919), 'The Effect of Foreign Trade on the Distribution of Income', *Ekonomisk Tidskrift* 21, reprinted in *Readings in the Theory of International Trade*, American Economic Association (1950), London, Allen and Unwin.

—— (1936), 'Mercantilism: Revisions in Economic History', *Economic History Review, First Series* 7, pp. 44–54.

—— (1955), *Mercantilism* Vols. I and II, M. Shapiro (trans.), revised ed. E.F. Soederlund, London, Allen and Unwin.

Heilbroner, R. (1980), 'On the Possibility of a Political Economics', *The Methodology of Economic Thought*, W.J. Samuels (ed.), New Brunswick, N.J., Transaction Books.

Helleiner, G.K. (1973), 'Manufactured Exports from the Less Developed Countries', *The Economic Journal*, 83, pp. 21–47.

—— (1977), 'International Technology Issues: Southern Needs and Northern Responses', ch. 12, *The New International Economic Order*, J.N. Bhagwati (ed.), Cambridge, Mass., MIT Press.

—— (1980), 'World Market Imperfections and the Developing Countries', ch.2, *International Economic Disorder: Essays in North–South Relations*, London, Macmillan.

—— (1981), *Intra-Firm Trade and the Developing Countries*, London, Macmillan.

—— and Lavergne, R. (1979), 'Intra-Firm Trade and Industrial Exports to the U.S.', *Oxford Bulletin of Economics and Statistics* 41, pp. 297–312.

Heller, P.S. (1976), 'Factor Endowment Change and Comparative Advantage', *Review of Economics and Statistics* 58, pp. 283–99.

Helpman, E. (1981), 'International Trade in the Presence of Product Differentiation, Economies of Scale and Monopolistic Competition: A Chamberlain-Heckscher-Ohlin Approach', *Journal of International Economics* 11, pp. 305–40.

Hendersen, P.D. (1982), 'Trade Policies and "Strategies" – Case for a Liberal Approach', *World Economy* 5, pp. 291–302.

Hesse, H. (1974), 'Hypotheses for the Explanation of Trade Between Industrial Countries, 1953–1970', *The International Division of Labour: Problems and Perspectives*, International Symposium, H. Giersch (ed.), Tuebingen, J.C.B. Mohr (Paul Siebeck).

Hexner, E. (1943), 'International Cartels in the Postwar World', *The Southern Economic Journal* 10, pp. 114–35.

——— (1945), *International Cartels*, Chapel Hill, University of North Carolina Press.

Hicks, J.R. (1959), 'National Economic Development in the International Setting', ch.8, *Essays in World Economics*, Oxford, Clarendon Press.

——— (1963), *International Trade: The Long View*, Cairo, Central Bank of Egypt.

——— (1969), *A Theory of Economic History*, Oxford, Oxford University Press.

Hilferding, R. (1910), *Finance Capital: A Study of the Latest Phase of Capitalist Development*, T. Bottomore (ed.), 1981 ed., London, Routledge and Kegan Paul.

Hillman, A.L. and Hirsch, S. (1979), 'Factor Intensity Reversals: Conceptual Experiments with Traded Goods Aggregates', *Weltwirtschafliches Archiv* 115, pp. 272–81.

Hirsch, S. (1967), *Location of Industry and International Competitiveness*, Oxford, Clarendon Press.

——— (1974a), 'Hypotheses Regarding Trade Between Developing and Industrial Countries', *The International Division of Labour: Problems and Perspectives*, International Symposium, H. Giersch (ed.), Tuebingen, J.C.B. Mohr (Paul Siebeck).

——— (1974b), 'Capital or Technology? Confronting the Neo-Factor Proportions and Neo-Technology Accounts of International Trade', *Weltwirtschafliches Archiv* 110, pp. 563–73.

——— (1976), 'An International Trade and Investment Theory of the Firm', *Oxford Economic Papers* 28, pp. 258–70.

——— (1977), 'Rich Man's, Poor Man's and Every Man's Goods. Aspects of Industrialization' Kieler Studien No.148, Tuebingen.

——— and Lev, B. (1973), 'Trade and Per Capita Income Differentials: A Test of the Burenstam–Linder Hypothesis', *World Development* 1, pp. 11–17.

Hirschman, A.O. (1961), 'Ideologies of Economic Development in Latin America', *Latin American Issues: Essays and Comments*, A.O. Hirschman (ed.), New York, The Twentieth Century Fund.

——— (1970), 'The Search for Paradigms as a Hindrance to Understanding', *World Politics* 22, pp. 324–43.

——— (1971), 'Introduction: Political Economics and Possibilism', *A Bias for Hope: Essays on Development and Latin America*, New Haven, Conn. Yale University Press.

——— (1977), 'A Generalized Linkage Approach to Development, with Special Reference to Staples', *Essays on Economic Development and Cultural Change in Honor of B.F. Hoselitz*, Supplement to *Economic Development and Cultural Change* 25.

——— (1980), *National Power and the Structure of Foreign Trade*, expanded ed., Berkeley, University of California Press.

Hobsbaum, E.J. (1968), *Industry and Empire: An Economic History of Britain Since 1750*, London, Weidenfeld and Nicolson.

Hobson, J.A. (1902), *Imperialism*, reprint 1965, Ann Arbor, University of Michigan Press.

——— (1920), *The Morals of Economic Internationalism*, Boston, Houghton Miffin Co.

Holzman, F.D. (1963), 'Foreign Trade', ch.7, *Economic Trends in the Soviet Union*, A. Bergson and S.S. Kuznets (eds.), Cambridge Mass., Harvard University Press.

——— and Legvold, R. (1975), 'The Economics and Politics of East–West Relations', *World Politics and International Economics*, C.F. Bergsten and L.B.

Holzman and Legvold (*continued*)   Krause (eds.), Washington DC, The Brookings Institution.

Homans, G.G. (1967), *The Nature of Social Science*, New York, Harcourt, Brace and World.

Hopkins, A.G. (1973), *An Economic History of West Africa*, London, Longmans.

Hopkins, T.K. (1979), 'The Study of the Capitalist World-Economy: Some Introductory Considerations', ch.1, *The World System of Capitalism: Past and Present*, W.L. Goldfrank (ed.), London, Sage Publications.

—— and Wallerstein, I. (1981), 'Structural Transformation of the World-Economy', ch.12, *Dynamics of World Development*, R. Rubinson (ed.), London, Sage Publications.

—— and—— (1982), 'Patterns of Development of the Modern World-System', ch.2, *World-System Analysis: Theory and Methodology*, T.K. Hopkins *et al* (eds.), London, Sage Publications.

Howe, W.S. (1978), *Industrial Economics: An Applied Approach*, London, Macmillan.

Hufbauer, G.C. (1965), *Synthetic Materials and the Theory of International Trade*, London, Duckworth.

—— (1970) 'The Impact of National Characteristics and Technology on the Commodity Composition of Trade in Manufactured Goods', *The Technology Factor in International Trade*, R. Vernon (ed.), National Bureau of Economic Research Conference Series No.22, New York, Columbia University Press.

—— (1983), 'Subsidy Issues After the Tokyo Round', ch.10, *Trade Policies in the 1980s*, W.R. Cline (ed.), Washington DC, Institute for International Economics.

—— and Chilas, J.G. (1974), J.G. (1974), 'Specialization by Industrial Countries: Extent and Conseqences', *The International Division of Labour: Problems and Perspectives*, International Symposium, H. Giersch (ed.), Tuebingen, J.C.B. Mohr (Paul Siebeck).

—— and Schott, J.J. (1983), *Economic Sanctions in Support of Foreign Policy Goals*, Policy Analyses in International Economics No.6, Washington DC, Institute for International Economics.

Hume, D. (1955), 'Of Commerce', Essays in Economics, *David Hume: Writings on Economics*, E. Rotwein (ed.), Edinburgh, Nelson and Sons.

Hutchison, T.W. (1977), *Knowledge and Ignorance in Economics*, Oxford, Basil Blackwell.

Hyde, F.E. (1973), *Far Eastern Trade, 1860–1914*, London, Adam and Charles Black.

Hymer, S. (1972), 'The Multinational Corporation and the Law of Uneven Development', *Economic and World Order: From the 1970s to the 1990s*, J.N. Bhagwati (ed.), New York, The Free Press.

—— (1979), 'Robinson Crusoe and the Secret of Primitive Accumulation', ch.4, *The Multinational Corporation: A Radical Approach*, Papers by S. Hymer (ed.) R.B. Cohen *et al*, Cambridge, Cambridge University Press.

Ianni, E.M. (1982), 'The International Treatment of State Trading', *Journal of World Trade Law* 16, pp. 480–96.

Independent Commission on International Development Issues ('The Brandt Commission') (1980) *North–South: A Programme for Survival*, London, Pan Books.

—— (1983), *Common Crisis: North–South Co-operation for World Recovery*, London, Pan Books.

Jacquemain, A.P. and de Jong, H.W. (1977), *European Industrial Organization*, London, Macmillan.

Johns, R.A. (1983), *Tax Havens and Offshore Finance: A Study of Transnational Economic Development*, London, Frances Pinter.

—— (1984a), 'Transnational Business, National Friction Structures and International Exchange', *Review of International Studies* 10, pp. 125–42.

——— (1984b), 'Colonial Trade: A Lacuna in the Explanatory Structure of Classical and and Neo-Classical International Trade Theory', *Department of Economics and Management Science Discussion Paper* No.47, University of Keele.

Johnson, H.G. (1964), 'Book Review of Linder (1961)', *Economica* 31, pp. 86–90.

——— (1967), 'International Trade Theory and Monopolistic Competition Theory', ch.9, *Monopolistic Competition Theory: Studies in Impact*, Essays in Honor of E.H. Chamberlin, R.E. Kuenne (ed.), New York, John Wiley and Sons.

——— (1968a), *Comparative Cost and Commercial Policy Theory for a Developing World Economy*, Stockholm, Almqvist and Wiksell.

——— (1968b), 'The Ideology of Economic Policy in the New States', ch. 8, *Economic Nationalism in Old and New States*, H.G. Johnson (ed.), London, Allen and Unwin.

——— (1969), 'The Theory of International Trade', *International Economic Relations*, P.A. Samuelson (ed.), London, Macmillan.

——— (1970), 'The State of Theory in Relation to the Empirical Analysis', *The Technology Factor in International Trade*, R. Vernon (ed.), National Bureau of Economic Research Conference Series No.22, New York, Columbia University Press.

——— (1975a), 'Technological Change and Comparative Advantage: An Advanced Country's Viewpoint', *Journal of World Trade Law* 9, pp. 1–14.

——— (1975b), 'Technology Superiority and International Trade', ch.3, *Technology and Economic Interdependence*, London, Macmillan.

——— (1977a), 'Technology, Technical Progress and the International Allocation of Economic Activity', ch.9, *The International Allocation of Economic Activity*, B. Ohlin, P-O. Hesselborn, and P.M. Wijkman (eds.), London, Macmillan.

——— (1977b), 'Changing Views on Trade and Development: Some Reflections', *Essays on Economic Development and Cultural Change in Honor of B.F. Hoselitz*, Supplement to *Economic Development and Cultural Change* 25.

Jones, R.W. (1974), 'Trade with Non-Traded Goods: The Anatomy of Interconnected Markets', *Economica* 41, pp. 121–38.

——— (1977), '"Two-ness" in Trade Theory': Costs and Benefits', *Special Papers in International Economics* No.12, New Jersey, Princeton University.

——— (1980), 'Comparative and Absolute Advantage', *Schweiz Zeitschrift für Volkswirtschaft und Statitz* pp. 235–60.

Junz, H.B. and Rhomberg, R.R. (1964), 'Prices and Export Performance of Industrial Countries', *IMF Staff Papers* 12, pp. 224–69.

Kahan, A. (1968), 'Nineteenth Century European Experience with Policies of Economic Nationalism', ch.2, *Economic Nationalism in Old and New States*, H.G. Johnson (ed.), London, Allen and Unwin.

Kalecki, M. (1976), 'Observations on Social and Economic Aspects of "Intermediate Regimes"', ch.4, *Essays on Developing Economies*, Hassocks, The Harvester Press.

Kane, E.J. (1977), 'Good Intentions and Unintended Evil: the Case Against Selective Credit Allocation', *Journal of Money, Credit and Banking* 9, pp. 55–69.

Kapp, K.W. (1954), 'Economics and the Behavioural Sciences', *Kyklos* 7, pp. 205–25.

——— (1976), 'The Nature and Significance of Institutional Economics', *Kyklos* 29, pp. 209–32.

Keesing, D.B. (1965), 'Labor Skills and International Trade: Evaluating Many Trade Flows with a Single Measuring Device', *Review of Economics and Statistics* 47, pp. 287–94.

——— (1966), 'Labor Skills and Comparative Advantage', *American Economic Review, Papers and Proceedings* 56, pp. 249–58.

Keesing (*continued*) (1971), 'Different Countries' Labor Skill Coefficients and the Skill Intensity of International Trade Flows', *Journal of International Economics* 1, pp. 443–52.
—— (1979), *World Trade and Output of Manufactures: Structural Trends and Developing Countries' Exports*, World Bank Staff Working Paper No.316, Washington DC, World Bank.
Kenen, P.B. (ed.) (1975), *International Trade and Finance: Frontiers for Research*, Cambridge, Cambridge University Press.
Keynes, J.N. (1930), *Scope and Method*, 2nd. ed., London, Macmillan.
Kidron, M. and Segal, R. (1984), *The New State of the World Atlas*, London, Pan Books.
Kindleberger, C.P. (1951), 'Group Behaviour and International Trade', *Journal of Political Economy* 59, pp. 30–47.
—— (1956), *The Terms of Trade: A European Case Study*, London, Chapman and Hall.
—— (1962), *Foreign Trade and the National Economy*, New Haven, Yale University Press.
—— (1966), 'The Role of the United States in the European Economy, 1919–1950', ch.14, *Europe and the Dollar*, Cambridge, Mass., MIT Press.
—— (1968), 'Foreign Trade and Economic Growth: Lessons from Britain and France, 1850–1913', *Economics of Trade and Development*, J.D. Theberge (ed.), New York, John Wiley and Sons Ltd.
—— (1969), *American Business Abroad: Six Lectures on Direct Investment*, New Haven, Conn., Yale University Press.
—— (1973), *The World in Depression, 1929–1939*, Berkeley, University of California Press.
—— (1978a), 'The Rise of Free Trade in Western Europe, 1820–1875', ch.3, *Economic Response: Comparative Studies in Trade, Finance and Growth*, Cambridge, Mass., Harvard University Press.
—— (1978b), 'Government and International Trade', *Essays in International Trade* No.129, New Jersey, Princeton University.
—— (1981), 'Dominance and Leadership in the International Economy: Exploitation, Public Goods, and Free Rides', *International Studies Quarterly* 25, pp. 242–54.
—— (1983), 'On the Rise and Decline of Nations', *International Studies Quarterly* 27, pp. 5–10.
—— (1984), *A Financial History of Western Europe*, London, Allen and Unwin.
—— and Depres, E. (1952), 'The Mechanism for Adjustment in International Payments – the Lessons of Postwar Experience', *American Economic Review: Papers and Proceedings* 42, No.2, pp. 335–44.
Kirschen, E.S. (1964), *Economic Policy in Our Time*, 3 vols., Amsterdam, North-Holland Press.
—— (1974/5), *Economic Policies Compared: West and East*, 2 Vols., Amsterdam, North-Holland Press.
Kitchen, J.S. (1980), *The Employment of Seamen*, London, Croom Helm.
Kleiman, E. (1976), 'Trade and the Decline of Colonialism', *The Economic Journal* 86, pp. 459–80.
Knorr, K.E. (1963), *British Colonial Theories, 1570–1850*, London, Frank Cass and Co. Ltd.
Kojima, K. (1970), 'Towards a Theory of Agreed Specialization: the Economics of Integration', ch.20, *Induction, Growth and Trade*, Essays in Honour of Sir Roy Harrod, W.A. Eltis, M. Scott and J.N. Wolfe (eds.), Oxford, Clarendon Press.
—— (1975), 'International Trade and Foreign Investment: Substitutes or Complements?', *Hitotsubashi Journal of Economics* 16, pp. 1–12.

———— (1981), 'A New Capitalism for A New International Economic Order', *Hitotsubashi Journal of Economics* 21, pp. 1–19.

Koo, H. (1984), 'World System, Class, and State in Third World Development: Toward an Integrative Framework of Political Economy', *Sociological Perspectives* 27, pp. 33–52.

Kostecki, M.M. (1979), *East–West Trade and the G.A.T.T. System*, London, Macmillan.

———— (1982a), 'State Trading by the Advanced and Developing Countries: the Background', ch.1, *State Trading in International Markets*, M.M. Kostecki (ed.), London, Macmillan.

———— (1982b), 'State Trading in Agricultural Products by the Advanced Countries', ch.2, *State Trading in International Markets*, M.M. Kostecki (ed.), London, Macmillan.

Krause, L.B. and Nye, J.S. (1975), 'Reflections on the Economics and Politics of International Economic Organizations', *International Organization* 29, pp. 323–42.

Kravis, I.B. (1956), '"Availability" and Other Influences on the Commodity Composition of International Trade', *Journal of Political Economy* 64, pp. 143–55.

———— (1970), 'Trade as a Handmaiden of Growth: Similarities Between the Nineteenth and Twentieth Centuries', *The Economic Journal* 80, pp. 850–72.

———— (1972), 'The Role of Exports in Nineteenth Century United States Growth', *Economic Development and Cultural Change* 20, pp. 387–405.

———— and Lipsey, R.E. (1971), *Price Competitiveness in World Trade*, New York, National Bureau of Economic Research.

Krueger, A.O. (1977), *Growth, Distortions, and Patterns of Trade Among Many Countries*, Princeton Studies in International Finance No.40, New Jersey, Princeton University.

Krugman, P.R. (1979), 'Increasing Returns, Monopolistic Competition and International Trade', *Journal of International Economics* 9, pp. 469–79.

———— (1980), 'Scale Economies, Product Differentiation and the Pattern of Trade', *American Economic Review* 70, pp. 950–9.

———— (1981), 'Intra-industry Specialization and the Gains from Trade', *Journal of Political Economy* 89, pp. 959–73.

Krupp, S. (1963a), 'Analytic Economics and the Logic of External Effects', *American Economic Review, Papers and Proceedings* 53, pp. 220–6.

———— (1963b), 'Theoretical Explanation and the Nature of the Firm', *Western Economic Journal* Summer, 1., pp. 191–204.

———— (1980), 'Axioms of Economics and the Claim to Efficiency', *The Methodology of Economic Thought*, W.J. Samuels (ed.), New Brunswick, N.J., Transaction Books.

Kuznets, S. (1960), 'The Economic Growth of Small Nations', ch.2, *The Economic Consequences of the Size of Nations*, E.A.G. Robinson (ed.), London, Macmillan.

———— (1967a), 'Quantitative Aspects of the Economic Growth of Nations: X – Level and Structure of Foreign Trade: Long-Term Trends', *Economic Development and Cultural Change* 15, No.2 Part II, pp. 1–140.

———— (1967b), 'Trends in International Independence', ch.6, *Modern Economic Growth: Rate, Structure, and Spread*, New Haven, Conn., Yale University Press.

Labys, W.C. (1982), 'The Role of State Trading in Mineral Commodity Markets', ch.4, *State Trading in International Markets*, M.M. Kostecki (ed.), London Macmillan.

Lake, D.A. (1983), 'International Economic Structures and American Foreign Economic Policy, 1887–1934', *World Politics* 34, pp. 517–43.

Lal, D. (1983), *The Poverty of 'Development Economics'*, I.E.A. Hobart Paper No. 16.

Lall, S. (1973), 'Transfer-Pricing by Multinational Manufacturing Firms', *Oxford Bulletin of Economics and Statistics* 35, pp. 173-95.
———— (1975), 'Is "Dependence" a Useful Concept in Analysing Underdevelopment?', *World Development* 3, pp. 799-810.
———— (1976), 'The Patent System and the Transfer of Technology to Less-Developed Countries', *Journal of World Trade Law* 10, pp. 1-16.
———— (1978), 'The Pattern of Intra-Firm Exports by U.S. Multinationals', *Oxford Bulletin of Economics and Statistics* 40, pp. 209-22.
———— (1979), 'Transfer-Pricing and Developing Countries: Some Problems of Investigation', *World Development* 7, pp. 173-95.
———— (1982), *Developing Countries as Exporters of Technology*, London, Macmillan.
Lancaster, K. (1957), 'The Heckscher-Ohlin Trade Model: A Geometric Treatment', *Economica* 24, pp. 19-39.
Lanyi, A. (1969), *The Case for Floating Exchange Rates Reconsidered*, Essays in International Finance No.72, New Jersey, Princeton University.
Lary, H.B. (1968), *Imports of Manufactures from the Less Developed Countries*, New York, Columbia University Press.
Latham, A.J.H. (1978), *The International Economy and the Undeveloped World, 1865-1914*, London, Croom Helm.
Laughlin, J.L. (1918), *Credit of the Nations*, New York, Charles Scribner's Sons.
Leamer, E.E. (1974), 'The Commodity Composition of International Trade in Manufactures: An Empirical Analysis', *Oxford Economic Papers* 26, pp. 350-74.
Leibenstein, H. (1978), *General X-Efficiency Theory and Economic Development*, New York, Oxford University Press.
Leff, N. (1973), 'Tropical Trade and Development in the Nineteenth Century: the Brazilian Experience', *Journal of Political Economy* 81, pp. 678-96.
Legarda, B. (1984), 'Small Island Economies', *Finance and Development* 21, No.2, pp. 42-3.
Lenin, V.I. (1917), 'Imperialism: the Highest Stage of Capitalism', in *Selected Works* Vol.1, 1960 ed., Moscow, Foreign Languages Publishing House.
———— (1920), 'Preliminary Draft of Theses on the National and Colonial Question', *Selected Works* Vol. 3, 1960 ed., Moscow, Foreign Languages Publishing House.
Leontief, W.W. (1953), 'Domestic Production and Foreign Trade: the American Capital Position Re-examined', *Proceedings of the American Philosophical Society* 97, republished (1954), *Economia Internazionale* 7, pp. 9-45.
———— (1956), 'Factor Proportions and the Structure of American Trade: Further Theoretical and Empirical Analysis', *Review of Economics and Statistics* 38, pp. 386-407.
Levcik, F. and Stankovsky, J. (1979), *Industrial Cooperation Between East and West*, M. Vale (trans.), London, Macmillan.
Lewis, W.A. (1949), *Economic Survey, 1919-1939*, London, Allen and Unwin.
———— (1978a), *The Evolution of the International Economic Order*, New Jersey, Princeton University Press.
———— (1978b), *Growth and Fluctuations, 1870-1913*, London, Allen and Unwin.
———— (1981), 'The Rate of Growth of World Trade, 1830-1973', ch.1, *The World Economic Order: Past and Prospects*, S. Grassman and E. Lundberg (eds.), London, Macmillan.
Leys, C. (1984), 'Relations of Production and Technology', *Technological Capability in the Third World*, M. Fransman and K. King (eds.), London, Macmillan.
Lind, J.D. (1978), 'The Long View of Economic Development: New Theories', *Development and Change* 9, pp. 667-81.
Lindbeck, A. (1975), 'The Changing Role of the Nation State', *Kyklos* 28, pp. 23-46.

—— (1977), 'Comment', ch.6, *The International Allocation of Economic Activity*, B. Ohlin, P-O. Hesselborn, and P.M. Wijkman (eds.), London, Macmillan.

Linder, S.B. (1961), *An Essay on Trade and Transformation*, John Wiley and Sons.

—— (1967), *Trade and Trade Policy for Development*, London, Pall Mall Press.

Lipsey, R.E. (1975), 'Review' of Grubel and LLoyd (1975), *Journal of International Economics* 6, pp. 312–14.

List, F. (1916), *The National System of Political Economy*, S.S. Lloyd (trans.), London, Longmans, Green and Co.

Loertscher, and Wolter, F. (1980), 'Determinants of Intra-Industry Trade: Among Countries and Across Industries', *Weltwirtschafliches Archiv* 116, pp. 280–93.

Lorenz, D. (1974), 'Explaining Hypotheses on Trade Flows Between Industrial and Developing Countries', *The International Division of Labour: Problems and Perspectives*, International Symposium, H. Giersch (ed.), Tuebingen, J.C.B. Mohr (Paul Siebeck).

Louis, W.R. (1984), 'The Era of the Mandates System and the Non-European World', ch. 13, *The Expansion of International Society*, H. Bull and A. Watson (eds.), Oxford, Clarendon Press.

Lowe, A. (1965), *On Economic Knowledge: Toward a Science of Political Economics*, New York, Harper and Row.

Lowinger, T.C. (1971), 'The Neo-Factor Proportions Theory of International Trade: An Empirical Investigation', *American Economic Review* 61, pp. 675–81.

Luard, E. (1977), *The Control of the Sea-Bed: Who Owns the Resources of the Oceans?*, revised ed., London, Heinemann.

Luxemburg, R. (1913), *The Accumulation of Capital*, reprint 1951, New York, Monthly Review Press.

Mabogunje, A.L. (1977), 'International Circumstances Affecting the Development and Trade of Developing Countries', ch.9, *The International Allocation of Economic Activity*, B. Ohlin, P-O. Hesselborn, and P.M. Wijkman (eds.), London, Macmillan.

McCalla, A.F. and Schmitz, A. (1982), 'State Trading in Grain', ch.3, *State Trading in International Markets*, M.M. Kostecki (ed.), London, Macmillan.

MacDougall, D. (1951), 'British and American Exports: A Study Suggested by the Theory of Comparative Costs', *The Economic Journal* 61, pp. 697–724.

—— Dowley, M. Fox, P., and Pugh, S., (1962), 'British and American Productivity, Prices and Exports: An Addendum', *Oxford Economic Papers* 14, pp. 297–304.

McEwen, W.P. (1963), *The Problem of Social Scientific Knowledge*, New Jersey, The Bedminster Press.

McGeehan, J.M. (1968), 'Competitiveness: A Survey of Recent Literature', *The Economic Journal*, 78, pp. 243–62.

Machlup, F. (1963), *Essays on Economic Semantics*, New Jersey, Englewood Cliffs.

—— (1966), 'Operationalism and Pure Theory in Economics', *The Structure of Economic Science*, S.R. Krupp (ed.), New Jersey, Prentice-Hall.

—— (1967), 'Theories of the Firm: Marginalist, Behavioural, Managerial', *American Economic Review* 57, pp. 1–33.

—— (1978), *Methodology of Economics and Other Social Sciences*, New York, Academic Press.

McIntyre, A. (1964), 'Some Issues in Trade Policy in the West Indies', *Readings in the Political Economy of the Caribbean*, N. Girvan and O. Jefferson (eds.), 1971 edition, Mona, New World Group Ltd.

McLean, D. (1976), 'Finance and "Informal Empire" Before the First World War', *Economic History Review, Second Series* 24, pp. 291–305.

McManus J. (1972), 'The Theory of the International Firm', *The Multinational Firm and the Nation State,* G. Paquet (ed.), Don Mills, Collier-Macmillan.

Maddison, A. (1962), 'Growth and Fluctuation in the World Economy, 1870–1960', *Banca Nazionale del Lavoro Quarterly Review* **61**, pp. 127–95.

——— (1982), *Phases of Capitalist Development,* Oxford, Oxford University Press.

Madeuf, B. and Michalet, C. (1978), 'A New Approach to International Economics', *International Social Science Journal* **30**, pp. 253–83.

Magdoff, H. (1969), *The Age of Imperialism,* New York, Monthly Review Press.

Magee, S.P. (1973), 'Factor Market Distortions, Production and Trade: A Survey', *Oxford Economic Papers* **25**, pp. 5–43.

——— (1977a), 'Information and the Multinational Corporation: An Appropriability Theory of Direct Foreign Investment', ch.13, *The New International Economic Order: the North–South Debate,* J.N. Bhagwati (ed.), Cambridge, Massachusetts, M.I.T. Press.

——— (1977b), 'Multinational Corporations, the Industry Technology Cycle and Development', *Journal of World Trade Law* **11**, pp. 297–321.

Majumdar, B.A. (1979), 'Innovations and International Trade: An Industry Study of Dynamic Comparative Advantage', *Kyklos* **32**, pp. 559–70.

Makler, H.M., Martinelli, A., Smelzer, N.J. (1982), 'Introduction', ch.1, *The New International Economy* H.M. Makler, A. Martinelli, N.J. Smelzer (eds.), London, Sage Publications.

Malmgren, H.B. (1977), *International Order for Public Subsidies,* London, Trade Policy Research Centre.

Manoilesco, M. (1931), *The Theory of Protection and International Trade,* London, P.S. King.

Marcy, G. (1960), 'How Far Can Foreign Trade and Customs Agreements Confer Upon Small Nations the Advantage of Large Nations?', ch.17, *Economic Consequences of the Size of Nations,* E.A.G. Robinson (ed.), London, Macmillan.

Marshall, A. (1923), *Money, Credit and Commerce,* London, Macmillan.

Marshman, J.C. (1867), *The History of India from the Earliest Period to the Close of Lord Dalhousie's Administration,* London, Longmans.

Masche, E. (1969), 'Outline of the History of German Cartels from 1873–1914', *Essays in European Economic History: 1789–1914,* F. Crouzet, W.H.C. Stern (eds), London, Arnold.

Mason, E.S. (1926), 'The Doctrine of Comparative Cost', *Quarterly Journal of Economics* **41**, pp. 63–93.

Mathias, P. (1969), *The First Industrial Nation: An Economic History of Britain, 1700–1914,* London, Methuen.

Matza, D. (1964), *Delinquency and Drift,* New York, John Wiley and Sons.

Mauro, F. (1961), 'Toward an "Intercontinental Model": European Overseas Expansion Between 1500 and 1800', *Economic History Review, Second Series* **14**, pp. 1–17.

Meade, J. (1955), *The Theory of International Economic Policy* Vol.II – Trade and Welfare, London, Oxford University Press.

Meehan, E.J. (1968), *Explanation in Social Science: A System Paradigm,* Illinois, Dorsey Press.

Meier, G.M. (1949), 'The Theory of Comparative Costs Reconsidered', *Oxford Economic Papers* **1**, pp. 199–216.

——— (1958), 'International Trade and International Inequality', *Oxford Economic Papers* **10**, pp. 277–89.

——— (1963), *International Trade and Development,* New York, Harper and Row.

Mendels, F.F. (1972), 'Proto-Industrialization: the First Phase of the Industrialization Process', *Journal of Economic History* **32**, pp. 241–61.

Merivale, H. (1861), *Lectures on Colonization and Colonies*, 1928 reprint, London, Oxford University Press.

Meyer, F. (1948), *Britain's Colonies in World Trade*, London, Oxford University Press.

Meyer, J.W. (1980), 'The World Polity and the Authority of the Nation-State', ch.6, *Studies of the Modern World-System*, A. Bergesen (ed.), London, Academic Press.

Michaely, M. (1964), 'Factor Proportions in International Trade: Current State of the Theory', *Kyklos* 17, pp. 529–50.

Michalet, C.A. (1982), 'From International Trade to World Economy: A New Paradigm', *The New International Economy*, H. Makler, A. Martinelli, and N. Smelser (eds.), California, Sage Publications.

Mill, J. (n.d.), *Essays*, reprints from the Supplement to the Encyclopedia Britannica, London.

Mill, J.S. (1909), *Principles of Political Economy, with Some of Their Applications to Social Philosophy*, W.J. Ashley (ed.), London, Longmans, Green and Co.

———— (1948), *On the Interchange Between Nations, Essays on Some Unsettled Questions of Political Economy*, London, London School of Economics Reprint.

Mills, F.C. (1924), 'On Measurement in Economics', *The Trend in Economics*, R.G. Tugwell (ed.), New York, A.A. Knopf.

Minabe, N. (1966), 'The Heckscher–Ohlin Theorem, the Leontief Paradox, and Patterns of Economic Growth', *American Economic Review* 56, pp. 1193–1211.

Minhas, B.S. (1962), 'The Homohypallagic Production Function, Factor-Intensity Reverses and the Heckscher–Ohlin Theorem', *Journal of Political Economy* 70, pp. 138–56.

Mises, L. von (1949), *Human Action*, New Haven, Connecticut, Yale University Press.

Modelski, G. (1983), 'Long Cycles of World Leadership', ch.5, *Contending Approaches to World System Analysis*, W.R. Thompson (ed.), London, Sage Publications.

Mommsen, W.J. (1981), *Theories of Imperialism*, London, Weidenfeld and Nicolson.

Mookerjee, S. (1958), *Factor Endowments and International Trade*, International Studies Occasional Papers No.2, Bombay, Asia Publishing House.

Morall, J.F. (1972), *Human Capital, Technology and the Role of the U.S. in International Trade*, Gainesville, University of Florida Press.

Moran, T.H. (1978), 'Multinational Corporations and Dependency: A Dialogue for Dependentistas and Non-Dependentistas', *International Organization* 32, pp. 79–100.

Moreland, W.H. (1923), *From Akbar to Aarangzeb*, London, Macmillan.

Moulton, H.G. (1946), 'Some Comments on Research Methods', *Economic Research and the Development of Economic Science and Public Policy*, New York, National Bureau of Economic Research.

Mun, T. (1664), *England's Treasure by Forraign Trade*, 1949 edition, Oxford, Basil Blackwell.

Myint, H. (1958), 'The Classical Theory of International Trade and the Under-developed Countries', *The Economic Journal*, 68, pp. 317–37.

———— (1969), 'International Trade and Developing Countries', *International Economic Relations*, P.A. Samuelson (ed.), London, Macmillan.

———— (1977), 'Adam Smith's Theory of International Trade in the Perspective of Economic Development', *Economica*, 44, pp. 231–48.

Myrdal, G. (1956a), *An International Economy: Problems and Prospects*, London, Routledge and Kegan Paul.

———— (1956b), 'The Cumulative Process of Economic Development within a

Myrdal (*continued*) National State', *Development and Underdevelopment: A Note on the Mechanism of National and International Economic Inequality*, Cairo, National Bank of Egypt.

—— (1968), *Asian Drama: An Enquiry into the Poverty of Nations*, London, Allen Lane.

—— (1970), 'The "Soft State" in Underdeveloped Countries', *Unfashionable Economics: Essays in Honour of Lord Balogh*, P. Streeten (ed.), London, Weidenfeld and Nicolson.

Nadler, M. (1937) 'Economic Interdependence, Present and Future', *American Economic Review* 27, pp. 1–11.

Nagel, E. (1963), 'Assumptions in Economic Theory', *American Economic Review, Papers and Proceedings* 53, No.2, pp. 211–19.

Nagi, M.H. (1982), 'Capital Flows to the Third World: the Outlook for the 1980s', *Journal of World Trade Law* 16, pp. 292–310.

Navarro, V. (1982), 'The Limits of World-Systems Theory', ch.3, *Socialist States in the World System*, C.K. Chase-Dunn (ed.), London, Sage Publications.

Nayyar, D. (1978), 'Transnational Corporations and Manufactured Exports from Poor Countries', *The Economic Journal* 88, pp. 59–84.

National Economic Development Council (1965), *Imported Manufactures, An Enquiry Into Competitiveness*, London, HMSO.

Nelson, P. (1970), 'Information and Consumer Behaviour', *Journal of Political Economy* 78, pp. 313–29.

Nelson, R.R. and Norman, V.D. (1977), 'Technological Change and Factor Mix Over the Product Cycle: A Model of Dynamic Comparative Advantage', *Journal of Development Economics* 4, pp. 3–24.

Nettels, C.P. (1934), *The Money Supply of the American Colonies Before 1720*, University of Wisconsin Studies in the Social Sciences and History No.20, reprinted 1964, New York, Augustus M. Kelly.

Newby, E. (1982), *The World Atlas of Exploration*, London, Artists House.

Nicholls, J. (1822), *Recollections and Reflections*, 2nd. ed., London.

North, D.C. (1958), 'Ocean Freight Rates and Economic Development, 1750–1913', *Journal of Economic History* 18, pp. 537–55.

—— (1984), 'Government and the Cost of Exchange in History', *Journal of Economic History* 44, pp. 255–64.

Nurkse, R. (1962), *Patterns of Trade and Development*, Oxford, Basil Blackwell.

Nye, J.S. and Keohane, R.O. (1972), 'Introduction' *Transnational Relations and World Politics*, R.O. Keohane and J.S. Nye (eds.), Cambridge, Massachusetts, Harvard University Press.

O'Brien, P.J. (1975), 'A Critique of Latin American Theories of Dependency', ch.2, *Beyond the Sociology of Development*, I. Oxaal, T. Barnett, and D. Booth (eds.), London, Routledge and Kegan Paul.

Odell, P. R. and Preston, D.A. (1978), *Economies and Societies in Latin America: A Geographical Interpretation*, 2nd. ed., Chichester, John Wiley and Sons.

Ohlin, B. (1933), *Interregional and International Trade*, Harvard Economic Studies 34, Cambridge, Massachusetts, Harvard University Press.

—— (1970), 'Model Construction in International Trade Theory', ch. 21, *Induction, Growth and Trade*, W.A. Eltis, M. Fg. Scott, and J.N. Wolfe (eds.), Oxford, Clarendon Press.

—— (1977), 'Some Aspects of the Relations Between International Movements of Commodities, Factors of Production and Technology, ch. 2, *The International Allocation of Economic Activity*, B. Ohlin, P-O. Hesselborn, and P.M. Wijkman (ed.), London, Macmillan.

—— (1979), *Some Insufficiencies in the Theories of International Economic Relations*, Essays in International Finance No. 134, New Jersey, Princeton University.

Olson, M. (1965), *The Logic of Collective Action*, Harvard Economics Studies 124,

Cambridge. Massachusetts, Harvard University Press.

——— (1982), *The Rise and Decline of Nations: Economic Growth, Stagflation, and Social Rigidities*, New Haven, Connecticut, Yale University Press.

Oteiza, E. (1979), 'Collective Self-Reliance: Some Old and New Issues', ch.13, *Transnational Capitalism and National Development: New Perspectives on Dependence*, J.J. Villamil (ed.), Sussex, The Harvester Press.

Owen, B.M. and Braeutigam, R. (1978), *The Regulation Game: Strategic Use of the Administrative Process*, Cambridge, Massachusetts, Ballinger.

Owen, R. (1981), *The Middle East and the World Economy, 1800–1914*, London, Methuen.

Page, S.A.B. (1981), 'The Revival of Protectionism and Its Consequences for Europe', *Journal of Common Market Studies* **20**, pp. 17–40.

Palloix, C. (1969a), *Problemes de La Croissance en Economie Ouverte*, Paris, Maspero.

——— (1969b), 'Imperialisme et Mode de Production Capitaliste', *L'Homme et La Société* No.12.

Palma, G. (1981), 'Dependency and Development: A Critical Overview', *Dependency Theory: A Critical Reassessment*, D. Seers (ed.), London, Francis Pinter.

Panic, M. and Rajan, A.H. (1971), *Product Changes in International Countries' Trade: 1955–1968*, NEDO Monograph No.2, London, National Economic Development Office.

Paquet, G. (1972), 'The Multinational Firm and the Nation-State as Institutional Forms', *The Multinational Firm and the Nation State*, G. Paquet (ed.), Don Mills, Collier-Macmillan.

Pares, R. (1937), 'The Economic Factors in the History of the Empire', *Economic History Review, First Series* **7**, pp. 119–44.

Parish, W. (1838), *Buenos Ayres and the Provinces of the Rio de La Plata: Their Present State, Trade, and Debt*, London, J. Murray.

Parry, J.H. (1966), *Europe and a Wider World, 1415–1715*, 3rd. revised ed., London, Hutchinson.

Passmore, J.A. (1953) 'Can the Social Sciences Be Value-Free', *Readings in the Philosophy of Science*, H. Feigl and M. Brodbeck (eds.), New York, Appleton-Century-Crofts, Inc.

Perkins, E.J. (1980), *The Economy of Colonial America*, New York, Columbia University Press.

Perlmutter, H. (1969), The Tortuous Evolution of the Multinational Corporation', *Columbia Journal of World Business* **4**, pp. 9–18.

Ping, H.R. (1980), 'Bargaining on the Free Trade Zones', *The New Internationalist* No.85, pp. 12–14.

Pistrowski, R. (1933), *Cartels and Trusts: Their Origin and Historical Development from the Economic and Legal Aspects*, London, Allen and Unwin.

Platt, D.C.M. (1972), *Latin America and British Trade, 1806–1914*, London, Adam and Charles Black.

Polanyi, K. (1957), 'Ports of Trade in the Eastern Mediterranean', *Trade and Markets in the Early Empires: Economics in History and Theory*, K. Polanyi, C.M. Arenberg, and H.W. Pearson (eds.), New York, The Free Press.

Pollard, A.F. (1909), *The British Empire: Its Past, Its Present, and Its Future*, London, League of the Empire, Caxton Hall.

Pollard, S. (1981), *Peaceful Conquest: the Industrialization of Europe, 1760–1970*, Oxford, Oxford University Press.

Posner, M.V. (1961), 'International Trade and Technical Change', *Oxford Economic Papers* **13**, pp. 323–41.

Postan, M.M. (1973), *Medieval Trade and Finance*, Cambridge, Cambridge University Press.

Pratten, C.F. (1971), *Economies of Scale in Manufacturing Industry*, Cambridge, Cambridge University Press.

Prebisch, R. (1950), *The Economic Development of Latin America and Its Principal Problems*, New York, United Nations.

―――― (1959), 'Commercial Policy in the Underdeveloped Countries', *American Economic Review, Papers and Proceedings* 49, No. 2, pp. 251–73.

―――― (1964), *Towards a New Trade Policy for Development*, New York, United Nations.

Pred, A.R. (1977), 'The Location of Economic Activity Since the Early Nineteenth Century: A City-Systems Perspective', ch. 4, *The International Allocation of Economic Activity*, B. Ohlin, P-O. Hesselborn, and P.M. Wijkman (eds.), London, Macmillan.

Preeg, E.H. (1970) *Traders and Diplomats: An Analysis of the Kennedy Round of Negotiations Under the General Agreement on Tariffs and Trade*, Washington DC, The Brookings Institution.

Rapp, W.V. (1975), 'The Many Possible Extensions of Product Cycle Analysis', *Hitotsubashi Journal of Economics* 16, pp. 22–9.

Rayment, P.B.W. (1983), ' "Intra-Industry" Specialization and the Foreign Trade of Industrial Countries', *Controlling Industrial Economies: Essays in Honour of C.T. Saunders*, S.F. Frowen (ed.), London, Macmillan.

Rejai, M. and Enloe, C, C. (1969), 'Nation-States and State-Nations', *International Studies Quarterly* 13, pp. 140–58.

Ricardo, D. (1951), 'On the Principles of Political Economy and Taxation', 1, *The Works and Correspondence of David Ricardo* P. Sraffa (ed.), Cambridge, Cambridge University Press.

Rinman, Y. and Linden, R. (1978), *Shipping – How it Works*, Stockholm, Rinman and Linden.

Rhomberg, R.R. (1970), 'Possible Approaches to a Model of World Trade and Payments', *IMF Staff Papers* 7, pp. 1–28.

―――― (1973), 'Toward a General Trade Model', ch. 2, *The International Linkage of National Economic Models*, R.J. Ball (ed.), Amsterdam, North-Holland Press.

Robbins, L. (1958), *Robert Torrens and the Evolution of Classical Economics*, London, Macmillan.

Robertson, D.H. (1928), *The Control of Industry*, revised ed., Cambridge, Cambridge University Press.

―――― (1938), 'The Future of International Trade', *The Economic Journal* 48, pp. 1–14.

―――― (1958), 'Stability and Progress: the Richer Countries' Problem', *Stability and Progress in the World Economy*, D.C. Hague (ed.), London, Macmillan.

Robertson, R.M. (1973), *History of the American Economy*, 3rd. ed., New York, Harcourt Brace Janovich, Inc.

Robinson, J. (1979), 'Reflections on the Theory of International Trade', ch. 13, *Collected Economic Papers* 5, Oxford, Basil Blackwell.

Robinson, R. (1956), 'Factor Proportions and Comparative Advantage', 2 Parts, *Quarterly Journal of Economics* 70, (a) pp. 169–92, (b) pp. 346–63.

Roepke, W. (1942), *International Economic Disintegration*, London, W. Hodge and Co.

Rosenberg, N. (1976), *Perspectives on Technology*, Cambridge, Cambridge University Press.

Ross, A.C. (1976), 'Emmanuel on Unequal Exchange: A Marxist Contribution on Trade Between Rich and Poor', *Journal of Economic Studies* 3, pp. 42–61.

Rostow, W.W. (1978), *The World Economy: History and Prospect*, London, Macmillan.

Rothschild, K.W. (1975), 'Export Structure, Export Flexibility and Competitiveness', *Weltwirtschafliches Archiv* 111, pp. 222–42.

Rowe, J.N.F. (1965), *Primary Commodities in International Trade*, Cambridge, Cambridge University Press.

Roxborough, I. (1979), *Theories of Underdevelopment*, London, Macmillan.
Royal Institute of International Affairs (1937), *The Problem of International Investment*, London, Oxford University Press.
Rustow, D.A. (1967), *A World of Nations: Problems of Political Modernization*, Washington DC, The Brookings Institution.
Safarian, A.E. (1983) 'Trade-Related Investment Issues', ch.18, *Trade Policy in the 1980s*, W.R. Cline (ed.), Washington DC, Institute for International Economics.
Sailors, J.W. and Bronson, W.D. (1970), 'An Empirical Study of the Ricardian Theory of Comparative Cost', *Indian Economic Journal* 18, pp. 1–16.
———— Qureshi, V.A. and Cross, E.M., (1973), 'Empirical Verification of Linder's Trade Thesis', *The Southern Economic Journal* 40, pp. 262–68.
Salamon, I.M. (1970), 'Comparative History and the Theory of Modernization', *World Politics* 23, pp. 83–103.
Salter, Sir A. (1936), *World Trade and Its Future*, Philadelphia, University of Pennsylvania Press.
Samuelson, P.A. (1948), 'International Trade and Equalisation of Factor Prices', *The Economic Journal* 58, pp. 163–84.
———— (1949), 'International Factor Price Equalisation Once Again', *The Economic Journal* Vol.59, pp. 181–97.
———— (1981), 'Bertil Ohlin, 1899–1979', *Journal of International Economics* Vol.11, pp. 147–163.
Sanyal, K.K. and Jones, R.W. (1982), 'The Theory of Trade in Middle Products', *American Economic Review* 72, pp. 16–32.
Saul, S.B. (1954), 'Britain and World Trade, 1870–1914', *Economic History Review, New Series* 7, pp. 49–66.
———— (1957), 'The Economic Significance of "Constructive Imperialism"', *Journal of Economic History*, Vol.17, pp. 173–192.
———— (1965), 'The Export Economy', *Yorkshire Bulletin of Economic and Social Research* Vol.17, pp. 7–18.
Saunders, C. (1978), *Engineering in Britain, W. Germany and France: Some Statistical Comparisons*, Sussex European Papers No.3
Savosnick, K.M. (1958), 'The Box Diagram and the Production Possibility Curve', *Ekonomisk Tidskrift* 60, pp. 183–97.
Sawnhey, B.L. and Di Petro, W.R. (1981), 'Monopoly Power, the Participation Theory and International Trade', *Economia Internazionale* 34, pp. 143–58.
Scammell, G.V. (1981), *The World Encompassed: The First European Maritime Empires C.800–1650*, London, Methuen.
Schiller, B.R. (1965), 'The Compatibility of the Theory of Comparative Cost with the Development Needs of Today's Economically Less-Developed Countries', *Indian Economic Journal* 13, pp. 1–12.
Schmitt, H.O. (1969), 'Integration and Conflict in the World Economy', *Journal of Common Market Studies* 8, pp. 1–18.
———— (1979), 'Mercantilism: A Modern Argument', *The Manchester School* 47, pp. 93–111.
———— (1980), 'Rejoinder on Mercantilism', *The Manchester School* 48, pp. 392–3.
Scitovsky, T. (1960), 'International Trade and Economic Integration as a Means of Overcoming the Disadvantages of a Small Nation', ch.18, *Economic Consequences of the Size of Nations*, E.A.G. Robinson (ed.), London, Macmillan.
Seers, D. (1981), 'Introduction', and 'Development Options: the Strengths and Weaknesses of Dependency Theories in Explaining a Government's Room to Manoevre', ch.6, *Dependency Theory: A Critical Reassessment*, D. Seers (ed.), London, Frances Pinter.
Seidman, S. (1983), 'Beyond Presentism and Historicism: Understanding the History of Social Science', *Sociological Inquiry* 53, pp. 79–94.
Sekine, T.T. (1973), 'The Discovery of International Monetary Equilibrium by

Sekine (*continued*)   Vanderlint, Cantillon, Gervaise and Hume', *Economia Internazionale* **26**, pp. 262-82.

Seligman, B.B. (1980), 'Philosophic Perspective in Economic Thought', *The Methodology of Economic Thought*, W.J. Samuels, New Brunswick (ed.), Transaction Books.

Semmel, B. (1970), *The Rise of Free Trade Imperialism: Classical Political Economy and Empire of Free Trade and Imperialism, 1750-1850*, Cambridge, Cambridge University Press.

Senghaas, D. (1974), 'Peace Research and the Third World', *Bulletin of Peace Proposals* pp. 158-172.

Shepherd, J.F. and Walton, G.M. (1972), *Shipping, Maritime Trade and the Economic Development of Colonial North America*, Cambridge, Cambridge University Press.

Shonfield, A. (1976), 'International Economic Relations of the Western World: an Overall View', Part I, *International Economic Relations of the Western World, 1959-1971* Vol.I - Politics and Trade, London, Oxford University Press.

Siebert, H. (1974), 'Trade and Environment', *The International Division of Labour: Problems and Perspectives*, International Symposium, H. Giersch (ed.), Tuebingen, J.C.B. Mohr (Paul Siebeck).

Singer, J.D. (1961), 'The Level-of-Analysis Problem in International Relations', *The International System: Theoretical Essays* K. Knorr and S. Verba (eds.), New Jersey, Princeton University Press.

Singh, A. (1977), 'U.K. Industry and the World Economy: A Case of De-Industrialization?', *Cambridge Journal of Economics* **1**, pp. 113-36.

Smith, A. (1950), *An Inquiry Into the Nature and Causes of the Wealth of Nations* (1776), E. Cannan (ed.) in 2 Vols., 6th. ed., London, Methuen.

Smith, A.D., Hitchens, D.M.W.N., and Davies, S.W. (1982), *International Industrial Productivity: A Comparison of Britain, America and Germany*, National Institute of Economic and Social Research Occasional Paper No. 24, Cambridge, Cambridge University Press.

Smith, M.A.M. (1979), 'Intertemporal Gains from Trade', *Journal of International Economics* **9**, pp. 239-48.

Smith, S. (1980), 'The Ideas of Samir Amin: Theory or Tautology?', *Journal of Development Studies* **17**, pp. 1-21.

Smith, T. (1979), 'The Underdevelopment of Development Literature: the Case of Dependency Theory', *World Politics* **31**, pp. 247-88.

Spiethoff, A. (1952), 'The "Historical" Character of Economic Theories', *Journal of Economic History, Second Series* **7**, pp. 131-39.

Steedman, I. (1979), 'Introductory Essay', *Fundamental Issues in Trade Theory*, I. Steedman (ed.), London, Macmillan.

Stein, S.J. and B.H. (1970), *The Colonial Heritage of Latin America: Essays on Economic Dependence in Perspective*, New York, Oxford University Press.

Stern, R. (1962), 'British and American Productivity and Comparative Costs in International Trade', *Oxford Economic Papers* **14**, pp. 275-96.

————— (1975), 'Testing Trade Theories', *International Trade and Finance: Frontiers for Research*, P.B. Kenen (ed.), Cambridge, Cambridge University Press.

Stewart, F. (1977), *Technology and Underdevelopment*, London, Macmillan.

Stewart, I.M.T. (1979), *Reasoning and Method in Economics*, London, McGraw-Hill.

Stigler, G. (1959), 'The Politics of Political Economists', *Quarterly Journal of Economics* **73**, pp. 522-32.

————— (1971), 'the Theory of Economic Regulation', *Bell Journal of Economics and Management Science* Spring, pp. 3-21.

————— (1983), 'The Process and Progress of Economics', *Journal of Political Economics*, **91**, pp. 529-45.

Stojanovic, R. (1978), 'Interdependence in International Relations', *International Social Science Journal* **30**, pp. 238–51.
Stolper, W.F. and Samuelson, P.A. (1941), 'Protection and Real Wages', *Review of Economic Studies* **9**, pp. 58–67.
Streeten, P. (1979), 'Development Ideas in Historical Perspective: the New Interest in Development', ch. 6, *Economic Growth and Resources* **4**, I. Adelman (ed.), London, Macmillan.
———— (1982a), 'A Cool Look at "Outward-Looking" Strategies for Development', *World Economy* **5**, pp. 159–69.
———— (1982b), 'Trade as the Engine, Handmaiden, Brake or Offspring of Growth?', *World Economy* **5**, pp. 415–22.
Sunkel, O. (1969), 'National Development Policy and External Dependence in Latin America', *Journal of Development Studies* **6**, pp. 23–48.
———— (1972), 'Big Business and "Dependencies"', *Foreign Affairs* **50**, pp. 517–31.
———— and Fuenzalida, E.F. (1979), 'Transnationalization and Its National Consequences', ch. 3, *Transnational Capitalism and National Development: New Perspectives on Dependence*, J.J. Villamil (ed.), Sussex, The Harvester Press.
———— and Paz, P. (1970), *El Subdesarrollo Latinoamericano Y La Teeria del Desarrollo* [quoted in Cardoso, 1982], Mexico Siglo XXI Editores.
Svennilson, I. (1954), *Growth and Stagnation in the European Economy*, Geneva, United Nations.
———— (1960), 'The Concept of the Nation and Its Relevance to Economic Analysis', ch.1, *Economic Consequences of the Size of Nations*, E.A.G. Robinson (ed.), London, Macmillan.
Szymanski, A. (1981), *The Logic of Imperialism*, New York, Praeger.
———— (1982), 'The Socialist World-System', ch. 2, *Socialist States in the World System*, C.K. Chase-Dunn (ed.), Beverley Hills, California, Sage Publications.
Targ, H.R. (1976), 'Gobal Dominance and Dependence, Post-Industrialism, and International Relations Theory', *International Studies Quarterly* **20**, pp. 461–82.
Taussig, F.W. (1928), *International Trade*, New York, Macmillan.
Thoburn, J.T. (1977), *Primary Commodity Exports and Economic Development*, London, John Wiley and Sons.
Thomas, G.M. and Meyer, J.W. (1980), 'Regime Changes and State Power in an Intensifying World-State-System', ch. 7, *Studies of the Modern World-System*, A. Bergesen (ed.), London, Academic Press.
Thompson, W.R. (1983a), 'World System Analysis With and Without the Hyphen', *Contending Approaches to World System Analysis*, W.R. Thompson (ed.), London, Sage Publications.
———— (1983b), 'Cycles, Capabilities, and War: An Ecumenical View', ch.6, *Contending Approaches to World System Analysis*, W.R. Thompson (ed.), London, Sage Publications.
Tilly, C. (1975), 'Western State-Making and Theories of Political Transformation', ch. 9, *The Formation of National States in Western Europe*, C. Tilly (ed.), New Jersey, Princeton University Press.
Tinbergen, J. (1965), *International Economic Integration*, 2nd, revised ed., Amsterdam, Elsevier Publishing Co.
———— (1978), 'Alternative Forms of International Co-operation: Comparing Their Efficiency', *International Social Science Journal* **30**, pp. 223–37.
Todaro, M.P. (1981), *Economic Development in the Third World*, 2nd ed., London, Longmans.
Tollison, R.D. and Willett, T.D. 'An Economic Theory of Mutually Advantageous Issue Linkages in International Negotiations', *International Organization* **33**, pp. 425–49.
Torre, H. de La, (1936), *El Antimerialisms Y El APRA*, Santiago [quoted by

Torre, H. de La (*continued*)   Hirschman (1961), p. 11].

Torrens, R. (1808), *The Economists Refuted; or, An Inquiry Into the Nature and Extent of the Advantages Derived from Trade*, London, Oddy.

United Nations (1947), *International Cartels: A League of Nations Memorandum*, Lake Success, N.J., Department of Economic Affairs.

———— (1970), *Science and Technology for Development: Proposals for the Second United Nations Development Decade*, New York, U.N.

———— (1973), 'Co-ordination of Road Transport with Other International Transport Media in South America', *Economic Bulletin for Latin America* 18, pp. 150–58.

Vaitsos, V. (1976), 'Power, Knowledge and Development Policy: Relations Between Transnational Enterprise and Developing Countries', *A World Divided: the Less Developed Countries in the International Economy*, G.K. Helleiner (ed.), Cambridge, Cambridge University Press.

Vakil, C.N. and Brahmananda, P.R. (1960), 'The Problems of Developing Countries', ch.8, *Economic Consequences of the Size of Nations*, E.A. Robinson (ed.), London, Macmillan.

Valenzuela, J.S. and A. (1979), 'Modernization and Dependence: Alternative Perspectives in the Study of Latin America Underdevelopment', ch. 2, *Transnational Capitalism and National Development: New Perspectives on Dependence*, J.J. Villamil (ed.), Sussex, The Harvester Press.

Vayrynen, R. (1978), 'International Patenting as a Means of Technological Dominance', *International Social Science Journal* 30, pp. 315–37.

Verheirstraeten, A. (1981), *Competition and Regulation in Financial Markets*, London, Macmillan.

Vernon, R. (1966), 'International Investment and International Trade in the Product Cycle', *Quarterly Journal of Economics* 80, pp. 190–207.

———— (1979), 'The Product Cycle Hypothesis in a New International Environment', *Oxford Bulletin of Economics and Statistics* 41, pp. 255–67.

Viljoen, S. (1974), *Economic Systems in World History*, London, Longmans.

Villamil, J.J. (1979), 'Planning for Self-Reliant Growth', ch.14, *Transnational Capitalism and National Development: New Perspectives on Dependence*, J.J. Villamil (ed.), Sussex, The Harvester Press.

Vincent, J.C. (1970), *The Extraterritorial System in China*, Harvard East Asian Monographs No.30, Cambridge, Massachusetts.

Viner, J. (1923), *Dumping: A Problem in International Trade*, Chicago, University of Chicago Press.

———— (1937), *Studies in the Theory of International Trade*, New York, Harper and Brothers Publishers.

———— (1950), *The Customs Union Issue*, New York, Carnegie Endowment for International Peace.

———— (1955), 'International Trade Theory and Its Present Day Relevance', *Economics and Public Policy*, Brookings Lectures 1954, Washington DC, The Brookings Institution.

———— (1958), 'Stability and Progress: the Poorer Countries', *Stability and Progress in the World Economy*, D.C. Hague (ed.), London, Macmillan.

Vines, D. (1980), 'Competitiveness, Technical Progress and Balance of Trade Surpluses', *The Manchester School* 48, pp. 378–91.

Wallerstein, I. (1973), 'Dependence in an Interdependent World: the Limited Possibilities of Transformation Within the Capitalist World Economy', Paper presented at Conference on Dependence and Development in Africa, Ottawa.

———— (1974), *The Modern World System Vol.1 –* Capitalist Agriculture and the Origins of the European World-Economy in the Sixteenth Century, New York, Academic Press.

———— (1975), 'Class Formation in the Capitalist World-Economy', *Politics and Society* 5, No.3.

———— (1979), *The Capitalist World-Economy*, Cambridge, Cambridge University Press.

———— (1980a), *The Modern World-System* Vol. II – Mercantilism and the Consolidation of the European World-Economy, 1600–1750, London, The Academic Press.

———— (1980b), 'Imperialism and Development', ch.2, *Studies of the Modern World-System*, A. Bergesen (ed.), London, The Academic Press.

———— (1983), 'An Agenda for World-Systems Analysis', ch.13, *Contending Approaches to World System Analysis*, W.R. Thompson (ed.), London, Sage Publications.

Walter, I. (1975), *The International Economics of Pollution*, London, Macmillan.

Walton, G.M. (1968), 'New Evidence on Colonial Commerce', *Journal of Economic History* 28, pp. 363–89.

———— and Shepherd, J.F. (1979), *The Economic Rise of Early America*, Cambridge, Cambridge University Press.

Ward, M.D. (1982), 'Changing Patterns of Inequality in a Changing Global Order', *Kyklos* 35, pp. 115–34.

Watkins, J.W.N. (1953), 'Ideal Types and Historical Explanation', *Readings in the Philosophy of Science*, H. Feigl and M. Brodbeck (eds.), New York, Appleton-Century-Crofts, Inc.

Wells, J.D. and Imber, J.C. (1977), 'The Home and Export Performance of U.K. Industries', *Economic Trends* No. 286, pp. 78–81.

White, A.S. (1899), *The Expansion of Egypt Under Anglo-Egyptian Condominium*, London, Methuen.

Whitehead, A.N. (1938), *Modes of Thought*, New York, Macmillan.

Whitman, M.V.N. (1977), *Sustaining the International Economic System: Issues for U.S. Policy*, Essays in International Finance No. 121, New Jersey, Princeton University.

Wilczynski, J. (1965), 'The Theory of Comparative Costs and Centrally Planned Economies', *The Economic Journal* 75, pp. 63–80.

———— (1969), *The Economics and Politics of East–West Trade*, London, Macmillan.

Wiles, P.J.D. (1968), *Communist International Economics*, Oxford, Basil Blackwell.

Willett, T.D. (1971), 'International Trade Theory is Still Relevent', *Banca Nazionale del Lavoro* 98, pp. 276–92.

Williams, G. (1978), 'Imperialism and Development: A Critique', *World Development* 6, pp. 925–36.

Williams, J.H. (1929), 'The Theory of International Trade Reconsidered', *The Economic Journal* 39, pp. 195–209.

Willmore, L. (1979), 'The Industrial Economics of Intra-Industry Trade and Specialization', *On the Economics of Intra-Industry Trade*, International Symposium 1978, H. Giersch (ed.), Tuebingen, J.C.B. Mohr (Paul Siebeck).

Winch, D.N. (1963), 'Classical Economics and the Case for Colonization', *Economica* 30, pp. 387–99.

———— (1965), *Classical Political Economy and the Colonies*, London, Bell and Sons.

Winkler, M. (1933), *Foreign Bonds, an Autopsy: A Study of Defaults and Repudiations of Government Obligations*, Philadelphia, Roland Swain Co.

Winston, A.P. (1927), 'Does Trade Follow the Dollar?', *American Economic Review* 17, pp. 458–77.

Worswick, G.D.N. (1972), 'Is Progress in Economic Science Possible?', *The Economic Journal* 82, pp. 73–86.

Wu, C-Y. (1939), *An Outline of International Price Theories*, London, Routledge and Sons.

Yates, P.L. (1959), *Forty Years of Foreign Trade*, London, Allen and Unwin.

Yeats, A.J. (1979), *Trade Barriers Facing Developing Countries: Commercial Policy Measures and Shipping*, London, Macmillan.

Yoffie, D.B. (1981), 'The Newly Industrializing Countries and the Political Economy of Protectionism', *International Studies Quarterly* **25**, pp. 569–99.

Zolberg, A. (1981), 'Origins of the Modern World System: A Missing Link', *World Politics* **34**, pp. 253–81.

Index

318   *Index*